THE UNTEACHABLES

THE
UNTEACHABLES

DISABILITY RIGHTS AND THE INVENTION OF
BLACK SPECIAL EDUCATION

Keith A. Mayes

UNIVERSITY OF MINNESOTA PRESS
MINNEAPOLIS • LONDON

Published by the University of Minnesota Press
111 Third Avenue South, Suite 290
Minneapolis, MN 55401–2520
http://www.upress.umn.edu

ISBN 978-1-5179-1026-6 (hc)
ISBN 978-1-5179-1027-3 (pb)

Library of Congress record available at https://lccn.loc.gov/2022039076.

Printed in the United States of America on acid-free paper

The University of Minnesota is an equal-opportunity educator and employer.

UMP BmB 2022

Contents

Note on Terminology

As a civil rights historian and scholar of race and racialization, I came to this book project from a deep curiosity about the historical mistreatment of black students and the labels associated with their academic struggle. I also came to this project as a nondisabled person but also as someone who has experienced near "brushes" with educational disability. I attended New York City public schools in the 1970s and 1980s, and I barely escaped being labeled "educable mentally retarded" (EMR) as I fit the profile of EMR students based on my race, social class, and poor record of achievement. My white educators considered me "culturally deprived," and both labels carried the racialized stigma of disability. The racial charge of these terms and their resonance in medicine, social science, and educational legislation in the twentieth century serve as a through-line in *The Unteachables*.

Out of topical necessity, I use several terms in the book that are problematic, repugnant, and outdated, including: "idiot," "imbecile," "moron," "handicap," "mentally retarded," as well as derivatives of these terms like "educable mentally retarded," "emotionally disturbed," and "emotionally handicapped." I employ scare quotes most of the time to indicate both the unseemliness of these words and my skepticism about their historical and sometimes contemporary usage. When I do not apply scare quotes, I do not subscribe to these terms and their meaning; rather, I am capturing the sentiment of a historical period and historical actors who espoused these words and believed in their putative authenticity.

By using these terms as they were employed and tracking their parlance, I seek not merely to adhere to the principles of historical precision but to chart how ideas of racial difference shaped objectionable terminology, harmful labels, and suspicious designations of disability. If we wish to continue to uncover, as the late Chris Bell wrote, "misrepresentations of black disabled bodies and missed opportunities to think about how those bodies transform(ed) systems and culture,"[1] then it is imperative to simultaneously document and critique these historical terms. This is the spirit with which I invoke these historical expressions of disability.

Abbreviations

ADD	Attention Deficit Disorder
ADHD	Attention Deficit Hyperactivity Disorder
ASPD	Anti-Social Personality Disorder
BD	Behavior Disorder
CD	Conduct Disorder
DBD	Disruptive Behavior Disorder
EBD	Emotional Behavior Disorder
ED	Emotional Disturbance
EMH	Emotionally Mentally Handicapped
EMR	Educable Mentally Retarded or Retardation
LD	Learning Disability or Disabled
MBD	Minimal Brain Damage or Dysfunction
MCD	Minimal Cerebral Dysfunction
MMR or MR	Mildly Mentally Retarded or Mild Retardation
ODD	Oppositional Defiant Disorder
SED	Seriously Emotionally Disturbed
SM	Social Maladjustment or Socially Maladjusted
TMR or TR	Trainable Mentally Retarded or Retardation

Introduction

In 1973, Michael J. Herrick presaged the history of black students in special education when he wrote: "I caution those who would be categorizers and decision-makers that we are not dealing with pieces of paper or money alone; we are dealing with a real, live population containing so many different children that we could injure a great many by the very act of labeling or by improper labeling."[1] Herrick's foretelling in 1973 was remarkable in that he, as did others, witnessed the early stages of a trend: the over-placement of black students in special education as "educable mentally retarded" (EMR). By the 1990s and early 2000s, the magnitude of black placement in EMR, learning disabled (LD), and emotional behavior disordered (EBD) classes made racial disproportionality in special education an acute problem and Herrick's prophesy biblical. *The Unteachables* charts the origins of black students in special education and examines the racialized labeling of African American students as EMR, LD, and EBD.

More than mere labels or disability categories, black special education raises historical questions about unteachability. Who is unteachable? The answer is no one; however, a host of historical actors has contributed to the fiction of unteachability: from medical doctors to psychologists and other social scientists; from school administrators and teachers to casual observers; and from the legislation of policymakers to the keystrokes of journalists. The unteachables conjure up perceptions of ghetto schools populated by at-risk students who are failing academically and struggling socially and emotionally. Experts claim that the unteachables come from broken families and neighborhoods marked by disorder. They often speak "nonstandard" English or a different language altogether. They are mostly, if not always, understood as poor or working class, black, indigenous, Latinx, but sometimes white and Asian. The unteachables are not always students with disabilities, but many disabled black and brown students are deemed unteachable. By all accounts, the racial and socioeconomic backgrounds of the unteachables in 2020 would seem the same as in 1960 or 1900. Read an essay or a book published in the early 1900s or the 1960s and compare it to writing on the subject today. The terms used to describe these students, such as "high-grade defective," "culturally deprived," "dullard," "backward," "educationally disadvantaged," and "at-risk" would be different in each era, but the ideas and arguments put forward regarding their unteachability are similar. Consider two statements separated by fifty-five years. In 1912 *The Psychological Clinic* reported, "It was decided to exclude from Detroit public schools all children in the idiot group and also those in the middle and low-grade imbecile groups. This rule has been rigidly adhered to, as it is considered a waste of public funds to attempt to teach children of these classes, who are regarded by all specialists as unteachable."[2] In 1967, anthropologist G. Alexander Moore wrote observantly, "For the ghetto school is marked not only by the obvious segregation of class and ethnic group, but also by the formal, official segregation within each grade by ability, and further, by an informal segregation within each according to behavior. Thus, many slum schools are divided into classes that are defined as teachable and nonteachable."[3]

The Unteachables is primarily a story set in the 1960s to the present, but to begin the history there is to pick it up in midstream. Indeed, the Supreme Court decision in *Brown v. Board of Education* (1954) and the Civil Rights Act of 1964 increased the growing presence of black students entering white schools throughout the 1960s and early 1970s. A black teacher in Milwaukee public schools remembered the panic exhibited by white teachers and their common refrain when black students started showing up to predominantly white schools: "They're coming! They're coming!"[4] This second wave of black students entering the general education system generated what some scholars called "second-generation discrimination," an assortment of techniques used by schools that resulted in ability grouping, curriculum tracking, and special education placement.[5] Though the point of origin is the modern special education system dating from the 1960s, black special education takes root in an earlier time when the first wave of black students entered the educational system in large numbers. The enactment and enforcement of compulsory attendance laws at the turn of twentieth century required all children to regularly attend public schools. The increasing number of black students from the factories and the fields triggered the creation of the special education system as a form of differential education for children deemed "subnormal" or "retarded" due to race, class, and academic underachievement.

Simply put, this book argues that compulsory education produced special education in the early twentieth century. Subsequently, racial integration of public schools further exacerbated black overrepresentation in special education after *Brown v. Board of Education* (1954). White educators and psychologists developed special education not to help "disabled" children but rather to protect the interests of white "normal" students who they considered the "future torchbearers of our civilization."[6] The fields of psychology and educational psychology constructed elaborate discourses praising white middle-class students while simultaneously denigrating students of color. As an early version of "risk management," special education emerged to prohibit students of color—and to a lesser degree, children of white foreign-born parents—from accessing general education classes. Indeed, the concept of educational risk has been misunderstood. Students of color were not "at risk" but exhibited perceived "risk" to middle-class white parents who wished for their children to learn in race- and class-segregated environments. These parents, along with physicians, psychologists, and school administrators, engaged in harmful discourses and racialized practices that built the intertwined structures of black intellectual disability and special education. Thus, black student placement in special education began when the system was first created. The system of special education was partially created for black and poor students twice over: once in the early 1900s and again in the 1960s.

Special education is an experiment in race and white middle-class privilege. Class is an important but overemphasized variable in the history of special education. As an analytical category, scholars have used class to explain the history of special education from its inception up through the 1970s, only centering race when the overrepresentation of students of color became apparent.[7] Class, indeed, has been paramount.

But if we do not hold race as a central analytical category in our analysis of special education, then we will fail to understand why so many black children were erroneously cast as unteachable. Special education is also a gender-based system in that more boys than girls have been over-represented historically. Schools, however, placed black girls in certain categories of special education at higher percentages than black boys by the end of the twentieth century and into the twenty-first century, demonstrating how disability, gender, and race emerged as set of interlocking categories and lived experiences.[8] But the numbers do not tell everything about the gendered nature of special education. There are other ways the system of special education is gendered, similarly in its disability discourses and punitive practices.[9]

Special education began as a system of white and able-bodied protection at the turn of the twentieth century. The system of special education protected young people from the dominant culture intrinsically considered "normal": white, upper and middle class, Anglo (or Anglicized), with an absence of physical and sensory "defects"—a "moral" designation that pushed numerous populations (e.g., black folk, immigrants, stutterers, epileptics, etc.) to the margins of public education and society.[10] In the early 1900s, children who limped or had Down syndrome became versions of unwanted deficiency.[11] If white middle-class children in general education had to be protected, then the needs of white middle-class students struggling academically, so-called white underachievers or slow learners, also had to be addressed. White middle-class parents believed it was anathema for their children to have scholastic challenges. White middle-class students who struggled would receive a different and more financially resourced version of special education. Not only was this belief baked into the system during its infancy, arguably the expectation remains of white middle-class families that children of color will receive a lesser education in both general and special education systems.

The civil rights decades introduced the public to recently integrated black "culturally deprived" children from the north and south. White families, psychologists, and educators also continued to search for solutions for white underachieving middle-class students deemed "slow-learners." Since IQ scores supposedly marked one's intelligence, the underachievement of white students at/or above median intelligence perplexed parents and educational professionals and sent them on what Bernadette Baker described as a "hunt" for new disabilities.[12] What parents and professionals settled on was a category called learning disabled (LD).[13] Social scientists joined white parents and educators to form what I loosely call the "educational disability rights movement."[14] Equal educational opportunity discourse opened a window for the educational disability rights movement to make the case for legislative recognition and new federal policies.

The Unteachables examines the racialization of educational disability, following the road psychologists and educators paved into mental retardation, and then out of mental retardation into LD and EBD. Although white psychologists and educators deemed black and white students mentally retarded, they disproportionately placed black students under this designation. I contend that the new LD label represented an intellectual white flight from mental retardation. LD materialized as an unstigmatized educational identity for white underachieving students while the theory of cultural deprivation kept black students under the classifications of EMR or MMR (mildly mental retarded) as educationally disadvantaged. Tracking disability labels reveal how special education was racialized from the early to mid-twentieth century, and how the educational disability rights movement in the 1960s not only worked on behalf of one student constituency but attempted to create categorical disability definitions that would only apply to white students. The attempt to racially segregate student populations within disability categories is borne out in the long histories of EMR, LD, and EBD.

Carving out privileged white spaces in each of these classifications, however, did not hold up for long. White student protection and advancement required the segregation of low-performing and "unruly" black children in a separate system. This separate, race-based system, with its accompanied disability discourses, created the foundation for black disproportional placement in special education. The pages that follow historicize how race shaped ideas about disability and then in turn how disability shaped ideas about race in a reinscribing feedback loop. Black students were not placed in special education because they were incontrovertibly disabled; they were placed there because they were incontrovertibly black. Far from being undeniably disabled, placement practices consigned black students to a resegregation scheme under the auspices of special education.[15]

The Unteachables explores the connections and disjunctions produced by two movements that often worked at cross-purposes: civil rights (racial integration and quality public schools) and educational disability rights (legislative recognition for white underachievers). The book asserts that the educational disability rights movement used the opportunity provided by the civil rights movement to make claims about white student invisibility and intellectual "handicaps" not covered in the law. As a movement that ostensibly included children from all racial groups, the educational disability rights movement focused its attention on the needs of white students. The integration of white public schools remained a focus of the 1960s desegregation campaigns of black civil rights advocates. White educational disability, on the other hand, tended to separate issues (e.g., unrecognized "handicaps," lack of funding, no legislation for white disabled students, etc.) and organized with different advocates (e.g., white parents, white social scientists, white special education lobbyists).

This bifurcated educational effort led to the civil rights and educational disability rights movements working both for and against each other's interests. Both movements found common ground in that physical, sensory, and intellectual disabilities affected all racial groups. At other times, both movements worked against each other in that black educational disability was understood mainly through the lens of race and poverty, which white people disassociated from themselves. Educational disability rights advocates identified deficits and applied labels to academically struggling black students that it did not apply to white "handicap" students. Borrowing the language of equality from the civil rights movement, the educational disability rights movement gained steam with small legislative victories in the 1960s and major ones in the 1970s, becoming part of a big tent social justice crusade that coalesced with the larger disability rights movement in the 1980s and 1990s. Though the disability rights movement leading to the Americans with Disabilities Act (ADA) is not a focus of this book, *The Unteachables* directs the reader to an early history of disability advocacy in the field of education that crossed paths with the black civil rights movement. Thus, within the context of a racially segregated social movement landscape, the concerns of black and white students were tended to in separate social justice communities and advocacy groups. But when it came to addressing the marginalization of black students in special education, the educational disability rights movement *was* and, for some, *still is* the civil rights movement.[16]

The overlap and tension between both movements are borne out in only a few historical treatments. With such rich lines of congruence and incongruence, I am amazed more historical monographs have not been produced on special education. Sociology has produced the most consequential scholarship on the subject outside of the various fields in education, particularly in the work of Sally Tomlinson.[17] Though there are several special education history surveys, there are only a few historical treatments of special education that are primary-source based, providing an in-depth perspective or describing the system of special education over a longer time span.[18] The only two studies that fit this description are Robert L. Osgood, *For 'Children Who Vary from the Normal Type:' Special Education in Boston, 1838–1930* (2000) and Jason Ellis, *A Class By Themselves? The Origins of Special Education in Toronto and Beyond* (2019).[19]

Broadly speaking, *The Unteachables* belong to the fields of disability studies and disability history as well as black disability studies and black disability history.[20] *The Unteachables* is also part of the rich tradition of black education history and civil rights education history, from studies on the educational pursuits of freed people and "freedom's children" in the late nineteenth century to studies on black children with exceptionalities and special needs in the late twentieth century.[21] In addition, the historiography of black education is a rich narrative examining African American school communities and the challenges they faced,[22] grassroots educational institutional formations,[23] various histories of desegregation and school reform,[24] the phenomenon of school resegregation,[25] and commemoration retrospectives on *Brown v. Board of Education.*[26] *The Unteachables* contributes to the civil rights education historical literature, which raises questions about the post-*Brown* promise of public schools without discrimination.[27] The broken "promise" of *Brown,* as it were, witnessed the continued violation of black students' civil rights immediately after the Supreme Court's decision and certainly throughout the 1960s, 1970s, 1980s, and 1990s. The problems black students faced (and still face) in special education and in public education broadly reflect an unfinished revolution in U.S. society and in public schools.[28]

As a history of special education categories, competing social movements, federal policy, and racial disproportionality, the book begins by asking the question in chapter 1, "Who Are the Unteachables? A Genealogy of Race, Retardation, and Intelligence." This chapter examines how the language of "unteachability" is interwoven in the genealogy of race, retardation, and intelligence. Psychologists constructed a hierarchy of teachability with the "moron" closer to the top of the normal distribution curve than the "imbecile" and "idiot." The black "moron," however, was still deemed unteachable. The identity of the "moron" changed to EMR when "feebleminded" categories fell out of favor. Nonetheless, the racialization of the "moron" cast black children with the lowest potential to succeed in schools. Chapter 1 places the beginning of special education into context if for no other reason than it raises questions about its sincerity as a system to help children beset with challenges that made learning in white schools difficult. The learning challenges black students brought to school were associated with the lived experience of being black in Jim Crow America. White psychologists and educators translated that lived experience into a discourse on retardation: "grade-level retardation" because black students often showed up to white schools two or more years behind scholastically and then called it "mental retardation" because their academic underachievement was deemed genetic and not based on their lived experience. Chapter 1 argues that psychologists created special education as a form of differential education. They invented and then applied disability categories to black and brown children to protect the interests of "normal" white middle-class children in public education. At the center of this story is how the discourse on mental retardation began and evolved in the early twentieth century.

Chapter 2, "The Road *from* Mental Retardation: Civil Rights, Disability Rights, and Equal Educational Opportunity," begins by examining the contested nature of mental retardation as an educational disability identity for some white families whose children were deemed uneducable, too. As a postwar concern, degrees of "mental retardation" divided populations and distinguished between the most and least redeemable. As a challenge to the fixity of hereditary intelligence, redeemability was predicated on which children held the greatest potential to learn and succeed academically. What emerges in the 1940s and 1950s was the label EMR (educable mentally retarded)—the highest stage of intellectual potential that "mentally retarded" children were thought to possess. This chapter explores how EMR evolved from previous labels associated with feeblemindedness and its racialization. Though important in its ability to address the intellectual potential among "retarded" student populations, some believed EMR failed to identify why other white students of "normal" or "superior" intelligence experienced subject-matter difficulties. While some white parents saw EMR as an identity breakthrough, other white parents and a growing number of social scientists believed EMR did not represent "non-retarded" white students who also struggled academically. This chapter examines why a small segment of white parents challenged EMR as the appropriate label for their children. Paralleling the civil rights movement, whose main pillar was the integration of public schools for black students, the educational disability rights movement included white parent organizations, psychologists, and school administrators advocating for legislative recognition in the U.S. Congress for white "slow learners." This chapter establishes how special education through the learning disabilities movement emerged as an exclusively white designation in the 1960s, moving away from the growing stigmatization of EMR.

Chapter 3, "Disabling Black Poverty, Supporting White Underachievement: Race and the Construction of Federal Special Education Policy," picks up where chapter 2 leaves off by examining the parallel development of early black special education through Head Start and Title I associated broadly with the civil rights movement and the War on Poverty. Black educational disability was established legislatively through the Economic Opportunity Act (EOA) (Head Start) and the Elementary and Secondary Education Act (ESEA) (Title I). While EOA and ESEA federally established black educational disability based on the prevailing presumptions of poverty's debilitating effects on black children, ESEA simultaneously made white educational disability a legislative priority and reality in separate parts of the law based on a belief of white "handicap" exclusion from these laws. This chapter demonstrates the bifurcated nature of equal educational opportunity discourse that produced two separate education movements that also in turn produced two distinct kinds of special education students whose legislative needs were articulated in separate parts of EOA and ESEA. Social scientists and public officials understood black educational disability through the racial and socioeconomic lens of the "culturally deprived" whose remedy were Head Start and Title I programs; equally they addressed white educational disability through ESEA titles III and VI, culminating in the Handicapped Children's Early Education Assistance Act 1968 and the Specific Learning

Disabilities Act of 1969. This chapter examines how social scientists, school administrators, special education lobbyists, and ultimately Congress racialized and promoted a distinct black disability identity known variously as the "culturally deprived" and "educationally disadvantaged" while simultaneously lifting the "white" learning disabled (LD) out of policy invisibility.

Chapter 4, "Challenging Special Education from Above and Below: Contestations of the 1970s and 1980s," examines the violence of labels and explores the minefields associated with EMR and LD from the late 1960s through the 1970s. As LD remained a designation that only represented a small number of exclusively white students, EMR continued to grow, with much of the increase resulting in African American students being classified as educable or "mildly retarded." Black parents filed lawsuits in cities like San Francisco and Chicago to contest the misclassification of their children as EMR. These lawsuits not only put public school districts, like San Francisco Unified and Chicago Public Schools under the spotlight for racist placement practices, the court cases also called into question the use of intelligence tests.[29] In the 1970s, the phenomenon of black over-representation in special education became politicized. As EMR was challenged at the grassroots level, LD was also being scrutinized for its definitional ambiguity and racial exclusivity by social scientists skeptical of its medical etiology. Some argued that LD was discriminatory, while others posited that LD was made-up. Many wondered what constituted a "learning disability." Could the black "culturally deprived" and the "educationally disadvantaged" also be considered "learning disabled"? And why did financial and other resources flow so freely to this population? This chapter ends by examining the impact of the challenge to EMR, and how the growing number of black students once labeled EMR were increasingly classified as LD by the end of the 1970s and early 1980s.

Chapter 5, "Emotional Behavior Disorder and Other Conduct Problems: The Intersection of Race, Research, and Policy," examines the second fixation of white psychologists, social scientists, educators, and politicians: black behavior. If "black intelligence" kept teachers and administrators in schools flummoxed and led to restriction and isolation of black students, so too did "black behavior." Like "black intelligence," "black behavior" was a product of white academic discourse, rooted in both genetic and environmental explanations that "pre-determined" not only the emotional states of black people but also whether black children were "predisposed" to "emotional disturbance" and "behavior disorder." Since the larger societal context for youth behavior was juvenile delinquency and social maladjustment, this chapter starts by charting how schools and society explained the racial differences in "bad" behavior. Black and white children were equally "delinquent," "maladjusted," "emotionally disturbed," and "behavior disordered," but there were racial differences, so the explanations went. Between the 1950s and the mid-1970s, special education lobbyists went to great lengths to avoid having black students covered by federal policy (what I term "legislating around black bodies"), accomplishing the feat once in 1963 and again in 1975 with the passage of the Education for All Handicapped Children Act. Scholars have argued that excluding the "socially maladjusted" from the law was accidental or an historical anomaly.[30] I question this position, for every utterance in behavior discourses made social maladjustment (SM) synonymous with black children, and some aspects of emotional disturbance (ED) synonymous with white children, which was ultimately covered by law. With federal law defining and covering children labeled seriously emotionally disturbed (SED), and not socially maladjusted, states created behavior categories, such as emotionally handicapped (EH), emotionally disturbed (ED), and behavior disordered (BD) that reflected their own needs. While some state definitions mirrored the federal one, others diverged from it. Federal policy did not always align with state practice, as teachers in districts within states placed thousands of black children who were classified as "emotionally disturbed," "behavior disordered," and "socially maladjusted" in what became collectively known as EBD at the state level.

Chapter 6, "The Implications of Unteachability: Special Education into the Twenty-First Century," compares the turn of the twenty-first century with the previous hundred years in special education history by asking: how did the system of special education become broken for black students, and can this educational harm be reversed? By critically examining ideas of risk, chapter 6 argues that "underachieving" and so-called bad black students are not "at risk" but rather *pose* a risk to white middle-class learners. Special education, and all the interests that propped it up, has convinced the public that children who struggle academically and behaviorally as well as socially and emotionally are disabled "medi-cally" and "administratively." Tragically, many of these students are conveniently African American and Latinx and are overdisciplined, pushed out, and criminalized. Thus, EMR, LD, and EBD have solidified as self-evident explanations for academic underachievement and so-called bad behavior.

1

Who Are the Unteachables?

A Genealogy of Race, Retardation, and Intelligence

Then came psychology: the children of the public schools were studied
and it was discovered that some colored children ranked lower than
white children.

—W. E. B. DU BOIS, "Race Intelligence"

Sometimes, our sciences create new kinds of people that in a certain
sense did not exist before. I call this "making up people."

—IAN HACKING, "Making Up People"

W. E. B. Du Bois's statement above, written in the passive voice, illu-
minates the history of "unteachability," race, and special education.
A more powerful description in the active voice would read, "psychology
'studied' and 'discovered' some black children ranked lower than white
children." But to turn Du Bois's choice of verbs from passive to active
only partially captures this long history. Psychology did not "study" and
"discover" black inferiority; psychology *invented* and *assembled* it. By
invoking the field of psychology, Du Bois implicitly correlated compulsory education with special education, revealing how U.S. society regarded
unteachability and who it represented. The "evidence" for black student
unteachability is found in the patently racist, classist, and misogynist discourses on intelligence and mental retardation produced in the nineteenth and early twentieth centuries. This chapter traces the early history
of mental retardation as it marked and marred innocent children, especially black learners. Mental retardation combined medical, social scientific, and educational theories into a composite discourse that not only

13

described student potential but fixed it on a probability curve. The belief in unteachability and individual differences in "intelligence" led to the practice of psychological or mental testing, which became the basis for "determining" educational disability for the next one hundred years. As the foundational discourse in special education, classifications of mental retardation putatively demonstrated black intellectual inferiority.[1] If black adults were supposedly unfit for citizenship, then certainly their children were deemed unsuitable for general education classrooms in American schools.

The Road to Mental Retardation:
Constructing Racial Underachievement and Disability

Compulsory education in the early twentieth century and desegregation in the mid-twentieth century triggered a spatial rearrangement of schools formerly built on racial exclusivity and family privilege. Both the early and mid-twentieth century manifestations of educational change were reactions to large numbers of students forced into the school system by law—compulsory attendance policies in the former, and *Brown v. Board of Education* and the Civil Rights Act of 1964, in the latter. The political context of the Progressive Era and the legal reach of compulsory attendance laws in the first decades of the twentieth century eventually mandated that children from all backgrounds attend schools, not just from "native" white, wealthy, and middle-class families. By 1930 working class and poor families whose children were immigrants or first generation from Europe, Asia, and Latin America as well as African Americans began attending public schools regularly.[2]

Compulsory education quickly came under fire. Children of color and students from poor white families were not welcomed into public schools with open arms, especially those defined as "feebleminded." Critics believed compulsory education attempted the unthinkable, for it tried to "teach everything to everyone" sending "all children to school regardless of their mental limitations."[3] The thought of an educational space where public schools would meet the academic needs of *all* students seemed anathema to a system that believed only white middle-class children were deserving of a quality education. Unimaginable were a variegated group of children at different levels of instruction and aptitude swelling public schools across the country. Edgar Doll, leader of the Vineland School in New

Jersey noted of the idea, "The public school with its program of mass instruction faces the impossible task of giving impartial attention to the most heterogenous aggregation of different social and intellectual classes that could possibly be imagined in a common gathering."[4] Thus, mass instruction ensuing from compulsory education, encouraged men like Doll and others to introduce a selective system that could separate students based on perceived ability.

If compulsory education insisted that children must attend school, special education appeared to differentiate and cordon them off inside schools. To guard the interests of white middle-class students, school superintendents worked to safeguard their well-being with the creation of "special" classes. During this inchoate period of special education, "special classes" contained student populations, rather than function as an intervention to help individual students with "disabilities." It is clear, said Doll, "that the special classes in public schools constitute the most important single measure for the social control of the feebleminded."[5] Special classes arose as an ableist response to underachievement and the appearance of racial and socioeconomic difference inside schools. James H. Van Sickle, superintendent of Baltimore Public Schools admitted as such when he wrote that large numbers of "retarded" and "unfortunate" students would "impede the regular progress of normal children."[6] The sporadic attendance due to children laboring in factories and on plantations could no longer be counted on to keep students of color and foreign-born youngsters out of school. If it was no longer possible for public schools to rely on the vagaries of the agricultural and industrial economy to keep poor children out of schools, then it was up to the special class to maintain the privilege afforded middle-class students to an exclusive general education. Superintendent Van Sickle appeared unabashed about this line of thinking when he stated, "Almost wholly as a protective measure, and in the interests of the normal children, it was decided to try experimentally their separation from other children."[7] As a preservationist measure on behalf of white middle-class students, the special class served as a barrier against the "hordes" of underachieving students entering general education classes. When it comes to "protecting the rights of the more capable children," Van Sickle continued, the creation and "enforcement of the compulsory attendance laws leaves no other course open."[8] Thus, special classes seemed less about helping a "disabled" student population not yet identified, and more about safeguarding the progress of "normal" white middle-class students. [9]

Protecting the rights of "capable" and "normal" students partly meant defining how black, brown, and poor white students were different. Invoking racial and class differences was one thing; impugning and ascribing intelligence and achievement differences based on poverty and life circumstances was another. Indeed, students are different, which begs the question: to what degree are students different? And are noted differences meaningful? Though the questions allow us to compare student ability and aptitude, they are not the right questions to ask historically. The historical question is: how was "difference" imposed on children and used against them as they entered school? "I have long been interested in the classification of people, in how they affect the people classified, and how the effects on people in turn change the classifications," wrote philosopher Ian Hacking. "We think of these people as definite classes defined by definite properties."[10] The "mentally retarded" is one such class. But the so-called retarded were not always "mental," and their so-called retardation changed with the emergence of psychology. The reasons for the variation in "retarded" or "feebleminded" perspectives is that most, if not all, of the discourses were products of ableist epistemologies.

Ableism is defined as a "pervasive system of discrimination and exclusion that oppresses people who have mental, emotional, and physical disabilities."[11] But ableism is so much more than rank discrimination against an oppressed or perceived minority—"the disabled." Ableism and the discourses it produces are more about creating binaries between who is "normal" and who is "pathological." Ableness is an ontological position of power that holds the most privilege in the polarity—the able-bodied or able-minded understood as normal. Ableism has historically been the "decider" (to use an old President George W. Bush term) of who in society constitutes the disabled, who occupies the "inferior" position. "Similar to other systems of oppression such as racism, sexism, classism, and heterosexism," Susan Baglieri and Priya Lalvani write, "ableism thrives on beliefs about the inherent superiority of some and the inferiority of others on the basis of group traits."[12] Ableism's power lies not only in deciding who is disabled but also determining those disabled groups' "traits."

Ableist discourses use the authority of science to "invent" disabled people, not "discover" them. Philosopher Ian Hacking identifies the human sciences as the fulcrum of the invention/discovery nexus. "We think of many kinds of people as objects of scientific inquiry . . . what sciences?" Hacking asked, "The ones I shall call the human sciences, which, thus understood, include many social sciences, psychology, psychiatry and, speaking loosely, a good deal of clinical medicine."[13] The sciences claim to neutrally "discover" by making observations, but in reality, scientists have their own biased motives in their pursuit of knowledge. Knowledge produced with the objective of "making up" people, Hacking argues, uses an avalanche of printed numbers to create human narratives. "Statistical analysis of classes of people is a fundamental engine," explained Hacking. In ableist mental retarded discourses, if people are deemed "subnormal," they are given properties, designations, descriptions, terms, labels, and diagnoses by an ableist fetish for hierarchization and numbering. It is a function of ableist discourses to demonstrate pathology through an overwhelming use of numbers relationally and in combination. "Enumeration demands *kinds* of things or people to count," noted Hacking. "Counting is hungry for categories. Many of the categories we now use to describe people are byproducts of the needs of enumeration."[14] One of the characteristics of disability enumeration is an obsession with the number of incidences (or occurrences) which can then be used to construct prevalence. Without the power to enumerate, ableist scientific discourses of disability would have no vitality or traction.[15]

Using Ian Hacking and Michel Foucault as points of departure, feminist philosopher of disability Shelley Tremain contextualized the politics of enumeration, impairment, and the predilection to "make up people" within an "apparatus of disability." The apparatus of disability deploys "dividing practices" and "technologies of normalization." If disability counts, divides, and pathologizes, then disability is less concerned with personal misfortune and is more so a function of biopower. Biopower is a "set of mechanisms through which the basic biological features of the human species became the object of a political strategy, of a general strategy of power, or in other words, how starting from the eighteenth century, modern western societies took on board the fundamental biological fact that human beings are a species."[16] Biopower encompasses the entire system of Western knowledge that represents the scientific version of the "natural order of things," producing "objects and rituals of truth."[17] Tremain sheds light on arguments that insist on a natural order or an inherent structure: "The world does not come divided into categories that humans must discover; rather, humans themselves organize and classify, constructing 'facts' and subsequently verifying statements about them. There are no natural kinds, nor is there a natural order."[18]

Mental retardation is not a natural condition; it is a "man-made" classification like all classifications. Historically, the road to mental retardation is paved with various explanations about impairment. In fact, impairment lies at the heart of all hard and soft disability categories, clinical and nonclinical. It would be nearly impossible to consider people disabled if some understanding of impairment did not underlie the diagnosis. But identifying an impairment does not constitute a truth, even if we are made to understand the visible manifestations of a "damaged" body or mind. Mental retardation associated with organic impairment and incurable genetic disorders like Down syndrome, do not confirm the precision or correctness of classification; it suggests that ableist scientific discourses built an edifice of mental retardation with clinical and syndromic impairments, like Down syndrome, serving as a foundation for future knowledge about other disabilities. From this foundational base, different etiologies describing types and causes led to additional suppositions about other kinds of mental retardation. If organic, clinical, or syndromic definitions of mental retardation referred to "maximum" brain injury (visible symptoms of pathology), then "mild" mental retardation and learning disability represented "minimum" brain injury (undetected pathology). But "undetected" or "invisible" pathology is an arbitrary diagnosis that relies on the whim of the person deploying the category, as was often the case with exclusionary disability definitions. The ability to convince the public that a pathology was present but undetected allowed for the arbitrariness of disability categories, like learning disability and emotional behavior disorder (EBD), to be defined by what they were not.

When examining early twentieth-century definitions of retardation, "underachievement" and academic lag in grade levels signified an impairment. "To say that a child is retarded, means simply that for his age he is not sufficiently advanced in his studies. . . . That retardation of school children in general terms expresses a *misrelation* between the age of the children, and the grades appropriate to their age is more and more a generally accepted proposition" wrote Roland P. Falkner in 1911, former superintendent of Puerto Rico Schools.[19] Consider another definition from 1914

that supports Falkner, both of which are like the discrepancy definition in learning disability: "There are two general definitions [of mental
retardation] used: the one based on *normal age,* and the other on *progress.*"[20] In 1965, Barbara Bateman, a scholar of learning disabilities, defined
what would become the centerpiece of learning disability theory when
she said that LD refers to students "who manifest an educationally significant discrepancy between their estimated intellectual potential and
actual level of performance."[21] Prior to Bateman, Marion Monroe, a scholar
of reading disabilities in the 1930s, was one of the first persons credited
with the notion of discrepancy between expected achievement and actual
achievement.[22]

Bateman's definition of discrepancy in 1965 and even Monroe's in 1932
was no different from early twentieth-century ideas of retardation: that a
student's intellectual potential was tied to what one should know at a certain age and grade level. What is a "misrelation" if it is not a discrepancy?
Is not "grade appropriate" the same as "grade expected?" The difference
here is that the aptitude—achievement misrelation or discrepancy—relied
on a student's actual age and grade-level progress and not on an IQ score
and an achievement test, at least not yet. The difference also is that in
practice "one could not be LD in 1900," because the classification did
not emerge until later in the century.[23] Many students who performed
below their actual age and intellectual potential were considered "pedagogically" or "academically" retarded. Curiously, the contrast between the
"pedagogically" or "academically" retarded from the "subnormal child who
had only limited potential" characterized the major difference between
LD and mental retardation in the second half of the century.[24] But that
would be then, and this was now. School leaders were so certain of their
conception of retardation in the first decade of the twentieth century
that James E. Bryan, superintendent of Schools for Camden, New Jersey,
wrote, "I believe that we are justified in defining retardation in terms of
school progress, no other definition of retardation has equal objectivity."[25] Thus, LD, as a *kind* of intellectual disability, was nothing more than
a refined version of mental retardation, an argument I take up in greater
detail in chapter 2.

Before intelligence testing transformed one's actual age and grade
level into a "mental disability," school officials were already deeming black
students "retarded" at the turn of the twentieth century. Their putative

retardation was rooted in the separate world white people created for them. Black educators understood that academic underachievement in white schools reflected black student exclusion not only from white schools but from white society. "The inauguration of separate schools, the motivation of the crises which force Negroes to accept, or even to ask for them, are not original with Negroes," said black scholar and educator Horace Mann Bond. "The basis for the separate school is apparently an unwillingness of the white population to accept the Negro as a full participant in the life of our Democracy."[26] The system of segregation and the entire Jim Crow experience reflected the desire of white people to cordon off white spaces from black people, be they geographical spaces (regions of the country or neighborhoods), labor market spaces (white jobs versus "Negro" jobs), and educational spaces (white schools versus "colored" schools). Excluding African Americans marked them as unfit associates of white people as neighbors, coworkers, and school companions. Oppressed economically, excluded politically, and separated socially, a determination of black retardation based on age progress or grade-level academic achievement began after black students arrived at white schools and struggled academically. If black and white schools were physically separated, then it stood to reason educational programs based on achievement within schools would be also separated. Thus, special education is a system that mirrored other systems of separation in the United States.

An elaborate taxonomy of "feeblemindedness" took shape between 1850 and 1910, which designated and separated people within society. Defined as a state of arrested mental development, "feebleminded" became synonymous with the word "retarded" and sometimes interchangeable with terms like "defective" and "deficient." Lightner Witmer, credited with founding the subfield of clinical psychology and the journal *The Psychological Clinic,* wrote, "In these severe forms of retardation, the mental defect usually rests upon some incurable brain defect."[27] Witmer distinguished between what he called "physiological" retardation—a form of arrested normal development that explained the incurable brain defect—and "pedagogical" retardation, which was the unrealized academic potential of students. Before the two were conflated, long before Witmer's influence was felt in the early twentieth century, it was the physiological retardation that produced the elaborate taxonomy we have come to associate with the history of feeblemindedness. As "classes or grades of retardation," feebleminded categories included the terms "idiot," "imbecile," and "moron," each graded as low, medium, and high.[28] But "idiot," "imbecile," and "moron" were not only categories or grades of retardation: with ableist psychologists, these terms began to refer to real people.

"An idiot," wrote G. E. Johnson, is "a natural born fool." Sounding more like a caricature today, medical doctors and scientists created the foundation for our understanding of idiocy as a medically diagnosed disability in the nineteenth century. "Idiocy is not a disease" that runs its course, said Johnson, who taught at Clark University, "but a condition in which the intellectual faculties are never manifested, or have never been developed sufficiently to enable the idiot to acquire such amount of knowledge as persons of his own age." The language of "never manifested or developed" stemmed from scientific notions of the "heritability" of natural (permanent) intelligence that marked individuals, families, and entire groups of people as "defective." If the "idiot" was a natural born fool, then it stood to reason that idiocy was genetic in nature. "Heredity plays a prominent part in the production of idiocy," Johnson continued. "There are whole families of idiots." Two scholars conducted "research" on a family of idiots and discovered, Johnson recalled, "five brothers and two sisters, all idiots."[29]

Scientists, medical doctors, and superintendents invoked heredity as the main source of idiocy due to its proximity with biology and physiology. If the accounts of the early history of retardation border on the absurd, it is because medical doctors went to great lengths to convince the public that "feeblemindedness is practically a permanent condition . . . that cannot be cured."[30] According to "experts" at the time, causes of idiocy were not always congenital (formerly referred to as "birth defects"); many were "acquired." Early understandings of congenital idiocy included neuroses, drunkenness, blood relationships of parents, and frequent sickness of the mother during pregnancy. Examples of acquired idiocy included meningitis, convulsions at teething, a blow to the head, rickets, measles, insanity, smallpox, typhus, brandy drinking, injury at birth, perverted training, epilepsy, inflammation of the brain, menstrual disorders, sunstroke or exposure to the sun, stroke of lightning, and fright. The range of ridiculous causes sometimes led to a "range" of idiots, classified by psychologists as "profound" or "absolute" idiots and "superficial" or "simple" idiots.[31]

Jean-Marc-Gaspard Itard's iconic "wild boy of Averyon" was a twelve-year-old "idiot" named Victor, who was described in the most disparaging terms. Located in the south of France and brought to Paris, Victor was portrayed by Itard as a "disgustingly dirty child affected with spasmodic movements and often convulsions who swayed back and forth ceaselessly like certain animals in the menagerie, who bit and scratched those who opposed him, who showed no affection for those who attended him."[32] Itard depicted Victor's intellectual capacity in similar terms, writing "his intelligence, the ability to produce a few incoherent ideas relative to his wants" made "his whole life . . . a completely animal existence."[33] Edward Seguin, a student of Itard, who was regarded as the most important theorist in the history of mental retardation, spent much of his career studying the behavior of so-called idiots. Seguin asserted that "idiots" are individuals, like Victor, who know nothing and can do nothing.[34]

Idiocy had a racial component, leading scientists and doctors to create pseudo-medical discourses about black and brown people. John Langdon Down, a medical doctor from England, whose name became associated with the syndrome, based his entire understanding of idiocy on racial and ethnic facial phenotypes. "I have for some time," Down announced, "had my attention directed to the possibility of making a classification of the feeble-minded, by arranging them around various ethnic standards." During his time at the Royal London Hospital and as medical superintendent at the Earlswood Asylum, Down found "among a large number of idiots and imbeciles which come under my observation . . . great divisions of the human race." Not to single out people of color, Down said, he understood that idiots "of course, are numerous representatives of the great Caucasian family." But Dr. Down claimed to notice something peculiar in idiots he saw in his practice. He explained, "Several well-marked examples of the Ethiopian variety have come under my notice, presenting the characteristics of malar bones, the prominent eyes, the puffy lips, and retreating chin. The woolly hair has also been present, although not always black." Dr. Down's description of each patient of color that entered his office was as if he was taking ethnographic field-notes on an anthropological safari. "Some arrange themselves around the Malay variety, and present in their soft, black, curly hair, their prominent upper jaws and capacious mouths, types of family which people the South Sea Islands." From Africa to Malaysia to the Americas, the "shortened foreheads, prominent cheeks, deep-set eyes, and slightly apish [*sic*] nose," from those people who "originally inhabited the American Continent" (indigenous peoples) were idiots but not prototypical. According to Dr. Down, Asian people were so-called prototypes, and it is where Down placed much of his attention. His findings meshed with the racial currency associated with Johann Friedrich Blumenbach's racial classification system that ultimately furthered a racist discourse on the so-called Mongolian race. "The great Mongolian family has numerous representatives" and a "very large number of congenital idiots are typical Mongols." With a "flat and broad face" and a "long and thick tongue," Dr. Down concluded, "these ethnic features are the result of degeneration."[35]

The purported degeneration was not particular to Asian people or any people of color but of an extra chromosome that made some children with the genetic disorder share facial characteristics projected onto Asian people. "Trisomy" at the twenty-first location is the medical term for the person having three copies of a chromosome instead of two. During a cell's division, geneticists discovered that it may split, resulting in "cells carrying additional chromatic material."[36] To underscore the arbitrariness of early discourses on the feebleminded, the medical community began to reconsider both the racial discourses associated with Down syndrome as well as its relationship with idiocy after the chromosomal basis of it was discovered in 1959. While the public still used the term "mongolism" to describe the genetic disorder through the mid-twentieth century, in 1961 scientists and genetic experts published an admonishing letter in the medical journal, *The Lancet*: "It has long been recognized that the terms *Mongolian Idiocy, Mongolism, Mongoloid,* etc. as applied to a specific type of mental deficiency have misleading connotations. We urge, therefore, that the expressions which imply a racial aspect of the condition be no longer used." How ironic that John Langdon Down's name was on the letter, who with eighteen other signatories urged that the term "mongolism" be abandoned in favor of "Langdon-Down's anomaly," "Down's syndrome or anomaly," "congenital acromicria," or "trisomy 21 anomaly." Despite the syndrome's disassociation with Asians and idiocy, the damage to people of color had long been done.[37]

The damage from racist, misogynist, and nativist classifications was incalculable, and no group was spared if it did not hold all the dominant subject positions in society. For so-called feebleminded women in general, able-bodied discourses proved equally unkind, positioning them as less than human and the most treacherous gender in society. Licia Carlson writes that

> mental retardation never became a "female malady" in the way that hysteria and other mental illnesses have become associated with women and feminine characteristics. However, in the first decade of this century, the "feebleminded women" became representative of the nature and dangers of the category of feeblemindedness as a whole. This was largely due to the intersection between conceptions of feeblemindedness and stereotypes of femininity. By virtue of her membership in two socially defined groups— women and the "feebleminded"—the "feebleminded woman" was singled out as a perversion of the former group and a symbol of the latter.[38]

For "feebleminded women activists" in the late nineteenth century considered "demagogues" as a class of suffrage agitators, Edward Seguin believed "they overburden themselves . . . and accept burdens unfit for them," making their children deranged. Dr. Walter E. Fernald equaled Seguin's misogyny when he said the "high-grade female imbecile group was the most dangerous class" because it is a certainty they will "become sexual offenders and . . . spread venereal disease or give birth to degenerate children." The children of these women (but ironically not the men who equally produced them) "become public charges" then later "juvenile delinquents . . . [and] adult paupers." "Strict sexual quarantine" was advanced as a solution of social control "because the institutions are overcrowded." Isaac N. Kerlin, another medical doctor, proposed that the "helpless classes—lunatics, imbeciles, and criminals . . . ranks run into one another," and it was increasingly hard to tell the difference between them. Kerlin acknowledged feebleminded native white populations posed a problem, too, increasing by 22 percent in Pennsylvania, but he saw an increase of "228 percent for imbeciles of foreign born" in the same state as the real problem in American society.[39] Fears of immigrants pouring into the United States, women participating in the public sphere, and criminals and the insane overwhelming institutions generated a similar anxiety about schools becoming infiltrated with defective, "underachieving" children.[40]

In the first two decades of the twentieth century, underachieving children were met with three developments that served as the foundation for special education: the mental testing movement, which would give rise to the Binet-Simon scale as a new tool for measuring students; the intelligence quotient (IQ) as evidence of student mental capacity (or in the case of black students, their inferiority); and the introduction of the "moron" to mental retardation classification, which would represent the prototype for the mildly or educable mentally retarded later in the century. Because of the congenital nature and mental capacity of "idiots," the "lowest" grade of feeblemindedness, ableist scientists and physicians believed that so-called idiots and many imbeciles were beyond of the pale of curability and educability, advocating institutionalizing and separating them from so-called normal members of society. Educators taught profoundly "feebleminded" children in separate training schools, which states began creating in the 1850s. But what about the less "defective" moron, or the deficient "dullard," "borderline," and "backward" child that may not have an incurable brain or genetic defect? Fictionalized as the majority, they would numerically come to represent most "mentally retarded" children in the United States. Byron Phillips, an early chronicler of Philadelphia public schools, suggested that morons, though less defective, were equally not suited for public education. "We must recognize that retardation is dependent to a great extent upon the natural inequalities of the human mind, which may be of any grade from the lowest to the highest intelligence. At one end of the series we have the profound idiot, at the other the genius. Somewhere between these extremes we find the average or 'normal' mind. Minds below the [normal] limit will not fit into a school system based upon this average, and a certain amount of retardation will always exist."[41] Trying to determine what to do with students whose "retardation," educators and psychologists like Phillips believed would always exist, emerged as a grand challenge in early twentieth-century public education.

Public education in the United States implemented a system of sorting "deserving" students from the "undeserving," the "normal" from the "abnormal," and finally, the "abled" from the "disabled." Consistent school attendance during the precompulsory era rested on family wealth and stability with the expectation that education was only for children from families with social standing. Between 1865 and 1920, all states passed compulsory attendance policies, prompting public schools to create special education programs for students that experienced academic challenges as soon as they arrived in schools.[42] Contending with the threat to "normality," schools employed more professionals to make sense of the welter of young people in public schools. New students generated new measurement procedures that led to newer experts. "With regard to defective children, these questions have been left largely to physicians," said Naomi Norsworthy of Columbia University in 1907, "but now they are beginning to attract the attention of the psychologist, too."[43] In addition to psychologists, special classes and special schools needed special teachers to make determinations about the abnormality of underachievers and what they could accomplish in life.[44] As Charles Scott Berry, educational psychologist at the University of Michigan noted, "Traditional education quickly discovers what the mental defective cannot do, but it is left to special education to discover what he can do."[45]

What the putative "mental defective" could not do was expect the same kind of education afforded to "normal" children. "Every child has a right to an education," said Superintendent George W. Twitmyer of Delaware Schools, but in no way "does it mean that all children should have the same education."[46] The type of education should be commensurate not only with a student's intellectual potential and distributed accordingly but also, as early twentieth-century educators believed, one's physical, medical, and mental ability. If students appeared unprepared to meet the academic challenges facing them, then the misfortune was their own no matter the source. Superintendent Twitmyer gestured toward a strategy of "disability" invention when he offered reasons why schools and parents should determine "causes" and potential "treatment." "Every school has some unfortunate children who cannot keep pace with their more fortunate neighbors." It was incumbent upon teachers to "discover the retardation, diagnose its causes, where possible, and suggest to parents the proper treatment."[47] Of all the so-called causes of mental retardation, structural discrimination and racial inequality in society and in the nation's schools were never mentioned but rather

irregularity in attendance and truancy; bad or indifferent domestic conditions and low ideals of life and conduct; want of parental care and discipline; vicious associates; malnutrition and fatigue; defective eyesight;

defective hearing; and such physical defects as catarrh, enlarged tonsils and adenoids; tobacco and alcoholic poisoning; the sequellae of scarlet fever; diphtheria, measles, whooping cough and typhoid fever; chorea and nervousness manifested in mental irritability; depression; emotional excitement; morbid fears; lack of self-control; persistent ideas; weakness of memory and concentration; exaggerated mobility; tremors and twitching movements of groups of muscles; stammering; stuttering, and other developmental defects.[48]

Every physical, mental, developmental, and emotional condition became a prima facie case for the causes of mental retardation along with ableist value judgments about the domestic realities of families and children. A 1914 survey covering a hundred cities in the United States reported 38 causes of mental retardation of which the most prominent were absence, mentioned by 26 cities; mental dullness, mentioned by 19 cities; physically defective, 18 cities; illness, 13; race, 13; late entrance, 10; change of school, 8; crowded school rooms, 7. From the 1950s through the early twenty-first century, one of the primary reasons given for the causes of black intellectual disability was poverty. In this 1914 study, poverty gets mentioned only once.[49]

Leonard Ayres, a trained statistician and former superintendent of Puerto Rico Schools, published in 1909 what many considered a classic text on retardation: *Laggards in Our Schools*. Securing a grant from the Russell Sage Foundation, Ayres studied schools nationally to determine the size, character, and the causes of retardation. He wondered why so many students fail to progress from grade to grade. Ayres believed "about this large group we need the facts":

Are they in their present condition largely because of removable physical disabilities, such as hypertrophied tonsils or adenoids, defective vision or hearing, or malnutrition? Do they drop behind in their school life because of illness? Are they behind because of late entrance into the schools? To what extent is irregularity of attendance a factor in delayed progress? Is compulsory labor after school hours an important factor? When do they drop out of school, and for what reasons? Are there any schools that succeed in educating an appreciably larger per cent of these children than do others? If so, how is it done?[50]

Laggards in Our Schools and other earlier studies demonstrated that pre-psychological conceptions of retardation rested on ill-health, sporadic attendance, and the demands of employment in the industrial and agricultural economy. The social class differences in poor health, attendance, and work kept working-class children from attending schools consistently. Instead of understanding this phenomenon objectively, ableist observers used it to construct a new social reality based on school progress and performance. Ayres's *Laggards* appeared during major changes in the academic disciplines. The *causes* of retardation moved away from basic social class difficulties to inherent intellectual and racial capacities of children from working-class and poor families. When psychologists entered the picture, the reasons why students struggled academically began to change, even though the life challenges faced by working-class and poor families remained the same.

In the early twentieth century, schools explicitly correlated race with intellectual disability and suggested higher rates of retardation existed because of the presence of black students in primary and middle grades. Philadelphia serves as a prime case in point. "When retardation in the colored schools is discussed," wrote Byron Phillips, an expert on Philadelphia schools, "it will be seen that in every case it is approximately from 10 to 20 percent higher than that for the district."[51] Philadelphia inventoried all students at the district and ward level, then at each individual school in the city, finding that retardation in white schools ranged between 30 and 50 percent, and in black schools, from 46 to 72 percent. Defined as at least two grades behind one's chronological age, retardation seemed to be a challenge in every district and ward. Philadelphia's business section sat in the center of the city, with the wealthier side of the city to the northwest, the factory district in the northeast, and south Philadelphia populated mainly by Italians, Russian Jews, and other immigrants. The report described, "District 3, almost entirely foreign, with a considerable colored element; District 4, business section, old aristocratic section, large colored element . . . District 5, residential, with a large colored element, [and] poor laboring class."[52] It then went on to say:

> We can readily see that District 3, composed almost wholly of foreigners, and District 4, with a large Negro element, have the greatest amount of retardation. District 7 has a low percentage of retardation . . . due to the . . .

absence of the Negro element. Each district, however, is composed of a number of political wards. . . . In District 4, with a retardation of 45.1 percent, the 7th ward has 62.2 percent (colored). District 6, with 37.2 percent of retardation, shows 45.1 percent in the 14th ward, which has a considerable Negro element besides a large number of foreigners.[53]

The report not only promoted the idea that black children in Philadelphia public schools increased the percentage of mental retardation across the district; it also argued that nine black segregated schools in Philadelphia offered additional evidence that black students were more retarded than any other segment of the school population.

The history of black separate schools in the North mirrored the South at the level of student demographics, where some schools were 100 percent black in Philadelphia. Despite a state law in 1881 that ended segregation in Pennsylvania, districts continued to maintain racially separate schools. But unlike the South, school segregation was not absolute. "In most of the schools of Philadelphia," wrote Phillips, "white and colored pupils are mixed in varying proportions" except in the nine schools that were exclusively black.[54] According to Phillips, the nine schools in Philadelphia were: J. Miller, Pollock, O. V. Catto, J. S. Ramsey, Purvis, R. Vaux, J. E. Hill, Meehan, and Wilmot. Out of the nine schools, three were located in District 4—Catto, Ramsey, and Purvis—where the percentages of retarded students were 67.3, 70.9, and 46.4 percent respectively. The highest number of so-called black retarded students existed at Hill where the report stated that 72 percent of the students in grades one through eight were retarded. For Philadelphia school officials, the higher number of retarded students in black schools proved to Phillips that black students were more retarded than all white students in the district, including recently arrived European immigrants to the city. Phillips wrote, "The foreign element raises the retardation above the average for the city, but not to as great an extent as the Negro element."[55] It is not clear if reading levels factored into Philadelphia's definition of retardation. W. E. B. Du Bois's study fifteen years earlier, *The Philadelphia Negro,* cast doubt on the claims of greater black retardation. He reported that Italians, Russians, Polish, Hungarians, and Irish all had higher illiteracy rates than black students in the seventh ward, with 63.6 percent of Italian students being the most illiterate population compared to only

18.6 for black students. Only children of German descent, said Du Bois, had a higher literacy rate in Philadelphia schools than black children.[56] Juxtaposing black retardation with the rest of the district, the Philadelphia retardation report marked black students with a permanent stamp of inferiority that questioned their ability to learn in Philadelphia public schools, as Phillips concluded: "It is a question whether the course of study is suited to the Negroes, as the educational results are so far behind those in the other schools, and it is very doubtful whether even a liberal interpretation of the course of study would meet the educational necessities of this group."[57] Thus, it is not an accident that white school administrators and psychologists correlated an increase in black student attendance, more than immigrant whites, with a need to proliferate special classes during the first two decades of the twentieth century.

In East Orange, New Jersey, the Board of Education and the Superintendent of Schools experimented with an "ungraded" class for thirty "backward colored pupils" in the primary grades. With three-quarters of the black student population attending two schools in the city—Eastern and Ashland—the board reasoned that a policy change was necessary due to the rise in "overage" black children, the classic definition of retardation. Black parents became indignant when school leaders began transferring average achieving black students from regular classrooms into the ungraded class. Out of eighty-seven black students that attended Eastern, twenty-three of them were initially moved, forcing parents to counter the district's argument that the placement was meant to improve black student performance: "If they bring the white boys and girls that are stupid," one parent chided, "then my child can stay there, but not otherwise." Black parents believed placing their children in ungraded classes was a way for the district to racially segregate them. The parents proved correct, as East Orange schools used the official policy of special classes to preserve general education classes for white students. The policy stated: "Whenever a sufficient number of Afro-American pupils are found in any one of the [first four] grades of any school, such pupils may be separately taught." After some black parents pulled their children out of East Orange schools and helped set up classes in the city's black churches, the board saved face by placing several white children in the ungraded class during the 1901–1902 academic year.[58]

The Making of the "Moron": Educational Psychology and the Mental Testing Movement

What have epistemology and scientific truth claims done to us? One answer is that epistemologies have taken us up an escalator discovering higher realms of truth. But our ability to produce new ways of knowing and understanding do not always lead to self-improvement or even a "total understanding of the various aspects of the cosmos," argued the late Joe L. Kincheloe, critical pedagogy theorist who taught at McGill University.[59] That is because our truths are partial at best. Perhaps even false. When Aristotle said, "To say of what *is* that it *is,* and what is *not* that it is *not* is true," was to place power at the center of truth-making.[60] The pragmatist philosopher William James said "truth *happens* to an idea. It *becomes* true, is *made* true by events," and by us. "Truth," James argued, "is a property" of the certainty of our ideas. "It means their 'agreement.'"[61] Epistemological breakthroughs and truth claims, especially in the psychological sciences, have been devastatingly harmful, and William James, as the first American psychologist, bears some responsibility. Kincheloe does not render a value judgment about psychology but rather on the entire Western scientific enterprise and the enduring belief that "if they [positivists] suppress their values while conducting their inquiry, they can produce universal axioms that transcend time or place."[62] Calling this at times epistemological "naivete," and at other instances, "hegemony," Kincheloe suggests that in our present moment "we are still staggering from the hangover of Western epistemology."[63] Thus, this begs another question. What have our epistemologies done to black people? In short, maimed, marginalized, vilified, tortured, oppressed.

In an aspirational essay written in 1892, William James said he "wished, by treating Psychology *like* a natural science, to help her become one."[64] James knew a great deal about achieving desired ends, as one of his foremost contributions to the development of psychology was his theory of the will. "If with the desire there goes a sense that attainment is not possible," he said, "we simply *wish;* but if we believe that the end is in our power, we *will* that the desired feeling, having, or doing shall be real."[65] James's dogged determination to "will" the discipline of psychology into a natural science rested on the concept called "mental states," of which he said is becoming "uniformly believed."

Whatever conclusions an ultimate criticism may come to about mental states, they form a practically admitted sort of object whose habits of co-existence and succession and relations with organic conditions form an entirely definite subject of research. Cannot philosophers and biologists both become 'psychologists' on this common basis? Cannot both forego ulterior inquiries, and agree that, provisionally at least, the mental state shall be the ultimate datum so far as 'psychology' care to go? . . . The attempt to get the undivided "mental-state" once and for all accepted by my colleagues as the fundamental datum for their science [means that] we *have* a "science" of the correlation of mental states with brain-states.[66]

But if mental states are associated with the mind, the "entity called mind lies no deeper than the entity called brain," said George Trumbull Ladd, one of William James's foremost critics.[67] Psychologists have insisted that thoughts and feelings are real, both separate from and a part of the brain. For the better part of a hundred years, psychologists have tried to convince a skeptical public that a science of the mind exists and that it is connected to the physical organ called the brain. As late as 2009, Lisa Feldman Barrett, distinguished professor of psychology at Northwestern University, captured this perpetual dilemma the discipline continued to find itself in. "Throughout our history, the link between the social (mind and behavior) and the natural (brain) has felt less like a solid footbridge and more like a tightrope requiring lightness of foot and a really strong safety net."[68]

Many have attempted to push psychologists off this tightrope since the discipline's beginning, arguing that psychologists were promoting an epistemology whose claims remained difficult to substantiate. "Let me, then, at once speak frankly and clearly," Ladd chided. "The conception of psychology as a natural science with which Professor James sets out, is—in my judgement—a wholly untenable conception."[69] But James took the position that when you have "your ruling idea" and the courage of your convictions, it is the "end of the matter." He also asserted, "You're in possession; you *know*; you have fulfilled your thinking destiny. You have obeyed your categorical imperative. Epistemologically, you are in stable equilibrium."[70] Ladd disagreed, believing the "science" of psychology was more a metaphysics, a philosophical discourse, hiding behind terms such as "cerebral physiology" when attempting to demonstrate general conditions of brain activity and functions of the brain. Ladd believed in the present state of knowledge on "cerebral hemispheres" that contributed to our understanding of limb function, but less convinced in the demonstrable research he saw in the "psychical vision,"[71] even less in how the brain contributed to "spoken or written language" (reading disability researchers like James Hinshelwood, Samuel Orton, and Marion Monroe would attempt causality). In addition, Ladd remained "very uncertain as to where are the so-called 'centres' of other sensory-motor forms of mental-life," questions pursued by psychologists Alfred Strauss, William Cruickshank, and others later in the century. Ladd impressed upon the reader that psychology was not "worthy to be dignified with the name of 'natural science,'"[72] and that the language of science, brain theory, and mental states was being employed by psychology in some kind of shell game. Ladd's cautionary tale to the public was simple: "When, then, Professor James maintains that his ... schematic descriptions of the brain-processes ... 'show what a deep congruity there is between mental processes and mechanical processes of *some* kind,' I must beg his pardon and flatly contradict him. They show nothing of the sort; they *show* nothing of any sort. They assume some sort of unknown congruity; they also serve to impress the uninitiated reader with the feeling that he is being shown something."[73]

But Ladd and other critics could not stop the growing chorus insisting on the importance of psychology and its application to human behavior. Psychologists claimed expertise not only in thoughts, feelings, and mental states but in all things relating to human nature. "A complete science of psychology would tell us every fact about every one's intellect and character and behavior, [and] would tell us the cause of every change in human nature," declared Edward Lee Thorndike, the founder of educational psychology.[74] In an essay published in 1910 entitled "The Contribution of Psychology to Education," Thorndike not only made a case for understanding human nature but also for controlling it. "Every advance in the sciences of human nature will contribute to our success in controlling human nature and changing it to the advantage of the common weal."[75] Thorndike likened the psychological "discovering," "measuring," and "controlling" of human nature to the physical scientist's discovery of the thermometer that determines temperature, the galvanometer's detection and measurement of electrical current, and the spectroscope's ability to measure the wavelengths and intensity of light. This analogy was not just absurd; it was patently false. Psychological claims purporting to understand human nature differentiated people in the United States based on flawed assertions about their character and intellect. When Thorndike announced in 1910 that the "first line of work concerns the discovery and improvement of means of measurement of intellectual functions," little doubt remained how this "science" would shape the perception of black people.[76] If one could not see where psychology was going from its declared "first line of work," Thorndike left little to imagine about psychology's "second line of work":

> The second line of work concerns race, sex, age and individual differences in all the many elements of intellect and character and behavior. These studies of individual differences or variability are being supplemented by studies of correlations. The extent to which the intellectual and moral differences found in human beings are consequences of their original nature and determined by the ancestry from which they spring, is a matter of fundamental importance for education.[77]

From its beginnings in the early 1900s, it seems educational psychology devoted much of its energy to mental capacity, measurement, and the differentiation of people.[78] Cornering the market on brain research, psychologists would build a body of neurophysiological knowledge, linking "damaged" and compromised central nervous systems to difficulties children experienced with reading, language development, and mental aptitude. "Feebleminded" perspectives now had the backing of a science that could be "empirically demonstrated" with mental and achievement tests. If William James and Edward Thorndike offered concepts like "mental states," then other psychologists, such as Alfred Binet, Henry Goddard, and Lewis Terman, inspired by the promise of psychometric testing, gave us "mental age." "Mental age" would transform over-age retardation born of economic hardships into a "mental retardation" located in the brain.[79]

Notions of mental retardation emerged at a time when white America debated the Negro "question." The so-called Negro question, however, became the Negro "problem," or more aptly, how white Americans conceived of black life, character, work, and citizenship. To turn it around and present it as the "Negro question" was to pretend to be impartial, to hold the "problem" at arm's length and provide an objective view that ignored the existence of racial prejudice. To invoke the Negro question was to address the race question, but skillfully imbed it in the language of human difference and not in white racial hatred. "The social and political questions connected to the African race in the United States," wrote Senator John T. Morgan of Alabama, "all relate to and depend upon the essential differences between the negro and the white man as they have been arranged by the hands of the creator." Morgan did not identify the problem as white racial antipathy toward black people but rather racial difference. Still not wanting to confront the obvious that the maltreatment of African Americans was motivated by racial animus, Morgan held that the differences characterizing black Americans and white Americans lay beyond what the eye could see. "Among these differences, the color of the skin, while it distinguishes the races unmistakably, is the least important," he continued. "The mental differences and differing traits, including the faculty of governing, forecast, enterprise, and the wide field of achieving in the arts and sciences are accurately measured by the contrast of the civilization of the United States, with the barbarism of Central Africa."[80]

The United States believed its civilization was manifestly destined to spread over the entire continent, conquering people of color to answer its "race questions." With the closing of the American frontier in the 1890s, the white man's burden and race questions revealed themselves in the Philippines in 1898. Representing the spirit of the times, this early twentieth-century civic nationalism promoted a form of "progressive" democracy that privileged efficiency and order in domestic and foreign life, from Theodore Roosevelt's so-called big stick diplomacy to Woodrow Wilson's efficiency in self-government. The growing industrial and manufacturing economy also created a need for efficient, better organized, and time-saving practices in institutions, but this "search for order" also included a heavy dose of racial nationalism. The practices of big business in the industrial age engendered Frederick Winslow Taylor's principles of scientific management and Henry Ford's production techniques. Political corruption led to the exposés of Upton Sinclair and Lincoln Steffens. And the welter of students produced by compulsory education necessitated the need for efficiency and order in public schools, inspiring psychological test makers to sort and differentiate between underachieving, normal, and gifted students. Psychological testing also addressed the Negro question by racializing underachievement, giving the results of the tests the green light to create special education, and to what liberal social scientists like Howard Odum believed about black children: "There are many negro children who have an almost total lack of mental perception, whose minds are so dense that they can scarcely learn anything. The percentage of such cases increases with age. Here are children who must cope with tremendous odds in inherited tendencies and environment. They are different in every particular from the white children; the basis on which their education must rest is different from that of the white children."[81]

The raw commentary and treatment of black people reflected and defined what historian Rayford Logan called the "nadir"—the lowest point for African Americans in U.S. history.[82] Bookended by the years 1877 and 1901, Logan framed the nadir conceptually within the context of lynchings and other forms of white mob violence. Logan's conceptual and temporal framing could easily extend to include the discursive violence exhibited by white professionals across the educational, medical, and political spectrum. This "enlightened" class of professionals continued to pose racial questions and repeatedly answer them, arriving at the same conclusions about black capability. In 1910, Howard Odum published *Social and Mental Traits of the Negro,* the same year the National Urban League began fighting on behalf of African Americans. This serve-and-volley between white degradation of African Americans and the black freedom struggle characterized the years between 1900 and 1930, extending Logan's notion of a nadir well into the new century. The first decade of the twentieth century did not see any curtailment of the behavior as white mob violence went unchecked. Race riots in Atlanta, Georgia (1906), Springfield, Illinois (1908), and the unjust imprisonment of black soldiers in Brownsville, Texas (1906), confirmed that white Americans would continue the racial status quo in the new century. In addition to the National Urban League, white supremacy also met the growing organizational strength of new groups like the Niagara Movement, the National Association for the Advancement of Colored People (NAACP), and the National Association of Colored Women—all visibly standing up to racial injustice. In an essay published in 1902 entitled "The Ethics of the Negro Question," Anna Julia Cooper wrote, "The colored people of

America find themselves today in the most trying period of all their trying history in this land of their trial and bondage. As the trials and responsibilities of the man weigh more heavily than do those of the infant, so the Negro under free labor and cut throat competition today has to vindicate his fitness to survive in the face of colorphobia that heeds neither reason nor religion and a prejudice that shows no quarter and allows no mitigating circumstances."[83]

The merciless colorphobia Anna Julia Cooper referenced above extended into the field of public education. Visible educational inequities reared themselves in school buildings and other facilities. But harmful policies like resource allocation, student placement, and ability grouping went unnoticed by the public, leaving the impression that racism occurred mainly at the level of individual acts. The work of historians John Cell, George Lipsitz, and Karen and Barbara Fields is helpful here, instructing us as students of U.S. history to pay close attention to racism, segregation, and whiteness, not only as visibly destructive forces but as deceptively and ambiguously self-contradictory ideologies and practices. Special education surfaced during the formative years of segregation; hence, special education is a product of segregation. As a system created by "well-educated and comparatively modern men" and not by hooded racists, Cell tells us segregation established "an impressive capacity for absorption, flexibility, and mystification."[84] Segregation promoted a fiction, and presented itself as a "positive, humane approach ... enabling each group to develop to its highest potential, at its own pace, in its own way, maintaining its distinctive cultural values."[85] Psychologists and educators continued to posture special education as a gesture of largesse to struggling students, an educational favor that segregated them from "normal" children to give them a chance to reach their academic potential at their own pace. But special education was neither altruistic as its proponents claimed, nor was it educationally beneficial. It obliterated the life chances of many students. Special education was a form of segregation that grotesquely based itself on racially perceived academic abilities and performances.

If segregation as a social system contributed to special education, then the "possessive investment in whiteness" as Lipsitz coined it, secured preferences for white children in an educational system that penalized some and rewarded others based on racially perceived academic potential and intellectual capacity. Invariably, children seen as "normal" or "gifted" in the early twentieth century were overwhelmingly white. Children deemed "mentally retarded" and placed in special classes were significantly black and brown. The absence of racism is not proven by the presence of white children in special classes. On the contrary, special classes taught a smaller percentage of the white public school age population. Most white students were educated in general education (i.e., "normal") and gifted classes. Special education is the very essence of the possessive investment in whiteness in that "systemic, collective, and coordinated [racist] behavior disappears from sight," said Lipsitz. What Lipsitz offers is a way to understand systemic and structural racism at the group level, arguing that "collective exercises of group power relentlessly channeling rewards, resources, and opportunities from one group to another, will not appear to be 'racist' from this perspective because they rarely announce their intention to discriminate against individuals. But they work to construct racial identities by giving people of different races vastly different life chances."[86] In U.S. society, racial group power produced different group opportunities. These group opportunities were racial opportunities that fixed two different starting positions in life for students of color and white children. Thus, the different fixed starting positions call into question the entire myth of meritocracy in public education.

If people of different races experienced different life chances because of white supremacy, powerful whites needed to convince the public that oppression had little to do with it. Keeping white oppression out of the discussion was paramount during the early days of special education. Whiteness was both hyper-visible and invisible. White power manifested in lynchings and other acts of white mob violence. But the leveraging of white privilege often went unnoticed in school policies and practices, especially by black children. A prime example was the development and use of psychological tests that converted underachievement into a "handicap." Turning underachievement into a "handicap" or "disability" invented who was "normal" and who was "impaired" or "pathological." But since special education was a product of segregation, psychologists racialized underachievement, making disabilities out of mental test results. Black "over-aged" retardation *before* the implementation of psychological tests became "mental" retardation *after* the administering of psychological tests. The *results* of the tests below 100 *indicated* a "handicap," the word being employed during this time for disability. The "disability" of racialized underachievement confirmed what Karen E. Fields and Barbara J. Fields described as "racecraft,"—a pervasive belief about black inferiority. They note that racecraft "is not a euphemistic substitute for *racism*, it is a kind of fingerprint evidence that *racism* has been on the scene." Racecraft consists of long-standing beliefs and "social facts" constantly recycled. Often, these beliefs hide only to reappear in another configuration or embodiment.[87]

Special education as an educational intervention must be questioned and considered suspect due to the racecraft that willed it into existence. Racecraft burrowed itself into the field of psychology, producing subspecialties variously known as educational psychology, clinical psychology, racial psychology, or framed as the psychology of the Negro, the inequality of the mind, the mental capacity of the American Negro, the comparative psychology of races, and the learning capacity of Negro children, to name a few. One is astounded by the sheer nonsense that passes as credible psychological research during World War I: that black students were inferior to white students; that "octaroons" (one-eighth black) were smarter than "quadroons" (one-quarter black); that quadroons were more intelligent than "mulattoes" (one-half black); and that mulattoes were smarter than "full-blooded Negroes." Psychology not only posited the notion of black inferiority but also advanced the position that the greater presence of intelligence was predetermined by the amount of white blood in African Americans. William Henry Pyle, an educational psychologist and an expert on learning theory observed the following in 1916: "In a former study of negro children, it appeared that negro children have about two thirds the mental ability of white children." After supposedly conducting his own "test" with a "new apparatus" he designed, and allegedly accounting for the "effects of experience and environment," Pyle concluded that black children proved smarter than he originally believed. He noted for example that "it appears that negro children have three fourths to four fifths the learning capacity of white children."[88] Later in the year, R. S. Woodworth advanced a learning theory of color when he identified a refinement in black intelligence, suggesting the "presence of mulattoes" improved black intelligence from two-thirds to four-fifths, raising the "standard of negro attainment."[89] The folly around "improved instruments" and the greater presence of white blood in black people demonstrated how color conscious white psychologists appeared. Thus, these pervasive beliefs, or racecraft, helped psychologists make two major claims during the dawn of special education: black people were intellectually inferior to white people in degrees according to skin color; and black children were more retarded than white children with foreign parentage.[90]

Special classes met the demand of compulsory education, which made grade-level retardation a problem for school districts to explain in the context of psychometric intelligence. Applying the field of psychology to education, psychologists transformed grade-level retardation into a retardation based on "mental" age rather than a student's chronological age, combining the two words into the term "mental retardation." Historian Douglas Baynton took careful note of the term's evolution when he wrote:

> While the term continued to be used in the older sense of "grade retarded" for several decades, at the same time a subtly different usage began to appear alongside it. Educators increasingly applied it not just to a child's progress, but to a quality that defined a particular category of persons—not the merely grade retarded, but the mentally retarded. . . . With increasing reliance on standardized testing, however, the term "retarded" gradually came to denote less an educational standing than an overall mental status. Children who were grade retarded when they could not keep up with their cohort became mentally retarded when they brought up the rear in a competitive testing system. Finally, they became retarded in the evolutionary race when heredity and eugenics entered the conversation.[91]

Psychologists abandoned the theory of "pedagogical" or "academic" retardation as the reason for underachievement and believed physical ailments no longer sufficed in explaining the cause of mental retardation. In 1906, Alfred Binet and Theophile Simon, the leaders of the mental testing movement in Paris, France, helped loosen the grip medical doctors held on determining retardation. They wrote, "If the physician gives a child a diagnosis of profound idiocy or of imbecility, it is not because the child does not walk, nor talk, has no control over secretions . . . [but] because he is affected in his intellectual development."[92] Rather than accepting the notion that the "subnormal" intellect was arrested due to physical or emotional conditions, psychologists promoted the idea that the "subnormal" intellect was inferior due to heredity. Binet and Simon argued that identifying the "causes" of retardation—from defective eyes, ears, enlarged tonsils, or the effects of illness such as typhus, scarlet fever, or emotional states like fright—"does not seem to us correct" and should be abandoned. A determination of inferior states of intelligence like idiocy is "a clinical classification to be made by means of psychology."[93] Characterizing Binet's position, Leila Zenderland wrote, "Where physicians went awry . . . was in their failure to distinguish sharply the body from the mind, and thus physical from mental impairment."[94]

University-trained psychologists, Henry H. Goddard, Lewis Terman, and Robert Yerkes, equally shaped the field of mental retardation.[95] In 1910, Goddard translated the Binet-Simon scale from French into English.[96] Goddard also introduced the "moron" to the feebleminded hierarchy, saying to a gathering of professionals, "I presume no one in this audience, certainly none of the superintendents of institutions need to be reminded that the public is entirely ignorant of this particular group. Our public school system is filled with them, and yet superintendents and boards of education are struggling to make normal people out of them."[97] Goddard believed morons "are a difficult class to recognize" because "they are often very handsome and otherwise attractive . . . and . . . are very affectionate." The belief that morons fooled superintendents and teachers because they were "normal-looking" did not mean they were normal in the eyes of psychologists. On the contrary, morons were still "feebleminded," representing a "great social menace." Goddard reasoned morons should be taken "out of the regular classes" and placed in "*special* classes," providing "them the kind of training which they can take."[98] J. D. Heilman, a psychologist at Colorado State Teachers College, agreed with Goddard regarding the placement of morons: the "aims must be very low . . . in weaving mats, caning chairs, and mending boots, but not in reading, writing and arithmetic."[99] By singling out the "moron," Goddard made outcasts of struggling students, dooming innocent children with academic challenges to a curriculum of low expectations.

In 1916, Lewis Terman, a psychologist at Stanford University, revised the Binet-Simon scale after Binet's death. Terman adopted the suggestion made by another psychologist, William Stern, who purportedly found a formula that determined people's intelligence. For Stern, intelligence became a single ratio: dividing a person's mental age (established by mental tests) by their chronological age. This number was called the "intelligence quotient" (IQ). Terman multiplied the intelligence quotient by one hundred to achieve a whole number. Psychologists then applied intelligence quotients to "feebleminded" categories, giving them broad ranges: 0–25 representing the "idiot"; 26–50 identified as the "imbecile"; and 51–70 branded as the "moron." This new taxonomy made mental retardation into a uniform system that internationally standardized "feebleminded" classification.

There has been an agreement to accept *idiot* as applied to the lowest state, *imbecile* to the intermediate, and *moron* to the state nearest normality. What importance can be attached to public statistics of different countries concerning the percentage of backward children if the definition

Figure 1. Lewis M. Terman published the *Stanford Revision of the Binet-Simon Scale* in 1916. "Stanford-Binet" tests determined the IQ scores of exceptional children. Photograph, National Library of Medicine (NLM): Image from the History of Medicine.

for backward children is not the same in all countries? How will it be possible to keep a record of the intelligence of pupils who are treated and instructed in a school, if the terms applied to them, feeble-minded, retarded, imbecile, idiot, vary in meaning according to the doctor who examines them?[100]

Terman's new IQ classification system also included an area between 70 and 90. In this area on the probability curve psychologists indicated different student identities variously identified as "dullard" "backward," or "borderline." By the mid-twentieth century, this same IQ range would be partially occupied by the learning disabled.[101] The range for normal or average intelligence fell between 90 to 110; superior intelligence between 110 and 120; very superior intelligence between 120 and 140; and the genius above 140.

The "moron" was the closest feebleminded person to normal and posed a problem for "idiots" and "imbeciles" over time. Walter Fernald, superintendent of the Faribault School in Minnesota, captured it succinctly in 1917 when he asserted, "When we talked of the feebleminded 25 years ago, we thought about imbeciles and idiots and not morons. When we discovered the moron, we doubled the number of feebleminded."[102] The "moron" was not "discovered"; the category was invented by psychologists. Made synonymous with the upper reaches of mental retardation, "morons" represented slightly subnormal children on the IQ scale. In closer proximity to "normal" children on the bell-shaped curve, the "moron" would generate the most rancorous debates in special education for the next hundred years, begun by Terman and fellow psychologists during World War I. "As far as the public schools are concerned," wrote Terman, "they never enroll idiots and very rarely even high-grade imbeciles. School defectives are practically all of the moron and borderline grades . . . and it is important teachers should be able to recognize."[103] Thus, the conception of the "moron" and the students it exemplified never changed. The individual deemed a "moron" evolved into other interchangeable labels like "borderline," "high-grade," "slow-learning," "educable mentally retarded," "mildly mentally retarded," "high-incidence," and "intellectually disabled." Thus, the medical doctor's "high-grade defective" (moron) in the late nineteenth century became the classroom teacher's "mildly" or "educable" retarded by the mid-twentieth century.

It is hard to prove whether the "moron" doubled the number of "feebleminded" individuals in the United States. The invention of the so-called moron did increase the total number of "mentally retarded" students and drastically changed the nature of prevalence. Though the total number increased, the percentages of mentally retarded students began dropping from the earlier ranges of 40 to 70 percent to a range of 2 to 5 percent.[104] With the making and placement of the moron alongside other "backward" children, special education classes began resembling what David L. Kirp called "a Noah's Ark of deviations from the school norm."[105] Except for a few special classes for "cripples and . . . stammerers," special classes included an assortment of diverse underachieving students, some who had chronic medical or academic challenges or both. Unwilling to manage different levels of student achievement, and feeling a crisis of identity, Detroit public schools used mental tests to help guide them through student maladies and low performance in 1910–11:

> For the past two years, the Binet-Simon tests for intelligence have been used as a basis to determine the mentality of backward children. Since September 1911, two hundred and fifteen pupils have been treated for defective vision and provided with glasses. A large number of cases of adenoids and enlarged tonsils have been operated upon and treated for nervousness, deafness, defective teeth, and infantile paralysis.[106]

If a student still experienced academic difficulties after physical ailments had been remedied, a Child Study Committee administered a "Binet test." If a Binet test "revealed" a student to be an "imbecile" or an "idiot," he or she was excluded from the special class and, in many cases, the entire school. The Detroit public school system described the situation in this way:

> Two years ago, the new classification, which includes in the feebleminded group three classes of children, the moron, imbecile, and idiot, each of which is subdivided into three grades, high, middle, and low, was adopted by the Child Study Committee. It was decided to exclude from Detroit public schools, all children in the idiot group and also those in the middle and low-grade imbecile groups. This rule has been rigidly adhered to, as it is considered a waste of public funds to attempt to teach children of these classes, who are regarded by all specialists as unteachable.[107]

Psychologists and educators projected "unteachability" onto so-called morons due to the growing number of underachieving students in public schools. But psychologists faced a major challenge with "morons." More often than not, according to psychologists, "morons" possessed no physical, sensory, or medical disabilities that could make their teachability a challenge like so-called idiots and imbeciles.

Psychologists correlated physical health challenges less with feeble-mindedness over time, not only because "morons" supposedly looked healthier than "imbeciles" and "idiots"; psychologists postulated that "morons" made up the preponderance of underachievers. If psychologists paid less attention to the health of "morons," it stood to reason that race factored into a new set of justifications for the moron's unteachability. "Moronic" black children became persona non grata in public schools, purposely taken out of general education classes and placed in special classes. Byron Phillips, the superintendent of Philadelphia schools put it bluntly: "If the Binet tests are at all a gauge of mentality, it must follow that there is a difference in mentality between the colored children and the white children, and this raises the question: should the two groups be instructed under the same curriculum?"[108] The answer to that question was unequivocally "no."

Race and the invention of the "moron" emerged as one of the most consequential endeavors for the mental testing movement. Terman alluded to the work he led at Stanford University during World War I, and the way his intelligence tests racially differentiated students. "At present we are at work on a new scale. . . . We are using the Stanford revision in studies of racial differences. . . . I believe that social and racial psychology in particular will soon have to be rewritten in the light of results which will be secured by the use of intelligence tests."[109] The U.S. entry into the war in 1916 set in motion the use of new group intelligence tests that included Terman's revision, now called Stanford-Binet, as well as tests developed by other psychologists. Robert Yerkes, a Harvard University psychologist, an Army major, and the president of the American Psychological Association (APA) assembled a group of psychologists, including Lewis Terman, to create the Army Alpha and Beta tests that determined a "workably accurate scientific classification of brain power of the manhood of the Army . . ."[110] The U.S. military chose university psychologists to ascertain the readiness of its fighting force and to make the Army more efficient. George Arps, Ohio State University psychologist and Army major, quipped, "psychology . . . the most youthful of the applied sciences, was able to place at the disposal of the Government a technique whereby a fairly accurate mental measurement could be made of each raw, prob-lematical recruit." The access to millions of recruits demonstrated how psychology further staked out its expertise in mental testing, deciding which recruits possessed "normal" intelligence and which ones did not. But Army recruits during World War I were no less "intelligent" than soldiers who fought in the Civil War or the Spanish-American War. Psy-chologists convinced the Army that weeding out the "feebleminded" from the "normal" was in its best interest. The Army believed the intelligence of recruits to be so low that it potentially constituted a "menace in the use of firearms and to the success of any military undertaking."[111]

The Army administered over two million intelligence tests to segre-gate the "mentally deficient from those capable of doing combatant ser-vice." The tests also determined what recruits can best perform "service in labor battalions." In addition, a score above normal positioned recruits for officer training. Black recruits poured onto Army bases to serve their country, but they were hauled into mental-testing facilities to receive an intelligence rating often deeming them morons. Adding insult to injury, black recruits were trained in segregated units and encountered racism on the battlefields in Europe from fellow white American soldiers. World War I may have made the world safe for democracy, but it unleashed a new level of racism during the war and in the immediate postwar period. Notwithstanding the discrimination black soldiers faced inside theaters of war, many African Americans lost property and their lives in the pogroms and race riots in East St. Louis, Missouri; Washington, D.C.; and Chicago, Illinois in 1919 and then in Tulsa, Oklahoma, in 1921.[112] When Army intelligence tests became public in 1919, they confirmed white people's long-standing beliefs about the hierarchy of American intelli-gence, meting out additional "violence" to black bodies and minds that held long- term implications for African American children in the class-room. The Army data also suggested much of the white military popu-lation fell in the range of "morons," too. But the data "revealed" native whites were smarter than soldiers from white immigrant families, and immigrant or first-generation white soldiers proved more intelligent than black American soldiers. "One of the most interesting results found by the psychologists who examined recruits entering the United States Army was the surprisingly low intellectual level of those members of the colored race who were examined," wrote M. R. Trabue, director for the Bureau of Educational Services at Columbia University.[113]

Far from representing the "truth" about intelligence, the Alpha and Beta tests resulted in a fait accompli.[114] Psychologists and politicians used test data to make empirically based arguments about Anglo racial deterioration from the presence of foreign whites and Asians. These ideas contributed to the passage of the Immigration Act of 1924. Psychologists and educators both used the results to denigrate black intelligence and call for the greater classification and differentiation in the public school population based on race and underachievement. "It would seem utter folly to try to transplant the system of schools which now exists for white people ... to the Negro race ... without condemning the millions of ordinary Negroes to a system of education in which they are absolutely certain to fail of success," said Trabue. IQ tests allowed psychologists to shift the burden from schools to the deficits students brought to schools. The Army tests defined black intelligence beyond military service and explained why special education emerged during this period. Trabue went on to admit that "our present school program is not fitted for the large mass of the Negro race, and for a considerable portion of our white race." If compulsory education insists on "morons" swelling our school ranks, Trabue continued, then differentiation must guide school-wide curriculum policies and practices moving forward: "Fundamental changes need to be made for the sake of those whose ability runs along the lines of personal service and bodily toil rather than in the juggling of words and ideas."[115]

Differential Education as Special Education in the Age of Intelligence Testing

The "making" of the moron and the emergence of mental testing provided proponents of differential education with additional ways to construct student identities and advance a discourse of racial underachievement. This compelled the black scholar Doxey A. Wilkerson to ask the question, "Which came first, racial differences in scholastic achievement or racial differences in test intelligence?"[116] Raising the question of why black students struggled academically, Wilkerson kept a critical eye on ableist education reform and its obsession with intelligence testing. For Wilkerson, the question was rhetorical, joining a growing chorus of black and white voices condemning the intelligence testing movement in the 1920s and 1930s. Racial differences in scholastic achievement came first, born out of decades of economic marginalization, political disenfranchisement, and educational exclusion and neglect. The racial predicament black students found themselves in, whether it was starting school for the first time at eight or nine years old or attending school intermittently, impacted their performance on ableist IQ tests. Psychologists, superintendents, and teachers assumed test results correlated with real intellectual endowment, confirming a growing belief that black students did not deserve to learn with white children in general education classes. If racial differences in scholastic achievement actually existed, then a lower black IQ score became prima facie evidence of inherited racial inferiority, which then became a prima facie reason to make differential education into race- and class-based special education.

But where is disability? Special education, in its nascent form as "differential" education, became the construction site of intellectual disability. The "refinement" of feebleminded classifications on a probability curve gave early special education a futurity to map various conceptions of mental retardation, learning disability, emotional behavior disorder, and other cognitive impairments not fully in existence.[117] Disability began to appear as psychologists increasingly transformed differential education into special education.[118] Distinctions between normality and subnormality gave differential education its meaning, leading to what Shelley Tremain termed an "apparatus of disability." And for disability to flourish, psychologists fetishized so-called normal children, believing that the "normal child is the future torchbearer of our civilization," as an editorial in the *Journal of Educational Psychology* put it in 1912.[119] If the statistical normal was white, middle-class, able-bodied, and of able-mind, then public schools guarded general education classes against an influx of struggling/subnormal students who were poor and destitute, working-class, black, Latinx, now judged "disabled." The general or regular class slammed its doors in the face of "subnormal" students, deeming them unworthy as newcomers into the system. This biased posture, to paraphrase Jennifer Scuro, widened the gap between children deemed "able-minded" and valuable (normal) as opposed to children defined as subnormal.[120]

In one of the most stunning admissions of differential education in 1924, Wallace Wallin advanced an ableist position that made special education the only solution to the growing problem of "subnormal" students:

> If the subnormals were given all the time they require in the regular grades, the normal and bright pupils would have to be neglected. This would seem like robbing bright Peter to pay dull Paul. After all, may not our highest obligation be to the great mass of normal and bright children, who are destined to become the leaders or organizers or the great balancing or leveling force of society? By removing the "clinkers" and the "drags," the regular grades will be thrown open to the normal progress pupils, thereby enabling these pupils to advance more rapidly, and materially reducing the extent of pedagogical retardation. This constitutes one of the strongest practical arguments in favor of the policy of organizing separate classes for children who cannot possibly keep up with the pace of the regular grades, and who serve as a brake on the progress of normal children.[121]

Stalling the progress of so-called normal children was verboten for psychologists and educators. But simultaneously lauding normality and decrying pedagogical retardation meant little without a solution. New classification systems and dividing practices appeared, justifying separate education for the "normal" and "subnormal." Thus, the justification of a separate education called "special education" created "disability." "Disability" did not create special education.

Differential education led to the creation of categorical disabilities where very few had existed previously. Far from being a "pre-given property of the human body," to use a turn of phrase by Fiona Kumari Campbell, disability functioned as an *outcome* of the practices of ableist psychology.[122] Disability was ostensibly a logical end point to a process that sought to segregate and hierarchize student learning. As Wallin confidently concluded, "The educator of today possesses instruments which enable him to diagnose and differentiate educational deviates, and prescribe for their educational treatment more intelligently than the educator of a few years ago."[123] Note the process Wallin identifies: the educator has "instruments" that can "diagnose" and "differentiate" "educational deviates." This subject-verb-object combination is revealing, as it establishes the power dynamic and the very process of creating disability out of what

Tremain identifies as a "diagnostic-style of reasoning." The ableist educator has an instrument (an intelligence test) that identifies (diagnoses) and tells apart (differentiates) the struggling student (educational deviate). Struggling students who seemingly could not keep pace with their peers received a new label (mentally retarded) and a new place in the educational landscape (special education).

Founded on the belief of differential education, special education emerged as a static education where psychometric tests "revealed" one's ability as permanent. Psychologists and educators not only believed in fixed intelligence (one's inherent capacity); what one acquired through the learning process, they believed, was equally fixed. Rudimentary or basic academic skills displayed by struggling students, psychologists alleged, served as "evidence" of their inherent abilities and not proof of a historic denial to learn. The ability to improve oneself academically over time was removed from the reasoning given by psychologists, for how one performed on IQ tests proved conclusive of current ability, future ability, and what kind of education such a student should be afforded. Frank O'Brien, psychologist and future leader of the New York City Bureau of Child Guidance professed as much in a 1923 edition of *Opportunity Magazine*, reasoning, "It must be admitted that the individual who can be trained to do nothing more than simple addition and subtraction in arithmetic has not the same degree of brain development as the individual who manipulates with ease, logarithms, cube-root, etc."[124] The judgment of abilities and skill sets was not an innocent project in scholastic differentiation; it was a way of racially and socioeconomically determining what kind of education black public school children received. IQ tests gave the green light to superintendents and teachers to develop a separate education curriculum based on race and class, arguably helping to inject the practice of low expectations into the educational system. Terman and other psychologists believed the IQ results served as proof for superintendents and teachers to offer dissimilar curricula for underachieving students. Lewis Terman wrote assuredly:

> If these intelligence-quotient differences represent actual differences in
> native endowment, it is sheer foolishness to attempt to arrange a single
> educational program which will serve the needs of all children. If these
> differences are real, the uniform, straight-jacket curriculum has no more

place in the first eight grades than in the last eight, in the first four than the last four.[125]

Terman's conditional "if-then" statements demonstrate the emphatic nature of the psychometric testing movement, even predicting himself that "intelligence tests will be the source of an enormous amount of controversy in the next twenty-five years."[126] Intelligence tests proved controversial for more than twenty-five years, if for no other reason, intelligence and achievement tests became the main mechanism to sort and classify students. The IQ and its accompanied classification system reveal how categorical disabilities emerged in special education. Underachievement created special education, which created novel disabilities. Finer distinctions of mental retardation classification led to other "disabilities," such as specific disabilities in reading, speech, and other general subject matter.

By the time the White Conference on Handicapped Children convened in 1931, six broad categories of disability existed: "blind," "partially-blind" (also called partially seeing children); "deaf," "partially-deaf" (also called hard-of-hearing children); "crippled;" "delicate" (defined as children with "anemia, tuberculous, and cardiac cases"); "socially maladjusted" (children who were "truant, incorrigible, or delinquent"); and "mentally retarded" (or "mentally deficient children")[127] Though still in currency in the 1920s and 1930s, gradations of "idiocy," "imbecility," and "moronity" began disappearing under the new disability classification system. Wallace Wallin, a psychologist who helped establish a "Psycho-Education Clinic" in the St. Louis Public Schools system, agreed as much, explaining that "the practice of applying the terms 'feeble-minded,' 'mentally defective,' 'imbecile,' and 'moronic' to the children in the special classes of special schools should be abandoned."[128] As the eugenics movement began to wane in the 1930s, the term "mentally retarded" came to represent older feebleminded categories and the only one not defined by a physical or sensory limitation. This "disability" would begin with a simple definition but grow into an elaborate discourse by the 1950s and 1960s. In the early 1930s, the sixth "handicap" category, "mentally retarded" was simply defined as *one whose mental ability is such as to make it impossible for him to profit by regular group classification.*[129] Vague, vacuous, and rather simple, the concept of mental retardation rested on the assumption that "regular," "general," or "mainstream" classrooms were not for certain segments of the school population due solely to what other people believed about their capability.

Existing as a projected identity, how mentally retarded children were "impaired" during the early days of psychometric testing never seemed clear. If a student was only a person whose mental retardation made it impossible for him or her to "profit" from being in general classrooms, then merely forecasting their failure in mainstream classrooms was no real explanation of impairment. Psychologists and educators needed to create a discourse of "impairment" through what I term an act of etiological mythmaking, a process that I examine in more detail in chapter 2. Only then could this new diagnostic style of reasoning produce "disability," a concept rarely found in the academic literature prior to the advent of psychometric testing. "Impairment cannot be thought of as prior to disability," argues Tremain, "because disability is required to think of impairment at all."[130] The foundation for "disability reasoning" lay in the "crippled," who were distinguishable by their physical challenges, and the "blind," "hard of seeing," "the deaf," and "hard of hearing," noticeable by their sensory adversities. But rarely was the word "disability" or "handicap" used to characterize people with physical challenges at the turn of the century, perhaps because little debate was needed to convince the public that they represented categories of impairment. With most physical and sensory disabilities easier to comprehend, impairment functioned less as a debate and required no plotting on an IQ scale. "Mental retardation," and later, "learning disability," required a greater leap of faith, not solely because they were "invisible handicaps" but because, to paraphrase Ladd, proponents of "mental retardation" and "learning disability" needed to convince the public that they were "real." It was paramount that "mental retardation" and "learning disability" possessed their own diagnostic style of reasoning.

These diagnostic styles of reasoning invent and magnify difference by measuring, comparing, and calculating intelligence and achievement gaps between students from dissimilar experiences, assigning children educational identities and new "handicaps." It was not enough to distinguish the so-called normal from the subnormal. The diagnostic style of reasoning offered a range of possibilities for psychologists and educators to construct and reconstruct subnormality, inventing then applying other "disabilities" to the IQ scale. Since many white middle-class students occupied the upper-left side of the bell-shaped curve where the "borderline," the "dullard," the "backward," and the "moron" were mapped, cognitive disabilities had to show up as distinct racialized disabilities. Accounting for variations in black and white student achievement required further differentiation, promoting the idea that a larger percentage of the black and brown student population in relation to their total numbers in schools were "mentally retarded," whereas only a smaller percentage of white students were "mentally retarded" in relation to their numbers.

Though white children were "mentally retarded," they were trapped inside the classification with black and brown children. By contrast, the "reading" and "learning" disabled seemed to be evolving as exclusively white. Very few black children were ever considered reading disabled in the first half of the twentieth century, which serves as evidence of how psychologists racialized the IQ scale. Since the majority of black children's IQ remained 70 and below, a "diagnosis" of "reading" disability was out of their reach. "It is quite futile to attempt to teach children or adults with I.Q.'s of 0.60 or less to read," said Arthur Gates, professor of educational psychology at Columbia University.[131] If children fell below 70, which is more than two standard deviations below the mean of 100, psychologists believed they were incapable of learning how to read because the children were "retarded" and "genetically" inferior. Edgar Doll observed that the "distinction between the high-grade moron and the lower-grade normal has developed almost entirely since 1920."[132] Samuel T. Orton said the distinction had been around longer than 1920 in "that children with a specific reading disability but with normal intelligence do exist and has been known in medical literature for approximately thirty years . . ."[133] Children with specific reading "disabilities" but with "normal" intelligence were overwhelmingly white. Children with reading difficulties or illiterate with "abnormal" or "inferior" intelligence were disproportionately black. Wallace confusingly announced that "a child may be specifically or generically, and permanently or temporarily, or inherently or accidentally pedagogically backward."[134] Either/or differences allowed for a race- and class-based separation in special education to take hold. Fabricating the distance between the "mentally retarded" and the "learning disabled" remained part of a changing diagnostic style of reasoning in special education.[135] The diagnostic style of reasoning needed thicker description, elaborate definitions, and finer distinctions that expanded disability discourse "at the borderline." This IQ "borderline/ borderland" of 70 to 90, an imagined intellectual terrain below "normality," operated as a hybrid space where psychologists and educators developed different causative explanations for the mapping of the "mentally retarded moron" and the "learning disabled."[136]

2

The Road *from* Mental Retardation

Civil Rights, Disability Rights, and Equal Educational Opportunity

In general, we have changed not concepts but words. Perhaps when we use the term *retardation* (compared with *defect*), we are trying to imply a more hopeful attitude.... It is ... dangerous to develop and use a terminology which appears to have a scientific basis but which hides vague and unprecise concepts.

—BENEDICT NAGLER, "A Change in Terms or in Concepts?
A Small Step Forward or a Giant Step Backward?"

The tendency to think in biological terms even when there is little or no evidence of organic pathology has been a particularly noticeable aspect of writing and thinking in the field of mental retardation.

—JANE R. MERCER, *Labeling the Mentally Retarded: Clinical and
Social System Perspectives on Mental Retardation*

The history of African Americans in special education is entangled with the history of intellectual disability and ideas about impairment. During the postwar era, white schools and districts labeled many African American children, who had been segregated in all-black schools, as "educable mentally retarded" (EMR) or "mildly mentally retarded" (MMR). In the 1970s, white teachers and school administrators frequently identified black students as "learning disabled" (LD), then increasingly as "emotional/behavior disordered" (EBD) in the 1980s and 1990s. While the disproportionate placement of black students in special education appears to be a late twentieth and early twenty-first-century phenomenon, unequal placement has been a common practice since the inception of special education. Indeed, special education became part and parcel of the broader intellectual disabilities movement that included students from all racial demographics. But the over-identification and placement of black students in special education *resegregated* them in America's public schools. Instead of being segregated *from* white schools before 1954, white educators segregated black students *within* white schools post-1954. In short, schools, districts, states, and the federal government forced African Americans to trade one form of segregation for another.[1]

To claim that racial integration created overrepresentation in special education is a provocative assertion. But it is no more suggestive to say compulsory education created the system of special education at the turn of the twentieth century. If compulsory education created the conditions for a separate, racialized special education system, then the overrepresentation of students of color in that system ensured their continued segregation in newly integrated schools some half a century later. Thus, a more apt explanation is racial integration swelled and intensified racist practices in special education in the name of equal educational opportunity.

Two developments stand out regarding equal educational opportunity and black students. One was the racial integration of public schools accompanied by the language of equal opportunity purporting to advance the educational interests of black and brown students. The other was equal opportunity's racialization by white psychologists, educators, and public officials that defined black special education students as "culturally deprived." As these "culturally deprived" and "disadvantaged" students integrated either exclusively or predominantly white schools, teachers and administrators increasingly placed and segregated them inside EMR classes.

Placing black and brown students in EMR classes also allowed white psychologists and educators to use equal educational opportunity as a form of interest convergence. Legal scholar Derrick Bell defined interest convergence as the point where black and white interests converged to make civil rights gains acceptable to powerful whites, especially in cases when white people perceived a personal or collective return to them. Interest convergence made equal educational opportunity appear attractive, not only for its value for black students, but for other student constituencies.[2] Equal educational opportunity not only became the dominant philosophy and policy outcome for racial school integration; it was broadened to support "disabled" student populations, known collectively for decades as "handicapped" children. Borrowing from what Allison Carey has called the "integration presumption,"[3] the educational disability rights movement tapped into the rights discourse that emerged from *Brown v. Board of Education*, which also challenged the exclusion of the intellectually disabled from schools and districts across the country. If black students were deprived of their constitutional rights, so too were the "mentally retarded," and the newly created student in the 1960s: the learning disabled.

The civil rights decades built the modern special education system and introduced the general public to black "culturally deprived" or "educationally disadvantaged" children. The 1950s and 1960s also introduced the public to underachieving white middle-class students who were deemed "slow-learners." Since IQ scores purported to measure one's "intelligence" on a scale, underachieving white students with IQs near the mean perplexed parents and education professionals, sending them on what Bernadette Baker described as a "hunt" for new disabilities.[4] The new terminology on which psychologists, parents, educators settled, therefore, was "learning disabled" (LD). Equal educational opportunity discourse opened a window for the educational disability rights movement to make the case for legislative recognition and new federal policies.

This chapter examines the road *from* mental retardation and pays close attention to the relationship between EMR and LD as categories of underachievement. I argue that the new LD label represented an intellectual white flight from "mental retardation." LD materialized as a less stigmatized educational identity for white underachieving students, while what some understood as so-called cultural deprivation kept black students educationally disadvantaged and saddled with the stigma of EMR. Within the context of equal opportunity discourse, examining the history of intellectual disability reveals how white psychologists created special education categories with some level of racial specificity, contributing to the disproportionate placement of black students in special education.

Differentiating Blackness, Normalizing Whiteness: Etiological Mythmaking and the Racialization of Disability

Mental retardation and learning disability have long and complex histories. As descriptions of children's intellectual potential and future place in American society, mental retardation and learning disability enjoyed the imprimatur of medical science and psychology. But more than a mere science of intelligence, behavior, and clinical diagnoses, mental retardation and learning disability segregated the educationally privileged from the underprivileged, the middle class from the working class, and white children from black and brown children. Though white psychologists and educators invoked race less often in the 1940s and 1950s than in the first three decades of the early twentieth century, race is the enduring elephant in the room—"disabling" the public school population in ways that held severe consequences for black and brown students later in the century.

Disability is unable to exist without etiology—the study of causation or origination. In the early 1930s, according to psychologists, a "mentally retarded" student could not profit in a class with "normal" students. The idea of "not profiting" from "normal" classes took on a distinct understanding enshrined in typological thinking that "there are large clusters of humans that differ fundamentally from other large clusters,"[5] especially in public schools. Psychologists believed it was essential to scientifically explain why "mentally retarded" students could not keep up with their peers in class. Thus, typologists began engaging in what I call etiological mythmaking. The etiological foundations of both mental retardation and learning disability spring, in many ways, from the same well.

Alfred Strauss, a medical doctor and arguably the most critical typologist in the history of special education, delineated the nuances of mental retardation and learning disability. Since mental retardation and learning disability belong to the broader condition psychologists called mental deficiency, Strauss focused on what he labeled "higher grade mental defectives, moron and borderline types without gross motor handicaps."[6] The children who fell into these categories were the same children Goddard and Terman labeled the most dangerous and deceptive ones because they *appeared* normal with IQs between 70 and 90. But Strauss's contribution to special education proved different than that of Goddard and Terman. Strauss normalized some children more than others by separating the "learning disabled" from the "mentally retarded." Between the early 1930s and the mid-1950s, Strauss provided an etiological framework for distinguishing the intellectually disabled, or the "mentally retarded," from the learning disabled. In doing so, Strauss also racialized special education by keeping most black and brown students, long deemed "mentally retarded," separate from a significant number of white students whose academic challenges increasingly fell under "learning disabled."

Alfred Strauss employed a "damaged" body-mind comparison when "scientifically" explaining mental retardation and learning disability. But since mental retardation and learning disability could not be seen, Strauss's theorizing required a leap of faith when it came to explaining how physical disability, a "malfunctioning" body, and mental "deficiency," a "malfunctioning" mind, were akin. Both mental retardation and learning disability used a medical model, a psychological portrait, and an educational essence rooted in science. Strauss asserts that these three "independent scientific fields have each contributed a typology. The medical field—classification according to etiological and clinical syndromes; the psychological field—classification according to I.Q. grade; the pedagogical field—classification of behavior and personality responses associated with educational difficulties."[7] Of the three, the medical model provided psychologists the greatest opportunity for etiological mythmaking by locating mental retardation and learning disability in the genes and the brain. Though "pedagogical" or "academic" retardation dominated the literature from 1900 to 1920, it proved increasingly hard to reconcile it with a retardation rooted in one's "mental." Regardless of how much medical doctors attempted to link enlarged tonsils and other illnesses with "pedagogical" retardation, these maladies could not rise to the level of a clinical abnormality. The older medical model of the nineteenth century constructed by physicians focused on infectious diseases and enlarged glands like tonsils as causative factors; the newer medical model of the twentieth century promoted by psychologists focused on brain science, offering concepts such as "brain-crippled" and analogizing such labels to physical disability. Alfred Strauss and his coresearcher at the Wayne County Training School wrote, "We suggest to characterize these . . . children as mentally crippled. . . . These children are damaged in the mental sphere during development in a similar way as the crippled children in the physical."[8]

The Wayne County Training School for Feebleminded Children opened in 1926, dedicated to the "rehabilitation" of "mentally retarded" children in Michigan. The school committed children from Detroit and the surrounding area. While psychologists and psychiatrists at the school accepted some students as known "imbeciles," the training school commits were mainly "morons" and borderline cases. But "training" and "rehabilitation" carried multiple meanings. Opening its doors only three years after the state passed its mandatory sterilization law, the Wayne County Training School conducted sterilization surgery on its so-called high-grade defectives to stop the spread of "mental deficiency." Professionals in psychiatric medicine believed "mental deficiency" was a "disease" that needed eradication. University of Nevada psychologist George Ordahl captured the way he and others thought about people labeled as such:

> It would appear that high-grade defective parents are responsible for the three grades of offspring, viz: 1. The imbecile and low moron, who become public charges. 2. The high-grade normal and dull-normal, who, for the most part, pass for normal, but nevertheless are responsible for the greater number of defectives in the next generation. 3. Normal children among whom, because of their defective heredity, there must be a large number of carriers of defect.[9]

Controlling "defective" people drove the eugenics movement to curtail the reproductive capacities of "moron" and borderline children. Hence, between 1926 and 1934, the Wayne County Training School sterilized over 900 children, 600 of whom were girls.

"Rehabilitation" at the Wayne County Training School also involved researching "moron" and "borderline" children. Alfred Strauss, a physician who received his medical degree from the University of Heidelberg, and Heinz Werner, a psychologist trained at the University of Vienna, both emigrés, arrived at the Wayne County Training School in the late 1930s. Their presence made the school the center of brain injury, mental retardation, and learning disability research. The school examined more than five hundred children and created detailed case records used to fashion developmental histories of individual children. From the data, Strauss and his colleagues combed for "mental deficiency" in the children's families, and they looked for any clinical signs and patterns of neuropathology. "Through a complex series of experimental and clinical investigations," said education historian Scot Danforth, "the Strauss-Werner partnership built the conceptual content of the Strauss Syndrome, a group of identifiable behaviors linked to an underlying brain etiology." So convincing and cutting-edge was the research that "the Wayne School research program gained a strong reputation in the psychological community," according to Danforth. Thus, what began as a school for high-grade "defective" moron and borderline children "would become central to the field of learning disabilities" and launched the careers of Newell Kephart, Samuel A. Kirk, William Cruickshank, Laura Lehtinen, and Ray Barsh. These scholars spent part of their early years at the institution and emerged as national and international experts on learning disabilities by the 1960s and 1970s. The Wayne County Training School studied hundreds of human subjects—black, brown, and white children—and produced an "intellectually lively environment." And through its research, the school combined the "fields of medicine, psychology, and special education."[10]

Bridging the fields of medicine, psychology, and special education yielded a bizarre set of discourses. One was the construction of learning disability theory as the "normal" form of "mental retardation." Theorizing the learning disabled proved impossible without accounting for the "mentally retarded" and, sometimes, the physically disabled. In the 1930s and 1940s, one could not understand learning disability etiology without thinking about "mental retardation." Their detachment today as two distinct disabilities belie the early history of their convergence. Strauss's research findings consistently proved this as he argued the case for the "brain-injured" child and the etiology that produced brain injury. Strauss shows the reader several strands of thinking, one, delineations of normality; two, what abnormalities are intrinsic to children versus those made from an external experience; three, how the central nervous system functions and is affected; four, what are motor and sensory handicaps; five, how behavior operates and should be interpreted in children; six, how brain function is localized; and finally, ultimately how perception and sensation are defined. With a dizzying array of theories related to the concept of brain injury, Strauss engaged in the same shell game as William James, one of the first to promote the idea of "mental state," and Binet, Goddard, and Terman, who all promoted the concept of "mental age." Brain injury or being "brain-crippled," like mental state and mental age, is difficult to visualize and must be taken at face value to be believed. One can visualize paralysis of the legs; one may not, however, "see" paralysis in the brain. Straus attempted to explain the concept through analogy, attributing certain observable behaviors that "indicated" brain injury: "Thus, the different behavior of the brain-injured child becomes a symptom of a condition *one cannot see, but which is just as crippling to his performance in normal society as motor paralysis.*"[11]

Strauss identified two types of brain-injured groups he called endogenous and exogenous. Each of their etiological roots comprises race- and class-based signifiers like "familial" and "normal." If the endogenous groups were rooted in a difference based on working-class and poverty-stricken blackness, then the exogenous would be rooted in a normalizing middle-class whiteness. Strauss's brain-injured children ranged from the high-grade defective moron to the dull-normal, 50 to 90 on the IQ scale. This range of mental deficiency allowed Strauss to statistically map, delineate, and define learning disability etiology against mental retardation:

> In the ensuing years, we published various other papers in which the term "exogenous type of mental deficiency" described a mentally retarded child who came from a normal family, who had suffered an injury to the brain before, during, or after birth, whose psychological make-up showed characteristics not found in the endogenous types of mental deficiency or in normal children and for whom we devised special educational methods based upon our knowledge of this child's peculiar psychological deviations. Gradually and erroneously the term "exogenous child" tended to become synonymous with the term "brain-injured child."[12]

Strauss marked learning disability as a category fundamentally dissimilar from mental retardation, not because it *was* different but because it was *made* different. Psychologists believed white academic underachievement at the borderline and near normal range on the IQ scale required different explanations than black and brown underachievement at a lower range. Strauss wrote that the endogenous and exogenous represented "two types of mental deficiency." The endogenous type was "any mental defective in whose immediate family (grandparents, parents or siblings) there occur one or more cases of mental defect, and in whose case history there is no evidence of brain disease or injury." The endogenous included so-called feebleminded morons, soon to be the educable mentally retarded (EMR), whose condition was believed to be passed down through the genes of the parents. This type, which Strauss named "familial," in "Typology in Mental Deficiency," "assumes the existence of a specific gene for mental defect which . . . follows the Mendelian ratio for recessive characteristics."

Much of the belief about black underachievement stemmed from the fiction of hereditary intelligence and black inferiority. The "hereditarians," as they were called, dominated the conversation during the first half of the twentieth century, setting the tone for special education discourse for years to come. Strauss agreed with the opposition to the hereditarians in describing the other possible cause of endogenous-familial mental retardation when he affirmed that "the alternate is that in the endogenous type, the 'mental defect' is the result of a form of social deprivation, a restriction of the sphere of social-cultural influence." Words like "deprivation" and "social-cultural influence," some psychologists believed, explained more convincingly how families, neighborhoods, and schools created, or "nurtured" mental retardation as opposed to nature creating it in the genes. Thus, the endogenous and the "mentally retarded" were synonymous, and the evidence of their "mental defect" for psychologists often consisted of a lower IQ score, and in addition, the case histories collected by institutions like the Wayne County Training School, and one's family racial and class composition.[13]

The second "mental deficiency" known as exogenous is the example of the brain-crippled child "who has a brain lesion acquired by trauma or inflammatory process before, during, or after birth." There is not much else that defines the exogenous child other than convincing the reader something has gone wrong inside the child's brain. What remains in determining the exogenous is a detailed comparison to the endogenous. This comparison "leads to the conclusion that the mental structure, intellectual impairment, emotional disturbances and personality deviations are fundamentally different in both groups. These conclusions lead to the assumption that the training of brain-crippled deficient children should be different from the training of the mind-run feebleminded child."[14] For Strauss, lifting up the "brain-crippled" or "brain-injured" over and above the "mine-run feebleminded" was not only useful in delineating typologies but also critical in establishing value judgments about which children deserved more from schools.

The normalization of the brain-injured/learning disabled child mirrored the normalization of the "moron" years prior. The "moron," according to Goddard, was distinguished from the "imbecile" and the "idiot" not solely by an IQ score but also by the lack of physical malformations. The moron appeared "normal" and showed no signs of "defect." The reason the "moron" showed no signs of defect was because they were never "defective." The moron was a descriptor of academic underachievement and established a disability where none existed. The fiction of unseen disabilities was increasingly becoming a feature of special education theory and practice, acknowledged by Wayne County Training School researchers and others. New research "has shown that much mental deficiency is not accompanied by any apparent corporal defect," wrote Strauss and Werner. "This is particularly true in that type of mental deficiency which has been variously called familial, hereditary or endogenous, and especially among the moron and the borderline group." Similarly, the "brain lesion" child will not show signs of a "visible defect in the motor apparatus." In fact, Strauss and Werner claimed, "The number of children belonging to the exogenous group who do not show gross motor disturbances exceeds the number who do show motor defects."[15]

Strauss's definition of the exogenous/learning disabled was quite simple. Filling out the definition with caveats, comparisons, provisos, and exclusionary criteria—then surrounding it with esoteric clinical and medical language—made the definition appear more complicated. But this definitional complexity was by design. The "brain-injured" could be defined by one set of neurological and behavioral attributes or different ones altogether. And the signs that accompany the brain-injured exogenous may be present in one child and absent in another. Furthermore, Strauss promulgated that the brain injury could occur during the embryonic stage, delivery stage, or the postnatal stage. The official definition by Strauss in his classic 1947 text read as follows:

> The brain-injured child is a child who before, during, or after birth has received an injury to or suffered an infection of the brain. As a result of such organic impairment, defects of the neuromotor system may be present or absent; however, such a child may show disturbances in perception, thinking, or emotional behavior ... Special education methods have been devised to remedy these specific handicaps.[16]

Within this convoluted definition exist seven different propositions. One, a child has suffered an injury to or an infection in the brain; hence the impairment is organic. Two, the brain injury occurred before, during, or after birth. Three, motor dysfunctions of the body, mainly legs, may be present *or* not. Four, challenges in perception (mainly perceiving words), thinking, and emotional behavior, occurring separately or together, may be observable. Five, IQ tests can determine if the disturbances are present. Six, the learning process has been compromised. And last, educational methods have been created to remedy the problems experienced by the brain-injured child.

By placing the exogenous brain-injured child in the long lineage of mentally deficient children, Strauss critiqued early mental retardation theorists. Strauss claimed Alfred Binet established the "permanence of the intelligence quotient" and that what the "feebleminded" knew academically "remained unchanged throughout his life." Strauss's exogeneous child was not so much a critique of Binet but more a critique of Goddard and Terman, as well as an answer to his own questions: "Was mental deficiency in truth an entity? Was the symptom 'inability to learn' a complete statement of the problem?" Strauss answered, "obviously not" for the brain-injured child proved different from the endogenous mentally retarded because a "new discovery of localization in the brain led, in the last few decades, to the isolation of a clinical syndrome in adults known as 'traumatic dementia.'"[17]

Traumatic dementia emerged from the research of Kurt Goldstein and Henry Head, two neurologists that Strauss studied in his formative years. Specifically, Strauss saw something analogous in their work on brain-injured adults. Goldstein and Head studied the brain trauma of American soldiers who suffered head injuries during World War I. Goldstein and Head observed that soldiers who experienced head injuries lost certain skills and abilities. Strauss was struck by Goldstein and Head's argument that the intelligence, personality, and behavior of brain-injured soldiers changed, writing that "since these patients were without a doubt functioning less intelligently as a result of their brain injury, they were customarily referred to as 'dements,' or more precisely, as 'traumatic dements.'" Traumatic dementia, however, did not have the same meaning as "senile" dementia, "although both showed a diminution of mental capacities." The major difference between the two was that senile dementia occurred from *general* deterioration of brain capacity, whereas traumatic dementia affected only a *specific* area in the brain. Again, a leap of faith is required to accept any portion of an analogy that advances a resemblance between brain-damaged soldiers and so-called brain-injured children whose neurological impairment is not evident. But the goal of brain-injury theorists like Strauss is to explain the skill, ability, and behavior differences in different groups and to provide a theory of intelligence in more privileged children. Thus, Strauss wondered "if the disturbances resulting from brain injury in adults might not be present in brain-injured individuals of younger age—in children? If these studies have changed the unitary character of our concept of dementia or loss of intelligence, did it not seem possible that the same clinical methods applied to children might not change our concept of mental deficiency or lack of intelligence?"[18]

Learning disability theory as an explanation for white underachievement has its roots in racial signifiers. This racialized theory distinguished between the *lack* of intelligence versus the *loss* of intelligence. In addition to the words *lack* and *loss,* amentia, and even dementia in the late nineteenth and early twentieth century, as a form of severe mental deficiency and deterioration had long been promulgated by psychologists as a black disease, associated with the history of feeblemindedness and denoting a general and permanent lack of intelligence, according to Arrah B. Evarts, in "Dementia Precox in the Colored Race." By contrast, amentia in brain-injured children is a *loss* of intelligence because it is *specific,* meaning the damage in the brain is *localized,* occurring only in one area. Strauss and Lehtinen reasoned:

> It was necessary to ask if amentia of the type found in brain-injured children is an acquired defect, would it not be better to differentiate these children as "early traumatic dements" from whose amentia was a continuation of the inferior endowments of their progenitors, with its origin therefore in ovo? In other words, should the diagnosis be mental deficiency, implying the lack of intelligence, or should it be early traumatic dementia, implying loss of intelligence? Whatever label should be attached to them, did those brain-injured children show the same psychological characteristics as the hereditary or familial type of mentally defective children, or did their psychopathological pattern of behavior rather resemble that of the traumatic dements as found by Head and Goldstein? How could these infantile dements be diagnosed? How could they be selected from other types of early mental impairments?[19]

Selecting clinical identities from existing mental impairments and using value-laden words like *lack* and *loss* established a form of impairment exclusivity or advantage. If white children were to be disabled, the "better" disability signifiers would apply uniquely to them.

Racial signifiers permeated both learning disability and mental retardation theory. To acknowledge their discursive nature is to understand how signifiers "float." As a discursive construct, Stuart Hall argued that race is a floating signifier. What that means, said Hall, "is that race works like a language ... and signifiers refer to the systems and concepts ... of classification" that make meaning. Racial signifiers "float" or "slide" because they are relational and not fixed. A racial signifier can never be "secured in its meaning," for it "floats in a sea of relational differences:"[20]

> It's only when these differences have been organized within language, within discourse, within systems of meaning, that the differences can be said to acquire meaning and become a factor in human culture and regulate conduct, that is the nature of what I'm calling the discursive concept of race. Not that nothing exists of differences, but ... what matters are the systems we use to make sense, to make human societies intelligible. The system we bring to those differences, how we organize those differences into systems of meaning, with which ... we could find the world intelligible.[21]

Intelligibility here is not desired for the sake of clarity but rather for purposes of classification and order. "Classification," says Hall, "maintains the order in any system," through the employment of signifiers.[22] Thus, when brain-injury theorists differentiated between *senile dementia* and *traumatic dementia*, they in effect identified which children were black and which were white. When brain-injury theorists argued that senile "dements" suffered from a *general* deterioration rather than a specific or local deterioration in the brain (like traumatic "dements"), that assertion fit the historical description of total black "defectiveness." Theorists placed this racialized "defectiveness" in contrast to white people who suffered from a past trauma-inducing experience. When brain-injury researchers compared some brain-injured children as *lacking* intelligence as opposed to *losing* intelligence, it signified that some children never possessed intelligence compared to others who had. And when brain-injury theorists separated the endogamous from the exogenous, they not only distinguished the mentally retarded from the learning disabled, but they also discursively racialized disability theory by remanding black children and white children under fixed categories. Floating signifiers do not require old designations of race like "black" or "white." The very nature of their ability to float allows them to readily function under racially signifying attributes, such as "familial" or "hereditary" for black children and "normal" and "brain-injured" for white children. Thus, this disability-making system was ultimately a meaning-making system, with one group holding a "much more positive value than the other group."[23]

The "brain-injured" child had a more positive identity than other disabled children. Strauss believed this child began life with normal brain potential. With all things proceeding normally or evenly in the brain, brain-injury theorists posited that only accidental destructive events could change a brain's development. Through no fault of their own, thereby "accidental," the child's brain injury disrupts intellectual ability and disturbs behavioral control. And even if the brain-injured child's intellectual ability appeared normal on a mental test, "bad" behavior indicated damage to the central nervous system from an assumed lesion in a local area of the brain. Etiologically speaking, Strauss and his fellow researchers understood colleagues in the field would question the idea of brain-injured mental deficiency. The challenge in front of Strauss and other brain-injury theorists was what the eyes could not see inside the brain. The question remained: could a conclusive clinical link between the academic performance of children at or near normal intelligence and the presence of brain lesions, brain tumors, and brain tissue damage be established? Strauss understood that to make a field-shifting statement and link white academic failure to the brain, he would have to neurologically prove "real" brain damage.

But brain-injury theorists could not establish this etiological link. Instead, they solved this conundrum by focusing mainly on the *behavior* of "brain-injured" children, calling the behavior signs "minimal brain damage," or "minimal brain dysfunction" (MBD). Sam Clements, professor of psychiatry at the University of Arkansas, identified the behavior and symptomatology of MBD: hyperactivity; perceptual-motor impairments; emotional lability; general coordination deficits; disorder of attention (short attention span, distractibility, perseveration); impulsivity; disorders of memory and thinking; specific learning disabilities in reading, arithmetic, writing, spelling; and disorders of speech and hearing.[24]

A clinical cornucopia of mostly behavioral characteristics would serve as evidence of brain-injured learning disability. Said Strauss and Lehtinen, "Behavior and learning . . . now beginning to be recognized, may be affected by minimal brain injuries without apparent lowering of the intelligence level."[25] Thus, behaviorally speaking, brain-injured children were "hyper-active, distractible and awkward individuals, poorly integrated in their motor performance, faulty in their perceptions, poorly organized and unpredictable in their behavior, who go to pieces on relatively slight prov-ocation."[26] The emphasis on the word *minimal* reduced the stigma car-ried by the term "brain injury" while retaining the scientific legitimacy of the disability. More importantly, the qualifier *minimal* implied that the brain injury was minor or arguably nonexistent. This claim only had to be asserted, never proven, because of MBD's proximity to medical science.

If the *behavior* of brain-injured children was isolated and explained as dissimilar to other mentally retarded children, then psychologists could suggest the *academic struggles* of the brain injured were unique to them, too. James Hinshelwood, Samuel T. Orton, and Marion Monroe estab-lished the criteria for evaluating reading failures in children, purporting that brain injury explanations along with comparisons to brain-injured adults could best distinguish learning disability from mental retardation.[27] Since the early twentieth century, scholars have researched the broad area of aphasia. The Mayo Clinic currently defines aphasia as a "condi-tion that robs you of the ability to communicate. It can affect your ability to speak, write and understand language, both verbal and written. Apha-sia typically occurs after a stroke or a head injury."[28] The current under-standing of aphasia carries over from its early twentieth-century iterations as a catchall word and a "broad general term to cover all losses in the use of language, including reading and writing as well as speaking and understanding speech," said Samuel T. Orton. "This is quite generally the use which is implied when the word is found in the plural as 'the aphasias,' while its use in the singular form, generally though not con-sistently, indicates a restriction of its meaning to the field of spoken lan-guage."[29] Thus, early learning disability theory is directly tied to the study of the aphasias, especially reading disability. In fact, the term "learning dis-ability" would not be used with any regularity or consistency until Samuel Kirk promoted it beginning in 1963. Prior to 1963, "learning disability" was considered a disability of the reading, speech, spelling, and writing varieties. It also included perceptual and motor deficits, hyperactivity, and distractibility. These varied disabilities were rooted in the theory of brain injury *after* being removed from the broad purview of mental retardation and mental deficiency.

Samuel T. Orton described the results of a 1920s study from the Iowa State Psychopathic Hospital in Greene County, Iowa, involving children who were "dull, subnormal, or failing or retarded in schoolwork." These "defective" children exhibited "congenital word blindness," "bizarre written productions," and wrote in alternate directions with letters that seemed to correspond more with "ancient documents." However, the psychometric ratings of 142 students garnered from mental tests revealed that 70 students had an IQ of 80 or above. The question arose whether these children should be referred to as "defectives" since it implied a general intelligence deficit. Since much of their speech, writing, and reading difficulties stemmed from isolated disturbances, "I have consistently attempted to make use of the word *disability* in describing this difficulty," said Orton. Their "reading disability does not correlate with a low intelligence," Orton continued.[30] This belief led Orton and other researchers

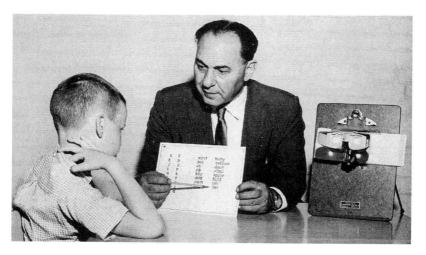

Figure 2. Samuel A. Kirk administering a Mirror Reading Test that reveals strephosymbolia, a type of dyslexia found in reading- and learning-disabled children. Photograph courtesy of the University of Illinois at Urbana-Champaign Archives, Record Series 26/4/1.

to look for "good reading cases," describing these cases as "normal." Orton differentiated "retarded" readers between good cases, "those who learn to read with great difficulty and those who never learn to read at all." Orton rendered the ultimate judgment against the latter, explaining "those whom no amount of ordinary teaching will train to read" were the true hereditary reading "defectives." For those who learned to read with great difficulty, the "explanation of the cause of the handicap rests on well-known facts of brain anatomy and brain pathology."[31]

Speech disability attributes also contributed to a discourse of permanent "retardation" based on heredity rather than temporary disability. Speech disability in "normal" children was understood as one of habit and tendency. William F. Lyons, a speech correctionist at the Newark State School in New Jersey, explained that the most prevalent speech problem he discovered among his students "is defective phonation from habit," mainly "the improper production of sound due to slovenly speech, left-over baby talk or an occasional tongue-tie."[32] Lyons added that lisping—the difficulty in learning how to make a specific speech sound—was "frequently encountered" among his "higher-grade patients."[33] Likewise, stammering and stuttering—problems with the normal flow of speech—were also tied to "defective phonation from habit" and understood as a higher-grade reading and verbal retardation issue often displayed in "normal" children. But "lalling," on the other hand, was understood differently. As an "infantile form of speech" characterized by the omission or substitution of sounds, lalling "is a defect in which the speech is unintelligible due to the omission of consonant sounds." Lyons said, "It is rarely found in normal children beyond the infantile age, but is often encountered among mental 'defectives,' especially in the lower grade."[34] These so-called lower-grade retarded cases, Lyons believed, were unsalvageable, and he thought that attention should be directed toward other students. Orton concurred, advocating that attention should be placed on children "under the suspicion of being 'dumbbells' but who were normal." Like the Iowa State Psychopathic Hospital, the Wayne County Training School "discovered" normal "retarded readers" whose "habits" appeared more "disabling" than "defective." The school published a report in 1932 authored by Thorleif Gruner Hegge, Richard Sears, and Samuel A. Kirk—the man who would formally place the two words "learning" and "disability" together thirty years later:

The problem of reading disability has hardly been touched upon in connection with the mentally retarded. We want to emphasize at the outset, however, that we do not advocate that all the reading cases belonging to this higher group should be treated without discrimination. On the contrary, we see the problem as one of selection. It is necessary to find those individuals who, while presenting a severe reading disability, appear especially deserving of treatment . . . and likely to profit educationally and socially by improvement in reading. . . . We have declared that good reading cases exist in considerable numbers in the mentally retarded group. . . . They should be trained to the extent to which training is profitable.[35]

When the theory of brain-injury took shape in the 1940s and 1950s, "mental retardation" underwent a major transformation "in view of the particularly urgent need for an etiological classification."[36] Throughout its history, mental retardation consisted of three elements: disease, hereditary defect, and being "overaged" for one's grade level. By the 1930s, being overaged for one's grade level was defined as an inability of children to profit from normal classes. But curiously, "mental retardation" was no longer considered a disease. According to Herman Yannet, it was just a "symptom or a condition which may result from a great variety of causes."[37] Seemingly, mental retardation could not go on as a purported disease. Diseases required impairment, and mental retardation had none, or at least none that were evident. Mental retardation did not cease being solely about overage-ness, but now being overaged for one's grade level and the inability to profit from a regular class would be described as "subaverage intellectual intelligence." Furthermore, mental retardation was still understood as a hereditary defect, with scholars, psychologists, and school administrators promoting two different ideas of hereditary mental retardation based on racial and class signifiers: one that was familial and subcultural (mainly black and brown students) and the other exhibited in cerebral, structural, or metabolic manifestations (mainly white middle-class children).

Early twentieth-century psychologists spent a considerable amount of time wresting conceptions of feeblemindedness away from medical doctors. Psychologists succeeded when Binet, Goddard, and Terman promoted the concept of mental age and "perfected," they believed, the measurement of hereditary intelligence. Psychologists progressively shaped the newer concept of mental retardation even while older feebleminded categories still circulated among professional circles and the lay public. With the term "mental retardation" having circulating for over fifty years, the American Association of Mental Deficiency made it an official designation in the late 1950s, announcing that "the term mental retardation, as hereafter, used, incorporates all of the meanings that have been ascribed historically to such concepts as amentia, feeblemindedness, mental deficiency, mental subnormality, idiocy, imbecility, and moronity, etc. Choice of the term *mental retardation* was predicated on the basis that it appears at present to be the most preferred term among professional personnel of all disciplines concerned."[38]

With official recognition, mental retardation still lacked an etiology, and to construct one, psychologists felt compelled to revise earlier associations of mental retardation with the medicalized body. The mind-body connection, therefore, had to be explained differently as advances in diseases placed mental retardation in a bind. No longer could psychologists purport that Down syndrome ("Mongolianism") was mental retardation, or that Gargoylism ("Dwarfism") and Tay-Sachs disease were mental retardation.[39] As the research of medical doctors advanced the knowledge about genetic diseases and other chronic disorders, mental retardation as a so-called disease was being questioned. Psychologists divested mental retardation of its classification of being a disease, but that did not stop the American Association of Mental Deficiency from trying to finesse the new understanding. "The system of classification presented here represents an attempt to develop a scheme which is consistent with the concepts of modern medicine," wrote educational psychologist Rick Herber. "For medical purposes, mental retardation is regarded as a manifestation of some underlying disease process or medical condition."[40] Mental retardation would no longer represent the disease itself but rather the symptom or the "manifestation" of a "real" disease. The relationship between mental retardation and organic diseases was one of "association." If the organic disease was debilitating enough to make a child's intellectual functioning subaverage, then mental retardation was associative or a symptom of the disease.

Under this new arrangement, mental retardation went from zero etiology to hundreds. "Well over a hundred different etiologies, diseases, and syndromes have been described in which mental retardation represents a more or less important syndrome," affirmed Herman Yannet, a pediatrician at the Yale Medical School.[41] Yannet admitted that the "organic determinants of intellectual inadequacy" rested squarely on diseases that "are extremely rare" with some being "medical curiosities." Not only were the diseases rare, Yannet acknowledged, but "they can be etiologically classified most effectively into three groups . . . (1) the pre-natal; (2) the natal and para-natal; and (3) the post-natal."[42] Ironically, the three potential periods or "groups" of disease causation resembled the same etiological timeline as Alfred Strauss's brain-injured exogenous learning disabled, proving again that mental retardation and learning disability were similar branches on the same underachievement tree. Thus, medical pathology still foundationally epitomized the conception of mental retardation despite its new reality as a "non-disease."[43]

In 1959, the American Association of Mental Deficiency issued its formal organizational definition recognized across professional disciplines. This definition stood for the rest of the twentieth century with only a few changes: "Mental retardation refers to subaverage general intellectual functioning which originates during the development period (pre-natal, natal, post-natal) and is associated with impairment in one or more of the following: (1) maturation, (2) learning, and (3) social adjustment."[44] The phrase "subaverage general intellectual functioning" is partly an ode to its past "in accord with the traditional concept of mental retardation with respect to age."[45] Subaverage meant a student's "performance greater than one Standard Deviation below the population mean of the age group involved on measures of general intellectual functioning."[46] On the IQ scale, one standard deviation below the mean (100) is 15 points, which in 1959 meant that mental retardation was any score below 85 on a mental test. The statistical definition existed independently of the medical definition, accomplishing something the organic medical model could not. "Normal" in the medical model meant the absence of an organic disorder; normal in the statistical model meant 100 on a psychometric exam. In organic cases, sick children were few and far between. In statistical cases, millions of children could be rendered "sick" after "failing" an IQ test. Sickness and psychometrics went hand in hand, possessing the power to "disable" children with the arbitrariness of a single value.

Mental retardation and learning disability theorists eventually realized that although a psychometric value was a powerful signifier in convincing the public that an impairment existed, this measurement alone could not adequately represent a disability. Thus, psychologists and educators added additional meanings to the official definition of mental retardation that manipulated and categorized children along the lines of race, class, and perceived academic abilities. Layering the definition increased the number of children labeled mentally retarded in public schools. Definitional "modes of manipulation" said more about the process of "contriving" and "inventing," and how children were brought into the mentally retarded fold. Hence, the concepts of "adaptive behavior," and the prevalence of mental retardation became the best tools of manipulation and invention.[47]

Midcentury changes in medical epistemology afforded psychologists the opportunity to layer even more definitions onto mental retardation, refine its multiple etiologies, and racialize its constituent parts. According to educational psychologist Rick Herber, the definition of mental retardation "specifies that the subaverage intellectual functioning must be reflected by IMPAIRMENT in ... adaptive behavior [and] ... it is inadequate intellectual functioning associated with impaired adaptive behavior which forms the essential basis of mental retardation."[48] Impaired adaptive behavior filled in the blanks of unknown etiology, allowing psychologists, teachers, and school administrators to "diagnose" mental retardation based on behavioral characteristics. Like the older conceptions of retardation at the turn of the twentieth century, the new iteration of mental retardation was equally infected with racism. If intelligence was hereditary, so too was behavior. Intellectual disability theorists attributed certain behaviors to specific racial groups based on false notions of heredity. Adaptive behavior, like intelligence, was racialized through the signifiers "familial" and "subcultural," which identified *impairments* in areas of "cultural conformity" and "interpersonal relations." To racialize impairment, theorists like Rick Herber and Herman Yannet differentiated between two distinct groups:

> In the first group, to which the term "familial" or "subcultural" retardation is applied, the genetic determinants might be properly called "physiological," in that they represent a part of the genetic pool which determines the hereditary transmission of normal intelligence. Intellectual inferior individuals in this category inherit from their parents those genes, undoubtedly

multiple in nature, which determine their position in the lowest levels of
the normal distribution curve of intelligence. These represent our intellectually marginal population whose social inadequacy will be closely
related to the nature and complexity of the society in which they live. . . .
Their problem is basically sociological. . . . The second group in our hereditary category represent an entirely different mechanism. The genetic factors involved in these patients are truly pathological in that they determine
abnormal, cerebral, structural, and metabolic manifestations. These conditions, which are fortunately, few in number although diverse in nature,
are due, as a rule, to single, mutant genes.[49]

Judgments about "bad" black and white behavior in "mentally retarded"
children would have different sources of origin: "familial and subcultural," stemming from a hereditary defect and manifesting "sociologi-
cally" in black behavior, in contrast to "metabolic manifestations" due
to a rogue genetic mutation describing sources of white behavior. Rick
Herber's offering rendered black impaired behavior as the inability to
adequately relate to fellow students, teachers, and other authority figures,
as well as behavior that did not "conform to social mores" and was "aso-
cial, anti-social, and/or excessively hostile."[50]

Statistically, mental retardation (now a substitute for describing
"morons," "imbeciles," and "idiots") sat comfortably below learning disability (later a substitute for "dullards," "slow-learners," and "brain-injured")
on the IQ scale. Learning disability would constitute an IQ score ranging
from 85 (one standard deviation below the mean of 100) up to around
110, buttressing and sometimes overlapping the higher end of mental
retardation. But the higher end of mental retardation and the lower end
of learning disability changed over time. By the 1970s, two standard deviations below the mean, or a score of 70, defined mental retardation,
and the floor for learning disability dropped as low as 80. The statistical
definitions of mental retardation and learning disability led to unending debates and muddled policies in special education during the 1960s
and 1970s.

In the minds of theorists, "impairment" is the absence of capability,
a loss, or a decrease in physical, emotional, or mental capacity measured against an established "normal" functioning. But beyond its medical understanding, impairment is a discursive property, belonging equally

(if not more) to our language systems. When Rick Herber purported "constructs and classifications are arbitrary language systems which vary according to their intended purpose,"[51] he underscored the belief that impairment, to paraphrase Michael Oliver and Shelley Tremain, is nothing more than a *description* of a person's physical body and perceived intellectual capacities.[52] Resting on suspicious intentions and poor research questions, the notions of impairment proved fundamentally untrue, existing primarily at the level of language and discourse. Psychologists like Herber often admitted as such, saying that constructs and classifications created more confusion than clarification.[53] The confusion seemed built into the process of inventing disabled children medically, statistically, and behaviorally. The arbitrary language systems provided the opportunity for various professionals in medicine, psychology, and education to "disable" children across different models.

With psychologists casting such a wide arbitrary net, it was difficult to know how many "mentally retarded" children existed in the U.S. population. Herschel W. Nisonger, president of the American Association of Mental Deficiency (AAMD) confessed that "it is difficult to conceptualize the size and characteristics of the retarded population in this country because of limited facts."[54] The "facts" were limited because they seemed to contradict other putative truisms about "mentally retarded" children. Studies in prevalence notwithstanding, the changing number of "mentally retarded" children varied widely "because of differences in definition, methodologies and measuring instruments used," Nisonger said in his presidential address to the AAMD in 1962.[55]

But the confusion allowed psychologists and educators to work the numbers.[56] Depending on the age group studied, mental retardation prevalence ranged from 1 to 3 percent of the population. School-age prevalence was thought to be higher than preschool or adult-age levels due to "intellectual demands" and compulsory "school attendance laws." Taking the top prevalence percentage in the 1950s, the widely promoted five million retarded children was reached and promoted:

Approximately three per cent of the school age population are found to be mentally retarded. It would be safe to say that at some time during their lives about three per cent of the population, especially at the school-age period, could be classified as mentally retarded. On this basis, the total retarded population in the United States would be approximately 5 million. Of this number ... 85 per cent are mildly retarded, 11.5 per cent are moderately retarded and 3.5 per cent are severely retarded.[57]

Five million retarded children in the 1950s increased to about six million by the 1970s until black, Latinx, and some Asian American families began taking school districts to court for the overrepresentation of students of color in special education. Legal challenges to the misclassification of black and brown EMR students slowed down the rates of prevalence. Although I argue the medical model existed as the greatest example of etiological mythmaking, it was the social (behavioral) and the statistical models that padded the numbers to five million. Of the five million cases, a vast 85 percent were "mildly" retarded, which demonstrated that the truly organic cases could not carry the fiction of the disability. It would be the "individuals who ... constitute a large proportion of the mild or educable retardation population ..." who we call "'familial' 'subcultural' and 'non-organic' [that] have ... characterized this group," wrote Nisonger.[58] If prevalence studies reported five million retarded children existed in public schools, then five million children were transformed into a new identity, becoming less about numbers and more about the equal rights of a new "minority" population.[59]

The Intersection of Civil Rights and Educational Disability Rights: From the Educable Mentally Retarded to the Learning Disabled

Setting a new course for the mentally retarded meant creating and clarifying a new identity in postwar America. Mental retardation as a classification of disability came of age between 1945 to 1963, garnering the attention of both public officials and ordinary people. As the struggles of the "mentally retarded" worked through different levels of society, an educational disability rights movement appeared and steadily gained momentum. The movement consisted of parent groups, psychologists, educators, special education organizations, and legislators. Though learning disability existed in its component parts (i.e., reading, spelling, etc.), and in placeholder identities like "brain-injured," "dull," "borderline," and "slow-learner," it would not be until the 1960s when public officials officially recognized the learning disabled (LD) as a "handicap" group. For now, advocating for the rights of the "mentally retarded" took precedence as parents with intellectually disabled children and professionals who worked in the field pressed for greater recognition. With five million deemed intellectually disabled, the "mentally retarded" became the largest "handicapped" group in the United States. Less stigmatizing than "idiot," "imbecile," and "moron," the term "mentally retarded" became an elevated designation from older feebleminded categories. This exalted identity gave its supporters and allies across the United States the confidence to pursue a social justice and civil rights agenda.

As a broad social justice crusade, the civil rights movement combatted white oppression by addressing long-standing inequalities, ranging from housing and employment discrimination to white mob violence and an under-resourced education. Inequities in education abounded, especially segregation in public schools and rampant racism in teaching, the curriculum and textbooks, and disciplinary practices. Though the South excluded black students from white schools, northern schools also engaged in segregation and racism as both policy and practice. Hence, the civil rights movement addressed many inequalities relating to black student well-being, engendering a righteous cause for freedom and justice in education through the middle and latter decades of the twentieth century. Black educational issues led the way in the struggle for civil rights; however, our collective memory neglects the ways in which educational disability rights developed a social justice agenda by creating a neglected "handicap" student identity. The tragic irony is that educational disability rights advocacy represented white disabled students in the 1950s and 1960s while claiming to represent all students. As a movement built on its own virtuous cause, educational disability rights found itself separating children based on race and class. Working in parallel formation in its temporal march through the 1950s, the educational disability rights movement and the civil rights movement began working toward contradictory ends in the 1960s and 1970s, leaving black families, black activists, and black professionals to fight specific educational inequities on their own, like the bias in IQ tests and the disproportionate placement of black students in EMR in the 1960s and the 1970s.

When the National Association for the Advancement of Colored People (NAACP) launched an assault on segregated education in the postwar years, the National Association of Retarded Children (NARC) developed a similar civil rights discourse. Invoking the U.S. Constitution in a journal article entitled, "A Bill of Rights for the Retarded," Richard Hungerford, a spokesperson for NARC, argued for a unique position, one based on the ideal of equality for the "mentally retarded." Hungerford and NARC did not begin this conversation; rather, Hungerford was one of the first to place the plight of all "handicapped" children in context of civil and constitutional rights. NARC linked the question of civil rights to a growing discussion about the educability of children considered "mentally retarded." NARC argued that because retarded children could learn like "normal" children, a refusal to educate them could be a violation of the Constitution. By adopting the language of rights from the U.S. Constitution, the educational disability rights movement emulated strategies used in the black freedom struggle, thus paralleling, and in some ways parodying, the civil rights movement.[60]

In a series of editorials, Hungerford lamented the ubiquity of the disabled as he traversed the streets of New York City. "As I walk to work mornings, I see the handicapped." Not wanting to appear hyperbolic, Hungerford admitted "I do not see all groups," clarifying, "but seldom is a week when I do not see someone blind, someone crippled, someone dull." Though the disabled constituted a "visible" presence on the streets, Hungerford seemed certain of the invisibility of the disabled, writing: "And I am certain that, among those who pass unnoticed, are an epileptic, free from the moment of seizure, a deaf man, using his vision as compensation, a cardiac, grateful for his respite, and delinquents, caught and the uncaught. All told they are so many walking the streets of the normal."[61] Hungerford imagined the anguish and frustration felt in the homes the disabled left before seeing them on the streets, placing himself in the shoes of their family members: "'Why feeblemindedness? I have kept Thy commandments; why did this come to me? Why did this happen to my son?'"[62] Speaking for himself, disabled people, and the parents, Hungerford argued that advocating for the rights of the disabled should be the responsibility of the larger society. "As responsible citizens we must be challenged to seek for the handicapped their right to live in spite of differences for the betterment of all."[63]

Improving the lives of disabled children reinforced the belief that they were normal, and as author Joseph Shapiro wrote, it was "not so much the disabled individual who needs to change, but society."[64] Discrimination from able-bodied people in society represented the typical experience of people who lived with disabilities. Able-bodied people who held privilege in society, as Hungerford understood, bore the burden of changing it. But since the majority of able-bodied people were white, the tone that advocates employed in speaking about the disabled is fascinating due to the use of the collective or universal "we." The conversation regarding disabled inclusion was not only a discussion about able (us) *versus* disable (them) but also about able (us) *and* disable (us) as members of the same ostensible white family. "As members of society, we must somehow learn to accept the 'mentally retarded' individual as one of our own group," wrote Arthur L. Rautman, a clinical psychologist and professor at the University of Florida. "Our education must enable us to accept the mentally defective individuals, limited though they may be in certain qualities, as citizens deserving of affection and respect—not for what they can do, or even for what they can be taught to do, but for who they are."[65] Phrases like "responsible members of society," and "as one of our own group" and "as citizens deserving of affection and respect" captured a certain kind of family politics that appeared inclusive but left people of color with disabilities outside of the conversation listening in. In white words and actions, people of color only mattered when interests converged as legal scholar Derrick Bell argued: "The interests of blacks in achieving racial equality will be accommodated only when it converges with interests of whites."[66]

Recognizing disabled children in society meant placing their plight alongside racial and religious groups, using the dichotomy of minority-majority racial groups to make the case for the "handicapped." John W. Tenny, president of the International Council for Exceptional Children (ICEC) advanced the argument that the "handicapped" comprised just another minority group oppressed by a powerful majority. "The term majority as used here does not necessarily imply a group larger in numbers," wrote Tenny, "but rather one which, in relation to a minority group, has greater prestige and power of decision and determination of human rights and opportunities." Identifying the majority as ableist and normal, Tenny recognized the various "limitations" imposed on disabled people that prohibited their advancement in society. The discrimination faced by the "handicapped" is "much like that of racial, nationality, and creedal minority groups," he wrote. Though acknowledging a commonality or similarity in struggle, Tenny abhorred that the "minority status of the handicapped is largely ignored." In a bold charge to the disabled community, Tenny asked, "Must we wait for the solution of the social problems of other minority groups before we scientifically attack the problem of society's attitude toward the handicapped?" Tenny wrote that waiting is not an option, exclaiming, "It is unthinkable that we should agree."[67]

After outlining the similarities between "racial minorities" and "disabled minorities," Tenny provided the reason why the "handicapped" should not wait until racial progress is made: "A handicap like other differences tends to produce social distance.... The handicapped, like other minorities, are often unfavorably portrayed in literature, in drama, and in slapstick humor.... The handicapped group like the Negro and other racial groups is frequently faced with segregation, particularly in schools." Tenny believed the struggle of the disabled should be placed above people of color because the "handicapped" have not taken to the streets, disrupted the public square, and demanded equal justice. Furthermore, Tenny surmised, the "handicapped" have not imposed their presence where it is not wanted, then explained, "Unlike other minorities, the handicapped do not create social-crisis threats. There is no threat of their [the handicapped] moving en-masse into so-called restricted residential areas. They do not threaten to take over certain desirable trades or business activities."[68] Tenny illustrated how the educational disability rights movement saw itself as different from the black and brown civil rights movement in the 1950s: leading with an advocacy approach built on "decency" and "decorum" and not with public agitation. Lee Marino, the president of the state council for the New Jersey Parents Group for Retarded Children, agreed with Tenny when distinguishing between the black civil rights struggle and educational disability rights. Unlike the civil rights movement for black equality, the members of educational disability rights organizations were not often an oppressed "minority" themselves or part of an oppressed "community." They were mainly professional advocates who represented the parents of "handicapped" children employing civil rights rhetoric. Often, these parents and professionals kept their distance from the African American civil rights community as Marino suggested. "We are not organized as a pressure group and do not intend to become one," wrote Marino. "We do think that mentally retarded children should be given a chance to be trained and to develop to the full extent of their capabilities. This is as much their God-given right as it is that of the normal child. But we also know that we will not achieve it merely by demanding it."[69] The educational disability rights movement functioned more as a lobbyist effort than a grassroots civil rights struggle. Its lobbyist orientation was much different than the groundswell grassroots disability rights movement of the 1970s and 1980s that produced the Americans with Disabilities Act in 1990.[70]

Educational disability rights and civil rights were parallel movements in that they both relied on the premise of equal educational opportunity for different student constituencies. While black children emerged from segregated educational institutions built on an edifice of racial exclusion, the postwar special education movement arose specifically to meet the needs of young people trapped inside the larger world of "mental defectives" and "deficients." The "mentally retarded" were part of the larger world of feeblemindedness that included categorical terms such as "moron," "imbecile," and "idiot." Though society today considers these terms to be pejorative, one hundred years ago, categories of "moronity," "imbecility," and "idiocy" existed as constructs to describe the mental and intellectual groupings of people. For example, "morons" possessed a mental age ranging from eight to twelve years old, the "imbecile" from three to seven years old, and the "idiot," from two years old or less. Their psychiatric labels ranged from mild, moderate to severe, and their social welfare labels included "marginally dependent," "partially dependent," and "totally dependent." Further accompanying these "degrees" of mental retardation was another describing the students' *potential* for education. This category contained subcategories, such as *noneducable* (representing no possibility); the *trainable* (representing some potential); and *educable*—characterizing the greatest hope for "liberating" the mentally retarded from the permanent confinement of feeblemindedness. Thus, the rise of postwar special education focused specifically on the latter two subcategories: trainable retarded (TR) and educable mentally retarded (EMR). Professor Charles Murdock wrote that "mentally retarded children of yesteryear who were excluded because they were 'unteachable' have recently become 'educable' or 'trainable'" with guaranteed rights.[71] Though the trainable and the educable were often addressed together, the educable mentally retarded held the greatest promise for the educational advancement of the intellectually disabled.[72]

The definition of "educability" rested on where a student placed on the intelligence quotient scale, with the ranges shifting over time: the profoundly retarded (IQ below 20); the severely retarded (IQ between 20 and 35); the moderately retarded (IQ between 35 and 50); and the mildly retarded (IQ between 50 and 75 but sometimes higher). According to sociologist Barry Cohen, the "profoundly and severely retarded as well as most of the moderately retarded are part of the category distinguished by central nervous system pathology." By the early 1970s, there were between "60 and 90 thousand profoundly and severely retarded children and adolescents who, if they were to survive, require constant closely supervised attention. By educational standards, these groups are uneducable, 'totally dependent' and represent the bulk of the total institutionalized retarded population." The second group made up of 300,000 to 350,000 individuals identified as moderately retarded in educational terms translated into the theory of "trainability" in that they "may attain an acceptable level of self-care, social adjustment to home or neighborhood, and a degree of economic usefulness via the home, residential facility or sheltered workshop." A life of self-dependent productivity "under supervision in a protected environment" was all this particular group might be able to achieve in society. And finally, numbering five million children in the United States, the "educable" mentally retarded were the "mildly" retarded, scorned for their "handicap" and championed for their potential.[73]

Parents of these students began to organize for their children's interests, creating a postwar educational disabilities movement that coexisted with the racial civil rights movement in the United States. As the civil rights movement gained traction in the 1940s and 1950s, historian Kathleen Jones noted, white "parent organizations demanded that local, state, and ultimately, the federal government live up to the liberal ideal of providing equally for the welfare of all its citizens."[74] Living up to the ideal of equal opportunity meant "normalizing" the "retarded" and providing the public with a more accurate portrait of the degrees of retardation. Since white students constituted the majority of the EMR population, many white families felt the impact of their children being misunderstood.[75] Thus, clarifying the rights and the needs of the "mentally retarded" fell on the shoulders of parents to organize and raise awareness. "I speak as a father of a mentally retarded child, and as state president of an organization of parents of these children," announced Lee Marino. "As an organization, the Parents Group must first of all endeavor to educate the parents of mentally retarded children to come out of their shell and get together with other parents who have similar problems." "There are no lists," Marino concluded, "no census of mentally retarded children, no way of knowing who are the parents of such children."[76]

The discourse on "educable mentally retarded" students materialized out of three aspects of the postwar intellectual disabilities movement. First, the movement represented one of the major social issues in the United States at the time; secondly, it captured the attention of psychologists and other professionals that worked with children; and lastly, disability rights in education was a family matter. The latter would propel the first two into action. The impossibility of raising "abnormal" children belied the ideals of middle-class domesticity in the 1950s.[77] Some middle-class white families insisted on raising their "abnormal" children normally even though they experienced pressures to institutionalize them. Guilt and shame would no longer consume families with "retarded" children. The main reason families felt less shame was that an IQ score between 50 and 80 suggested that retardation was only partly hereditary and therefore perhaps reversible.

The perception of "mentally retarded" persons began to shift when the public discovered that many of them served bravely in World War II, and that not all cases of retardation were severe. The "mentally retarded" and their families had to overcome the perception promoted by exposés on institutions like Letchworth Village, and the popularity of "retarded" confessional literature, like the book, *The Child Who Never Grew*. The most prominent account from the early twentieth century, Henry Goddard's *The Kallikak Family*, about severe "mental retardation," was still etched in the public's mind. With the "mentally retarded" representing an eclectic and diverse population by the 1950s, there was a drive toward greater public awareness about their normality and the absence of civil rights legislation on their behalf. Historian James Trent wrote, "As a group, families with retarded members could demonstrate their normality far better than such families of previous generations. They would not be the Kallikaks; rather, they would be ordinary post-war families."[78]

The National Association of Retarded Children (NARC) grew out of local efforts of white middle-class families that began organizing around the country in the 1950s and aligning themselves with psychology professionals. Three of the earliest local organizations consisted of parents from Bergen, Passaic, and Essex counties in New Jersey, the Association for the Help of Retarded Children in New York City, and the Parents Council for Retarded Children in Rhode Island.[79] Judges, professors, realtors, secretaries, and housewives served as members in the local affiliates. Possessed with a zeal for volunteerism and civic engagement, parents developed what sociologist Allison Carey called a "family agenda," asking, "What specifically did parents want for their children and themselves?"[80] The families protested conditions at state institutions for the retarded, demanding quality residential centers, community clinics, vocational training, and special education classes. Primarily, NARC parents wanted "to give each and every retarded individual the opportunity . . . to develop his or her fullest capacity."[81] Offering children the opportunity to develop at their highest levels required parents to work with educators and legislators from their respective states, as well as psychologists affiliated with national organizations, such as the American Association of Mental Deficiency. Kathleen Jones argued, "parent activism on behalf of physically and mentally handicapped children appeared during the 1940s and 1950s in part because of the interest of psychologists and educators."[82] The convergence of sustained parent activism and the interest of professional groups forced both lawmakers and superintendents of public schools to act forthrightly for the needs of retarded students and find ways to support their educational advancement.

In just a few years following the onset of parental activism, special education classes at the state level proliferated around the country and marked an important step in rendering services to a previously ignored student population. Most states legally created special education classes for the educable and the trainable "retarded" in the 1950s, although "special classes" in schools have existed since the early twentieth century. In 1947, California became the first state to legally mandate "special training schools or classes."[83] "By 1951," noted historian Margret A. Winzer, "a total of 39 states provided some form of mandatory or permissive legislation that provided subsidies to local districts for the education of children with exceptionalities. The most pronounced increases in the newly developed special education services seemed to be in the field of mental retardation."[84] Speaking to a local advocacy group in 1950, the governor of Minnesota, Luther Youngdahl, told an audience, "The retarded child has the right to social assistance in a world in which he cannot possibly compete on an equal footing. He has a right to special education and special institutions."[85] In 1957, the Minnesota legislature passed a special education law relating to the education of "handicapped" children in the state: "Minnesota's program of special education provides services for educable mentally retarded children through the establishment of a special class or special services in the pupil's district of residence."[86] Vernon L. Nickell, superintendent of public instruction for the State of Illinois understood the absence of state-mandated special education classes for the "mentally retarded" as a dereliction of duty, writing, "A school board that disregards this problem is disregarding a constitutional privilege and duty. An administrator who claims to have no obligation to the handicapped child is sidestepping a moral mandate of the 'People of Illinois, represented in the General Assembly.'"[87] Ten years after special education classes were created in Illinois, James Redmond, general superintendent of schools in Chicago lauded the success of children with intellectual disabilities when he commented: "In the decade 1954–64, the number of classes for the educable mentally handicapped has tripled. The educable mentally handicapped child has shared in the improvement of services, which have been brought to every child the Chicago public schools in the past decade. The Board of Education has recognized the importance of special education classes for handicapped children. In these classes, the quality of instruction may well make the difference between a life of dependency and a life of contributing citizenship."[88] Though special education classes grew in school districts across the United States, rhetoric always seemed far ahead of reality.[89]

The effectiveness of EMR classes served as a source of much debate. The issue of stigmatization sat in direct contrast to the growing popularity of special education classes. Five million children (and growing) were classified as educable mentally retarded by the early 1960s. Though the classification, "educable mentally retarded" functioned as a more encouraging term than "moron." Barry Cohen observed that EMR students "performed poorly in regular classes," could not be "promoted with their age cohort," and were the "major constituents of special education classes."[90] Epitomizing the intellectual disability with the most potential, EMR, like the "special class" public schools established in the early twentieth century, quickly became a dumping ground for students who struggled academically, socially, and emotionally. "Every large city finds, among the thousands of children enrolled in elementary and high schools, the pathetic misfits," decried Herold Hunt, superintendent of Chicago Public Schools.[91] EMR, indeed, was understood as a step above the "lowest" retarded populations; it was nonetheless a place to warehouse academically challenged students who could not be "adequately educated" in regular classes. According to Minnesota's assessments of its EMR students, they can only "profit from some degree of academic instruction," allowing them to "maintain themselves economically and socially in open society."[92] As a former superintendent of Massachusetts schools put it, "If society does not keep mentally deficient children busy in a *constructive* way during the whole of their school lives, they in a *destructive* way will keep society busy during their adult life."[93] Racially, it is hard to determine who is being referred to here because taken together, EMR classes represented a racial cross-section of the United States. In the 1960s, however, the overrepresentation of black students in EMR classes became more apparent to educators and the public, arising as a source of controversy. The percentage of black students considered mentally retarded steadily grew since the inception of special classes in the early 1900s, and in many respects, black students have always been "overrepresented" percentage-wise in comparison to their total number in a particular class, school, district, or state. Overrepresentation in special classes appeared well before states legalized the creation EMR classes in the 1950s. At the heart of black overrepresentation were perceptions of black intelligence—ideas cemented by Henry Goddard and Lewis Terman in the early 1900s—that raised the stakes again in the 1950s and 1960s when desegregation efforts began shifting more black students into white schools that led to greater overrepresentation in EMR, consequentially leading to the problem of racial disproportionality in special education.

Breaking the Dam of Hereditary Intelligence: *Brown v. Board,* Deprivation Theory, and the Black Freedom Struggle

The history of race, disability, and civil rights made for strange associations and movement responses. First, the civil rights movement cared deeply about the oppressive forces of a segregated and excluded education that rendered black schools, students, and teachers under-funded and thoroughly marginalized. Black organizations, administrators, and teachers fought for quality education alongside desegregation, which required transforming the entire public education system in the United States. But the black racial struggle never quite cohered with the educational disability struggle because special education operated as part of the larger oppressive system that African Americans, Latinx, Indigenous, and Asian American students experienced. Black learners became the victims of intelligence tests and special class placement. Once again, black students often found themselves segregated inside the very institutions they had just integrated.

The overwhelmingly white educational disability rights movement cared little about the issues that affected black and brown students. Ironically, the educational disability rights movement used the philosophy of equal educational opportunity to great effect in achieving its goals. If we mark the postwar period as the starting point for both civil rights and educational disability rights, then interest convergence characterizes the relationship between the advocacy communities. The Supreme Court's decision in *Brown v. Board of Education* in 1954 served as the imprimatur for educational justice in the United States. In addition, southern black activism led to the passage of the Civil Rights Act of 1964, breaking the legislative and legal back of segregation by reviving the Fourteenth Amendment's equal protection and due process clauses. By contrast, white parent organizations and the lobbying efforts of special educators and psychologists did not engender any significant legal achievements for educational disability rights in the late 1950s and early 1960s. With no meaningful case law or statutory law, the educational disability rights movement made progress where it could by attaching its legislative demands to the Elementary and Secondary Education Act (ESEA) on behalf of white disabled students. The ESEA of amendments of 1966, 1968, 1969, although essential steps on the road to disabled students' rights, merely laid the foundation by adding new title amendments. It would not be until the early and mid-1970s, after the black civil rights movement established a legal structure for "minority" rights, that educational disability rights began experiencing case law victories. Court cases like *Pennsylvania Association for Retarded Children (PARC) v. Commonwealth of Pennsylvania* (1971), *Mills v. Board of Education of District of Columbia* (1972), and new laws, such as the Rehabilitation Act of 1973 and P.L. 92–142—the Education for All Handicapped Children Act in 1975 used *Brown v. Board of Education* and the Civil Rights Act of 1964 as legal and statutory precedent to make the demand for the full inclusion of the "mentally retarded."[94] "From the surge of recent litigation," said Charles W. Murdock, professor of law at the University of Notre Dame, "it appears that the civil rights movement has at least discovered another oppressed minority—those persons encompassed within the rather unhappy label 'mentally retarded.'"[95]

African Americans fought against racial exclusion from schools and society and against the belief in their mental retardation. The perspective that the "civil rights movement" discovered another "oppressed minority" in the 1970s was amusingly tongue in cheek but revealing about how whiteness commandeered educational disability rights discourse. But the long black freedom struggle and its supporters had tenaciously pushed back against the idea of "mental retardation," the belief in hereditary intelligence, and the tests purported to measure it. American journalist Walter Lippman wrote, "Since intelligence, or rather 'performance' on a mental test, was not fixed by heredity, then tests could never measure fixed 'intelligence.'"[96] Horace Mann Bond advised and counseled black people to find "every detail of the operation, use and origin of these tests, in order that he might better equip himself as an active agent against the insidious propaganda." Bond went to the heart of the matter, arguing that the tests scientifically promoted the belief that "certain races are intellectual paupers; they have not made very great contributions to civilization within historic times, and that is because they are naively inferior and, moreover, that inferiority cannot be rectified."[97] Charles Johnson concurred with Bond, stating that measuring intelligence represented only half the aim of IQ tests; the other purpose was to scientifically prove that African Americans lacked the ability to acquire it.[98] E. Franklin Frazier cited history, placing theories of intelligence alongside other discourses that provided similar disparaging perspectives about the black mind. Frazier mused, "At one time the Bible was invoked to prove the inferior position of the Negro among the human races." "When this type of authority declined," Frazier added, social Darwinists' "evolutionary hypothesis was brought in to [*sic*] the support of prevailing sentiments and beliefs." Frazier argued that the baton of black inferiority discourse passed from religion to the social sciences, which "at the present time" via mental tests "are affording a basis for the rationalization of beliefs concerning the Negro's mental capacity."[99] Horace Mann Bond concluded, "Never before has the literature of psychology witnessed so determined an effort to establish, as a fact, the proposition that there are 'native differences between Negroes and whites as determined by intelligence tests.'"[100]

If the early twentieth century served as the era of feeblemindedness—which mapped the categories of "imbecile," "moron," and "idiot" onto real people—it also functioned as the era of intelligence tests and their purported capacity to measure innate acumen. Though the environmentalists believed it was "nurture" and not "nature," the hereditarians, like Goddard and Terman, dominated the debate for decades. The fixation with measuring intelligence made performance scales and tests, such as the Stanford-Binet, Weschler, and Otis tests, supposed yielders of irrefutable results. Simultaneously, however, environmental explanations, rather than heredity, gained traction in intelligence research. The examination of "deficits" produced by one's environment represented a major turning point in the 1930s and 1940s. Environmental explanations linking race and poverty pulled many researchers away from scholarly findings associated with hereditary notions of intelligence.[101] The publicity of sterilization abuse and state eugenic reproductive policies coupled with Nazi atrocities during the Holocaust also greatly diminished the hereditarian position. Though both black and white scholars embraced the environmental position, some black thinkers argued that white oppression and lack of educational opportunities impeded black intelligence. Since African Americans generally scored lower on both intelligence and achievement tests, black academic retardation was often regarded as an immutable given. These ideas began to change as African Americans migrated North.[102]

An essay in the *Journal of Negro Education* identified rural black migration to southern and northern cities as the source of public school troubles. "It was shown that as soon as immigration [*sic*] was restricted," wrote Alicia Doran in the *Journal of Negro Education*, "the vacuum thus created drew hundreds of thousands of Southern Negroes to the industrial cities, and shifted 20 percent of the Negro children of school age in the South to city schools."[103] Unlike all-white southern schools that restricted access to black students until desegregation, northern school districts experienced demographic transformations decades earlier and fashioned themselves unable to accommodate the influx of black students.

Doran taught in the public schools and further observed, "Chicago, with its many industries, brought great numbers of them [black students] to its public schools, where they are largely in the underprivileged class, with the retardation existing among them constituting one of the important phases of the general problem of retardation."[104] Doran recalled the findings of a research project undertaken at a Chicago junior high school in 1933. Psychologists administered to 212 eighth-grade students the Otis Classification Test for achievement and intelligence, as well as the Stanford Achievement Test in paragraph meaning, word meaning, language usage, history, civics, and arithmetic computation. The "tests" revealed a large percentage of black students were "below the normal level in both intelligence and achievement."[105] Doran not only concluded that the "lack of mental ability and achievement ability were probably important factors in the retardation of the group"[106] but also argued that environmental factors must always be taken into consideration: "They lived crowded together, in a very congested neighborhood under the most unsanitary conditions, with hardly a tree or a blade of grass in the entire community. Most of their families were on relief, and except for a few, economic status and the standard of living were very low." Doran and others staunchly believed impoverished black living conditions impacted academic performance. "It may reasonably be presumed that they [environmental factors] were important in the determination of the school progress of these children."[107]

Concurrent with the rising environmental thesis was whether northern black students were more intelligent than their southern black and white counterparts. Otto Klineberg posed this question in *Negro Intelligence and Selective Migration*.[108] Klineberg's research examined the grades and intelligence test scores of black students who migrated to New York City from Birmingham, Alabama; Nashville, Tennessee; and Charleston, South Carolina. Klineberg observed, with the increasing length of residency in New York, the test scores of black southerners tended to mirror those of native black New Yorkers. Rising black intelligence did not manifest upon arrival. Subsequent years in New York increased the likelihood that the performance of former southern black students would match their northern black counterparts. Advancing the theory of regional differences in intelligence, however, precluded Klineberg from asserting that black intelligence equaled that of whites in northern cities. His belief in northern regional differences in racial intelligence allowed northern black students to proximate northern white students, while exceeding white southerners. This position lent credence to Klineberg's conclusion that the social environment was a critical factor in the improvement of black intelligence: "There seems to the writer to be no reasonable doubt as to the conclusion of this study. As far as the results go, they show quite differently that the superiority of the northern over the southern Negroes, and the tendency of northern Negroes to approximate the scores of the Whites, are due to factors in the environment, and not to selective migration."[109]

The question of environmental factors permeated discussions concerning black education and shaped how courts, schools, and social scientists addressed the problem of black mental retardation.[110] Prior to the first Great Migration during World War I, the perception of lower black intelligence was premised on innate black intellectual incapacity. The first Great Migration, along with the parallel movements of the second Great Migration and public school desegregation in the 1940s and 1950s, elevated the explanation of poverty and neighborhood environment alongside innate black inferiority. The two explanations—inherent black inferiority and environmental deficits—shaped the national debate. These twin explanations became a popular area of study across various social science disciplines and a driver of special education policy in the 1960s. The Supreme Court's opinion in *Brown v. Board of Education* gave environmental theorists the power to push back against the hereditarians. *Brown* elevated the theory of cultural deprivation, adding a new dimension to special education discourse and policy.

While the *Brown* case is known for overturning *Plessy v. Ferguson* (1896) and eliminating segregation in law, *Brown* also contributes to our understanding of black mental retardation. The Supreme Court identified educational deprivation as an outcome in the long history of black schooling. When *Brown* invoked the idea of "detrimental effects" on black learning, the Supreme Court placed itself squarely in the intellectual disabilities debate, connecting educational deprivation with black academic retardation. The Court inferred that segregation created educational deprivation, which in turn stunted black mental development. "Segregation with the sanction of law," the Court wrote, "has a tendency to retard the educational and mental development of African American children and to *deprive* them of some of the benefits they would receive in a racially integrated school system." The famous line in *Brown*, "separate educational facilities are inherently unequal" concerned the physical condition of schools and "nonexistent" programs. Still, this line also concerned those conditions southern state laws created: mentally retarded black children *deprived* of white resources, white opportunity, and as many scholars argued, a larger white middle-class world. Thus, the deprivation the Supreme Court identified in *Brown* was twofold, one, a deprivation based on the denial of opportunities and another based on the denial of legal recourse under the U.S. Constitution: "Segregation of children in public schools solely on the basis of race deprives children of the minority group of equal educational opportunities . . . [and] segregation is a deprivation of the equal protection of the laws guaranteed by the Fourteenth Amendment."[111]

Through its reasoning in the *Brown* case, the Supreme Court agreed with black scholars of public education who continually stated that segregation compromised the learning of black students.[112] The Supreme Court invoked the word "non-existent" to describe southern black education.[113] In the South, argued the Supreme Court, the "curriculum was usually rudimentary; ungraded schools were common in rural areas; the school term was but three months of year in many states; and compulsory school attendance was virtually unknown."[114] Black high schools were few in number until the 1920s and 1930s, forcing historically black colleges and universities, like Morehouse and Spelman, to educate African American high school students for a protracted period.[115] Approximately 64 public high schools existed for African-Americans students in 1915–16; by 1935, there were 2,305. "In spite of the phenomenal growth of secondary education facilities for Negroes," black scholar Ellis O. Knox wrote, educational opportunities for black students still proved grossly inadequate in the South.[116] Public education for black students in the North fared no better, eventually attracting the attention of the northern civil rights movement. Thus, black mental retardation born out of white oppression, as understood by *Brown*, provided environmentalists the evidence to push back against the hereditarians. "Elementary education for Negroes in states where four-fifths of them live is devastatingly below that offered to any other racial group in the United States," wrote Howard Long. "Illiteracy among Negroes is nearly four times higher than among white persons," Long continued. Environmentalists believed a direct correlation existed between black educational inequities and black educational outcomes. "The limitations condition the achievement of the secondary pupil ... and thus the group is retarded as compared with standards set by pupils with normal backgrounds. ... To the problems of the underprivileged we must add color caste when we consider the plight of Negro youth."[117]

Most black students suffered from subpar educational resources and opportunities, and these inequities came to a head when black parents and civil rights organizations demanded improvements in black education. Though the term "de facto segregation" is generally applied to the North to contrast it with southern "de jure segregation" in the law, the racial reality for African Americans in cities like New York City, Boston, Philadelphia, Chicago, Cleveland, and Los Angeles mirrored that of southern cities.[118] "We will go to jail and rot there, if necessary, but our children will not go to Jr. High Schools 136, 139, or 120," said Mrs. Viola Waddy of New York City.[119] Mrs. Waddy was a member of a black parents organization that protested racial inequities in education. When change appeared elusive, a group of black mothers boycotted the New York City Board of Education by refusing to send their children to schools, thereby openly defying compulsory school attendance laws. The board took the parents to court, but in confronting the actions of the parents, the board had to answer questions about the poor quality of school buildings, overcrowded classrooms, and a growing number of inexperienced and substitute teachers assigned to classrooms attended by black and Puerto Rican students. The board, white teachers, and administrators relayed to black parents and civil rights leaders that segregation did not exist in New York City public schools. Such denials of segregation and discrimination were refuted by the conditions themselves and in multiple studies published on the state of public education in New York and across the country. The actions of black parents and the reports' conclusions went unaddressed, with few localities heeding the warnings to make the institutional changes necessary. As a result, tensions arose nationally in the first few years of the 1960s. Black and Latinx middle and high school students staged walkouts and massive boycotts of schools in New York City, Los Angeles, and in midwestern cities.[120]

What separated the civil rights struggle from educational disability rights advocates was the denial of systemic racism and a critical mass of white allies. In the context of demanding institutional change, skin color and class privilege mattered profoundly. For black parents, white teachers and school administrators rarely retreated from their adversarial posture, perceiving black community members as undeserving at best and a threat to white schools at worst. By contrast, school authorities welcomed white parents as allies in the pursuit of equal educational opportunity for their disabled children. Black students, families, and civil rights organizations remained at the mercy of white boards of education, teachers, and superintendents, having to determine the best way out or around the resistance. When allies seemed few and far between, a deficit philosophy, like the theory of "cultural deprivation," sometimes proved to be the only effective weapon. Nothing epitomized a "deficit" philosophy more effectively than the newer environmental deprivation thesis argued in *Brown* and thereafter in the social science literature.

The two dominant schools of thought about mental retardation causality—hereditary intelligence and cultural deprivation—became the way teachers, administrators, and social scientists approached the problem of black retardation, as well as the remedies they advanced. Cultural deprivation argued that the source of black mental retardation was not genetic but rather the "environment"—a function of impoverished neighborhoods and the lack of middle-class family values. Though black hereditary "stupidity" remained a leading perspective, *Brown* opened the door for cultural deprivation theorists to recalibrate the debate around black intellectual disability. Cultural deprivation/environmental arguments not only led to the desegregation of white public schools but also promoted compensatory education as *the* solution to black mental retardation. Writing about the impact of the environment on black student disabilities in 1958, Benjamin Pasamanick, professor of psychiatry, and Hilda Knobloch, associate professor of pediatrics, both at Ohio State University's College of Medicine, wrote in the *Journal of Negro Education,* "We think it has been and would be possible to indicate that Negro school children are not as bright, have more specific learning disabilities and behavior disorders than white school children. Indeed, considering the environment in which they are conceived and reared, it would be surprising if they did not."[121] To acknowledge black intellectual disabilities in 1958 by invoking possible "specific learning disabilities" and "behavior disorders" proved a remarkable admission given the racial disproportionalities in these two areas later in the century. Pasamanick's statement foreshadowed a special education dilemma that existed below the surface but not yet openly politicized in the 1950s. His words also cast doubt on hereditary black mental retardation, raising the possibility that black children had other kinds of "disabilities." Thus, the slow shift from innate intellectual capacities to black cultural deprivation had indeed turned a corner after the *Brown* decision.

After thirty social scientists submitted a statement to the Supreme Court supporting the plaintiffs in the *Brown* case, the environmental position began to displace the hereditary intelligence thesis as a causal explanation for black inferiority. In 1957 eighteen prominent social scientists—including Otto Klineberg of Columbia University, Allison Davis of the University of Chicago, and Kenneth Clark, of The City College of New York signed a joint statement published in the *American Journal of Orthopsychiatry* speaking to the issue of environmental deficits in the context of the immediate post-*Brown* years. An excerpt from the statement read:

> In connection with the process of school desegregation and the difficulties with which it has been accompanied in certain areas, the question has again arisen as to the existence of innate differences in intelligence between Negroes and Whites. The present statement is directed to that question. Those who have signed it are not on this occasion taking sides with regard to the problem of desegregation as a whole, nor with the manner or the rapidity with which it should be accomplished. They are for the moment concerned only with the facts and conclusions accepted by scientists with regard to racial comparisons in inborn intellectual capacity.[122]

In the post-*Brown* period, lower black intelligence and the correlative or causative explanation regarding depressed environments influenced the making of black educational disability policy at the state and federal levels. Admittedly, black students represented a significant segment of those labeled "mildly" retarded, with "educable mentally retarded" (EMR) emerging as a catchall designation for all intellectually disabled students regardless of race. However, the two dominant discourses still differentiated black and white intellectual disability in the 1950s and 1960s. The postwar shifts that reconfigured the "origins" of intellectual disability provided a unique moment that could not be a lost occasion for the families of the white intellectually disabled. Black and brown families took advantage of equal educational opportunities produced by the *Brown* decision and the civil rights movement. White parents, psychologists, and educators especially seized upon the moment, advancing a separate educational disability rights movement. Such a movement could potentially identify more educationally and legislatively underserved white students.

If the educable mentally retarded (EMR) found themselves trapped inside the larger world of "mental defectives" and possessed only a modicum of hope for a fulfilling life, then a new set of white parents and professionals believed another segment of the white student body went overlooked, too. In the postwar years of proliferating disabilities, EMR sat at the top of the mental retardation hierarchy, garnering the attention of school districts and the nation. Thus, in the late 1950s and early 1960s, a wholly different parents' movement emerged, along with special education experts like psychologist Samuel Kirk, who identified and "liberated" a segment of the student population from EMR categorization and stigmatization. These so-called neurologically handicapped and brain-injured students would no longer be linked to the "mentally retarded" but rather have an identity of their own: the "learning disabled" (LD).

When Learning Disability Was White: Samuel Kirk and the Politics of Special Education

The educational disability rights movement produced a second visible and vocal white middle class that advocated for their "slow-learning" children. Similar to the early generation of EMR parents, this coalition represented doctors, lawyers, accountants, sales clerks, and teachers in every region of the country. While many were college educated, some held stable blue-collar jobs in the manufacturing and retail sectors of the labor market. What united them was a collective sense that their children were different from the previous generation of "mentally defective" students and should be afforded special treatment. Thus, their children's difference hinged on the idea that this new group of parents and professionals *believed* that their students were not "classically" retarded. Like their previous counterparts, the race and socioeconomic status of their parents provided them a platform to mobilize and organize. This combination of class privilege and professional background allowed parents to challenge their children's "underachiever" identity. As self-organized families, they were determined "to bring about greater knowledge and better physical and social-psychological treatment for their ill or handicapped child."[123]

In the beginning period to recognize the "learning disabled," parents took the lead simply because they shared a common problem that very few people seemed capable of addressing; they wanted professional answers to questions beyond their own lay understanding. Having little access to policymakers who could affect change, they relied on their own circles since few institutions for "brain-injured" students existed.[124] Public schools refused to provide resources to the few students identified nebulously as "neurologically handicapped." Certainly, the number of special education classes increased for the "mildly" retarded, but classes for the learning disabled did not address this particular student population. Politicians were uninformed and indifferent to the problem of intellectual disabilities beyond mental retardation, and there existed no sense of urgency from a constituency that could not bring pressure to bear on local and national lawmakers. But by the late 1950s and early 1960s, this lack of attention changed.

White middle-class parents emerged from basements and vacant storefronts demanding institutional modifications in the field of special education.[125] They moved from informal commiseration to formal advocacy, giving themselves names like the California Association of Neurologically Handicapped Children, the Minnesota Association for the Brain-Injured Children, the Milwaukee Society for Brain-Injured Children, the New York Association for Brain-Injured Children, Fund for Perceptually Handicapped Children of Central Kentucky, Michigan Children's Neurological Development Program, and the Alabama Foundation to Aid Aphasoid Children, to name a few. Though officially organized into groups under phrases like "neurologically handicapped" or "brain injured," parents did not fully understand the "science" behind their children's disorders, which reflected vast differences in local organizational development.[126]

While some of these organizations proved more advanced in their mobilization, others were just getting started. "Our program has been primarily one of understanding, a little on education, and we haven't delved into research yet," wrote a member of the Minnesota organization. The monthly or bimonthly gatherings designed to increase membership were all some groups could muster. Still, others struggled to maintain a decent level of parental involvement. One parent advocate asked, "Our problem in Milwaukee is . . . how can we get the parents interested in doing something for their children?" Members of the Chattanooga, Tennessee organization spent time collecting information and literature from other groups around the country while soliciting advice from local psychologists and bringing in brain-injury experts, such as Syracuse University professor William Cruickshank, and Richard Lewis, author of *The Other Child*.[127] Despite the fact that the Minnesota organization had not "delved into research yet," the support of empirical research would be crucial for parents in brain-injury organizations.[128] The union between white families and white psychologists placed academic research front and center of their decision-making, as they both sought a solution to the protracted problem of white student underachievement.[129] Dr. Samuel Kirk and Dr. William Cruickshank received their training in educational psychology. They both emerged as consequential figures in the neurological "handicapped" children's movement, forcing the country to pay attention to the nuances of mental retardation. Heavily influenced by Alfred Strauss and the research established at the Wayne County Training School in Northville, Michigan, the premier residential and research center for the educable mentally retarded, Kirk and Cruickshank cultivated their academic interests in the broad field of learning disorders. The field of neurology, specifically brain theory research, focused on reading and language challenges as well as perceptual and behavior disabilities of "retarded" children. As Samuel Kirk remembered, "Pathological brain dysfunction was proposed to explain many of these aberrations."[130] He told an audience of conference attendees to resist getting bogged down in scientific concepts.

The educational disability rights movement and the civil rights movement literally and legislatively crossed paths in the 1960s. Dr. Samuel Kirk delivered the morning address at the Conference on Exploration into the Problems of the Perceptually Handicapped Child in Chicago on Saturday April 6, 1963, the same day civil rights leaders Fred Shuttlesworth and Charles Billups led a group of marchers from the A. G. Gaston Motel to the Birmingham City Hall. Though the Birmingham movement was miles from Chicago, and the two events occurred simultaneously, the march and the speech encapsulated the two lanes black civil rights and white educational disability rights traversed in the sixties.

Civil rights and educational disability rights served different racial constituencies. The two movements competed for Congress's attention. Led by men and women connected to the black church and labor organizing, the civil rights movement focused on integration of public schools, voting rights, public accommodations, employment discrimination, and fair housing. By contrast, the educational disability rights movement was white-parent led, white-student focused, and white-professional driven, with an emphasis on achieving rights and recognition for white slow learners. As the civil rights movement sought to integrate southern institutions and procure constitutional rights for African Americans, the educational disability rights movement "medicalized" white academic failure. Both movements looked to lawmakers in Congress to help them in their respective undertakings.[131]

The theme at the Conference on Exploration into the Problems of the Perceptually Handicapped Child set the tone of the proceedings and centered its attention on white children. "The purpose of this conference is to obtain information, share ideas and open channels of communication with all groups who are interested in the PERCEPTUALLY HANDICAPPED CHILD [*emphasis in original*]. We will move toward investigation of the child who has average or above average intelligence but is not learning."[132] Not only was it important for the conference to spotlight the "appropriate" child, but it was equally important to relay the most basic of facts: the purpose of the conference was to serve young people who were of average and/or above average intelligence but were unable to learn at the rate of their fellow white peers. Using the discourse of equal educational opportunity, the call to action for white disabled students seemed resolute, urgent, and momentous. "This is a new frontier in education," wrote Dr. Oscar M. Chute, superintendent of elementary schools in Evanston, Illinois and cochair of the conference. "Regardless of the psychological and/or medical reasons for severe learning difficulties, we do have an obligation to find out how such children with persistent deep-seated learning difficulties can be helped." Believing it would require a "teamwork approach of medical, psychological services, and teachers" to get to the root of matter, Chute looked at the problem through the prism of equal educational rights when he concluded, "I think all of this is consistent with the basic idea that our public schools are for all children of all the people."[133]

The 1963 conference merged medical science with equal educational opportunity, producing a fresh discourse for the nonretarded white slow learner. Psychologists from mental health clinics, neurologists from medical schools, executive directors and supervisors from departments of education, counselors and teachers from schools across the country attended the conference. Academic experts marshaled hard science to provide explanations about the difficulties plaguing slow-learning white children. Many believed the portrait of white slow learners required the backing of science to understand their academic struggles in schools. "The services of a pediatrician, neurologist, ophthalmologist, otolaryngologist, and child psychiatrist," wrote Wretha Petersen, supervisor of special education in Montgomery County, Maryland, "are needed in order to get as complete a picture as possible."[134] Brain-injury researchers provided varying opinions on the realities of neurological damage due to central nervous system dysfunction. Despite clinical interpretations, the medical diagnoses describing slow learners were not always helpful. Parents, teachers, and administrators were often confused, especially when clinical monikers, such as brain injury and perceptual disorder, were used interchangeably. A goal of this conference would be for participants, including academics, teachers, and parents, to find a simple and common label describing white slow-learning students.

Kirk remembered earlier struggles with educational classification in the late 1940s and 1950s. "The term 'slow learner' has been applied to children with greatly different characteristics," he wrote. Though psychologists typically used "slow-learner" when referring to "near-normal" children, "it has been used by different authors to refer to all children who are not making adequate educational progress regardless of the cause."[135] Kirk felt the need to rethink the category of slow learners and limit the definition to students he considered slightly below average to above average intelligence. He answered, "The term 'slow learner' should be restricted to the child who does not have the capacity or potentiality to learn intellectual things, such as reading, at the same rate as average children."[136] Kirk wanted to develop a better understanding of white underachievement. Slightly reconfiguring and repositioning the slow learner on the IQ scale would provide greater clarity for parents and educators. "At most," he wrote, the term "slow learner" "should include the dull and border-line children, with intelligence quotients of approximately 75–90, and if we stretch the term, the mentally handicapped, with intelligence quotients from 60 to 70 or 80."[137] According to Kirk's new proposed definition, this would partly include the EMR student population. However, Kirk was more interested in the slow-learning population at the top of this IQ range. These children with the higher IQ he believed should receive greater attention.

For Kirk to construct a new category called "learning disabled," he began disaggregating the "slow-learning" population. In an essay entitled, "Reading Problems of Slow Learners," Kirk racialized the slow-learning student population when he identified two distinct groups that required "different educational or remedial programs." The first group of slow learners were "those with a variety of psychological handicaps caused by a possible cerebral dysfunction." Exhibited manifestations included problems with auditory and visual reception of words, vocal and motor expressive disabilities associated with verbal communication, and disorientation in space. The second group, and the largest segment of the slow-learning student population, according to Kirk, was "what we might designate as culturally produced slow learners. This group is probably inherently normal . . . but because of cultural deprivation, inadequate child-rearing practices, and inadequate intellectual stimulation, they score below average on intelligence tests and are retarded in reading . . ." These culturally deprived black "slow learners" resided in the "deprived areas of the cities where the home and neighborhood environment and the quality of schooling is below average." Kirk's solution to black slow learning was not to determine the causes and solutions to their academic challenges but rather to proffer "community rehabilitation, slum clearance, and other social and economic measures that will raise the economic and cultural levels of a community."[138]

The racialization of slow learners is as old as the early twentieth century and is traceable during the civil rights era to Rudolf Flesch's influential book, *Why Johnny Can't Read* published in 1955.[139] The subject still resonated in the early twenty-first century with the *New York Times* bestseller, *Why Bright Kids Get Poor Grades and What You Can Do About It.*[140] For decades, this literature questioned why capable white middle-class students were failing basic academic subjects. In the 1950s and 1960s, the educational disabilities movement addressed this question by constructing paradigms of normality and white underachievement couched in the language of disability. To convincingly advance the argument of white

"normal" underachievement, white failure had to be seen as not possessing any contributing influences. "White," "middle class," and "student
failure" were contradictions in terms because "bright" white children
don't fail. In reference to struggling white students, Robert Thorndike,
professor of psychology at Columbia University, wrote in the 1960s, "It
seems obvious that we can only have underachievement in relation to
some standard of expected or predicted achievement. So perhaps we
should begin by asking where that standard of expected achievement
comes from"[141] White expected achievement comes from white middle-
class privilege—a sense of social entitlement that has always coincided
with white advancement. To the extent parents and scholars would locate
white underachievement in academic failure, they would call it a subject-
matter disability, rarely a retardation, and never an environmental disadvantage.[142] While white underachievement was made synonymous with
reading failures, black underachievement was rarely associated solely with
subject-matter failures but with being black, growing up in a black family, or living in black neighborhood settings.[143]

   Kirk confronted the dilemma of defining the problem at the 1963 conference. Kirk took his audience through an exercise detailing what disabilities should be excluded when identifying slow-learning children. "As
I understand it," he wrote, "this meeting is not concerned with children
with sensory handicaps, such as the deaf or blind, or with children who
are mentally retarded, or with delinquent or emotionally disturbed children caused by environmental factors." Kirk omitted "the deaf" and "the
blind" not because they constituted sensory disabilities but because he
did not want to suggest that sensory disabilities were necessarily comorbid with brain damage or neurological impairments. Kirk also eliminated both forms of mental retardation as the appropriate way to frame
the problems children experienced. Mental retardation "marked . . . intellectual deficits" associated with central nervous system impairment that
manifested in total dependency throughout a lifetime, institutionalization, and/or extensive medical and nursing care."[144] Neither was Kirk talking about the educable mentally retarded, the largest segment of special
education students in the 1960s, or the culturally and educationally disadvantaged synonymous with African American and Latinx students.
These were not Samuel Kirk's children. The Hannah Harts throughout
the country were his primary concern.

In the book, *Where's Hannah: A Handbook for Parents and Teachers of Children with Learning Disorders,* Beverly Jones and Jane Hart introduced the world to an eleven-year-old "pretty," "slim, silky-haired charmer" named Hannah who happened to be the daughter of one of the authors. Jane Hart challenged the results of all the psychological tests that repeatedly diagnosed and rendered Hannah as mentally retarded. Refusing to accept her daughter's IQ score and the label of mental retardation that accompanied it, Jane Hart knew that Hannah "couldn't learn as *fast* as the average child, although this did not mean she couldn't learn most things *eventually.*"[145] Jane's determination resulted in Hannah's placement into a perceptually "handicapped" class that would become synonymous with the new learning-disabilities movement. Jane was not only an advocate for her daughter; she "refused to accept the idea that she was not normal"[146] despite the fact that Hannah was "hyperactive . . . moody, excitable, distractible, distracting, and destructive to an unusual degree."[147] Jane, like other parents, realized that she was not the mother of an unusual child. Ray H. Barsch, another influential scholar in the field of learning disabilities, wrote that Hannah Hart "is only a single representative of a large percentage of the nation's children who are lost in space. Diagnostic precision is unfortunately lacking to identify accurately the specific etiological factor in these spaces. A host of labels are applied in general practice; but few, if any, are sufficiently precise to generate a well-defined program of action . . . Children wander. Parents wander. Both search."[148]

Samuel Kirk did not want parents to search any longer. He had been toying with the idea of using the term "learning disabled" to describe developmental difficulties in reading, communication, and social interaction deemed neurological. One year before the conference, Samuel Kirk used the phrase "learning disability" for the first time in an article published in the journal *Exceptional Children.* In this groundbreaking essay, Kirk and his student Barbara Bateman defined this new term. "A learning disability," they wrote, "refers to a retardation, disorder, or delayed development in one or more of the processes of speech, language, reading, writing, arithmetic, or other school subjects." The next task was to establish that learning disabilities were due to "possible cerebral dysfunction and/or emotional or behavioral disturbances." For Kirk and Bateman, it was important to state unequivocally that learning disabilities did not result from "mental retardation, sensory deprivation, or cultural or instructional factors."[149] Learning disabilities included brain injuries linked to basic subject skill deficits born out of internal "defects" and not the culture, family, neighborhood, or environment of the student.

Samuel Kirk was fond of recalling a story about a four-year-old boy he met at a state institution in Illinois. Entering the institution with an IQ of 60, the boy received six hours of preschool training per day, which raised his IQ to 90. At five and a half years of age, the boy was deinstitutionalized and placed in a foster home and in a community school. "At age six and a half," said Kirk, "he tested 104 IQ on the Stanford-Binet and was placed in regular first grade rather than a special class." "It was soon discovered," Kirk wrote, "that in spite of his average IQ, he was having difficulty in learning to read." The student underwent additional evaluation that revealed "some major deficiencies in the integration of sounds, and in the ability to learn words." After tutoring in reading using a "systematic phonic method," "he progressed through the grades in an adoptive home with average performance." Kirk surmised the boy eventually graduated from high school with above average grades and attended college earning Bs and Cs. Kirk admitted the case was unusual but that it demonstrated the existence of another previously unknown segment of the public school population. "How many children classified as mentally retarded, would not be mentally retarded if we viewed the condition from a remedial vantage point?" "How many children classified as mentally retarded by professional opinion could be better classified as cases of learning disabilities?"[150]

Though Kirk grounded his definition of learning disability in science by describing the etiology—that is, the study of causation—as brain dysfunction, he wanted desperately to move parents and others away from describing learning disabilities in medical terms for no other reason than "it is often difficult to determine whether or not there is a cerebral dysfunction." Kirk let the proverbial cat out of the bag by admitting the difficulty in linking brain injury with learning disabilities. The inability to discover a causal link would form the basis of many critiques of learning disability in the 1970s as an "invented" medical diagnosis. For now, Kirk wished for parents and educators on the front lines of the learning disabilities movement to concern themselves "primarily with behavioral systems of deficits rather than with the location or extent of brain damage."[151]

Though Kirk provided a new term, he remained suspicious that both new and old labels produced confusion and impeded comprehension. When Kirk spoke at the 1963 conference, a friend approached him for a more appropriate term that could apply to brain-injured children. "Last night a friend of mine accosted me with the statement, 'We're going to ask you to give us a term.' I didn't know how to answer his question."[152] Kirk explained to the audience that he had used the term "learning disabilities" a year prior to avoid over-medicalizing learning difficulties. "We seem to be satisfied if we can give a technical name to a condition. This gives us the satisfaction of closure. We think we know the answer if we can give the child a name or label—brain injured, schizophrenic, autistic, mentally retarded, aphasiac," he wrote.[153] Kirk's issue with technical terms lay in their lack of specificity. If he were to use labels at all, he preferred they characterized observed behavior. Even then, he cautioned the Chicago audience:

> I should like to caution you about being compulsively concerned about names and classification labels. Sometimes names block our thinking. I would prefer that people inform me that they have a child that does not talk instead of saying to me their child is dysphasic. People apparently like using technical terms. I have received letters from doctors and psychologists telling me that "we are referring a child to you who has strephosymbolia." I would prefer they tell me that "the boy has been in school two years, and he hasn't yet, learned to read even though his intelligence is above average."[154]

The audience understood Kirk's purpose and adopted a relatively new label that had been circulating loosely. For psychologists and doctors in the context of their offices, institutions, and journals, children could be dysphasic or strephosymbolic, but to parents, teachers, administrators, and the public, they were just the learning disabled (LD). Kirk's label possessed the power of science but the simplicity of language in identifying a new special education student.

Kirk's contribution to a new way of thinking gave parents as well as professionals a sense of organizational purpose. New local groups were created, and older institutions immediately changed their terms from "brain-injured" to "learning disabled." A national organization emerged using the new label. "We are happy to report that since the date of that meeting," wrote Walter Goodman, president of the Fund for Perceptually Handicapped Children in Illinois, "most of the primary details have been worked out; contact has been made with the people who agreed to become the nucleus in the formation of a national association for children with learning disabilities."[155] The new organization was named the Association for Children with Learning Disabilities (which later became the Learning Disabilities Association of America—LDA). Some conference attendees returned home to establish new organizations. Conference participants from Washington state recalled: "In 1964 a small group of parents in Edmonds, Washington, concerned about their learning disabled children, formed the first chapter of the Washington Association for Children and Adults with Learning Disabilities, or WACLD. The association was incorporated in 1964 and became the Washington State affiliate of the National Association for Children with Learning Disabilities (ACLD). That same year the Seattle Chapter was also started by a group of 75 parents and professionals intensely excited about a new field—learning disabilities. This chapter and its first officers later became the State-based association."[156]

The years between 1963 and 1965 were pivotal years in the civil rights movement but equally transformative for educational disability rights. Like the leaders of the civil rights movement, Samuel Kirk began appearing on Capitol Hill and at the White House in the mid-1950s and 1960s. Kirk's appearances in Washington, D.C. were on behalf of all "handicapped" students, those with intellectual disabilities as well as physical and sensory disabilities. Kirk's lobbying efforts contributed to the passage of four policies: Public Law 83–531 in 1954, which provided $1 million for educational research with a focus on mental retardation;[157] Public Law 88–164 in 1958, the Mental Retardation Facilities Construction Act, which authorized another $1 million for the training of teachers and administrators of the mentally retarded; and Public Law 87–276 in 1961, which allowed colleges and universities to prepare teachers of "deaf" students for two years at $1.5 million. In 1963, Congress expanded Public Law 88–164, which provided financial resources for research and community mental health facilities.[158] With a drastic increase from the mere $1 million allotted in 1958, Title III allocated $47 million for a three-year period for educational agencies, schools, colleges, and nonprofit organizations to all "handicapped" children.[159] The 1963 act specifically appropriated $10.5 million for the "training of personnel in all areas of special education." Samuel Kirk lent his influence directly to the passing of the 1961 and 1963 laws, during which President Kennedy appointed him head of the Division of Handicapped Children and Youth. Kirk shared that he "was privileged to be the Director of this program during its initial stages in the U.S. Office of Education and was in a position to observe the response which it received from the country as a whole."[160] In 1964, Representative John Fogarty of Rhode Island read one of Kirk's speeches on the floor of the House, lending support to a reauthorization of the 1963 legislation.[161]

When Representative John Fogarty read Samuel Kirk's speech from the House floor on June 16, 1964, Andrew Goodman, James Cheney, and Michael Schwerner had disappeared from a rural Mississippi county, where the three missing civil rights workers investigated the burning of a black church.[162] Freedom Summer, the civil rights campaign Goodman, Cheney, and Schwerner participated in, was in full swing, and so was the push to eliminate racial discrimination across the country. Though Goodman, Cheney, and Schwerner were found dead in August, Freedom Summer bridged Birmingham and the March on Washington a year earlier in 1963 to the Selma movement occurring later in 1965. During Freedom Summer, President Johnson signed the Civil Rights Act of 1964 into law after a full year of congressional wrangling over key provisions. Leading up to this historic law, the black freedom struggle made the final push for the right to vote, resulting in the Voting Rights Act of 1965. Civil rights legislation in 1964 and 1965 provided African Americans legislative victories but obscured and overshadowed a fight being waged on behalf of disabled students.

Despite recent increases in congressional appropriations for the mentally retarded, Kirk posited that "programs for handicapped children are minority operations." "It must be remembered," Kirk continued, "that any minority group, unless protected, tends to be swallowed by the majority," underscoring an earlier point made by Tenny. Kirk believed, heretofore, that the efforts of the federal government should be applauded, but a real commitment to addressing mental retardation lacked federal attention. A year later, Samuel Kirk was back in front of a House education subcommittee bringing its attention to another "minority group" in the United

States: the learning disabled. On June 15, 1966, he stood and announced: "My name is Samuel A. Kirk. I serve as Professor of Special Education and of Psychology, and as Director of the Institute for Research on Exceptional Children at the University of Illinois. I appreciate the opportunity to appear before this Committee and to discuss with you the problems of children with learning disorders. Children with learning disabilities have only recently begun to receive the attention that they deserve from parent groups and public schools."[163] Learning disabilities as a congressional priority would have to wait; Congress and the president were preoccupied with black educational disability associated with the War on Poverty. Kirk entered this discussion as well, drawing distinctions between the group he represented and the group the black freedom struggle brought to the nation's attention, which is the subject of the next chapter.

3

Disabling Black Poverty, Supporting White Underachievement

Race and the Construction of Federal Special Education Policy

Law has been used by special educators and parents of handicapped
children as a "sword of Damocles" to force an unwilling educational
system to direct resources to the establishment of special programs
for handicapped children.

—FREDERICK J. WEINTRAUB, "Recent Influences of Law Regarding
the Identification and Educational Placement of Children"

If extensive research and documentation can demonstrate that culturally
deprived children behave educationally, emotionally, and socially in
the school similarly to the learning-disabled child ... [then] why is the
culturally disadvantaged student excluded from consideration by the
field of special education?

—MICHAEL J. HERRICK, "Disabled or Disadvantaged:
What's the Difference?"

In his speech at the White House Rose Garden on May 18, 1965, President Johnson spoke to the nation about the U.S. failure to address
poverty and its victims. He stated, "Five and six-year-old children are
inheritors of poverty's curse and not its creators. Unless we act these
children will pass it on to the next generation, like a family birthmark."[1]
This was not the first time President Johnson addressed poverty; he
spoke about the issue over the fifteen months since becoming president
after the assassination of John F. Kennedy. Confident after his electoral

victory over Senator Barry Goldwater, Johnson declared a War on Poverty in his State of the Union address in January 1964: "This administration today, here and now, declares unconditional war on poverty in America, and I urge this Congress and all Americans to join me in this effort."[2] President Johnson's goal was not merely to provide relief from poverty "but to cure it—and above all—to prevent it."[3] In proposing a panacea for poverty, he called on the nation to join him in the effort, knowing it would not be easy. President Johnson recognized the policy challenges when he said, "No single piece of legislation . . . is going to suffice."[4] Later that year, Congress passed the Economic Opportunity Act (EOA) of 1964 and the Elementary and Secondary Education Act (ESEA) of 1965, making poverty, cultural deprivation, and educational disadvantage the foundation of black special education policy in the United States. By addressing poverty as a policy issue in addition to a social concern, the Johnson administration constructed a distinct black educational disability category based on race and social class.[5]

Though the Johnson administration constructed black educational disability at the federal level through EOA and ESEA, these laws also determined the future of white educational disability. A few years removed from the signing of ESEA, President Johnson recalled the significance of the policy for educational disability rights: "Three years ago, upon the occasion of my signing the Elementary and Secondary Education Act, I said that no other law bearing my signature would ever mean more to the future of America. Subsequent additions to that act have provided new services and opportunities for over 5,000,000 of the Nation's handicapped children and youth."[6] Serving all disabled students became a proxy for addressing the needs of white "handicapped" students. Lifting white "handicapped" people from policy invisibility, Samuel Kirk and other special education interests engaged in a vigorous form of legislative advocacy, seizing the opportunity provided by the civil rights movement and the War on Poverty to make learning disabilities (LD) recognized under the law.[7] If EOA-Title II and ESEA-Title I defined black educational disability, then ESEA titles III, V, and VI emerged as policy opportunities to address all "handicapped" students. The ESEA congressional debates provided moments for school administrators, academics, organizations, and even lawmakers themselves to make arguments about educational inequities for white disabled children and produce policy on their behalf. Because of the polarizing nature of 1960s racial politics, Congress reproduced this polarization through separate policy titles that addressed different handicapped student constituencies. Since white students from middle-class families sat outside the purview of Head Start and Title I—the two programs most associated with black and brown students—the drive to address white underachievement would make learning disabilities legislation a centerpiece of ESEA-Title VI, becoming as significant as Title I by decade's end. Hence, this chapter argues that the federal government racialized special education policy by constructing and promoting two distinct intellectual disability identities: one for students of color, the other for white students. This policy bifurcation would lay the groundwork for the overrepresentation of black and brown students in special education.

Creating Black Disability with Head Start and Title I: The Culturally Deprived and Educationally Disadvantaged

Sargent Shriver, the director of the Office of Economic Opportunity, led the federal government's effort in the war against poverty. As the government's poverty administrator, Shriver played a key role in articulating President Johnson's agenda. "We look to the War on Poverty as a system of mutually reinforcing programs breaking through the mutually reinforcing causes of poverty which keep people poor," noted Shriver.[8] Representing an ambitious panoply of programs and interventions, the major facets of the government's focus were summarized by Shriver in 1964:

> The major parts of our system include programs for job opportunity, programs for educational opportunity, and programs that attack other social and economic factors which cause a man to be poor. These include systems to attack the problems of health, housing and equal justice in the courts of our land. All of these programs are necessary as part of our total system. Because our primary objective is opportunity for people to remove themselves from poverty, the *jobs programs* are essential. Economic opportunity ... means the opportunity to work at gainful employment. But *educational opportunity* is necessary to make job opportunity meaningful, because much of the employment problem of the poor is caused by inadequate education. Other social and economic program[s] which attack

poverty are necessary because neither education nor employment comes easy to someone who lives in the degrading environment of the slum. Neither education nor a job can bring someone out of poverty who lives in a broken home with no wage-earner in the house, insufficient food, no medicine, no books and not even basic knowledge of family planning available most Americans.[9]

According to Shriver, an interlocking set of realities made the experiences of the impoverished unique. Shriver and other officials distinguished the poor as a people set apart from the rest of society. To comprehend the poor's economic, health, housing, and education experiences was to view them in tandem through the prism of poverty. Even when separated and explored as independent variables, the Johnson administration arrived at the same conclusion: black Americans were "handicapped" by their racial identity but also, and more importantly, by the jobs they held, the houses they lived in, the schools they attended, and the lifestyles they led. Thus, deprivation, in all its manifestations, informed the federal government's approach to black special education.

The black freedom struggle in the 1950s and 1960s helped bring attention to poverty discourses. President Johnson and his administration tapped into an enormous body of literature that defined poverty, explained its root causes and its deleterious effects on people of color and white people in various geographical regions. Describing and assessing poverty, however, focused much of the attention on African Americans who lived in or were still migrating to the urban core, or as it was called in the 1960s, the "gray areas" of big cities.[10] Parsing black urban living conditions as deficient and defective, black poverty discourse became an intellectual showcase describing various deficits. For the president, congressional lawmakers, social scientists, and cultural critics, large cities were not just places African Americans called home but geographical spaces—filled with social, cultural, and educational deficits that represented degeneration and societal decay.[11] Poverty discourses proliferated within white middle-class America to explain black debility. For white society, black debility ranged from a culture of poverty, neighborhood disorders, and family dysfunctions to crowded integrated city schools with an increasing number of culturally deprived and educationally disadvantaged students frustrating and burning out white teachers.

The new concern with fighting black poverty emerged from the political will sparked by the civil rights movement. At the same time, the movement's challenge to poverty contested long-standing beliefs about hereditary intelligence. The *Brown v. Board of Education* decision not only argued against the constitutionality of the separate-but-equal doctrine, it advanced the "conception of intelligence as a product of the individual's encounters with his environment."[12] A growing body of social science research located the source of an individual's "lack" of intelligence and reduced self-concept to his or her unstable environment. Environmental deficits, and not "bad genes," the argument went, made African Americans and other poor people of color veritable failures at school and in life. Thus, despite its victim-blaming posture, the deficit perspective proved a big breakthrough, shifting paradigms away from arguments that promoted innate hereditary intelligence.[13] Outdated theories of scientific racism continued to resurface into the 1960 and 1970s, with several scholars still peddling a discourse of hereditary intelligence based mainly on IQ tests.[14] While Samuel Kirk focused his attention on white slow learners, other social scientists dedicated themselves to the problem of the social and cultural disadvantaged, leading to a hyperfocus on the black poor and their shortcomings.[15] For black students, special education interventions evolved into a variety of compensatory programs that the Johnson administration adopted from existing state and city models, which were then expanded and promoted within the legislative confines of the Economic Opportunity Act and the Elementary and Secondary Education Act, according to Adam Nelson in *The Elusive Ideal*. Thus, the origins of federal special education for black students began with Head Start and Title I.

The racialization of special education can be traced to the steady conflation of related terms: race and ethnicity became conflated with social class and culture. Lower-class culture emerged as a proxy for race, which equated to African Americans, Latinx, and other people of color. The combination of race and ethnicity with a lower socioeconomic status evolved into the special education moniker: culturally deprived. Sociologist Norman Matlin and psychologist Carlos Albizu-Miranda argued, "The concept of cultural deprivation is a syncretic notion lumping together two basic groups: minorities and the poor."[16] Although social scientists and public officials tended to classify black students as educable mentally retarded (EMR), their designation as socially or culturally deprived came to define the source of their disadvantage and their particular brand of mental retardation.[17] Mical Raz, professor of Public Policy and Health at the University of Rochester wrote in an important study, "The rise of deprivation as a distinct etiological factor" in the mental retardation of black and brown children "reflected a growing acceptance both in medical and social policy discourse."[18] In some states, like California, EMR and cultural deprivation were seen as different categories of black learners, but in some states, they were perceived as the same.[19] Prominent social scientists and educational organizations attempted to clarify many of the categories associated with African American students. The National Society for the Study of Education understood the larger problem of conflation when it announced that the members of its "committee were aware of the large variety of terms used to describe these groups. Within the past few years, such pupils have been referred to by such terms as 'culturally deprived,' 'socially disadvantaged,' and 'educationally disadvantaged.'" Robert J. Havighurst and Thomas E. Moorefield were charged by the National Society for the Study of Education with differentiating "between the terms 'educationally retarded' and 'disadvantaged,'" in an attempt to "specify the boundaries of what is called 'retardation' and what is called 'disadvantaged.'"[20] They concluded that a student could be disadvantaged but not retarded, retarded but not disadvantaged, and both disadvantaged and retarded. Havighurst and Moorefield used hypothetical examples to explain the differences.

According to the identities explained by Havighurst and Moorefield, Michael was a ten-year-old boy in fifth grade whose school was in a "laboring-class section of town." His mother stayed at home raising two other children, and his father worked as a truck driver earning a steady income but was constantly on the road. Michael's mom and dad would have liked to live in a "better" part of town with "nicer" children, where there were less "Saturday-night fights" but were unable to afford those privileges. Michael was placed in an experimental second-grade class when he was seven years old after failing reading in the first grade. By Thanksgiving, Michael was reading at grade level with an IQ of 97. The experimental class was accompanied with frequent trips to the library where Michael checked out twenty books during the school year. Michael and the family incurred a fine for a few overdue books, prompting his mom to forbid him from visiting the library again. From the third to fifth grades, Michael's grades were average; he was well behaved, and projected as likely to graduate from high school. According to Havighurst and Moorefield, Michael "is not retarded in relation to his age group ... he is disadvantaged ... [H]is disadvantage led to his retardation in the first grade which resulted in his being given a brief period of compensatory education."[21]

In the second illustration by Havighurst and Moorefield, Jerry was also a ten-year-old student but was placed in a class for EMR. Jerry's mother graduated from high school and was currently taking care of three other children. Jerry's father worked as a post-office clerk after junior college. It took Jerry longer than average to learn how to talk, dress himself, and play with other children. Jerry did not learn to read in the first grade and was retained. During his second year in school, Jerry still did not learn to read and was subsequently placed in a "special slow-learning group for his third school year." After an examination by a school psychologist, Jerry's IQ tested at 70, resulting in his placement in a room for the "educable mentally handicapped." "Jerry is retarded," asserted Havighurst and Moorefield, "but not disadvantaged by any home or other social factor." "In our present state of knowledge," they continued, "we infer that he is innately retarded and that he will go through life as a marginal person, able to earn a living at a simple job."[22] Michael and Jerry both came from challenging family and neighborhood circumstances that impeded their academic progress in school. Because the challenges they experienced manifested in only a single condition (disadvantaged and retarded, respectively), the impact on Michael and Jerry was limited. The boys' ability to recover should have led to more productive lives. A boy named Sam, Havighurst and Moorefield's third example, however, was not so privileged and fortunate as Michael and Jerry:

> Sam is a ten-year-old boy in the fourth grade of school in a deteriorated section of a large city. He lives with his mother and four other children in a two-bedroom flat. His mother gets a monthly welfare payment from Aid to Dependent Children. His father deserted the family five years ago, and the last two children have other fathers who did not marry his mother. Sam's home life has been chaotic: his father and mother quarreled a great deal when he was very young and Sam was left to fend for himself. Nobody read or paid much attention to him. He played with other children in the

back yard of the run-down houses or apartments in which he happened to live. His mother did not send him to kindergarten. In the first grade, he was placed in a "slow" group, and was not reading when he entered the second grade, still in the slow group. Finally, he began to read, but not at all well, and remained in slow sections through the fourth grade, which he repeated. He has been mischievous and unruly for the last two years, and his teacher asked for a psychological examination of him. This examination disclosed that he had an I.Q. of 80. The examiner suggested that Sam probably could do better if he had some systematic tutoring. The examiner did not approve of sending him to a class for the emotionally maladjusted and thought he was within the range of "normal" intelligence. However, he was reading at only a second-grade level.[23]

Though the respective racial identity of each boy is never mentioned, we can infer that Sam is a black student and that Michael and Jerry are white. Given the family background provided by the authors, Michael and Jerry could be black if their narratives stood alone. With Sam's narrative placed alongside Michael and Jerry's, however, the researchers have clearly attached racial inferences to academic failure, welfare, neighborhood deterioration, and illegitimacy, making Sam's racial and class identity more contributory to his academic challenges. According to Havighurst and Moorefield, "black" Sam was "both *retarded* and *disadvantaged*. We assume that the disadvantages he suffered at home have retarded his mental development." Havighurst and Moorefield delivered their final assessment about Sam in comparison to the other two students: if Sam were not the victim of his race and poverty, "his I.Q. would probably be substantially higher if [he] had been brought up in Jerry's home."[24]

Havighurst, along with Lindsey J. Stiles, conceptualized the so-called culturally deprived more precisely by distinguishing between four different segments of the American student: the "academically superior," the "middle two-thirds," the "handicapped," and the "alienated." The academically superior represented 15 percent of young people whose IQs were above 115, epitomizing "good college material." "These young people," say Havighurst and Stiles, "have to be regarded as a precious resource which must be cared for and cultivated to the fullest." In this study, the "middle two thirds" of students do reasonably well in life, with most graduating from high school. The students in this group that leave high school without a diploma "manage to get jobs at the age of sixteen or seventeen, or to marry at those ages, and to grow up to adulthood in a fairly acceptable manner." The "handicapped" students represent the 2 to 3 percent of boys and girls who have an IQ of 75 and possess mental or physical disabilities defined as the "educable mentally handicapped." State special education services focused more of their resources on this group through stand-alone classes. The third alienated group, according to the authors, has many monikers, such as "the uneducables, the non-learners, [and] the hard-to-reach." With IQs ranging from 75 to 90, the alienated could be the growing classification "learning disabled," mainly at the higher-end IQ level of 80 to 90. The other descriptors tied to the alienated, however, belie this assumption, wrote Havighurst and Stiles, "They tend to come from broken homes, or homes which are inadequate emotionally and culturally.... This is a group whose start in life has been poor because of the disadvantages its members face. Their families have been inadequate." Not only have they been unable to meet the "standards ... of behavior, of learning in school ... they are hostile and unruly ... and have quit learning and have dropped out of school psychologically two or three years before they can drop out physically." Finally, not only do alienated students represent a large portion of "juvenile delinquents," they are "members of underprivileged racial or immigrant minorities.... Thus Negroes, Mexicans, and Puerto Ricans make up a large proportion of alienated youth in the industrial cities of today."[25]

As cringe-worthy as these statements come across today, in the mind of most white people, indeed, students of color made up the largest segment of the "culturally deprived" in the 1960s. For all intents and purposes according to white society, they *were* the culturally deprived. Much of the social science literature on race and poverty "identified" a variety of deficits found in these groups, even by scholars of color. The research findings supported the education policy debates and programmatically shaped every pilot program implemented in the 1960s. Cultural deprivation and compensatory education research became a growth industry with a significant focus on some aspect of the urban black and brown poor. Foundationally, cultural deprivation research drew from the work of E. Franklin Frazier whose focus on black family dysfunction inspired policymakers and sociologists like Daniel Patrick Moynihan and Nathan

Glazer. While Moynihan and Glazer's report on the "Negro family" captured the greatest public attention, equally cited authors from this period detailing the challenges facing black culturally deprived students also included Frank Reisman, Martin Deutsch, Robert Havighurst, Kenneth Clark, Harold Passow, and Oscar Lewis, to name a few.[26]

Theories of cultural deprivation and the culture of poverty emerged as a convenient explanation for both scholars' and lay people's understanding of black and Latinx underachievement and societal woes.[27] Kenneth Clark called the theories "fashionable," generating catchall synonyms, such as the "culturally disadvantaged, the disadvantaged, minority groups, socially neglected, socially rejected, socially deprived, school retarded, educationally disadvantaged, lower socio-economic groups, socio-economically deprived, culturally impoverished, culturally different, rural disadvantaged, the deprived slum children."[28] As seductive terms that articulated more about the growing popularity of deficit thinking than about students themselves, the names raised more questions than they answered.[29] Nonetheless, advocacy groups and social scientists draped black student underachievement in cultural deprivation theories, holding conferences, producing reports, and sharing members and expertise among different organizations. Groups like the Great Cities Program for School Improvement (composed of superintendents and school board members from the largest cities), the National Education Association (NEA) (the largest lobbying organization for public school education), and President Kennedy's Committee on Mental Retardation did more than most groups to link cultural deprivation to a specific brand of black "mental retardation."[30] Great Cities focused on the educationally disadvantaged since the mid-1950s. By 1963, the Research Division at the NEA had conducted forty-two experimental projects on disadvantaged students. And in the same year, Kennedy's Committee on Mental Retardation focused the nation's attention on the white "mentally handicapped" and the black "educationally disadvantaged."[31]

Cultural deprivation experts, through their influence and links to presidential administrations and Congress, helped shape the Economic Opportunity Act and Title I of the Elementary and Secondary Education Act. Edward Davens, a subcommittee chairman on mental retardation prevention, remembered the rich conversations between the research experts and his task force and what he believed was the significance of their work on congressional policy:

> During our many discussions of preventative opportunities, extensive readings of the scientific literature, and the frequent conferences with experts from many disciplines all over the nation, Dr. Nicholas Hobbs, then of the Peabody College, now Provost at Vanderbilt University in Nashville, persistently brought to our attention the growing body of data on severe degrees of social and cultural deprivation that are a major cause of mental retardation. He provided the Task Force with an excellent statement prepared by an associate from Peabody, Dr. Susan Gray, who has devoted many years to research and study of the effects of social and cultural deprivation on normal growth and development of the child. For this and numerous other reasons, Task Force I proposed a major recommendation that was accepted and that in my view was an important forerunner of the initial Head Start program of the summer of 1965.[32]

By 1965, research projects and regular conferences on the "educational disadvantaged" and the "culturally deprived" seemingly consumed the academy and every corner in Washington, D.C. "Culturally deprived" and "mentally retarded" were now broadly promoted identities that defined black educational disadvantage as a disability. An essay by Frederick Bertolaet, executive secretary in the Research Council of the Great Cities Program for School Improvement, synthesized the current literature, becoming one of the most widely referenced articles during congressional hearings.[33]

Sergeant Shriver credited academic experts with helping him think about what a federal policy in black special education could look like. He remembered coming across the same influential research on black cultural deprivation that Davens conducted, particularly an early childhood education project "run by a brilliant psychologist, Susan Gray, at the George Peabody Teachers' College," and the research by Bettye M. Caldwell, professor of Child Development and Education at Syracuse University. Shriver was particularly convinced by the research on mental retardation that pointed to the malleability of IQ scores, which had long been used as evidence of unchangeable and unalterable intelligence in children. Surprisingly, the subjects were black. "When I first heard about this, I was dumbfounded," Shriver remembered. "Well that bit of information just sort of rolled around in the back of my skull."[34] Shriver liked the findings about the potential to raise IQ scores. He equally appreciated the findings related to the possible reduction of racial antagonisms between black and white people, specifically white antipathy for the black poor. "I hoped that we could overcome a lot of hostility in our society against the poor in general, and specifically against black people who are poor, by aiming for the children," he expressed.[35]

The black special education vision of Shriver, Johnson, and the federal government seemed rooted in a single understanding of black improvement cloaked in a framework of cultural deficit thinking.[36] African American students did not harbor subject-matter deficiencies like white students—they experienced deficiencies in life chances. Thus, programs that emphasized early intervention would become highly attractive for the construction of federal policy initiatives. "So, I went back to the office and said, 'look, we've got to get a program going, and this is the theory behind it," Shriver remembered. "The theory is that we'll intervene early; we'll help IQ problems and the malnutrition problem; we'll get these kids ready for school and into the environment of a school."[37] Getting black children ready for school did not start with questions about the lack of good reading, math, or speech skills. Black special education started and ended with assumptions about the race of a people who happened to be poor. Black students were disabled because their lives were disabled, according to Shriver:

> Maybe the child doesn't have the right clothes, the right books, the right haircut, or whatever. There are a huge number of psychological problems. And I said, "let's get these youngsters *ahead* of time, bring them into school and 'culturally' prepare them for school: for the buildings and teachers, desks, pencils and chalk, discipline, food, etc. At the same time, we'll give them the books ahead of time, show them what they are like, and what you do with books. We'll find out where they stand in reading, and find out if they need 'shots.'" Some of them have eye problems, but their parents are so poor they've never taken them to a doctor, so they don't *know* [if] they've got eye problems. Often the kid can't see the blackboard. So we figured, we'll get these kids into school ahead of time; we'll give them food;

we'll give them medical exams; we'll give them the shot or the glasses they need; we'll give them some acculturation to academic work—we'll give them a *head start*.[38] (emphasis in original)

This line of thinking laid the groundwork for the program called Head Start, which became a child development enterprise designed to confront all of the so-called disabilities associated with being black, not solely a preschool program for millions of poor black children.[39] The concept behind Head Start mirrored how "black retardation" was understood at the turn of the twentieth century, not merely school deficits, but life deficits. Head Start and Title I funding in ESEA became the philosophical and programmatic centerpiece of federal black special education policy in the United States and the site of legislative debates about black intellectual disability.[40]

While conflating disability and black poverty seemed obvious to educators and federal administrators like Shriver,[41] certain lawmakers proved harder to convince during the EOA and ESEA hearings. EOA and ESEA merged three risk factors into a single black federal special education identity: low-income, low IQ, and race. But questions about who exactly the laws targeted remained. Senator Robert Kennedy and other lawmakers sought to clarify who constituted the "educationally deprived." Senator Dominick had specific questions about whether poor children could be educationally deprived if they attended school in a wealthier district. Congress grilled the commissioner of education, Francis Keppel, who answered questions from Senator Kennedy: "Senator, the definition of educational deprivation [was] devised by the superintendents of the 15 biggest school systems . . . [You] may recall there was a statement that . . . one-third of pupils in their school system they described as educationally deprived." The answer provided by Commissioner Keppel proved unsatisfactory to Senator Kennedy. "How do you reach that conclusion?" he asked. "That is the number, but what is an educationally deprived child?" Kennedy queried again. Feeling pressured to provide specific information about black "handicapped" students, Keppel offered the standard description of black educational disability in 1965:

What I can say is this. It is children whose home backgrounds do not include encouragement for the study that is normal . . . in the sense that there are books at home, there is encouragement to learn to read as a child. In particular I think it is fair to say, sir, that the educational deprivation for children from low-income families involves the lack in all too many cases of preschools to get them ready for the first grade. The charts that the Secretary [Celebrezze] showed about reading comprehension, for example, would in those central Harlem figures suggest educational deprivation of serious order by the time of the third grade. That is, educational comprehension was so notably low. There would be other deprivations that I think would be included in this. They need the kind of special help on reading which comes from an uncertain grasp in their own lives of the English vocabulary. They tend not to have the kind of experience in arithmetic computation which is quite normal in children who come from homes where the child is always encouraged to add or subtract. But I suppose in the deepest sense, Senator, the superintendents were describing educational deprivation in terms of the overall life of these young children, sometimes the lack of food, the weariness, in addition to the total lack of encouragement in their homes. And then to be sent to schools which in many cases are overcrowded, in many cases have the temporary teacher rather than the most highly skilled teacher. That deprivation runs through their lives at home and their lives in school. I'm sorry that one can't give a definition except in the whole life of the individual child, but that is precisely what the President's program is aiming at.[42]

Senator Kennedy seemed only partially satisfied with Keppel's answer. Kennedy believed that the longwinded definition may have been a product of social science and school administration speak, but a simpler definition that captured the role schools played would have provided a better picture of the source of the problem beyond poor people themselves. Senator Kennedy followed up. Has not the "school system itself . . . created an educationally deprived system,?" "I am sorry to say that is true," Keppel responded. Sensing an opening to opine some more, Kennedy asked:

Would you not agree . . . that one of the really great problems we have in the country, being blunt about it, is that school boards in some of these communities, in some of these States, and the commissioners of education in some of the States, that they are just not going to take the necessary steps to deal with the problem? And then I come to this other point, that if you are placing or putting money into a school system which itself creates this problem or helps to create it, or does nothing, very little to alleviate it, are we not just in fact wasting the money of the Federal Government and of the taxpayer and putting money in areas and investing money where it really is going to accomplish very little if any good?[43]

Though Senator Kennedy was critical of the way states administered their systems of education, he too fell in line in the end and voted for the passage of ESEA. President Johnson signed the Economic Opportunity Act into law on August 20, 1964. In less than a year, he signed the Elementary and Secondary Education Act on April 11, 1965.

The establishment of black educational disability united both Title II of EOA-1964 (Community Action—Head Start) and Title I of ESEA-1965. Head Start emerged as one of the greatest manifestations of "community action." Poor people now controlled early childhood education programs themselves—from development to implementation—the culmination of "maximum feasible participation" as the law required.[44] Head Start served poor students from ages three to five. EOA-Title II's language on black educational disability focused attention on "special remedial ... educational assistance ... and other evidence of low educational attainment" of culturally deprived children.[45] ESEA-Title I also gave a legislative call to action to "programs and projects which are designed to meet the special educational needs of educationally deprived children."[46] ESEA Title I empowered local education agencies (LEAs)—mainly school districts—who worked with schools to develop programs for students from families earning $2,000 or less per year. "Local school districts are required to develop proposals for projects to be funded under their allotments which the state education agencies (SEAs) are to approve under regulations and guidelines established by the U.S. Commissioner of Education."[47] In their language, both policies referenced the "educationally" and "economically" disadvantaged as the target student population, emphasizing societal handicaps that impeded the cognitive development of poor students. Several lawmakers perceived a natural synergy in the policies' focus on the early childhood education of culturally deprived students. During the legislative hearings, Representative Albert Quie of Minnesota drew a connection between Head Start and Title I when he asserted, "The educationally deprived child being talked about for these two days in the bill . . . are the ones who have been lost before they ever reached school for first grade. The children who are poverty stricken and result in the unemployed; the ones we were trying to reach last year in the antipoverty bill for the most part, were lost before they ever attended public schools."[48]

Some lawmakers believed Head Start represented the best blueprint for a comprehensive early childhood program for all children and that its ideas should be expanded after its transfer from the Office of Economic Opportunity to the Office of Education. Shriver was against this suggestion, reminding Congress that Head Start "is a child development program," and not a preschool program. If there are some Head Start programs that wish to run theirs that way, "they may . . . do that," Shriver wrote.[49] In some ways, Shriver reinforced the idea that black disability was defined by poverty and not solely by the absence of basic academic skills. Unlike a typical preschool program, policymakers designed Head Start for a particular student population based on the presumptions of a white middle-class majority. But the same white middle-class presumptions prevailed in Title I. Bureaucrats then transferred Head Start to the Office of Education in the early years of the program's existence. Due to the focus on students with similar backgrounds, Head Start and Title I programs became aligned in many states across the country.[50]

Bound together, Head Start and Title I made financial resources available to communities and districts without fully understanding the needs of black disabled students. From the standpoint of social justice activists, the community focus of Head Start seemed like a policy victory. But from the standpoint of tackling real educational disabilities, Head Start and Title I lacked the professional experts needed to truly serve black students who were experiencing unique academic challenges. In contrast to white disabled students, ESEA emerged as a beacon of opportunity and opened real possibilities for the educational disability rights movement. White advocates of the "handicapped" used ESEA title amendments to train a panoply of white special education professionals. The construction of white intellectual disability included the culturally deprived and educationally disadvantaged when white intellectual disability was defined *against* black deprivation and black disadvantage.

ESEA and the Problem of White Underachievement: The Culmination of Learning Disability Policy

Along with the Civil Rights Act of 1964 and the Voting Rights Act of 1965, EOA and ESEA represented two additional "progressive" social policies linked to the civil rights movement and the War on Poverty.[51] But ESEA's singular focus on education, and its appearance of racial neutrality beyond Title I, made it different from other laws. Though ESEA's Title I was overwhelmingly associated with the uplift of black and brown children, few in the American public recognized ESEA's potential to help the white middle class. Edwin W. Martin Jr., policy expert in the 1960s and future assistant secretary of education for Special Education and Rehabilitative Services in the Carter administration (and others like him), invoked the law's ability to help another overlooked group, writing that ESEA "amendments affecting the lives of the minority group known as handicapped children attracted little attention from the press."[52] After the initial passage and signing of ESEA in April 1965, the educational disability rights movement immediately advocated for ESEA revisions. The amendments occurred in the first few years, producing the Aid for Education of Handicapped Children in State Operated Institutions (PL 89–313), the Education for Handicapped Children Act in 1966 (PL 89–750), the Pre-School and Early Education Act of 1968 (PL 90–538), and the Specific Learning Disabilities Act of 1969 (PL 91–230). Martin recalled how ESEA's amendment process consumed the attention of congressional committees on behalf of white disabled students: "Twice in the less than 14 months between late October 1966, and December 15, 1967, members of the House and Senate committees responsible for educational legislation came to Room EF 100 to form a conference committee. These conferees were charged with resolving differences in the 1966 and 1967 Elementary and Secondary Act amendments which, among their many purposes, promised to change dramatically the course of education for handicapped children in the United States."[53]

But the additional titles led to further policy separation in how ESEA served racial groups differently, exacerbating the distance between black and white special education students. The separation culminated when the Education for All Handicapped Children Act in 1975 intentionally excluded "culturally deprived" and EMR students. The consequence of this racialization in federal special education policy not only created a hierarchy of disability categories but also, in service allocation, the availability of financial resources and the continuing presence of stigma. Hence, the policies that generated opportunities for white "handicapped" students as part of the growing educational disability rights movement simultaneously protected them from black and brown special education students.[54] When it came to black special education students, the civil rights movement and the educational disability rights movement began to work at cross-purposes.

After 1965, the educational disability rights movement would no longer sit at the margins of the civil rights movement and the War on Poverty. The momentum generated by the black freedom struggle that achieved policy outcomes in EOA and ESEA Title I provided opportunities for the white educationally disabled too. Frank Withrow, director of the Division of Educational Services in the Bureau of Education for the Handicapped, U.S. Office of Education, put it in stark historical and contemporary terms when he announced:

Thomas Paine's advice to the American revolutionary in the eighteenth century is appropriate advice for the American special educator in the latter half of the twentieth century. For the first time, the special educator in America has the chance to develop a quality education program for the handicapped child. Today, there is a widespread support for special education, which is partly the result of an educational revolution which recognizes the right of all children to a universal education. Secondly, the civil rights movement has awakened our country to an individual's right to self-determination. Both universal education and self-determination create an atmosphere that assures the handicapped person a place in society. The handicapped person can no longer be shunted aside into custodial institutions. As a result of these factors, the special educator must make many critical decisions during the next few years. These decisions may determine the nature of education for the handicapped child for the remainder of this century. Therefore, it is imperative that these decisions be made through maximum level of information input.[55]

Though mental retardation had entered national public policy discourse, no major piece of legislation directed at the intellectually disabled materialized as part of the new federal education laws.[56] With white handicapped people at the center of potential disability policy outcomes, changed seemed imminent, even though advocates seemed frustrated. Equal education opportunity produced both disappointment and hope: disappointment due to white "handicapped" invisibility but hope because educational disability rights incubated inside the Economic Opportunity Act and the Elementary and Secondary Education Act.

Despite its focus on eliminating black and brown poverty, ESEA, as it was originally constructed, still paid dividends for white "handicapped" students. If ESEA gave the civil rights movement and the War on Poverty a legislative lift with a central focus on black special education students, then ESEA also provided "handicapped" students more reasons to press their own civil rights claims. Supporters like Samuel Kirk and the Council on Exceptional Children saw the passage of ESEA as an opportunity to address the policy needs of "handicapped" students in the different titles of the law. Romaine P. Mackie, whose title was chief of education of handicapped in low-income areas in the U.S. Office of Education, and a member in the Council of Exceptional Children, put it succinctly when she invoked the new federal policies: "Let us be on the alert to determine what we can gain" from them.[57]

Romaine P. Mackie understood the potential gains for "handicapped" students in ESEA. She wrote several articles in the journal *Exceptional Children,* the most pertinent entitled "Converging Circles: Education of the Handicapped and Some General Federal Programs."[58] In the article, Mackie distinguishes between "people-oriented" policies generated by the civil rights movement and what was now needed legislatively to serve intellectually disabled students: different "categorical" policies. This categorical legislation generally focused on "clinical" conditions, marking these new laws as distinct from "people-centered" laws. Instead of targeting African American or Latinx students disabled by poverty, categorical legislation identified the specific disability and addressed it from a medical vantage point. Mackie's delineation is an admission of categorical segregation. The racialization of federal education law created a hierarchy in special education categories through title segregation. Title II of the Economic Opportunity Act and Title I of the Elementary and Secondary

Education Act were categorical in nature because poverty signaled disability. The "disability of poverty," however, was overwhelmingly associated with black and brown bodies, which diminished their categorical intent, making them, according to Mackie, "people-centered," and thus less of a priority.[59]

In the article, Mackie described the evolution of federal education policy up to 1965 through the visual metaphor of converging circles in a Venn diagram. She believed it was time to put "handicapped" children at the center of all discussions regarding special education students. Mackie entitled the intersection, "Education of Handicapped Children and Youth (Exceptional Children)"—a policy under congressional debate in 1966, the same year Mackie wrote her article. Mackie's other circles included existing policies produced in the civil rights era and the War on Poverty: the Juvenile Delinquency and Youth Offenses Control Act of 1961; the Manpower Development and Training Act of 1962; the Vocational Education Act of 1963; and the Economic Opportunity Act of 1964. These four "people-oriented" policies encircled or "converged" around the categorical legislation, which Mackie believed only tangentially addressed special education students. Inasmuch as they partially addressed "handicapped" students, Mackie believed the movements that produced the people-centered policies still contained lessons for special education: "There are now a number of national movements that have been given impetus by recent federal legislation and budget which may open the doors of educational opportunity much more rapidly to 'handicapped' children. Some of these people-oriented programs have the potential for converging favorably with our categorical programs for the education of handicapped children and youth ... What can we as special educators gain?"[60]

Though Mackie and the Council of Exceptional Children named four policies produced by the "national" civil rights movement, the ESEA mainly provided the educational disability rights movement the greatest opportunity to expand services to a broader segment of the "handicapped." When President Johnson signed ESEA into law in April 1965, special education advocates pored over every title to understand the implications of the law for the disabled student population. The Council of Exceptional Children released a detailed report enumerating the potential benefits. "The purpose of this report," wrote Morvin A. Wirtz and

James C. Chalfant, "is to alert the field of special education to the significance of the Elementary and Secondary Education Act (Public Law 89–10) for the education of handicapped children and youth."[61] More than an alert, the report was meant to clarify the titles and demonstrate how school districts should use each title for "handicapped" students. Though Title I reflected the Johnson administration's focus on poverty and black students, Wirtz and Chalfant reminded its readers that on paper, Title I also "includes those children who are handicapped because of physical, mental, or emotional impairment."[62] Wirtz and Chalfant argued that the right of "handicapped" students is "supported by Senate Report No. 146 on the bill," which "indicated that educationally deprived children include those who are deprived because of handicapping conditions as defined by Title III of Public Law 88–164,"[63] such as the "deaf," "hard of hearing," "speech impaired," "visually handicapped," "seriously emotionally disturbed," "crippled," "mentally retarded," or other health-impaired persons. Ostensibly, ESEA Title I covered the culturally/educationally deprived without other disabilities *or* those who had any of the additional comorbid disabilities above. Though ESEA Title I covered a broad spectrum of disabled people, the targeted disabled student population was still too racially focused on poor black students. One observer commented, "It was apparent . . . that the basic thrust of ESEA was toward the economically disadvantaged . . . and that more direct sources of support for the handicapped would be necessary."[64]

President Johnson's signature was barely dry on the original April 1965 bill before the educational disability rights movement sought to revise ESEA, pushing for amendments that focused on "handicapped" students generally and learning-disabled students in particular. The legislative breakthrough occurred when Congress amended Title I (PL 89–313) in November 1965, seven months after the original (PL 89–10) was passed, to aid "handicapped" children in state-operated institutions. Public Law 89–313 not only changed the mission of state-operated "handicapped" institutions from a custodial care model for children to an educational model, but it also became the "building block toward the total construction of categorical aid for the education of handicapped children."[65] Beyond the law's concentration on institutionalized children, PL 89–313 reflected how Congress positioned "disability rights" in relationship to "civil rights," both as similar and distinct. Civil and disability rights were "the same" because ESEA as a whole served disabled children who were considered another "minority" group whose "civil rights" needed to be acknowledged, addressed, and protected. The two movements were "different" because the racialization of ESEA's titles was apparent in various congressional debates with special educators, thus creating a minority group *within* a minority group. Public Law 89–313 was the first legislative salvo that placed racial distance between black and white disabled children, a fitting end to arguably one of the most important years in both disability rights and civil rights histories.[66]

But 1966 sparked more robust debates over the expansion of ESEA. At a hearing on September 16 and 17, 1966, before the United States Commission on Civil Rights, Samuel Kirk was asked to assess ESEA's Title III regarding its efficacy for disabled students. Kirk echoed the sentiments of Wirtz and Chalfant, affirming, "Title III of the ESEA of 1965 provided for innovative and exemplary projects in all areas of education, including the education of the handicapped children." Similar to Wirtz and Chalfant's Title I argument, Kirk also believed that there was no facet of education, whether it be "subject matter, curriculum, state programs, counselling" that could not be "adapted to the education of handicapped children." While Kirk lauded the flexibility of Title III, when asked directly by Representative Carey whether "we have a national policy with regard to the education and training of the handicapped," Kirk admitted that the United States did not. "When a country as great as the United States can fly to the moon and can do all the things it does," said Kirk, "this seems to me to be a very minor problem. I see no problem in reaching the goals, if we are willing to do it, and if we set up a national policy."[67] Kirk identified gaps in Title III and the absence of a national "handicapped" policy, one of which was the lack of "provisions for children with learning disabilities."[68]

Heeding the sentiment of Kirk and others who believed the United States should do more for disabled students, Congress created additional policy layers and greater coordination between states and the federal government. The first additional stand-alone amendment in ESEA pertaining to disabled students was Title VI (PL 89–750), the Hugh Carey–Wayne Morse bill, passed in November 1966. Title VI funds were "specifically earmarked for handicapped children and youth."[69] Title VI also included the establishment of "administrative supervision at the federal level through a National Advisory Committee on Handicapped Children and a bureau for the education and training of the handicapped in the US Office of Education."[70] Called "one of the most significant pieces of legislation to date affecting the education of handicapped children," PL-89–750 provided grants to the states to "assist in the initiation, expansion, and improvement of special educational and related services . . . at the preschool, elementary, and secondary school levels."[71] Though ESEA Title VI provided more funds to the states to expand services to its "handicapped" student population, it was not the national policy some in the educational disability rights movement sought. The most significant issue remained that PL 89–750 did not name the learning disabled as part of its definition of "handicapped," rendering them invisible in Title VI. Title VI tucked the learning disabled away "under the part of the definition referring to 'other health impaired.'" The term "other health impaired" was a setback for Samuel Kirk. Lawmakers told Kirk that the learning disabled could be served by Title I and Title IV, and did not need to be named. E. W. Martin wrote that Samuel Kirk could not convince "key congressional staff persons that the definition of LD was so broad that it could not include any economically disadvantaged child whose circumstances resulted in educational problems. They argued that such children, already assisted by the Congress through Title I of the Elementary and Secondary Education Act, would use up all the resources needed by children who were, in fact, disabled."[72]

To make a stronger case, special education lobbyists like Samuel Kirk needed to present sharper distinctions between the learning disabled and black "handicapped" students covered under EOA-Head Start and ESEA Title I. In June 1966, the Meredith March against Fear gripped the attention of the country, for it marked the beginning of the Black Power movement. James Aubrey Norvell, a white supremacist, shot civil rights advocate James Meredith on the second day as he and a few other black men walked on a 270-mile, twenty-one-day journey from Memphis, Tennessee, to Jackson, Mississippi. Stokely Carmichael, Dr. Martin Luther King Jr., and others picked up where he left off as Meredith recovered from his injuries. Inside the Capitol, during the ESEA amendment hearings, at the very moment Black Power changed the tenor of the civil rights movement, Samuel Kirk counseled Congress to understand differences between disabled student populations. While the Meredith

March against Fear attempted to dismantle racial barriers for African Americans, Samuel Kirk worked, albeit unwittingly, to erect different barriers that separated segments of the special education population. "When you talk about disadvantaged children, particularly under the antipoverty program, and Headstart," said Kirk, "I think we have a little different picture than we do in the field of handicapped children."[73]

The picture Samuel Kirk and others painted for Congress included a two-tiered special education system, the first born out of civil rights and black empowerment.[74] Kirk believed the civil rights movement forced Congress to act hastily on behalf of black disabled children. "Because Headstart is a very new program," Kirk continued, "we included thousands and thousands of children under Headstart last summer. You could not train people that fast." Kirk had long advocated for the formal training of special education teachers by increasing the number of graduate programs in special education. University-trained teachers for white disabled students were a major part of Kirk's special education vision. By contrast, black special education evolved differently. Since policymakers used the framework of poverty to legislate for black special education, special education advocates of the white "handicapped" like Kirk lacked the interest to invest in resources in highly trained teaching personnel for the so-called culturally deprived. Sending college-and-university-trained teaching professionals to work with black Head Start preschoolers did not function as part of the early vision for serving black special education students. "So, under the Headstart program," said Kirk, "it was necessary to bring people in . . . and give them a week or two weeks of training and assign them to someone that could guide them in the development of the Headstart or preschool program." Much to the astonishment of Representative James Scheuer, the "experts" brought in to teach black special education students were teacher aides: "Let me interject a moment. We are using teacher aides in Headstart?" "Yes," Kirk replied. "Instead of doing nothing, it was the best you can at the time."[75]

Doing "the best" for black special education students meant employing para-professionals in classrooms with black students.[76] Unlike the learning disabled, Kirk believed the culturally deprived student did not need professionally trained teachers in classrooms to help them with "their clothes, to keep records, to . . . help them with their coloring books, to help them with their lunch, and to help them on and off with their galoshes and their coats ... and do a lot of other than professional chores in the course of the teaching day." A teacher's aide or educational assistant was thought to be enough. In Kirk's view, the primary difference between the culturally deprived and the learning disabled was the "role in the management of the day." Kirk reminded Congress that there was nothing unusual about using educational assistants for classroom management purposes. "That practice has been in vogue for some time," said Kirk. "For disadvantaged kids?," Scheuer asked in response. "Not for disadvantaged children," Kirk said, "but for mentally retarded kids." "This exists in many programs throughout many states," Kirk continued. "I see no reason why aides cannot help teachers and relieve them of certain tasks throughout the day," he concluded.[77] Deeming black children "culturally deprived" at the policy level served much more than symbolic functions—the label produced pedagogical drawbacks for black classrooms and missed learning opportunities for black students. In this instance, constructions of cultural deprivation generated material deprivation.

The Select Subcommittee on Education held a hearing in 1968 to debate a bill authorizing preschool and early education programs for "handicapped" children.[78] Similar criticisms of Head Start emerged, and similar racially implied distinctions between disabled white and black students prevailed. John W. Kidd, President of the Council for Exceptional Children, and William C. Geer, the council's executive secretary, appeared before Congress to convince members that a new law was required to address the needs of disabled preschool children between the ages of two and five. With Head Start theoretically providing for the similar needs of black and brown special education students, the Council for Exceptional Children had to address stark differences in preschool education programs. Like Samuel Kirk, the council insisted on a racially bifurcated understanding of disability. "I think one of the shortcomings so far as handicapped children are concerned with the Headstart program is that it really was not planned for them," said William Geer. "If I have understood the prevailing philosophy of that program, it has not been designed for the child who is handicapped." Representative Quie from Minnesota pressed both Geer and Kidd for further clarification on the subject when he asked:

Dr. Kidd, in your statement you included a policy statement issued by the Council for Exceptional Children. Let me quote from it. "Exceptional children include children and youth with special learning needs and, categorically, the term includes the gifted, the blind, partially seeing, deaf, hard of hearing, crippled and other health impaired, speech impaired, mentally retarded, emotionally disturbed, delinquent, and neurologically impaired." Then you mention the culturally disadvantaged. Do you believe that if we are to help substantially the culturally impaired and culturally disadvantaged that we should be considering them as and including them with other handicapped or exceptional children? Or, would it be wiser to assume that they have different problems than other exceptional youngsters?[79]

Kidd responded by saying that he believed the research is conclusive about the damage caused to culturally deprived students from their environments. "I certainly respond in the affirmative to your statement. I think we can agree with many sources that the disadvantaged present a unique problem and that permanent damage is done perhaps by age 1, certainly by age 5."[80] Kidd's response seemed indicative of a racialized "needs" perspective created by white special education advocates and the lawmakers who supported such positions. Not only did a racially bifurcated needs viewpoint permeate special education thinking, but black professionals often found themselves working within this difference.

At the same hearing for preschool and early education "handicapped" programs, Dr. Frank Wilderson, a black educational psychologist from the University of Minnesota, advocated for black culturally deprived students in the legislation under consideration. "My principal concern," Wilderson told members of a House committee, "will be expressed for the handicapped child who is also deprived of educational opportunity and rendered more susceptible to a continuation of his handicapping conditions due to poverty, racial discrimination, and geographic location within a state."[81] In some ways, Wilderson found himself on the outside looking in, trying to make a case for black special education students while providing the House committee with a nuanced understanding of racist educational politics. Wilderson understood that the financial benefits would flow greater in the direction of white special education students, aiding them more than black disabled students. He admitted:

Since it is well known that there is an increased incidence of most handi-capping conditions in populations stricken by poverty, separated by race, and occupying a disadvantaged location in our country, it would be neces-sary for a bill such as this one that is before this committee to build in a great deal of assurance that early preschool programs located near the centers where large numbers of handicapped children could be expected to be found. By this, I mean that a sufficient number of these centers be located near poverty pockets and near racial minority ghettoes.[82]

Wilderson was one of the last witnesses to testify before the committee. The Handicapped Children's Early Education Assistance Act passed as ESEA amendment Title V Part C. After the bill went into effect beginning in 1969, seventy demonstration projects or pilot programs occurred in a two-year period mainly for white non–Head Start pre-K disabled chil-dren. By contrast, the Urban League established four projects in four dif-ferent cities, serving black disabled students.[83] Though Wilderson helped establish a pilot program in Minneapolis for emotionally disturbed stu-dents, it was hardly the number he hoped would serve black students.

As "handicapped" students gained policy momentum with the passage of each ESEA amendment, Samuel Kirk and the educational disabilities movement finally turned Congress's attention toward the learning dis-abled. The final phase of Kirk's legislative advocacy transformed law-makers into "learning disabled" advocates. On July 8, 1969, the first day of hearings for the House Committee on Education and Labor, Rep-resentative Quie set the tone of the proceedings when he announced: "We now move into the area of learning disabilities. A good constitu-ency has developed in a number of categories of the handicapped, be it mental retardation, cerebral palsy, or deaf and blind. I think it is impor-tant now that we do . . . move into the area of learning disabilities and have programs specifically designed for it."[84] The committee humanized the learning-disabled student. Chairman Roman Pucinski believed, here-tofore, schools and teachers rushed to judgment when encountering such students in the class: "There was a time when children who had difficulty learnings (sic) were shunted aside or described as 'incorrigible' by teach-ers and parents alike. Teachers often devoted their time to good students—and good students usually meant submissive. . . . Anyone not classified in the 'good' category was dismissed as mentally deficient or a discipline problem." He argued that the impact of false projections and bad decision-making regarding students with cognitive disabilities had repercussions beyond what teachers could know: "We will never know the devastation these ignorant judgments made on the lives of children who were unable to defend themselves." With new knowledge and greater awareness "to the countless factors which determine human growth, the child who is having difficulty learning is no longer written off as lazy, stupid, or merely defiant. We now know that his inability to learn may be related to a variety of perplexing maladies."[85]

Inasmuch as the education subcommittee hearings concerned preparing the groundwork for the passage of the new LD law, the hearings also provided supporters the opportunity to construct and promote the concept of the LD student. Again, echoing the separation of the "normal" "moron" from the "abnormal" "imbecile" and "idiot" at the beginning of the twentieth century, much of their argument tapped into the discourse of normalization that, in some ways, held together two competing phenomena inside the same individual: normal and "handicapped."[86] Robert Russell, president of the Association for Children with Learning Disabilities, equated disability invisibility with "normal" learning-disabled children. "Although children with learning disabilities have been with us throughout history," he said, "they experience a rather invisible kind of handicap. They look normal and it is very easy to forget them."[87] One of the sponsors of the bill, Representative Joshua Eilberg from Pennsylvania captured the seeming paradox nicely when he said, "One of the major reasons I sponsored the Children with Learning Disabilities Act is because the definition of 'handicapped' which we have been using is not accurate. This definition speaks only of medically-determined handicaps that a child might have while to all medical appearances he is normal."[88]

In a stunning example of normalization provided at the hearing, Dr. Jeanne McRae McCarthy, president-elect of the Division for Children with Learning Disabilities in the Council for Exceptional Children, told the subcommittee that many learning disabled students were misclassified as mentally retarded only to be reassigned after a battery of tests and consultations. She used an example of a young boy once in her care: "The first year I tested him he had an IQ of 65. It would have been very simple to put him in a class with the mentally retarded. This is what has happened to many of our learning disability kids. But the only thing I could say at the time was he didn't feel mentally retarded. Everything I was getting in the way of test data confirmed a functioning level of 65. Instead we put him in our learning disabilities program." McCarthy's testimony was profound in that it was rare for even a white student whose IQ was more than two standard deviations below the mean to be conceived of as LD. McCarthy also testified on behalf of another young person named David whose IQ rose from 65 to 77, then from 77 to 83, then from 83 to 94 due to his placement in a council-sponsored LD program. Not only did McCarthy believe that David's remarkable progress was evidence that he "no longer falls within the range of the mentally retarded" but that programs for the learning disabled could reclassify students and prevent "costing the public a great deal more per year for . . . mentally retarded" programs.[89]

The testimony by McCarthy, Eilberg, and many others during the hearing demonstrated how educational disability rights advocates envisioned LD for white students. A black "culturally deprived," special education student in the 1960s with an IQ of 65 would likely not have been reclassified as LD. The transfer of African American students from EMR to LD only began in the mid-1970s after black families and grassroots movements challenged the misclassification of EMR black students in the courts. Representative Eilberg said that the LD label was not for black and brown students but "I do not want to be misunderstood . . . I have supported programs which are designed to help our disadvantaged citizens. . . . But I really do believe," he continued, "that too many of our educational programs have been overly directed to reaching the poor."[90] Representative Pucinski supported the position of his colleague more bluntly by invoking race, financial appropriations, and recent public policy when he added: "This country had better wake up to one fact: We are going to continue spending billions of dollars on public aid programs, on various programs dealing with social disorders, crime in the streets. We have no hesitancy in appropriating $1 billion for Title I, and various other programs. We had better start thinking about priorities."[91] Pucinski's dog-whistle response indicated both racism in the movement for educational disability rights and a growing confidence that advocates for the "handicapped" no longer needed to rely on the black freedom movement to open up legislative opportunities.

By 1969, Congress made LD a top educational priority. As a new categorical program, LD had to be distinguished from mental retardation, especially designations associated with African Americans. Harold J. McGrady, director of the Program in Learning Disabilities at Northwestern University, submitted a prepared statement to the House Committee and then offered direct testimony to congressional members about LD and race. McGrady argued that the LD student "is not disadvantaged." "This is to say that a particular disadvantaged child may not have a learning disability. Any . . . condition may occur in combination and a disadvantaged child may also have a learning disability. But a learning disability is not the result of disadvantage per se. The learning disability child needs a program different from the disadvantaged."[92] Dr. McGrady's statement was placed in the public record, thereby giving congressional members a chance to ask follow-up questions about how LD proved different from black EMR.

Representative Quie raised the issue of race with McGrady, suggesting that more learning "disabilities" may be found in students from lower income backgrounds than in students whose families are middle class. "I could ask the question on the race of the people, too," Quie said. He added, "I know it is very difficult to talk about that." Given the volatility of racial issues engulfing the country and the policing power of the Civil Rights Act of 1964 that monitored institutional practices of discrimination, Quie quipped, "We aren't too free" to talk about race. Nonetheless, McGrady felt compelled to answer Quie's question, stating, "This is a very important question. It is a question I don't believe anybody has really begun to answer with bare statistics." Instead of providing a few possibilities on the question of race and learning disabilities, McGrady fell back on a class analysis of learning disabilities, explaining, "One could hypothesize that in lower income groups—and I would state it on the base of socioeconomic level rather than in terms of a racial issue here— that at lower socioeconomic levels, with health conditions not being adequate, that there would be more propensity towards learning disabilities because of the conditions which cause these disabilities. Nutrition is being recognized as a very important cause."[93] McGrady's remarks tapped into an old strategy that proxied class or low socioeconomic status, poor health, and nutrition to refer to black people. Desiring to reserve the LD designation for the student population not "degraded" by poverty, blackness, and any accompanying risk factors, Grady hinted at the possibility of some overlap: "So one could hypothesize that there will be a higher

incidence of specific learning disabilities among disadvantaged populations, yes. But we certainly would not say that every disadvantaged child
has a specific learning disability. It is a subpopulation."[94] The same hairsplitting that distinguished the white "mentally retarded" from the "culturally deprived" was happening once again between the white "learning
disabled" and the "culturally deprived." The parsing of categories served
the same purpose: to racialize and continue to separate two segments of
the special education population in the United States.

The racialization of LD also required clarifying its legal definition, as
advocates sought to achieve separate categorical status before Congress.
Samuel Kirk had the privilege of defining the term "learning disabilities"
as early as 1962 when he explained that "a learning disability refers to a
retardation, disorder, or delayed development in one or more of the processes of speech, language, reading, writing, arithmetic, or other school
subject resulting from a psychological handicap caused by a possible cerebral dysfunction and/or emotional or behavior disturbances. It is not the
result of mental retardation, sensory deprivation, or cultural and instructional factors."[95] For the most part, Kirk's original definition was held
firmly in place with the added concept of a "discrepancy between their
estimated potential and actual level of performance related to the basic
disorder in the learning process," articulated by his former student Barbara Bateman in 1965.[96] By the time the learning disabilities hearings
commenced in 1969, most scholars and LD organizations accepted this
as the standard definition. The National Advisory Committee on Handicapped Children adopted this definition in its first annual report, which
Congress used as the starting point for the floor debate in July:

Children with learning disabilities means those children who have a disorder in one or more of the basic psychological processes involved in
understanding or using language, spoken or written, which disorder may
manifest itself in imperfect ability to listen, think, speak, read, write, spell
or do mathematical calculations. Such disorders include such conditions
as perceptual handicaps, brain injury, minimal brain dysfunction, dyslexia,
and developmental asphasia. Such term does not include children who
have learning problems which are primarily the result of visual, hearing,
or motor handicaps, of mental retardation, of emotional disturbance, or of
environmental disadvantage. The present bills incorporate this definition

in essentially this form. The National Advisory Committee on Handicapped Children has advised us that they feel the term used to identify these children in legislation should be "specific learning disabilities."[97]

At the heart of LD's meaning is what it is not. LD is not generated by mental retardation, physical handicaps, culturally deprived factors, or poor teaching. According to the definition, LD is a subject matter failure in one or more academic areas. Subject matter failures were supposedly caused by brain dysfunction, as Representative Pucinski described early in the deliberations, or in the body's central nervous system, as Dr. James Gallagher reported at the hearing. According to Pucinski, "His brain may have been slightly injured at birth, causing real—but often minimal—interference with his ability to perceive letters, colors, and figures as other children do." Also, "he may have imperfect speech."[98] If medical researchers could not find a consensus on causation, it would be hard to reach a consensus during a legislative hearing. Dr. Gallagher advised members on the House committee that a "practical problem associated here is that definitive neurological diagnosis is not always possible for such minimal problems. The conscientious physician may not give a clear and unequivocal diagnosis on such a child. Given the usual medical clearances, which are routine procedures for school and special program admission, children should not have to forego specialized instruction on the basis of a medical category that experts report to us is very hard to determine with certainty."[99] When asked to elaborate on the question of medical uncertainty by the committee, Dr. Gallagher answered straightforwardly: "If you took a group of youngsters who would now be in a class in the State of Illinois, of 10 children, you could probably get positive neurological findings on five of them. Another five, you probably couldn't find anything or it would be ambiguous."[100] Despite Dr. Gallagher's pronouncements about causal factors, LD was still promoted using a medical framework (which led to rabid criticism in the 1970s and 1980s). Inserting the adjective "specific" in front of the label "learning disabilities" was designed to do three things: maintain the medical model, to use the medical model to explain specific academic failures in subject areas, and to promote LD's categorical importance as the hearing moved toward final passage of the Children with Specific Learning Disabilities Act.

The question of categorical legislation placed ESEA, once again, at the heart of the debate. Questions proliferated about whether LD would absorb much of the handicap appropriations already earmarked for other disabled groups. Tied to this question was another concern: should specific learning disabilities be placed in Title VI of ESEA as a general amendment or a special category called Title VI-Part G? "The committee is going to have to make a very difficult decision here, as to whether we want to move in the direction of just amending title VI, or whether we want to set up this special category," chairman Pucinski announced.[101] Representative John Dellenback interjected, addressing the dilemma, saying, "One of the concerns that some of us have had is that every time a new idea comes along we create a new category. We then create a whole authorization and a whole appropriation for that new category."[102] Samuel Kirk long advocated for a separate category "for the simple reason that when you place something that needs a push under something else, it doesn't get off the ground."[103] Kirk believed that LD would remain beneath other disabilities, and that keeping LD confined within "other health impaired" categories or placed in existing parts of Title VI would render it a lesser priority. Dr. Gallagher concurred with separating LD, saying in the hearings that integrating LD into other parts of Title VI could be problematic, warning, "but I must caution you that, when you go that route, you are going to have to compete against eight or nine existing programs which are now trying to take care of 11 million children with a $30 million recommendation."[104] Kirk and others argued for LD's "institutionalization," not only in name but also in categorical separation on a new branch of the ESEA Title VI policy tree. They prevailed.[105]

By the time PL 91–230 (Children with Specific Learning Disabilities Act) was introduced in the Senate and House in February and March of 1969, respectively, and signed by President Nixon on April 13, 1970, a new policy branch was erected onto ESEA Title VI called "Part G—Special Programs for Children with Specific Learning Disabilities," authorizing $12 million for fiscal year (FY) 1970; $20 million for FY 1971; and $31 million for the next two fiscal years. Samuel Kirk's legislative advocacy paid off. The learning disabilities rights movement culminated in a major legislative victory for special education in general, and white underachievers, specifically. Representative Carl Perkins from Kentucky noted that the failure to include LD in previous legislation was a "serious omission." Representative Ogden Reid of New York added, "To permit the exclusion of these [i.e., learning disabled] children from Federal programs for the education of the handicapped to continue for even one additional day would not only be unfair, it would be inhuman." Representative Steiger of Wisconsin summarized ESEA Title VI-Part G, saying PL 91–230 "is presented not as one more shot in the arm, but as a major link in the structure of enabling legislation for improving educational opportunity for handicapped children." Representative Pucinski of Illinois said that the new law would do away with stigma for good: "The child who is having difficulty learning no longer will be written off as lazy, stupid, or merely defiant." And Senator Ralph Yarborough of Texas argued the law finally forced Americans to understand the uniqueness of learning-disabled students: "Coming to terms with these children . . . is going to help us realize that children have individual learning styles and characteristics and that we are going to have to do more than pay lip service to these individual differences."[106]

Educational Disadvantage as Racialized Disability in EOA and ESEA

ESEA finally advanced the interests of white "handicapped" students, increasing their visibility and legitimacy within the expansion of statutory special education law. With ESEA foregrounding white educational disability, EOA and ESEA legislatively trapped African-Americans inside a system of disability categories, of which "cultural deprivation" described all their nonacademic disorders, and "educational disadvantaged" made their identity distinct from white "handicapped" students. "It is claimed that these children do not learn because they come from 'poor homes,' 'broken homes,' 'culturally deprived backgrounds,' or are inhibited by a host of community problems," wrote the organization Harlem Youth Opportunities Unlimited (HARYOU) in an essay in *Integrated Education*. "Specifically, there is no conclusive evidence to demonstrate a consistent relationship between 'poor homes' or 'broken homes' and the ability to learn to read. Poor children, culturally deprived children, can learn if they are taught."[107] Furthermore, EOA and ESEA cemented black students in their "place" within the disability hierarchy: at the bottom. When it mattered the most legislatively, public officials and advocates for the white "handicapped" completely excluded the category of cultural deprived or educationally disadvantaged from policy consideration in the new law. "The tendency on the part of some educators, and others," wrote HARYOU, "to lump all children in a racial ghetto under one heading of 'culturally deprived,' and therefore 'uneducable,' is an insidious form of stereotypic thinking and is a contemporary version of the earlier contentions that Negroes are innately inferior."[108] Though desegregation of public schools remained the focus of the civil rights movement, education disability rights advocates constructed the idea of "exceptionality" for all children "above" the statistical normal (the talented and gifted) and "below" it (the educationally disadvantaged). Also racialized, the concept of "exceptionality" promoted categories of learning that provided white children with the best chances to succeed: talented and gifted for academically exceptional white students on the one hand and learning disabled for white students who struggled academically on the other. Invoking national social movements was a way to tie the Economic Opportunity Act's Title II and Elementary and Secondary Education Act's Title I to black and brown learners, and ESEA's Title VI and the Children with Specific Learning Disabilities Act to white "handicapped" students. Racializing "exceptionalities" led to federal policy segregation. In spite of the fanfare associated with Head Start and Title I from a War on Poverty standpoint, African American special education was conceived out of highly racialized policy initiatives that lacked the programmatic importance given to "mainstream" disability legislation and white underachievement.[109]

A *Journal of Special Education* symposium brought this dilemma front and center when Michael J. Herrick posed a basic question in his essay, "Disabled or Disadvantaged: What's the Difference?" The five respondents and Herrick's rebuttal appear in retrospect as the most important cautionary tale in the history of race and special education. Assessing the learning and behavior characteristics of both the learning disabled and the culturally deprived student, Herrick argued that he began to see one student, not two. "I began to understand," mused Herrick, "that the specifics of differentiating these two students were simply degrees of the same behavior."[110] Agreeing with the differences on the extreme ends of the respective labels, it was the "mild" middle where Herrick saw one student and the categorizations he most questioned. In seeing one student and not two, Herrick wondered about their separation in Bateman's definition of the learning disabled, in the EOA and ESEA legislation, and in the definition provided by experts like Samuel Kirk, Patricia Myers, and Donald Hammill. Herrick's frustration was evident when he explained:

> I seldom question the distinction when the behavior of a child in either group is extreme or completely different from the normal. However, as a regular classroom teacher, I am too often faced with the *mildly* disabled and/or disadvantaged student. Thus, it does not help me to know if the students are *really* learning disabled or *really* disadvantaged. However, the literature and my graduate training indicate that I should know the differences because they *really* exist![111]

If the differences really existed, Herrick argued, "Why don't they investigate cultural disadvantage as a causal factor of learning disability *equal to* the causal factor of central nervous system dysfunction? Certainly, special education professionals should be concerned about such a cause, if, as Myers and Hammill speculate, 'between 25 percent and 50 percent or better of the urban, center city school children would qualify for learning disability programs (emphasis added)'"[112] The importance of distinguishing between the learning disabled and the culturally or educationally deprived seemed to hinge on this important fact: that an acknowledgment of the culturally deprived as also and equally learning disabled could infringe on the growing white special education movement. Black special education, as it was invoked and underscored by special education experts, contained secondary and tertiary elements associated with nonschool environmental influences.

To debate the finer points of an august piece of legislation like ESEA or EOA would belie the real damage caused by racial legislative segregation. What went on inside of Congress (and journal symposia) failed to capture fully what took place inside schools. The racial violence of separate policies, different labels, tracking, and other sorting practices cohered inside classrooms in ways few legislators could or attempted to imagine. Keeping track of abilities in schools also functioned as a way to keep track of disabilities in districts as well.[113] *Hobson v. Hansen,* one of the earliest special education cases, brought attention to the problems of separate educational designations and racial sorting systems. This trial not only occurred a few blocks from the offices of national lawmakers, but also

during the period legislators debated the minutiae of cultural deprivation and learning disabilities. The Washington, D.C. public school system
became emblematic of how the correlation between race and socioeco-
nomics was manifested in differential policies and practices. So too did
the cases *Larry P. v. Riles, Pace v. Hannon* and *Corey v. City of Chicago*
reflect unequal special educational practices, demonstrating how EMR
remained an intractable issue in segregating black students in places like
San Francisco and Chicago, as explained in the next chapter. In addition
to the grassroots struggles waged by black students and their families to
contest the misclassification and overrepresentation of black students
in EMR, challenges to the LD label in the 1970s and 1980s also defined
some of the starkest divisions in special education and demonstrated all
that had gone awry with special education. Indeed, the federal government's bifurcated disability polices and their polarizing effect during the
1960s contributed to the racial disproportionality in special education in
later decades.

4

Challenging Special Education from Above and Below

Contestations of the 1970s and 1980s

We must face the reality—we are asked to take children others cannot teach, and a large percentage of these are from ethnically and/or economically disadvantaged backgrounds.

—LLOYD DUNN, "Special Education for the Mildly Retarded—
Is Much of It Justifiable?"

We now have what may be called a 6-hour retarded child—retarded from 9 to 3, five days a week, solely on the basis of an IQ score.

—President's Committee on Mental Retardation,
The Six-Hour Retarded Child

The culmination of LD had been achieved. Lawmakers and special education proponents celebrated the passage of the Specific Learning Disabilities Act. "By passing the Children with Specific Learning Disabilities Act," stated Howard S. Adelman, professor of psychology, "Congress has added its official sanction to this category of exceptionality."[1] The official sanction by Congress also meant placing legal distance between LD and EMR. The separation that Samuel Kirk and others desired now placed the two disability categories in the spotlight, allowing many to question their practicality and legitimacy. Many believed these categories became another way for the white educational establishment to racially segment disabled student populations. Within the language of equal rights for the inclusion of all disabled students lurked the strategy of educational segregationists—some who perpetuated a special education system that marginalized black students and promoted white students in the name of equal educational opportunity. It was no wonder that in the 1970s, special education became a site of struggle, with pitchfork battles waged on many fronts. The challenge to EMR and LD from above and below involved a cross-section of people and organizations looking to make special education live up to the promises of educating all disabled students equally.

This chapter examines the power of labels and explores the politics surrounding EMR and LD. It argues that the racialized critique of EMR, waged by black parents and civil rights advocates, worked to discount the legitimacy of special education. At the same time, social scientists deemed LD ambiguous, which cast doubt on the white exclusivity of the label. As LD began its career as an implicit identity for white students, EMR continued to claim a greater percentage of culturally deprived African American students. Black parents filed lawsuits in cities like San Francisco and Chicago to contest the misclassification of their children as EMR. These lawsuits not only put public school districts like San Francisco Unified and Chicago Public Schools in the spotlight for racist classification practices but also called into question the use of intelligence tests—the very instruments used to define black students as "mentally retarded" since the turn of the twentieth century. For the first time, the phenomenon of black overrepresentation in special education became highly politicized, garnering the attention from the civil rights movement. As EMR was challenged at the grassroots level, LD was also being scrutinized for its definitional ambiguity and racial exclusivity by social scientists skeptical of its medical etiology. Some argued that LD was discriminatory against black students while others posited that LD was invented.[2] Many wondered what defined a "learning disability."[3] Could the culturally deprived and the educationally disadvantaged also possess learning disabilities? And why did financial and other resources flow so freely to this population? This chapter ends by examining the impact of the challenge to EMR and how the growing number of black students once labeled EMR were increasingly classified as LD by the end of the 1970s and early 1980s.

The Politics of Labels: Challenging the Racialization of Special Education Categories

In the seminal 1968 essay "Special Education for the Mildly Retarded—Is Much of It Justifiable?," Lloyd Dunn, professor at the George Peabody

College for Teachers at Vanderbilt University, shook the foundation of special education by suggesting that the system was broken. Dunn observed that schools warehoused "blacks, American Indians, Mexican, Puerto Ricans, non-standard English speakers, and students from broken, disorganized, and inadequate homes" in "self-contained special schools and classes." Representing between 60 to 80 percent of the "mildly retarded" student population, Dunn believed tracking these students into separate classes was too expensive and raised "serious educational and civil rights issues which must be squarely faced." Dunn's seminal article appeared after a spring and summer marked by political unrest: from the assassinations of Martin Luther King Jr. and Senator Robert Kennedy in April and June, respectively, to the antiwar protests during the Democratic National Convention in August. Dunn was not the first to observe the danger of misclassifying students of color as EMR; he was one of a few white scholars in the 1960s to say the practice must end: "It is my thesis that we must stop labeling these deprived children as mentally retarded. Furthermore, we must stop segregating them by placing them into our allegedly special programs."[4]

By the time Dunn had issued his cautionary tale, black and brown urban education was synonymous with mental retardation. In 1969, the President's Committee on Mental Retardation organized the Conference on Problems of Education of Children in the Inner City and assembled administrators, psychologists, education commissioners, teachers, and college presidents to address the issues that beset urban education. The conference advanced the notion of the "six-hour retarded child," signifying a correlation between race and academic underachievement between the hours of 9 a.m. and 3 p.m. Though cultural deprivation exemplified mental retardation all day, many believed the "six-hour retarded child" defined urban black and brown students whose experience in public education was one of frustration and failure. The conference's report stated, "Within the last decade there has been a mass migration to the large cities. Among 'immigrants' are large numbers of low-income families from minority groups, whose children often fall further behind with each school year. A large number of these children score low enough on individual tests of intelligence to be classified as mentally retarded."[5] The President's Committee set itself up to address the problem and perhaps to find a solution to so-called educable mental retardation. But like other well-meaning people in the field of urban education, the professionals who gathered never imagined themselves to be part of the problem. Thus, the "six-hour retarded child" was more than the theme of the conference or the identity of black and brown school children but represented the embodied practice of a special education system established to segregate students of color.

The "six-hour retarded child" symbolized a politics of white resistance in education post-*Brown*. For example, the curriculum track system in Washington, D.C. Public Schools was a racially conceived special educa- tion policy in differential education, created and implemented after the *Brown* decision to segregate black and white students who attended classes in the same building. In 1955, school authorities in the District of Columbia turned their dual racially segregated system into a single differential one based on educational tracks. Washington, D.C.'s track system ranged from the "lowest" to the "highest": basic or special academic track (the retarded); general track (the average); honors/gifted track (the above average); and at the high school level, the regular track (college preparatory for honors and gifted students).[6] With a number of black students moving from all- black schools to racially mixed learning environments, Washington, D.C. Public Schools authorities defined them as "mentally retarded" and placed a disproportionate number of black students in the basic/special academic track for EMR students. Judge Wright noted this phenomenon after Julius Hobson, a local resident and a member of the Congress of Racial Equal- ity (CORE) sued Washington, D.C. Public Schools and prevailed:

> Until that time no one was aware of the overall achievement level of Negro students because achievement scores had not been reported on a city-wide basis in the old Division II (Negro) schools. However, soon after integra- tion Dr. Hansen, then Assistant Superintendent in charge of senior high schools, began to receive "reports of very serious retardation in achieve- ment in the basic skills." The low achievers were predominantly from the Division II schools. It was the discovery of this large number of academi- cally retarded Negro children in the school system that led to the institu- tion of the track system.[7]

Judge Wright's ultimate decision to abolish the track system as discrimi- natory proved easy. The plaintiffs in the case used a mountain of available evidence—one of which was the words of D.C. Superintendent Hansen himself. Hansen revealed that the primary reason for instituting the track system was the growing presence of black students in white schools, conceding that "to describe the origin of the four-track system without reference to desegregation in the District of Columbia Public Schools would be to by-pass one of the most significant causes of its being. Racial integration was a precipitant of the four-track development in the District's high schools."[8]

Special education served as a racial battleground by the late 1960s and early 1970s. Professor David Franks's study of eleven Missouri school districts during the 1969–1970 school year revealed two separate classes for EMR and LD students. Franks desired to know whether EMR self-contained day classes functioned as depositories for students of color and low-income families. His research revealed that black students made up 34 percent of the EMR classes, while white students constituted 66 percent. Alternately, black students constituted only 3 percent of the LD classes in Missouri while white learners comprised a whopping 97 percent of the student population, attesting to the fact that African American students were not the original targeted population for LD classes.[9]

Franks's findings in Missouri were supported by Christine Sleeter's research. Sleeter examined national LD data first collected in the late 1970s. Twelve of sixty-one LD studies examined by Sleeter reported the racial composition of their samples, revealing that LD classes were 98.5 percent white and only 1.5 percent students of color. In addition, 16 of the 61 LD studies examined by Sleeter reported the class composition of their samples, showing that 69 percent of the students were middle class or higher, while 31 percent represented lower middle class or below. Twelve out of the sixteen studies reported student samples whose families were at least 90 percent middle class or higher. Sleeter concluded, "The learning disabilities category probably was not consciously established just for white middle-class children, even though it was populated mainly by them. It was established for children who, given the prevailing categories used to describe failing children, did not seem to fit any other category."[10] Indeed, placing students in LD served as a way to help white underachieving students while simultaneously containing underachieving black students in EMR classes.

A handful of researchers, such as psychologist Edith Grotberg, challenged the racial exclusivity associated with an LD "diagnosis."[11] Many psychologists and educators theorized the white, "slow learning" LD student not only as middle class but also as "neurologically impaired." A white student's normal IQ and his or her subject-matter failures in school defied belief. Psychologists historically linked neurological brain damage to explanations of white middle-class underachievement.[12] Grotberg and others raised an additional set of questions that held implications for other students: "While we tend to agree that learning disabilities include neurological factors, we do not understand the relationships of these symptoms to different socio-economic groups."[13] In other words, if we take LD as real and objective category, then why are white middle-class students the only demographic group that can be labeled as "neurologically-impaired"? To maintain the whiteness of LD, Grotberg argued, was to only look for "clean, uncluttered elements with a neurological base and no confounding variables, such as culture or nutrition."[14] The likes of Grotberg, Edmund Gordon, Ray Barsch, H. Birch, J. F. Cawley, C. M. Drillien, and N. Munro attempted to diminish LD's racial and class exclusivity by exploring other correlates of learning disabilities in addition to the "neurological" markers.[15] Using black Head Start "low-income children who demonstrate the symptoms of learning disabilities but have symptoms confounding the diagnosis," these scholars examined malnutrition, visual perception, eye-motor coordination, and sensory deprivation to search for answers that could explain black academic challenges. "Internal conditions of the organism generated by birth trauma," argued Grotberg, "and external stresses generated by socioeconomic and ethnic patterns contribute to learning disabilities. The neurological elements may well be affected by both sources of experience."[16]

Similarly, two medical doctors and a researcher from Baltimore, Maryland, raised the question about learning disabilities and black students. "Too little attention has been focused on the specific learning disabilities of individual children who live in deprived neighborhoods," wrote Murray Kappelman, Eugene Kaplan, and Robert Ganter.[17] This team examined 306 educationally disadvantaged students in the black section of the city and found that most suffered from a spectrum of learning disorders linked to nutritional deficits, prenatal deprivations, childhood accidents, and chronic illnesses. They concluded, "It is simply not adequate to label the poor achiever in the inner-city classroom as culturally deprived and allow this all-inclusive term to explain his poor approach and response to the learning experience."[18] Thus, scholars began asking probing questions about learning disability theory as much as they did about the practice of placing one racial group in LD over others.

If LD's inherent whiteness became increasingly questionable in the early 1970s, then EMR's growing blackness was evolving into a conspiracy. Between 1965 and 1975, the African American student population integrating white school districts increased exponentially. This rise in the black student population challenged white teachers and administrators who often lacked an understanding of black culture and family dynamics. Thus, the integrated classroom became a way station—an educational checkpoint for white teachers to ascertain the academic challenges and cultural "baggage" black students carried with them into white schools. John L. Johnson, a professor of special education at Syracuse University, captured the growing sentiment developing around the racial bifurcation of general and special education:

> General education, by definition, is supposed to be capable of teaching all children, but when confronted with inner-city Black children, it has failed.... The current plight of the Black is, in fact, a direct result of the regular school's failure to cope with individual and collective differences in learning and conduct of an increasing number of pupils. Regular schools have been the major force for accommodation of the "regular" Blacks and special education receives the "hard to break" Blacks. It is an unwritten pact between the two. Special education is part of the arrangement for cooling out students. It has helped to erect a parallel system which permits relief of institutional guilt and humiliation stemming from the failure to achieve competence and effectiveness in the task given to it by society. Special education is helping the regular school maintained its spoiled identity when it creates special programs for the "disruptive child" and the "slow-learner," many of whom for some strange reason, happen to be Black and poor and live in the inner city.[19]

An astute promoter of black studies as an academic discipline during its infancy, Johnson's racial critiques of special education in 1969 paralleled later concerns about overrepresentation in the 1990s and early twenty-first century. The difference between critiques in the 1960s and 1970s and the ones rendered forty to fifty years later were the number of African

American students overrepresented by the turn of the twenty-first century. For many critics, the story was the same. Special education did not improve black educational outcomes; rather, it served as a way to keep black students segregated from mainstream classrooms. M. Stephen Lilly from the University of Oregon said forthrightly, "It is with regard to these children that we as special educators have trouble justifying our practices both socially and morally, and this is the area in which we must spend a considerable time and energy examining both our actions and our motives."[20] When examining the number of black and brown students placed into special education in the last three decades of the twentieth century, it is clear that the motives were questionable at best and insidious at worst.

Like Lloyd Dunn and John Johnson, Lilly offered a strong indictment and issued a strident position about a system that appeared broken in its infancy. "It is the position of this writer," explained Lilly in 1970, "that traditional special education services as represented by self-contained special classes should be discontinued immediately for all but the severely impaired . . ." Lilly's call to discontinue self-contained classes emerged from his questioning of research that promoted the efficacy of special education for the mildly disabled. Commenting on the growing body of research literature, Lilly admitted that "these studies have produced conflicting evidence concerning special class programs, with the weight of the evidence suggesting that special programs have produced little that is superior to what is produced in the regular class setting." Like Dunn, Lilly did not mince words, calling special education perpetually ineffective based on efficacy studies: "To avoid exhaustive argument with regard to research design and confounding variables in these efficacy studies, let us accept the statement that they are inconclusive to date. It must be added, however, that in the true spirit of research they will be inconclusive forever."[21]

Maynard Reynolds and Evelyn Deno of the University of Minnesota also emerged as two of the staunchest critics of a racially bifurcated and flawed system. As professors in the Department of Special Education, Reynolds and Deno worked directly with local schools in Minneapolis and served on national bodies, like the Council of Exceptional Children. As experts on educational disabilities, Reynolds and Deno also served as the director and codirector, respectively, of the Leadership Training

Institute in the U.S. Office of Education, and trained the next generation of special education teachers. Their privileged positions notwithstanding, Reynolds and Deno embraced their identity as detractors of the current special education system. Known for rendering systems-oriented critiques of the growing edifice of special education, Reynolds and Deno understood special education and general education to be inextricably linked. They sensed the field of special education beginning to set itself apart from general education with its conceptual models, myriad categories, and arcane language. They warned special education practitioners to resist feeling haughty, for if general education experienced systemic failings, so too did special education. Reynolds and Deno believed that special education took the word "special" too seriously, with the word being exclusively applied to "problems" with students rather than with the general education system that made them problematic. "The pot is in no position to call the kettle black," wrote Deno. "Special educators must ask themselves whether they are justified in continuing to try to fix up the children that an inadequate instructional program has maimed so they will fit better into a system that should be adjusting itself to the learning needs of the children rather than expecting children to adjust to them."[22] And even if the special educator helped "disabled" students and not students in general education, Reynolds argued special educators should never see themselves on an island unto itself but rather part of a larger community of educators: "Hopefully, every special educator sees himself as a resource for his entire school and not as one who takes his own little group to some special closet."[23]

Deno raised existential questions about special education. She queried, "Does special education need to exist at all as a separate administrative system" especially if its current measure of success is "judged by how many more children are enrolled in special education programs this year than were enrolled last year or 10 years ago?"[24] Deno took aim at the notion long supported by special education advocates—that many underserved students awaited to be identified. Sharp increases in sensory disability categories like the "blind" may not garner as much attention as sudden spikes in mental retardation. But that was the narrative promoted by special education advocates: that there existed so many "unidentified" and "underserved" students who had not yet been located. Deno, Reynolds, and others witnessed this growing contradiction that posited the notion that disabled students were waiting to be placed in special education. This idea was being promoted while the field of special education as well as special education policy advocated for "mainstreaming" "disabled students," defined as the "process of educating handicapped children in regular classrooms."[25] "Mainstreaming" proved both a strange term and an odd borrowing of a concept, demonstrating the cross-wiring of education disability rights and civil rights. It allowed the integration of disabled students into general education classes, while integration functioned as the mainstreaming of black students into those same classes.[26]

The mainstreaming movement held different objectives for different student constituents. As educators overidentified students of color as "special," advocates of handicapped students believed school districts failed to respond adequately to the disability needs of white students, which represented a significant thrust of the Education for All Handicapped Children Act. "Abolishing" special education and funneling students back to general education classes could address the problem of black student resegregation; however, an emphasis on black and brown misclassification would fall short of addressing the educational rights of white disabled students who, as it was repeatedly surmised, often remained unclassified or unidentified. Indeed, special education was at an impasse in the 1970s and felt the sting of criticism for over-labeling too many black and brown learners on one hand and not enough white students on the other. "There is disquieting evidence that these classes serve as a holding operation for many racial and economically deprived students who could receive a better education sharing classrooms with other students whose talents and backgrounds vary greatly," noted Wilton Anderson. He continued, "The question dealt with here centers around what is unfair in the separation of disadvantaged students into special education classes; and what can be done to get them back into the regular classroom, and what can be offered them once they are there."[27] Placing black EMR students into general education classrooms was indeed a "mainstream" concern and another dimension in the long fight for black equal education opportunity.[28]

Identifying white disabled students for special education services, however, had become the thrust of mainstreaming and a focal point of a new kind of equal educational opportunity. Equal educational opportunity, the pillar of black and Latinx civil rights in the 1950s and 1960s, shifted to the white intellectually disabled in the 1970s. In 1971, the Pennsylvania Association for Retarded Children (PARC) sued the Commonwealth of Pennsylvania in U.S. District Court for excluding retarded children from all educational programming and services if psychologists determined students to be "uneducable and untrainable."[29] As one of the Pennsylvania statutes read, "When a child is thus certified, the public schools shall be relieved of the obligation of providing education or training for such child."[30] In the following year, partly as a result of the elimination of the track system, another "right-to-education" federal lawsuit was filed in Washington, D.C. The plaintiffs in *Mills v. Board of Education of the District of Columbia*, alleged that "mentally retarded" and "emotionally disturbed" students were excluded from the D.C. public schools and denied educational services due to the claim of insufficient funding. As two of the most important civil rights cases in the early 1970s, *PARC* and *Mills* argued that the refusal to render services to students with developmental disabilities and behavioral issues constituted a violation of their rights under both the equal protection and due process clauses of the Fourteenth Amendment. Extending the logic of *Brown, PARC,* in a consent agreement, employed language that would become the foundation of disability legal discourse: "It is the Commonwealth's obligation to place each mentally retarded child in a free, public program of education and training appropriate to the child's capacity."[31] *Mills* extended *PARC* by arguing that insufficient district funds "cannot be permitted to bear more heavily on the 'exceptional' or handicapped child than on the normal child."[32] Thus, phrases such as "free and appropriate education (FAPE)," "least restrictive environment (LRE)," and an "individualized education plan (IEP)" emerged as the bedrock of disability education and the cornerstone of mainstreaming philosophy in statutory law and congressional policy.

The judicial victories in *PARC* and *Mills* culminated in the Education for All Handicapped Children Act of 1975 (EHA) (P.L. 94–142).[33] *PARC* and *Mills* did for the Education for All Handicapped Children Act (EHA) what the *Brown* decision did for the Civil Rights Act of 1964. Case law, born out of activism and advocacy, produced new statutory law. The connective tissue leading from case law to statutory law was important, for it served as the final span in the bridge that connected the civil rights and educational disability rights movements, according to the *Peabody Journal of Education*: "The civil rights movement had laid a constitutional foundation that could be used to argue for expanded and different educational services for handicapped children."[34] But the connection should be understood as one of interest convergence. The demand for educational disability rights was essentially a demand for civil rights, a claim that disability rights advocates made repeatedly but were unable to make without the precedent of *Brown*. "As the last frontier of equal educational opportunity," the Education for All Handicapped Children Act advanced similar arguments found in the *Brown* decision and the Civil Rights Act of 1964 based on the inherent civil and human rights of disabled children. The *Peabody Journal of Education* concluded:

> The issue in *Brown*—the ending of racial segregation through integration of schools and classroom—is a cornerstone decision in the education for the handicapped children although it may at first appear only tangentially related. Both the legal questions upon which *Brown* was decided and the policy developments that came from it laid the foundation for the judicial role in special education reform. It established the applicability of constitutional protections to public education, bringing educational issues within the realm of civil rights. In addition, it legitimized subsequent anti-discrimination legislation, and provided an entry for the federal government into education policy. Finally, the plaintiffs' argument in *Brown* relied on both the stigma and detrimental educational consequences of segregation. These precedents established by the *Brown* decision were successfully applied by advocates for the handicapped in later cases.[35]

Trumping all legal attempts in the previous decade to help the physically, sensory, and developmentally disabled, the Education for All Handicapped Children Act extended "protections to a previously neglected segment of the population," and emphatically delivered the message that all children can benefit from an education and have a right to one. The EHA encapsulated smaller legislative responses enacted two years prior. First, Section 504 of the Rehabilitation Act of 1973 represented a stop-gap measure to withhold federal funding from any institution that discriminated against the disabled. Law professor Kathryn Coates noted, "In 1974, an interim statute was enacted to enable Congress to analyze the handicapped situation."[36] And in 1975, Congress nearly spoke in one voice, passing the EHA "with large margins and little floor debate."[37]

Though the Education for All Handicapped Children Act appeared inclusive in protecting the rights of all disabled youth, the law came up short for disabled students of color. Black and brown students received the short end of the legislative stick, arguably left outside of the policy looking in. In essence, educational disability rights used black and brown constitutional claims to augment the boundaries of democracy for itself only to allow the legislative gates to close on black and brown special education students. The EHA did not cover the overwhelmingly black and brown educable mentally retarded. The EHA protected the learning disabled but added an exclusionary provision that left out students who experienced "cultural" or "educational disadvantage," which again marginalized black and brown students. The EHA also excluded those with "social maladjustment," an educational disability applied to black children, but protected the "emotionally disturbed," who were mostly white up to 1975. The *Peabody Journal of Education* recognized the omission: "The concerns involved in educating mildly retarded children—by far the most numerous and those most likely to attend regular public schools—were only sporadically addressed in the hearings on P.L. 94–142."[38]

EMR did not make it into the EHA as a federally recognized disability, and LD was covered with caveats. The principal provisions of the new law provided a summary: "The definition of 'children with specific learning disabilities' would be clarified to exclude children whose learning problems are the result of cultural or economic disadvantage."[39] Black and Latinx, Asian American, and Native American students labeled EMR or deemed culturally or economically disadvantaged could not benefit from the law.[40] Similar to the Specific Learning Disabilities Act in 1969, the EHA was only interested in learning problems associated with psychological disorders that made it difficult for a student to use spoken or written language or complete mathematical calculations. Indeed, many black students struggled with learning problems that made it difficult for them to listen, think, speak, read, write, and spell. There was, however, a purported difference according to special education experts and disability researchers.

The learning problems black students experienced became exclusively associated with their race and class, and only potentially presented as a "learning disability." Poverty (or what the law deemed as economic and environmental disadvantage) and being black (what the law understood as a cultural disadvantage) did not signify "disorders" like perceptual handicaps, brain injury, minimal brain dysfunction, dyslexia, and developmental aphasia.[41] Black difficulties with reading, writing, speaking, and performing mathematic calculations were understood to be signs of educable mental retardation. Thus, lawmakers and special education lobbyists put forth the rationale that federally funded Title I and Title III programs created in ESEA already served black and Latinx special education students, respectively. It was not necessary to cover them again. "Consequently, under the present criteria and guidelines," Kenneth A. Kavale remarked about the EHA, "the cultural disadvantaged (CD) child is essentially left with only two categories of special education service, educable mentally retarded (EMR) or behaviorally disordered (BD)," both of which were not covered under EHA.[42] Black students were left at the mercy of states and districts across the country.[43] In the mid-1970s, neither Congress, the states, nor the districts took seriously the issue of misclassification and overrepresentation of black students in EMR. Even as the educational disabilities rights movement scored its biggest victory for white students in 1975 with the passage of EHA, black families realized their fight for equal education opportunity in general and special education must continue.

Confronting Special Education in the Courts and in the Streets: From *Larry P. v. Riles* to *PASE v. Hannon*

Though the quest for equal educational opportunity began with the *Brown* decision, integration did not start in earnest until ten years later with the Civil Rights Act of 1964. In fact, during the Black Power era, the movement for equal education opportunity expanded, bringing together a series of civil rights groups and professional coalitions that included black educators, psychologists, social workers, counselors, and mental health workers. Black professionals believed their academic training positioned them to address the ills of black neighborhoods, including schools. For black social scientists, closing ranks around their professional interests stymied white supremacy inside their respective disciplines. They also used their roles as black professionals to serve a wounded black public. Founded in 1969, the Association of Black Psychologists and the Association of Black Social Workers joined civil rights groups, like the NAACP Legal Defense Fund, the Urban League, La Raza, and local legal organizations to fight on behalf of black EMR students across the country.[44]

The Association of Black Psychologists (ABA) immediately went to work, issuing strident positions against the American Psychological Association (APA) and targeting intelligence tests that damaged the self-concept of young black students.[45] Robert Williams, the first president of the ABA, admonished white psychologists to "stay out of Negro neighborhoods." Feeling as if white psychologists and governmental officials used black neighborhoods as research laboratories, Williams announced vociferously, "Don't come around here with your Mickey Mouse antipoverty programs." Well aware that antipoverty programs were sites for black "culturally deprived" students, he bemoaned the fact that special education had become a racialized system of advantages and disadvantages with social science being weaponized against black children. Thus, Williams extended his argument to the whole gamut of intelligence, aptitude, and achievement tests, believing the white world identified black academic deficits with the intent of keeping black students from accessing educational opportunities. He and the ABA called for a temporary cessation of these tests:

> The Association of Black Psychologists calls for a moratorium on the repeated abuse and misuse of the so-called conventional psychological tests, e.g., Stanford-Binet (Form L-M), the Wechsler, Scholastic Aptitude Test (SAT), Stanford Achievement, Iowa Basic Skills, Graduate Record Examination (GRE), the Miller Analogies Test and many others. For more than two decades, we have known that these conventional tests are unfair and improperly classify Black children. In spite of the abundance of facts, nothing has been done to correct this abuse. Thus, the Association of Black Psychologists, dedicated to preventing further exploitation of Black people, calls for an immediate moratorium on all testing of Black people until more equitable tests are available.[46]

Williams rose to his own challenge, developing a series of "counter-intelligence" tests, as he called them, that are "*biased in favor* of black people." Based directly on the experiences of black people, "the name of the instrument is the 'BITCH' test, which is translated 'Black Intelligence Test Counterbalanced for Honkies.'" BITCH, Williams noted, is the "adult form." He revealed that another test was in development for children titled,

"The S.O.B. Test." "At first blush," Williams warned, "you perhaps consider these tests as humorous."[47] But Williams was not joking.

Beyond Robert Williams's tongue-in-cheek humor sat a larger question: who gave white people a monopoly on determining what constitutes intelligence? It was a question directed at the tradition of ablest white psychology from Goddard and Terman to Arthur Jensen, Gordon Reed, and all white standardized tests. For Williams and other critics of psychological tests, intelligence was situational, endemic to the primary environment to which black people were exposed. He asked rhetorically, "Is it more indicative of intelligence to know Malcolm X's last name or the author of Hamlet?" "I ask you now," Williams continued, "When is Washington's birthday?" The question served as another rhetorical trap for a potential white test-taker, designed to highlight how intelligence tests are racialized. "Perhaps 99% [sic] of you thought February 22," he answered facetiously. "That answer presupposes a white norm. I actually meant Booker T. Washington's birthday, not George Washington's." The questions were apropos. The creators of intelligence and achievement tests had little interest in tapping into the "native" or relative intelligence of black students, only establishing something called an intelligence quotient from questions that appeared less relevant to their history and experiences. Since the days of Lewis Terman, white educators used intelligence tests to segregate black students and provide differentially inferior services in special classes.[48] Black psychologists objected to, perhaps more than anything, the ways in which intelligence tests disproportionately marked students of color as mentally retarded. The fight against the misclassification and overrepresentation of black students in EMR would bring the issue of special education placement based on IQ test results front and center in *Larry P. v. Riles* and *PASE v. Hannon*.

On November 23, 1971, a class-action complaint was filed against the San Francisco school board and extended to the entire State of California three years later. Wilson C. Riles, superintendent of public instruction for the State of California, was the named defendant. The plaintiffs—Larry P. and elementary students attending San Francisco Unified School District (SFUD)—challenged the defendant's use of IQ tests for placement of students in educable mentally retarded classes. They argued that the actions of SFUD and the State of California were unconstitutional. The court determined the tests were indeed culturally biased, favoring white middle-class students. In addition, the plaintiffs asked for a re-evaluation of all black students in EMR classes. If administrators placed black students in EMR classes, argued the attorneys for *Larry P.,* then black student enrollment should be proportional to their total number in the district. The plaintiffs also asked that the district provide supplementary assistance to help black EMR students return to general education classes. In California, enrollment in special education classes peaked at fifty-eight thousand by the late 1960s. Twenty-seven percent of EMR students in special education were black. Black students, however, only accounted for 9 percent of the state's school population. The federal district court granted a preliminary injunction in favor of the plaintiffs, which the defendants immediately appealed to the Ninth Circuit. In August 1974, the Court of Appeals for the Ninth Circuit affirmed the lower court's decision. It was at this point that the order was modified to include all black children in EMR classes across the state of California.

The plaintiffs also used the existing language in the California EMR code to argue that the law promoted an inferior curriculum. The state's EMR law clearly spelled out the goals of EMR classes, one of which was not to emphasize the teaching of basic skills: "The educational goals for the educable mentally retarded are not reading, writing, and arithmetic per se."[49] The California EMR law explicitly stated that "the primary instructional goals for the mentally retarded are set forth in Education Code Section 6902 as 'social adjustment' and 'economic usefulness.'"[50] These classes emphasized the importance of living skills in personal care rather than higher-order thinking and comprehension skills. Black students placed in EMR classes learned very little that could advance them toward a college-bound education. Reading as well as writing and math were considered secondary learning objectives in the EMR curriculum. As the California statute stated, "The pupil should be able to do some reading." The language in the California statute and in the EMR program literature bore some resemblance to the explicit beliefs of Stanford University professor Lewis Terman. In 1916, Terman advocated for the segregation of students deemed slow and feebleminded: "Children of this group should be segregated in special classes and be given instruction which is concrete and practical. They cannot master abstractions, but they can often be made efficient workers, able to look out for themselves."[51] Critics recognized that inferior, separate classes trapped black and brown students inside a "special education" built on low expectations. The slow pace of the curriculum made it nearly impossible for black EMR students to return to regular classes after placement.[52] San Francisco Unified and the State of California found themselves in the position of having to defend not only an inferior EMR curriculum and racist placement practices, but seventy years of arguments about hereditary intelligence.

The trial forced the San Francisco Unified School District and the State of California to provide an explanation for the significant black presence in EMR classes. The defendants had two options: either to argue that the disproportional placement was indeed based on hereditary intelligence or reject this long-standing belief altogether. Rejecting the idea of hereditary intelligence proved impossible, as the idea had long ago constructed the notion of "feebleminded" people, shaped our beliefs about them, and justified decades of mistreatment.[53] While environmental critiques against fixed notions of intelligence proved powerful, hereditary views of intelligence remained influential. Arthur Jensen, educational psychologist at the University of California at Berkeley, and the greatest proponent of the idea of fixed intelligence in the 1960s and 1970s, advanced the thesis that heritability is 80 percent genes and 20 percent environment. Professor Arthur Jensen submitted a detailed brief to the *Larry P.* case supporting the notion that intelligence is hereditary and can be measured by IQ tests. Jensen's signature essay in 1969, much of which made its way into the case, posed the question, "How much can we boost IQ and scholastic achievement?" Jensen's answer: very little. Believing that African American intelligence existed one standard deviation below the mean of white people, Jensen argued that 80 percent of race differences could be explained in "genotypes" along with the interaction of phenotypes (an individual's physical attributes—appearance, structure, and body functions; a person's physiological state as either normal or pathological; and a person's sociocultural background). Though genotypes, according to Jensen, are "the totality of factors that make up the genetic complement of the individual," what is ultimately inherited or passed on to an individual is the "proportion of phenotypic variance due to the variance in genotypes."[54] Jensen's argument, supported at trial by Professor Robert A. Gordon, stated that "natural selection has resulted in black persons having a 'gene pool' that dooms them as a group to less intelligence."[55] The defendants in *Larry P. v. Riles,* invoking the research of Jensen and others, claimed there was a higher rate of mental retardation in black and English language learners.

The fetish of the IQ score worked against the defendants in *Larry P.* A careful analysis of the politics of black student placement in EMR classes, and the scientific reasoning behind it, discredited Jensen's arguments, making it difficult for the state and its subdivisions to defend at trial. Since the late 1960s, the California State Department of Education had been under pressure from the civil rights, Black Power, and Chicano movement organizations about the overrepresentation issue, forcing the state to enact House Resolution 444, which called for "the study of the problem of over enrollment of minorities in EMR classes." Fred Hanson, a state board administrator with no expertise in IQ scoring, was questioned on the appropriateness of placement methods. He was unable to provide a rationale for the use of IQ tests, although IQ scores played a substantial role in the placement of students into EMR classes. Hanson told the court it was only one of several determinants. His testimony was contradicted by Robert Whiteneck, the director of special education in the Berkeley schools from 1965–1975, who asserted that the district was overreliant on IQ scores and felt "that the number has some sort of very definite magic-determining effect on their decisions." Professor Alice Watkins, an expert in the study of EMR classes at California State University Los Angeles, agreed with Whiteneck. Professor Jane Mercer of the University of California at Riverside found a strong correlation between IQ test scores and the overenrollment of minority students in her own research. A study conducted by the California State Department of Education on EMR placement concluded that "the record of the I.Q. score was clearly the most scrupulously kept record, and it appears to have been the most important one." Judge Wright, who worked on the *Hobson v. Hansen* case, commented that the entire placement process revolves around the IQ test. "Retardation is defined in terms of the I.Q. test"[56]

The case revealed that it was not only IQ tests that misclassified students but also the definition of mental retardation itself. In the early 1970s, the American Association of Mental Deficiency (AAMD) changed the statistical meaning of mental retardation. Demonstrating the whimsical nature of the concept of mental retardation, its statistical definition from the 1959–1961 Manual on Terminology and Classification was based on the stated definition of mental retardation as "subaverage intellectual functioning." In a decade, the criteria for mental retardation changed from one standard deviation below the mean (IQ 85) to two (IQ 70). The court reported in the *Larry P.* case that "in the 1973 revision of the AAMD Manual . . . the definition was changed to 'significantly subaverage general intellectual functioning,' now meaning two standard deviations below the mean. The AAMD's decision essentially reduced the number of mentally retarded Americans from 15 percent to 2 percent" overnight.[57] California Senate Bill No. 33 announced: "No minor shall be placed in a special education class for the mentally retarded if he scores higher than two standard deviations below the norm."[58] California immediately saw a decrease in new classification cases of EMR students, but many current black and Latinx students were still stigmatized by the label and they remained in EMR classes.

In spite of the AAMD's statistical change, the issue of culture was at the heart of *Larry P.* The plaintiffs marshalled evidence to support the claim that IQ tests were culturally biased. First, a statement by Dr. David Wechsler, who developed the WISC test in the 1940s, and served as a plaintiff witness, conceded that IQ tests were culturally biased when he first standardized his test in 1944: "Though we have tested a large number of colored persons, our standardization is based upon white subjects only."[59] In addition, the sub-tests in WISC and Stanford-Binet that purported to measure vocabulary failed to account for the various ways in which people understood and employed the English language. Dr. Asa Hilliard, a plaintiff witness, argued, "Vocabulary is not standard, even when people use the same word. So even before you are able to . . . figure out the answer to a problem, you first have to ensure that the examiner and the examinee understand the word in the same way."[60] Related to vocabulary subtests, the court argued that "cultural differences can also be found in specific test items."[61] For instance, a WISC test contained a "fight item" on it, posing a question to students "what would they do if struck by a smaller child of the same sex?" The correct answer was that it is wrong to hit the child back. It was reported at the trial that "black children aged six and seven missed this item . . . twice as often as their white counterparts." "The difference," said the court, "can only be attributed to a cultural variation at that age."[62] "Similarly," the court concluded, "it may be that such questions as who wrote *Romeo and Juliet*, who discovered America, and who invented the light bulb, are culturally biased."[63] Each question elicited different cultural responses from black students who perhaps had never heard of William Shakespeare; who understood that indigenous people were in the Americas before Columbus; and Louis Latimer's invention of the filament made him equally as important to the invention of the light bulb as did Thomas Edison. Sociologist Robert Williams raised this point to the American Psychological Association in proposing to introduce a black intelligence test, what he called BITCH, to raise awareness about inherent cultural bias on IQ tests.

The issue of biased standardized intelligence tests did not make California unique. In fact, the late civil rights movement made fighting racial bias in intelligence testing an essential priority, implicating other school districts such as Chicago Public Schools and Boston Public Schools. As in *Larry P.,* black parents challenged the IQ tests, the disproportionate number of black students in EMR classes, the EMR placement process, and the district's (and state's) continued use of IQ tests. Black parents argued that their children's rights were violated under the equal protection clause of the Fourteenth Amendment, Title VI of the Civil Rights Act of 1964, section 504 of the Rehabilitation Act of 1973, and the Education for All Handicapped Children Act of 1975. Challenges to the entire system of misplacement sometimes worked out favorably for black plaintiffs as in *Larry P.*; at other times, they lost in court. Special education emerged as another discriminatory system that elicited a new round of black social activism. Multiple voices began to agree that black students should receive appropriate educational and academic support, and if some black students are indeed disabled, then a more accurate diagnosis of their disability should come forth. The decisions rendered by judges, favorably and unfavorably, in the 1970s onward marked the beginning of an increasing number of black students identified as LD.

While the Northern District of California ruled in favor of the plaintiffs in *Larry P.,* the United States District Court for the Northern District of Illinois rendered a different decision. The case of *Parents in Action on Special Education (PASE) v. Hannon* was tried over a three-week period in January 1980.[64] Parents of children placed in EMR classes challenged the use of IQ tests as a method of classifying and placing black and Latinx students in EMR classes. Similar to *Larry P.,* the plaintiffs claimed that intelligence tests were racially biased. But unlike the conclusions in *Larry P.,* the court argued the Chicago Public Schools system did not have a specific objective to discriminate against children when it misclassified them as mentally retarded. Like California, the politics of black student misplacement functioned with the imprimatur of state law. The Illinois school statute required classes for students diagnosed as mentally retarded. If students were incapable of learning "profitably and efficiently," in a regular classroom, the state provided classes for educable mentally handicapped (EMH) students "designed to make them economically useful and socially adjusted."[65] The EMH curriculum taught students at a slower pace with "subject matter . . . oriented toward socialization, language skills and vocational training."[66] The EMH program in Chicago Public Schools also provided a certificate after graduation, but this diploma did not qualify the student for college. Thus, not only were EMH classes in Chicago Public Schools grossly overpopulated with black students, but the program also allowed white students an extra advantage in general education classes. While the court accepted some of the facts concerning black misplacement and overrepresentation, it nevertheless declared that Chicago Public Schools did not *purposely* aim to misplace and overrepresent them.

In the late 1960s and early 1970s, a major part of the local civil rights movement was already confronting problems inside Chicago Public Schools. Black activism stubbornly addressed segregated conditions black students faced within an "integrated" system. The movement to improve education in Chicago led to the filing of *PASE v. Hannon*. The question before the court was straightforward: was there an unlawful intent to segregate students of color from their white peers through the *intentional* misclassification of lower income black and Latinx students? This question formed part of the broader one posed by desegregation lawsuits across the country. While courts addressed the question of the *intent* to segregate in schools and classrooms, the civil rights movement dealt with the question of segregation's effect, and from that standpoint, the answer to the question was a resounding "yes." Segregation had devastating impacts on black students and their families. Civil rights groups, like the Woodland Organization, United Neighborhood Organization, People's Coalition, as part of the broader Coordinating Council of Community Organizations, applied pressure on the issue of differential conditions in black and white schools. Although segregation had been illegal in Chicago, a de facto system endured. White children attended half-empty schools with better conditions, while Chicago Public Schools packed black students into overcrowded "temporary units." Superintendent Benjamin Willis favored neighborhood schools, which allowed segregation to persist. Black activists equally persisted in the 1960s, leading to Willis's removal from his position.

With Willis's two successors proving no better, Chicago school reform became increasingly encumbered by central administrative bureaucratic politics. Superintendents James Redmond and Joseph Hannon favored the well-being of middle- and upper-class white families over low-income black families, appeasing city hall at every turn. The top-level administration of CPS held close ties to Mayor Richard Daley and his successors, Michael Bilandic and Jane Byrne, and mayors held significant influence over the appointments of school administrators and contracts. The few appointees who strove to reform Chicago Public Schools had no support. The powerful Chicago Teachers Union, a staunch critic of Chicago Public Schools' administrative bureaucracy, remained locked in wage and fiscal crises that saw shifting and misplaced funds contributing to the unequal conditions of schools and educational programming in Chicago Public Schools. Parents and community organizers were not satisfied with the pace of the administration's attempted reforms of a broken system, and neither were they sympathetic to the larger reform issues. Black students were still learning in segregated schools and educators continued to label them "mentally retarded" at disproportionate rates compared with white students.

Rendering a decision against intentional misclassification seemed likely when, in the 1978–1979 school year, black students comprised 62 percent of the school population in Chicago Public Schools but accounted for 82 percent of EMR classes. In addition, plaintiff witnesses presented current research perspectives on the problems with IQ tests. Both the plaintiff and the defendant made similar arguments in *Larry P.* and trotted out the same supporters to strengthen their position. The *PASE* side argued that students labeled "mentally retarded" carried a serious social stigma and that the tests were racially biased. Dr. Leon J. Kamin of Princeton University argued that the tests measure "current performance." Dr. George Albee, professor of psychology from the University of Vermont, argued that the tests measured a student's familiarity with white culture. Dr. Robert Williams, from the Association of Black Psychologists, demonstrated how each test question manifested a cultural bias. The defendants countered, affirming that the tests gauged a child's current skill level and that the scores "correlate significantly with his prospects of succeeding in schools."[67] Two other defendant witnesses, school psychologists Dr. Terrence Hines and Elmer Smith, agreed that the tests indicate "the areas of a child's mental strengths and weaknesses."[68] The judge concluded that, overall, the tests (Stanford-Binet, WISC and WISC-R tests) contained only one culturally biased question, believing it was not enough to significantly affect student scores. Judge Grady called out the judge in the *Larry P.* case, explaining, "Judge Peckham heard a number of the same witnesses who testified here, including Professors Kamin, Albee and Williams and Dr. Gloria Powell. He found their testimony persuasive. As by now obvious, the witnesses and the arguments which persuaded Judge Peckham have not persuaded me."[69] After Grady's decision, Chicago Public Schools continued its racialized practice of misplacing students in EMR classes. Though Chicago Public Schools prevailed, the Chicago grassroots movement for educational change and a federal desegregation lawsuit forced Chicago Public Schools to pay some attention to the issue of misclassification and overrepresentation.

Designs for Change (DFC) was a nonprofit organization aimed at improving the basic public school experience for children in Chicago and greater Illinois. Founded in 1977 by attorney Donald R. Moore, DFC became known nationally for their research and advocacy in public education on behalf of "low-income, minority, and handicapped students."[70] DFC focused on "improving the quality of 'special education' programs for handicapped children; improving the capacity of public schools to teach children to read; and improving the way school districts use their financial resources."[71] In December 1982, the DFC published a report entitled *Caught in the Web: Misplaced Children in Chicago's Classes for the Mentally Retarded*. The report called the misclassification problem in Chicago schools a "blatant injustice" and sought to expose every aspect of the practice. "Chicago has been the largest misclassifier of students assigned to classes for the mentally retarded in the United States," the report said. CPS has "more than 12,000 children in EMH (educable mentally handicapped) classes for the last decade, almost twice as many children as another school system in the country." DFC believed of the twelve thousand students, "approximately 7,000 ... do not belong in them and could ... move back into the regular school program." The DFC then made a startling discovery. Out of the twelve thousand students, "more than 10,000 of the students in Chicago's EMH classes are black."[72]

After the *PASE* lawsuit, Chicago Public Schools agreed in theory to work toward nondiscriminatory placement practices in their schools as part of an agreement with the federal government to settle a desegregation lawsuit. The Department of Health, Education, and Welfare (HEW) threatened to sue the City of Chicago for delaying a two-decade effort to desegregate Chicago Public Schools and required busing as the means to do so. Unlike the judge in *PASE,* an Office of Civil Rights/HEW report "concluded that Chicago school officials intentionally created and maintained a racially discriminatory and dual school system."[73] Some Chicago schools in certain neighborhoods were either predominantly black or overwhelmingly white. The federal government desired to break up this racial concentration by reducing enrollments to no "more than 50 percent white and 65 percent black."[74] Despite "settled" lawsuits and other coercive measures by the federal government, Chicago Public Schools continued maintaining racially imbalanced schools, which had taken place under the supervision of three different Chicago Public Schools superintendents, all who capitulated to white families that threatened to leave the city for the suburbs if desegregation efforts were not at least voluntary.[75] The same was true when it came time to change special education placement practices as DFC noted: "The school system indicated that it would change the testing procedures used to place children in EMH classes, retest all children currently enrolled in EMH, and provide transitional help to those children who were misclassified and should be returned to regular classrooms."[76] The district did not make significant changes in special education practices either. The class-action lawsuit *Corey H. v. Board of Education of the City of Chicago* filed in the early 1990s continued the struggle parents had waged since the 1960s. The case "demonstrated beyond doubt that the Chicago public schools have been and continue to be saddled with archaic notions of educating children with disabilities in restrictive placements determined more by the categories of their disabilities than by their individual needs."[77]

In Boston, black parents mobilized in the Parents' Association for South End Schools and the United South End Settlement organization, which helped craft and release a report entitled *End Educational Entombment* in 1968.[78] This report alleged that Boston Public Schools misdiagnosed black students as mentally retarded, effectively placing them in EMR classes instead of providing proper resources. To prove this was indeed the case, black parents forced Boston Public Schools to reexamine twenty-two children diagnosed as mentally retarded by the district. In a follow-up report titled *End of Educational Entombment II*, which revealed the results of the reexaminations, sixteen of the twenty-two students were found to be misplaced. Instead of being placed in EMR classes, the report concluded the students needed resources to help with their learning disabilities, remedial reading, speech, and/or emotional disturbances. Emboldened by the results of this small reappraisal, the parents of the sixteen students demanded Boston Public Schools and the Massachusetts State Department of Education reexamine all students in EMR classes as well as provide appropriate resources to any misplaced student. By the end of 1969, an internal group called the Boston School Committee, composed of district and state educational officials, passed a series of resolutions in response to the report. The resolutions called for "better testing practices; intensive-in-service training programs for special class teachers and principals; and a Special Class Assistance Council . . . composed equally of parents, mental health professionals, and community agency representatives."[79] The committee did not agree to reexamine all students classified as EMR, and neither did they make good on their set-forth resolutions. Though the original sixteen children found misclassified were placed in mainstream classes or classes for the emotionally disturbed and the learning disabled, the Special Class Assistance Council failed to diligently aid in the students' transition process.

Attempting to reverse racist placement practices held several implications, one of which was the inherent contradiction in equal educational opportunity discourse and practice. On the one hand, the main thrust of the civil rights movement was to "de-concentrate" segregated, under-resourced schools attended overwhelmingly by poor black and Latinx children. On the other hand, educational disability rights meant providing special and compensatory education services in the form of special classes to students identified as educable mentally retarded or culturally deprived. Equal educational opportunity did not break up hyper-segregated schools over the long term, nor did it stop the terrible practice of misplacing black students in EMR classes. Equal educational opportunity emerged as an aspirational ideal that never fully manifested. Adam

Nelson took note of this paradox, writing, "For minority students in these classes, it was not always clear which aspect of their placement ensured equal educational opportunities: was it placement in a racially balanced school or placement in a racially imbalanced special-compensatory program?"[80] Another contradiction appearing in the 1970s that would have consequences in the 1980s and 1990s was the idea that black students could be learning disabled (LD). This belief went against conventional wisdom until teachers, administrators, and even judges used LD to explain black unteachability in similar ways as they did EMR. When Judge Grady in the *PASE* case argued the "court found that the children did not score poorly on the tests because of their race. They scored poorly due to their learning disabilities that the tests actually revealed," his opinion spoke volumes to the arbitrary character of special education placement and the shell-game practices of teachers, administrators, and psychologists.[81] The belief that a learning disabled student could be black or brown marks not only a shift in the racial demographics of LD but also the belief that scores on an intelligence test and ranges on an IQ scale can be equally arbitrary, contradictory, and politicized from one decade to the next.

Politicizing Underachievement: Shifting Black Students from Educable Mentally Retarded to Learning Disabled

As families and grassroots organizations kept the spotlight on EMR in the courts, the number of new black EMR cases began to diminish slightly in some states.[82] While the legal challenges to EMR forced school districts to examine their placement practices, scholars in the 1970s and 1980s applied greater scrutiny to the definition of EMR and questioned its meaning.[83] Concomitant with a decrease in new EMR cases, the number of black students identified as learning disabled increased rapidly between 1969 and 1979, causing one observer to label it an "epidemic."[84] At the heart of the decline of EMR and the rise of LD was the reracialization of disability categories.[85] Black students began shifting from EMR to LD due to the way in which underachievement, behavior, and mild retardation were reconceptualized in relationship to learning disability.[86] Some argued that functional similarities existed between the learning disabled and "mildly retarded."[87] Others contended that a relationship existed between learning disability and cultural and economic disadvantage.[88]

The placement of black students in LD also spoke to the issue of how the federal government defined LD and how the states utilized the category.[89] Just as EMR proved to be an ambiguous category, so too was LD.[90] LD was often defined by what it was not (its exclusionary clauses), allowing challenges to its previous racial and socioeconomic exclusivity and to its overreliance on the medical model. Like EMR, any close examination of LD in the 1970s and early 1980s reveals the number of cautionary tales about its ambiguity, subjectivity, and racialization. Policymakers, state educational agencies, administrators, teachers, and scholars alike appeared flummoxed by the process of identification, classification, and placement. Following the debates in the 1970s, one is surely left with the impression that both the systems of general and special education believed many black students were "unmainstreamable" and unteachable.

The larger story of EMR and LD is the story of white resistance to school integration. Professors James Ysseldyke and Bob Algozzine wrote candidly, "A fundamental mission of American schools is the education of all students, regardless of race, religion, sex, national origin, or creed. Yet it is apparent that either schools fail to educate significant numbers of students, or significant numbers of students fail to profit sufficiently from schooling."[91] Failing to educate students could mean poor instruction, low teacher expectation, or a dull curriculum. Failing to educate could also mean structural impediments that entangle and entrap students in separate systems. Separate systems like special education purportedly promoted positive educational outcomes. In the early twentieth century, psychologists and educators heralded differential education as a positive transformation in school restructuring due to the enforcement of compulsory attendance laws. Though differential education constituted the birth of black special education, the outcome for black students in a separate system proved anything but positive in the long twentieth century.

In the 1960s and 1970s, equal educational opportunity emerged as the latest example of progressive reform in eliminating segregated schools and providing new services to white "handicapped" students. But progressive educational reform in the 1960s and 1970s resulted in the same outcome as it did in the early 1900s: the (re)segregation of black students. The willingness to use white-imagined disability categories like LD to resegregate black students in the name of equal educational opportunity made the identification of LD more suspect since LD was never designed for them in the first place. The twin manifestation of equal educational opportunity and resegregation exhibits the extent to which people in power will maintain the status quo. LD performed the work of corralling bodies and separating black students from the mainstream even when black students were not LD's intended audience. The tragedy is that many students have real disabilities that need addressing. However, in a racist educational context, ill-defined and ambiguous disability categories provided an opportunity for indifferent teachers, administrators, and psychologists at best (or racist ones at worst) to remake the disability categorical landscape. In the larger context of equal educational opportunity, shuffling, labeling, and transferring bodies from one disability category to another became the solution for dealing with black students few wanted to teach on a regular basis. Adam Nelson, professor of educational policy studies, described the double-edged sword of equal educational opportunity in Boston with the law Chapter 766 that mandated "services to meet the special needs of all children." As black families fought the misplacement of their children in special education, white psychologists and teachers, Nelson argued, "refused to place minority students in regular classes when their diagnosis clearly showed that they could benefit from isolated remedial programs."[92] Thus, in the 1970s, not only did equal educational opportunity hold different meanings for different student constituencies, but equal education opportunity also produced different outcomes.

In 1975, several months before Congress passed the Education for All Handicapped Children Act and it was signed into law by President Ford, concerns of a learning disability epidemic proliferated. In January of that year, a critical *New York Times* article noticed the groundswell of national concern about learning disability. The paper explained, "A decade ago almost no one heard of the malady. In the early seventies, it was estimated that 3 to 10 per cent of the school population had learning disabilities; and now responsible spokespersons are saying that up to 40 per cent of our youngsters are so afflicted." Unlike EMR in the 1960s, LD enjoyed the strong support of policymakers and scholars, which secured federal funding for states and districts across the country. Indeed, from 1963, when the identity of learning disability was born, to 1969, when the Specific Learning Disabilities Act passed, LD became the categorical house that Samuel Kirk built. Narrowly defined as a "minimal brain dysfunction" and mainly serving students slightly below and above normal on the IQ scale who happened to be white, LD endured scrutiny from many corners, and its defenders had some explaining to do to the American public. *The New York Times* noted that "the movement takes most of its cues from medicine. The children first described as 'learning disabled' were those who shared some behavior with brain-injured children but had no organic damage. The children behaved eccentrically despite a background of good homes or read poorly despite adequate I.Q.'s, it was hypothesized, because of some undefined disorder—faulty physiological wiring, a chemical imbalance, a central nervous lag." Then the dam broke. Almost overnight, the ranks of the learning disabled swelled, according to the *Times,* allowing students with "minimal brain dysfunction to bad manners" to become classified. One LD practitioner quipped, "If a child got through our screens without something being picked up, we'd call him Jesus Christ."[93]

To be sure, a new policy and the availability of federal money hastened the professionalization and proliferation of learning disabilities. But at the very moment LD gained greater legitimacy, people inside and outside of special education questioned its current state of knowledge. Building on the work of neurologist Herbert J. Grossman, professors John T. Neisworth and John G. Greer argued that mild mental retardation and learning disability were functionally similar, writing "there has been no convincing evidence that mild or educable mental retardation is associated with organic dysfunction. Likewise, research on the relationships between brain injury or dysfunction and learning disability is characterized by inconclusive and contradictory findings. Too often, when an inference of brain injury cannot be authenticated, it is then called *minimal cerebral dysfunction.*"[94] Both EMR and LD had relied on MCD (minimal cerebral dysfunction) or MBD (minimal brain dysfunction) science. The operative word has always been "minimal," as the term signified medical certainty, although it was unable to explain both the etiologies of mental retardation and learning disability. Nevertheless, challenges surfaced. Herbert Grossman was one of the first to make this observation in 1966 in an essay entitled "The Child, the Teacher, and the Physician." Neisworth and Greer quoted the neurologist, writing, "There is no syndrome, no aggregate of neurological signs, that can be correlated with any specific learning and/or behavior disorder."[95]

Samuel Kirk could not have anticipated how the passage of the Specific Learning Disabilities Act in 1969 and the Education for All Handicapped Children Act in 1975 would change who was identified as learning disabled. Title VI-G of the Specific Learning Disabilities Act, carrying over to the 1975 law, created Child Service Demonstration Centers (CSDCs) across the country. Between 1971 and 1980, at least 97 centers operated in the United States. The CSDCs exposed the distance between LD, as defined by the likes of Samuel Kirk, and the practice of identifying new LD cases among students of color. However, this is where the proverbial definitional rubber of LD met the projected road of the presumed LD student. Though Kirk insisted that the LD student population hovered around 1 to 3 percent, CSDCs identified a higher percentage. Undoubtedly, many of the students identified as learning disabled by the CSDCs were white, but many more were unexpectedly African American, Latinx, and Indigenous students. After collecting and analyzing the data, CSDC observers found the results surprising. "The overall impression," reported a study on the demonstration centers, "is supportive of the conclusion that many of the CSDC's efforts (perhaps a majority) were directed towards the provisions of services to the culturally handicapped pupils ... to direct services to unserved and underserved populations. This meant a focus on inner city pupils and rural pupils—both of whom are likely to have larger minority constituents."[96] Arguably, the CSDCs marked the beginning of students of color being classified as learning disabled in larger numbers. At this critical point in the history of special education, the exclusive whiteness of LD remained uncertain as black and brown LD cases increased across the states. A group of researchers examining the centers' data inferred that "certainly, learning disability services, as constituted by the various CSDCs, did not constitute a white preserve of educational privilege."[97]

The criteria used by the CSDCs tell us a story of how LD expanded racially and definitionally. The four broad areas of diagnostic measures were academic (low achievement), behavioral (attendance and behavior problems), cognitive disabilities (language difficulties), and possible retardation (developmental lag). One of the strongest points made by the team of researchers was that the CSDCs' data did not support the definitional exclusivity of learning disabilities as defined by Samuel Kirk and the federal government. The researchers argued that the CSDCs expanded the notion of what constituted a learning disability. From the perspective of CSDCs, the criteria matched the profile of students walking through their doors. Since the Specific Learning Disabilities Act was passed in 1969, and the CSDCs opened in 1971, there were "protests that, despite the definition, learning disabilities were often environmentally induced, that behavioral disorders were a frequent if not a necessary correlational problem of learning disabilities, that the distinction between learning disabilities and mental retardation was artificial." "We can have," the authors of the study noted, "learning disabilities with cultural deprivation, learning disabilities with behavior disorders, learning disabilities with neurological problems, etc."[98] The authors rendered their final judgment about LD: "Any consensus on the definition of LD, if indeed one ever existed, has, of course, dissipated since 1971."[99]

Surveyed in both 1975 and 1981, learning disability experts revealed deeper fissures in special education through their responses. The most prominent researchers in the field were asked four broad questions:

Do you believe that "learning disabilities" is a viable classification for handicapped children? Do you believe that learning disabilities are clinically identifiable by specific symptoms or by a constellation of various symptoms which differentiate them from other problems associated with learning (e.g., cultural diversity, lack of educational opportunity, etc.)? What do you believe to be the probable percentage of school-age children with identifiable learning disabilities? How old do you feel a child must be before such a learning disability can be positively identified with assurance that the symptoms observed are not simply a reflection of developmental lag or other confounding developmental conditions?[100]

While the first two questions in the 1975 and 1981 surveys yielded high affirmative responses (78 and 88 percent, respectively), commentary from those who answered "no" spoke to the courage of a handful of researchers. "No one (professional educator or otherwise)," said Bob Algozzine, at the University of Florida, "has been able to demonstrate to me that a specific, distinctly unique group of behaviors differentiate LD children from many of their classmates (often called other names). To build an empire on such a foundation is very dishonest."[101] Jim Ysseldyke of the University of Minnesota, reiterated Algozzine's position when he said,

"It is literally impossible to differentiate LD from ED, low achievers, etc."[102] LD had long been thought of as a disability of middle-class children with normal IQs, which allowed Kirk and others to conclude that LD was race neutral. But when the question was asked in the reverse, LD's whiteness and EMR's blackness seemed irrefutable. Jean Kealy and John McLeod wanted to know whether there was a "higher proportion of children diagnosed as learning disabled from families from higher socioeconomic status than there is from families of lower socioeconomic status?"[103] Their sample revealed this was indeed the case. Kealy and McLeod also posed a similar question about the relationship between socioeconomic status and mild mental retardation, discovering the opposite was true: that more children from poorer families were diagnosed as mildly retarded than middle-class ones. Kealy and McLeod placed a finer point on it when they added, "Diagnostic personnel must themselves guard against the prejudgment that low achievers in inner city schools are common retardates while their cousins in the suburbs are 'learning disabled.'"[104]

Samuel Kirk vehemently rejected both the expansion of LD and any major changes in its exclusionary definition. He reminded the public that he had coined the term "learning disability" for the very first time in 1962, which was subsequently adopted by the Association for Children with Learning Disabilities (ACLD) in 1963. Kirk exercised his privilege as the "originator" of the concept, and he received the support of a variety of disability organizations, such as the National Advisory Committee on Handicapped Children (NACHC). Kirk and the NACHC's definition was adopted by the United States Office of Education and by Congress in both the Specific Learning Disabilities Act (1969) and in the Education of All Handicapped Act (1975). The original definition in 1962 stated:

A learning disability refers to a retardation, disorder, or delayed development in one or more of the processes of speech, language, reading, spelling, writing, or arithmetic resulting from possible cerebral dysfunction and/or emotional or behavior disturbance and not from mental retardation, sensory deprivation, or cultural or instructional factors.[105]

The 1969 definition presented to Congress added the term "specific" and elaborated further:

The term "children with specific learning disabilities" means those children who have a disorder in one or more of the basic psychological processes involved in understanding or in using language, spoken or written, which disorder may manifest itself in imperfect ability to listen, think, speak, read, write, spell, or do mathematical calculations. Such disorders include such conditions as perceptual handicaps, brain injury, minimal brain dysfunction, dyslexia, and developmental aphasia. Such terms does not [sic] include children who have learning problems which are primarily the result of visual, hearing, or motor handicaps, of mental retardation, or emotional disturbance, or environmental, cultural or economic disadvantage.[106]

Though this became the standard federal definition for learning disability, a 1976 survey revealed only 57 percent of the states adhered to the federal definition along with new federal guidelines.[107]

The Education for All Handicapped Children Act brought to the surface what Kirk saw as the most important aspect of learning disability: the "discrepancy between the child's achievement and his capacity to learn." The 1975 Act and the federal guidelines etched in stone the discrepancy between ability and achievement, arguing that the difference between the two must be "severe" for a student to be considered learning disabled.[108] The discrepancy issue (ability versus achievement or expected performance versus actual performance) added another layer to the debate in the 1970s and 1980s, raising the issue of identifying students as learning disabled.[109] Samuel Kirk and his wife W. D. Kirk represented a group proposing that the discrepancy issue make its way into a new definition of learning disability. At a 1975 Division of Children with Learning Disabilities conference, the Kirk group announced that a "specific learning disability is a serious impediment to cognitive functioning that (a) is manifested in such wide discrepancies among developmental and/or school achievement areas that special, remedial, and/or compensatory teaching is required; and (b) exists independently of, or in addition to mental retardation, sensory deficits, emotional disturbance, or lack of opportunity to learn."[110] In the following year, Congress asked the Office of Education to refine the 1969 definition. Though the Office of Education could not produce an agreed-upon definition from the experts that included the word "discrepancy," it tried to create a discrepancy-based formula that school districts could use to identify students who struggled with learning disabilities. The Office of Education put forward a 50 percent discrepancy formula; however, special education lobbyists rejected it in favor of an understanding of discrepancy deemed "severe." The federal guidelines in 1977 announced a school team may determine that a child has a specific learning disability if: "(1) the child does not achieve commensurate with his or her age and ability levels in one or more areas: oral expression; listening comprehension; written expression; basic reading skill; reading comprehension; mathematics calculation or mathematics reasoning, and (2) the child has a *severe* discrepancy between achievement and intellectual ability in one or more of the following areas."[111]

Though discrepancy emerged as the cornerstone of LD identification, "severe" served as the operative word. But since no definitional criteria for "severe discrepancy" was provided by the federal government in its guidelines, school districts had to decide what severity of underachievement represented a learning disability. An analysis of the federal regulations debates sheds light on what position remained the strongest: "While the application of the proposed LD regulations had been based on a formula, the overwhelming opposition to the use of the formula led to the elimination of both the formula and the specification of a specific severity level for eligibility."[112] The LD debate remained one of the most controversial topics in the 1970s and early 1980s, not solely because of its complicated formulas and regulations but also because it was losing its exclusive association with white middle-class students. Contested definitions of LD made one thing clear: those struggling students represented a cross-section of young people in the United States irrespective of race and class. Samuel Kirk's insistence on LD's distinctive difference from the brand of "underachieving" caused by mental retardation revealed its continued racialization. A growing skepticism emerged in the special education research literature about the differences between LD and EMR. Professors Algozzine and Ysseldyke noted: What remained unsettled was the "extent to which learning disabled children could be differentiated from low achievers and the nature of identified differences."[113] Samuel Kirk attempted to settle the debate by conducting his own research on Child Service Demonstration Centers, asking, "Will the real learning-disabled student please stand up?"[114]

Kirk was convinced that many students identified as LD in the 1970s were indeed low achievers, but they were "mildly retarded" low achievers, not learning-disabled ones. "To some," Kirk wrote, "mentally retarded children are considered to have 'generalized' learning disabilities, and attempts have been made to change the label 'mental retardation' to 'general learning disabilities.'"[115] To prove that students in the centers were more EMR than LD, Kirk averaged the IQ of all the students and found that 35 percent had scores below 90, with "eleven states reporting a small percentage of their children as having IQ's of 69 and below." Kirk also asked teachers if the students they served were severely learning disabled, moderate, or mild. An analysis from twenty-one states revealed that the "median percentage of children rated as severe was 54 percent with a high of 84 percent and a low of 13 percent." Kirk also examined a discrepancy criterion used in the original CSDC data set, revealing 25 percent of children assessed had a severe learning disability. After Kirk finished analyzing the CSDC data, he reaffirmed his long-stated position about LD and who the disability represented. "It would appear from the data that the majority of children in the projects, although underachieving to some degree," wrote Kirk, "would not qualify as specific learning-disabled children, since many of the children were retarded equally in reading, spelling, and arithmetic and were therefore not specific but general in academic retardation."[116] For Kirk, "specific" academic retardation in subject areas applied to the white learning disabled; "general" academic retardation in all school matters, including academic subjects and behavior, applied to black and brown students. And if the black "educable retarded" can be identified now as learning disabled, Kirk conceded they should only be identified as general learning disabled, not the one codified in the 1969 and 1975 law.

Similar to the 1960s when Kirk lobbied vociferously for LD legislation by comparing it against EMR, he found himself once again arguing that black and brown underachievement was different from white underachievement. The "culturally deprived" of the 1960s and 1970s were now labeled "at-risk" students in the 1980s. The new term encapsulated the same mildly retarded children, indicating, according to Martinez and Rury "that the term 'at-risk' was introduced as a manner of describing children from poor or minority backgrounds with respect to their prospects of educational success."[117] "At-risk" could describe both a "disabled" black student that carried an individualized education plan (IEP), or it could refer to any struggling black student in public schools. Samuel Kirk could not disagree more. The thinking that black underachievement was pervasive kept many black students "at-risk," and in the mind of Kirk, not deserving of a specific learning disability identification and placement. Kirk called black academic struggles, "problems," suggesting that a prolonged association with academic failure should never be understood as a disability. "It was obvious that they were not dealing with specific learning disabilities," Kirk asserted, "but rather with a *general learning problem* [emphasis in original] in a number of subject areas as is generally found with (a) slow learning children, or (b) children from disadvantaged environments who have had unequal opportunities to learn."[118] This form of chronic underachievement, Kirk surmised, had been recognized in separate federal policies required to meet the needs of black and brown slow learners. "Admittedly, these children—slow learners, disadvantaged children, and others—need attention from compensatory programs under Title III or Title I" of the Elementary and Secondary Education Act.[119] The Board of Trustees of the Council for Learning Disabilities agreed with Kirk, announcing in 1986 that the significant increase in LD incidence rates was largely due to the "inclusion of students whose low achievement or underachievement reflects factors other than a learning disability (e.g., depressed intellectual functioning, lack of motivation, inadequate or inappropriate instruction, environmental disadvantage, cultural differences)." After the board took this position, it issued the following recommendation to state boards of education and school districts across the country: "Nonhandicapped low-achievers and underachievers who have already been misdiagnosed and misplaced should be removed immediately from learning disability services."[120]

No evidence indicates that states and districts withdrew any learning disability services from children during the 1980s. Quite the contrary, incident rates of students of color in LD increased during this period despite a growing chorus of scholars questioning LD's use of the discrepancy criteria. Several scholars suggested that LD represented a white disability "entitlement" program that Kirk and others went to great lengths to wall off from other students. "We believe it is wrong to argue that discrepancies are the best and only way of determining which low achievers should be eligible for special education," Algozzine and Ysseldyke suggested.[121] A discrepancy criteria functioned less as an identifier of learning disabilities and more of a regulator of controlling who should be included in the categorization. Algozzine and Ysseldyke were critical of both LD and the mechanisms used to keep certain students underrepresented, charging, "We think discrepancies have become a popular tool in the process of limiting a number of students who receive special education."[122] Vague definitions that use words like "psychological processes," "brain injured," "minimal brain and central nervous system dysfunction," along with "discrepancy formulas" treat LD as if it were a "technical problem." "It is not!" Algozzine and Ysseldyke continued:

> Rather, it is a social-policy problem. Students with learning disabilities can be found; they can be found in hundreds of ways, some of them incredibly sophisticated. Yet, little consensus will be achieved on how this ought to be done. Eligibility decisions are entitlement decisions; they are essentially third-party payment decisions. Highly qualified professionals with elaborate practical skills and knowledge (e.g., counseling, instructional design) are asked to make entitlement decisions. We believe it is a waste of professional time and effort.[123]

The more LD seemed embattled, the more entrenched it became with greater layers of complexity. Greater complexity made LD more difficult to define and understand, making the questioning of the disability less likely in the future.[124] "I believe that if we continue trying to define learning disabilities by using ill-defined concepts, we will forever be frustrated, for it is an illusive concept," concluded T. T. Lovitt, an expert on learning disabilities from the University of Washington. "We are bamboozled. It is as though someone stated a great hoax by inventing the term then tempting others to define it. And lo and behold, scores of task forces and others have taken the bait."[125]

Some observers went further in their critique of LD, calling it an imaginary disease. To say that LD is constructed is to trace its genealogy, to know much about both its present history and its trajectory back to the past. To invoke LD as imaginary disability, however, is to underline it as a myth as Thomas Finlan humored: "You may think LD exists since more than two million school children have currently been identified with this federally legislated disability, but LD does not exist anymore than there are witches in Salem, monsters in Loch Ness, or abominable snowmen in the Himalayas." Beyond the tongue-in-cheek wit, Finlan wanted to make a larger point about LD's subjectivity and nebulously defined concepts in the name of science but more so in the promotion of myth. Finlan's critique proved unforgiving when he surmised that "LD is a movement based on supposition, analogy, and guesswork. There never has been any scientific evidence that LD exists.... LD theory and practices keep changing to accommodate current research most of which contradicts previous LD guesswork." LD seemed like an attractively packaged legend to describe students "unable to learn what their peers learn." But instead of simply defining students who do not learn at the same pace as their peers, or are unable to profit from the same instruction or retain information differently, LD became an edifice of invention that described student challenges as "disorders" in the "psychological processes." Finlan's juxtaposition of the simple and the complex is a reminder of what Ray McDermott and colleagues wrote about researchers coming along and making things worse.[126] When Finlan began his career working closely with LD students, he experienced an epiphany that forced him to question his professional training and practice. "I began my training as a school psychologist in 1974 when LD was gaining favor. I was beset with doubts. I have struggled with the concept of LD since that time. For a long time, I was confused by the jargon and immobilized by my naivety, but eventually I came to one inescapable conclusion— *There is no such thing as LD.*"[127]

Despite the handful of heretics, LD was here to stay because the "monolithic bureaucracy of education" will keep the "myth intact."[128] Also here to stay were black and brown students searching for equal educational opportunities in a system that pinned inaccurate labels on them. If Algozzine and Ysseldyke were correct about learning disabilities evolving as both a social policy and disability problem, which meant a black and brown version based on *social policy* and a separate white one based on *disability*, then the future of LD required more hairsplitting by proponents and opponents alike. Learning disabilities could be "specific," "severe," and "general." Lloyd Dunn advanced the concept of "mild general learning disabled" (MGLD) as a potential place where the black and brown educable retarded can go to remove the educational stigma.

But Dunn's definition is not an example of stigma removal inasmuch as it another example of reifying racist thinking in special education:

> As contrasted to the general school population, these children were more likely (1) to have met defeat, frustration, and rejection in the regular grades where they were first placed; (2) to have exhibited substantial behavior disorders in general education; (3) to be from racial or ethnic minority groups; (4) to have parents who place little value on education; (5) to have inadequate health and nutritional provisions; (6) to be unclean and unkempt; (7) to live in poverty and deprivation; (8) to be boys rather than girls; (9) to come from broken or disorganized homes; (10) to be seriously retarded in schools; (11) to have restricted oral language skills in standard English; (12) to have obtained IQ scores ranging between 65 and 78 on individualized tests of verbal intelligence administered in standard English.[129]

Dunn may have issued a clarion call in the late 1960s about overrepresentation of students of color in EMR, but his counter-proposal only yielded a reshuffling from EMR to what he called MGLD. MGLD never became a category of disability. Yet it did signify the movement of black and brown students into LD with greater frequency. The mere fact that confusion and scrutiny continued to follow these students indicated that in no way was the system of special education finished with maligning them. As the ranks of black LD students swelled in many states, other characteristics of these students became a major focus of attention. "In spite of the innumerable combinations of disabilities which exist, mild retardation associated with emotional disturbance has been one of the most frequently found in special classes for the mildly retarded."[130] Emotional disturbance, social maladjustment, juvenile delinquency, and other kinds of behavior stood as "disabling" experiences on their own, leading to further misclassification and black student overrepresentation in the system of special education.

5

Emotional Behavior Disorder and Other Conduct Problems

The Intersection of Race, Research, and Policy

The term "seriously emotionally disturbed" includes children who are schizophrenic. It does not, however, include children who are socially maladjusted, unless it is determined they are also seriously emotionally disturbed.

—U.S. Congress, Education for All Handicapped Children Act of 1975, Pub. L. No. 94–142, 89 Stat

An emotional or behavioral disorder is whatever a culture's chosen authority figures designate as intolerable. Typically, it is behavior perceived to threaten the stability, insecurity, or values of that society.

—WILLIAM C. RHODES and JAMES L. PAUL, *Emotionally Disturbed and Deviant Children*

White inventions of "bad" behavior proved to be one of the most harmful fabrications of blackness. This made-up belief was, and remains, a product of other constructions about black bodies and minds.[1] Racist ideology framed black bodies as syphilitic, black minds as schizophrenic, and black behavior as delinquent and socially maladjusted.[2] This tripartite discourse about diseased bodies, inferior minds, and deviant behavior partly explains the overrepresentation of black students under state criteria for emotional behavior disorder (EBD), and under the federal designated category, seriously emotionally disturbed (SED).[3] The problem of overrepresentation today can be located in the circulation and recirculation of ideas about black emotions and behavior stemming from a composite of black people. Prior to the modern legal and administrative system of special education, white authorities judged black emotions and behavior as defective, deviant, and delinquent in the early to mid-twentieth century. These judgments flowed into EBD disability categories from the 1970s to the present. Black overrepresentation in EBD was not an oversight. An age-old discourse that defined African Americans as a conduct-disordered people created the disproportionate number of black EBD students.

Special education disability categories, such as seriously emotionally disturbed (SED), are replete with exclusionary definitional criteria. These categories are as much about what and whom it leaves out as what or whom it includes. For example, federal disability legislation, SED, excluded "social maladjusted" as a category deserving of protection. Special education scholars have described this particular exclusion as an "accident of history."[4] This exclusion of the "socially maladjusted," however, was not accidental. The omission of the "socially maladjusted" was Congress's way of denying disability services to black students who many believed exhibited the most antisocial behavior, thereby granting schools greater power to punish that behavior. Thus, understood at various times as incorrigible, antisocial, defective, delinquent, unruly, emotionally disturbed, and behavior disordered, black student behavior sat at the heart of special education thought and practice from the early twentieth century to the present. This chapter traces the history of black behavior from the 1950s through the late twentieth century and demonstrates how SED/EBD was historically determined to become disproportionately black.

Black Behavior in the Era of Equal Educational Opportunity

American history is marked by innumerable examples of white-defined black behavior. White people considered black behavior problematic when Africans resisted captivity on ships during the transatlantic slave trade. "Drapetomania" described enslaved blacks who frequently attempted to escape slavery. Early twentieth-century psychiatry, psychology, and other social sciences laid the groundwork for present-day notions of "bad" black student behavior and educational disability. From psychoanalytic theories to sociological and legal-criminological frameworks, these scholars shaped the debate about black emotion and behavior. They also gave us our common understanding of social maladjustment and delinquency against other kinds of comportment. Though people of all races, classes, and genders exhibited "bad" or questionable behavior, "hard core" social deviancy was attached to black, and mostly male, personhood. This perspective, fleshed out over decades, provided an understanding for legislators, teachers, school administrators, and lay people to distinguish between bad behavior and not-so-bad behavior, between "social maladjustment" and the more benign "emotionally disturbed."

Where we are today regarding black behavior and emotion is where we were yesterday. In an article from 1939 entitled, "Why the Presence of the Negro Constitutes a Problem in the American Social Order," the sociologist Edward B. Reuter answered his own question with a mix of profundity and simplicity: "The Negro is a problem in the American social order because his aspirations . . . are oriented toward a goal that a dominant [white] majority does not want to realize."[5] In foreclosing full-fledged black citizenship, white America continued to distort black life and culture by making the argument about black people's inability to adjust to white society. If black people were wholly or partly what white people proclaimed, then the variables remained, singly or in combination, black neighborhoods, black families, and black behavior, never what created the conditions—white systemic racism and exclusion.

Discrimination and exclusion in the labor and housing markets, political disenfranchisement, and denied educational opportunities placed African Americans on the lowest rung of the social order. Deficit-thinking perspectives found in influential medical and social science research justified this order. Marred and haunted by either biological or social pathological frameworks (or both), African Americans were victimized in the areas of research and policy. Research and policy worked in tandem to produce the system of special education through constructed ideas of black intelligence and behavior. Thus, white supremacist thinking influenced the research that eventually made its way into policy. Richard Valencia called deficit-thinking research "1) a mind-set molded by the fusion of ideology and science; 2) a dynamic form of social thought allegedly accounting for between-group behaviors; 3) an actual way of thinking to combat problems."[6] Invoking William Ryan's classic text, *Blaming the Victim,* Valencia concluded, "It follows logically from Ryan's (1971) analysis of 'victim-blamers and victims' that deficit thinking is a form of oppression."[7]

Biological and scientific ideas of inherited intelligence and behavior contrasted with social pathological models that described African American life and culture. While the biological model dominated during the early decades of the twentieth century, social-pathological schools of thought gained credence by the mid-century, which identified environmental factors linked to impoverished neighborhoods as the cause of black circumstances. By relocating the source of black intellectual incapability and mental incapacity to poor families and neighborhoods, the social-pathological model was posited as a scholarly upgrade from the ideas of heredity, intelligence, and behavior. Despite this paternalistic turn, the conclusions reached about black people were the same.[8]

Gunnar Myrdal's classic book, *An American Dilemma: The Negro Problem and Modern Democracy* (1944) examined the liberal creed of freedom and equality against the reality under which black Americans lived in the United States.[9] Instead of a dilemma in political creed and social practice, Helen McLean, of the Chicago Institute for Psychoanalysis, studied the psychodynamic dilemma she believed shaped black behavior. The dilemma resided in the psychic imbalance of being black in the United States. McLean argued that black behavior was rooted in internalized white prejudice, positing that "there is a complex psychological relationship, in which many of the constituent elements are unconscious."[10] Unconscious psychodynamic racial factors produced frustration and anxiety in African Americans, manifesting in antisocial behavior. The externalizing behavior of black people is a product of an impaired "emotional health" and a "neurotic character disturbance," which is no fault of their own. McLean surmises the "hatred which the Negro feels for the white majority largely arises out of the real injustice meted out to him. His crime lies in being born a Negro, in other words, fate, and not he, is responsible. Therefore, the guilt for his hostility can be externalized."[11] Thus, many midcentury psychoanalysts believed black antisocial behavior was an attempt to restore psychic balance by eliminating or reducing neurosis. Though McLean's work represented the "better" social-pathological interpretation of black behavior, these scholarly accounts are difficult to condone in the twenty-first century.

Reading the social science literature leads one to conclude that African American life was synonymous with social maladjustment and delinquency. In fact, social maladjustment and delinquency were often used interchangeably to describe black behavior. To be a "delinquent" was to be a "neurotic," a mental "defective," and a mental "retardate." "We have said that the earliest studies of the general intelligence of juvenile delinquents emphasized their retarded mentality as a class," wrote Harry Manuel Shulman, professor of sociology and one of the foremost experts on the subject. Summarizing other experts in the field "led to the conclusion that at least one-half of juvenile delinquents were mental defectives."[12] Juvenile delinquents are found everywhere, but they are "drawn in disproportionate numbers from (a) lower socio-economic groups, (b) Negroes, (c) foreign-born parentage, (d) groups disproportionately high in indices of mental disorder."[13] In a place like Los Angeles, the majority of "mentally deficient delinquents" were of "Mexican-born and Mexican ethnic stock children of presumed bi-lingual backgrounds."[14] Sociologists Clifford R. Shaw and Henry D. McKay, in their classic but highly racist "magnus opus in criminology" entitled, *Juvenile Delinquency and Urban Areas* (1942) used crime data and neighborhood maps in Chicago to spatialize black antisocial behavior.[15] Their spatial analysis of impoverished neighborhoods populated by poor African Americans and European immigrants "discovered" group patterns of delinquency. "The delinquency data presented graphically on spot maps and rate maps," noted Shaw and McKay, "give plausibility to the existence of a coherent system of values supporting delinquent acts. In making these interpretations it should be remembered that delinquency is essentially group behavior."[16]

Group behavior pivoted around the axis of deviant/normal to dichotomize the behavior of people of color versus whites. Social science scholars often accounted for "bad" white behavior (normal) and explained it against so-called bad black behavior (deviant/delinquent). Scholars performed this feat by racializing offenses and linking them to intelligence. Shulman explained, "Forgery and fraud have been associated with higher levels of intelligence, and crimes of violence with lower levels."[17] If behavior is revealing of one's intelligence, then the "offense chosen is typical of the individual who commits it . . . thus an individual with a low IQ will usually commit a simple theft such as breaking in through a window and taking some insignificant object, or stealing a car, leaving it and running away."[18] Simple theft or violence was not only claimed to be beneath the dignity of whites, but these offenses were believed to be below their intellectual station. Intellectualizing behavior as racially predictable humanized white people, allowing them social respectability in society as well as more privileged diagnoses in schools. Normalizing criminal behavior was tantamount to normalizing disabilities as Columbia University clinical professor of psychiatry John Levy observed in 1931, "Bright children tend toward personality problems and dull children toward conduct disorders."[19]

The behavioral characteristics used to construct delinquency and social maladjustment fell into neat sociological categories like "socialized" and "unsocialized." These perspectives reveal how behavior characteristics were not only racialized but gendered. Psychiatrists Richard L. Jenkins and Sylvia Glickman created behavior traits for boys and girls, ranking their attributes by levels of severity and order of frequency. For "socialized delinquent" boys, it included stealing, truancy from home, truancy from school, police arrest, staying out late at night, associating with bad companions, running around with a gang, smoking, loitering, lying, incorrigibility, and leading others into bad conduct. If "socialized delinquent" girls exhibited the same behavioral characteristics as boys, the frequency of the characteristics occurred in a different order: staying out late at night, truancy from home, truancy from school, police arrest, lying, sex delinquency, stealing, over-interest in the opposite sex, incorrigibility, associating with bad companions, and loitering. Traits identified in girls, but not boys, are noteworthy. The rapacious appetite of boys who engaged in "sex delinquency" or exhibited an "over-interest in the opposite sex" must have gone unnoticed in Jenkins and Glickman's research.[20]

Locating group delinquent behavior also required explaining it in terms of social class and family composition. The practice of separating and walling-off referents such as "delinquents," "families of delinquents," and "parents and siblings of delinquents" was designed to mark the black family and to show that deviance did not exist solely at the individual level. Sociologist Thorsten Sellin demonstrated this tragically when he affirmed in 1951:

Families of delinquents had changed domicile more frequently; they had poorer sanitary facilities in the home; home was more crowded, less clean and neat, more disadvantaged economically, having fewer breadwinners; average weekly income per person was less and earning came more frequently from illicit sources. Delinquents lived less often with both parents and their parents lived together less frequently. Mothers of delinquents had more frequently been raised in poor economic circumstances and mental retardation, emotional disturbances, drunkenness, and criminality in her family showed higher proportions. This was also true of emotional disturbances and criminality in the homes in which the delinquents' fathers had been raised.[21]

Sellin added that the parents of delinquents suffered from more physical and mental disabilities, they relied more on social services, worked more often in unskilled jobs, and "had poorer work habits and did not do equally well in managing the family income" compared to parents of nondelinquents. When it seemed like his diatribe could not get any worse, it did:

Parents and siblings of delinquents showed more serious physical ailments, mental retardations, emotional disturbances and criminality. Families of delinquents had . . . more contacts with social agencies and more financial aid from public sources for less worthy reasons. The fathers of the delinquents were more likely to have unskilled and casual jobs, had poorer work habits and did not do equally well in managing the family income.[22]

The families of the delinquents showed fewer elements of cultural refinement, less self-respect and ambitiousness and poorer standards of conduct. Conjugal relations were poorer. Mothers worked outside the home, all or part-time, more frequently and gave less supervision to children. Family group recreation was less marked among families of delinquents. Parents knew less about the leisure time activities of the boy, were more averse to having him bring his friends home and made fewer provisions for home recreation. The cohesiveness of the families of the delinquents was less marked.

In school, the delinquents showed less attainment, attended more schools, repeated more grades, and were more often retarded, and in special classes. They "liked" fewer subjects and disliked most, had poorer grades, were poorer at reading and arithmetic, disliked school, showed less ambition for continuing their education, poorer adjustment to school mates, misbehaved more frequently (especially truancy) and at an earlier age, and were more disorderly, stubborn, disobedient, impudent, disinterested and inattentive.[23]

Beyond projecting low expectations onto black students before they walked into school, these ideas communicated to current and future teachers that black youth came from a conduct-disordered culture. Social scientists projected that poor black and brown caretakers reared their children "pathologically," which explained their delinquency and conduct disorders. Middle-class white children reared "normally" expressed behavioral characteristics, but they were more apt to have personality and emotional disorders and not antisocial ones. Shulman racialized behavior characteristics in this way when he concluded, "The lower-class child, reared permissively, but frustrated in his status aspiration in a democratic society, and subjected to temperamental and culture clashes in his family environment may react to his frustrations by conduct disorder, while the middle class child, reared strictly, but with less frustration of his status aspirations, may react to frustrations in opportunity for self-expression and to temperamental and culture clashes in his family environment by anxiety and personality problems."[24]

The shades of gray between delinquency and social maladjustment made the two categories hard to distinguish, and social scientists and psychiatrists often used the terms interchangeably to describe human behavior. Denotatively, however, there was a difference. They defined delinquency and applied to it to youth who encountered law enforcement and the juvenile justice system, particularly the courts. A "delinquent" was socially maladjusted, but a "social maladjusted" youth was not necessarily a delinquent. Regarding behavioral characteristics, a consensus emerged that both were one in the same, though the "social maladjusted" youth, not under the purview of the courts, was often characterized as a "pre-delinquent" or a "potential delinquent."[25] In essence, they were on their way to being under court supervision.

As a concept, maladjustment is best understood without its prefix. Adjustment in an individual meant being satisfied with one's environment. That environment could be society, school, or a neighborhood. By contrast, a maladjusted individual is not only someone who is dissatisfied

with his or her environment but so conscious of the "gap between his present real condition and the desired condition," that the person develops a
level of frustration that he or she begins to "act out."[26] Acting out mani-
fests in misconduct, which "implies maladjustment to the demands of
society" or more specifically, the status quo.[27] "Maladjustment is the result
of the failure to identify oneself with the aims and purposes of a particular group or society," explained sociologist Manuel Lopez-Rey, "or of the
inability to participate actively in conformity with these aims and purposes, or of unsuccessful attempts to achieve individual goals or meet the
expectations of a group or society."[28] Delinquency among African Americans was believed to be a social response to neighborhood, family, school,
and societal norms, and represented the "substance of the adjustment," or
a capitulation to it—a "maladjustment." This (mal)adjustment to harsh
living conditions (delinquent acts) was not permanent by any means, but
they were projected as typical for black people.

In the social science literature, scholars provided race and class explanations of black behavior in a much different way than it did for white
people. The cumulative explanations posed long-term consequences for
black youth entering schools. Crimes committed by the white middle
class remained unracialized and unnoticed, allowing certain axioms and
"statements of fact" about black youth to thrive and flourish. Social scientists linked fraud directly to white persons and higher IQs, as well
as kickbacks, fixing, rigging, and other kinds of "white-collar" crimes.
Lopez-Rey admitted that "the ironic fact is that while those involved in
such unethical and corrupt practices are seldom branded and treated as
offenders, juveniles 'borrowing' a car, or running away, or smoking without permission, or being more or less difficult, are branded as maladjusted
and treated as offenders."[29] A decade-long study in the 1950s at Yale University revealed how maladjustment and delinquency applied to young
black and brown people:

> Delinquency was found to be significantly associated with several individ-
> ual characteristics (nonwhite, male, low intelligence, and leaving school)
> that were considered as indicators of barriers to legitimate opportunity
> that produce anomie and delinquency. Delinquency was also significantly
> related to characteristics of deviant families (illegitimacy, absent parents,
> and delinquent siblings) and to characteristics of deviant neighborhoods

(public housing and high delinquency rates). These characteristics were considered to be indicators of access to illegitimate opportunities that increases delinquency rates.[30]

The data assembled by the Yale study inferred that being black or Latinx doubled the probability of delinquency; being below-average intelligence tripled one's probability; and being a male quadrupled a person's chances of becoming a delinquent.[31] If delinquency and social maladjustment were the fate of black and brown people, then white education stakeholders sought to seal off white youth from this stigma.

Equal opportunity discourse allowed the educational disability rights movement to distinguish student constituencies and their needs inside schools and in policy. But the discourse of equal educational opportunity cut in different directions. *Brown v. Board of Education* promoted equal educational opportunity to eliminate dual school systems in the South and provide quality schools in the North. The discourse also functioned as the perfect vehicle for the educational disability rights movement to address the needs of exceptional children. Generally, while the civil rights movement featured organizations and activists who took to the streets to demand that lawmakers act on behalf of African Americans, the educational disability rights movement featured parents who consulted with clinicians, researchers, and school officials regarding the white "handicapped." White parents, clinicians, and school officials vied for the same attention from lawmakers in Congress, and since the civil rights movement focused attention on African Americans, the educational disability rights movement attempted to make the disabled white student visible through the "rights of the handicapped" discourse. Samuel Kirk promoted learning disability (LD) as a *new* category, racially and cognitively distinguishing it from the black and brown educable mentally retarded (EMR). Emotional disturbance (ED), as a *label already in existence,* complicated the ability of researchers and policymakers to racialize ED as a white category because it could not be easily disassociated from social maladjustment and delinquency. Notwithstanding the difficulty in reserving ED for white students did not mean, however, that psychiatrists, psychologists, educators, and politicians would not try.

As juvenile delinquency and social maladjustment in schools became a top legislative priority, "special classes" inside public schools and alternative "special day schools" educated students under those categories.

Special classes emerged inside public schools, and the "same objectives for educating normal children hold for educating socially maladjusted children" noted Edward Stullken, one of the most prominent voices in special education at mid-century.[32] Separate, special day schools also developed for the same purposes as special classes but administrators designed these schools to educate more "difficult" children, often referred to as the "socially handicapped," "truants," "incorrigibles," and "delinquents." Teachers educated these so-called difficult students in alternative settings. Stullken saw no problem with this kind of separation: "The special school is an important provision which must be made for the more severely emotionally disturbed children and for those children with the more fixed patterns of bad behavior. They should be created in all communities containing a sizable number of emotionally disturbed or delinquent children."[33] Written in 1953, Stullken's words rang eerily similar to those of avid segregationists.

Special day schools proliferated in every major city in the United States and drew attention from people inside and outside of education. "Educational practices with maladjusted children are attracting widespread interest," stated Jack W. Birch, director of special education for Pittsburgh Schools. In the 1950s, educators often confronted the problem of the poorly behaved student by willfully ignoring the harm of separate learning environments for "maladjusted" students. Birch attempted to paper over the detriments of separate classrooms by highlighting the false progressivism of this measure: "There is much public and professional concern about emotionally and socially maladjusted children and about special provisions for them in the public schools. Correspondence with school officials in the 50 largest cities in the United States confirmed that public school systems are making important and impressive forward steps in fostering positive adjustment in all children. Emphasis is placed on the prevention and correction of maladjustment . . . and special schools and classes."[34] Writing in 1956, Birch was just one of many white administrators who used alternative placement as an insidious form of resegregation of classrooms during the era of *Brown*.

Special classes in public schools and separate special day schools were racially diverse, serving an eclectic mix of emotional and behaviorally challenged students. In some cities, special day schools were predominantly black. One would find, in both special schools and classes, "aggressive, hostile, and contentious behavior which has been labeled at various times, conduct disorder, unsocialized aggression, or psychopathy," according to psychologists Herbert Quay, William Morse, and Richard Cutler. Other students appeared "anxious, withdrawn, introvertive" and exhibited other personality problems or "neuroticism." A few more seemed preoccupied, lacked interest, or they were sluggish, lazy, and "daydreamy" of which the "labels of inadequacy-immaturity and autism have been suggested."[35] Though separate schools and classes were racially heterogeneous, certain behaviors applied to particular students. For the "part played by race in determining social maladjustment has not been settled," wrote Edward Stullken. However, Stullken continued, "Delinquency is more common among Negroes and the children of newly arrived immigrants."[36] In the discourse of education specialists like Stullken, "delinquent" and "Negro" were bound together in ways that made the terms appear inextricably linked and allowed for the legal marginalization and containment of "delinquents" in the era of desegregation.

Edward Stullken was not only the founding principal of Montefiore Special School in Chicago, which served a disproportionate number of Polish, Italian, and African American children, he was one of the leading theorists in the country on educating socially maladjusted and delinquent students.[37] As a participant in the White House Conferences on Child Welfare in 1930, 1940, and 1950, Stullken was active on its committees on special education. He was instrumental in describing the role special classes and special day schools should play in the education of the maladjusted and delinquent student. He believed schools could prevent delinquency by resocializing troubled students.[38] According to Stullken, schools had a socialization/citizenship function as well as an academic one, for "schools today recognize that it is the purpose of education not so much to teach pupils what otherwise they would not know as it is to teach them to behave in a way in which they would otherwise not behave."[39]

Stullken was a staunch proponent of a particular brand of behavior readjustment. He promoted early detection of delinquency for the purposes of prevention by changing said behavior through less punitive strategies. If schools had "the proper philosophy" for understanding "truancy, misbehavior, delinquency, and other bad behavior," they would be less apt to dismiss and punish it. "It is well to remember," Stullken claimed, "that the school is society's best legally constituted agency to deal with children as children rather than having them dealt with as adults by some legal agency, and that the school must show understanding rather than exert force."[40] Ironically, Stullken's positions contributed to early special education theory that influenced the direction of special education classes inside public schools as much as alternative day schools like Montefiore. Instead of the separate day school approach in which the clinical model dominated, educational disability rights insisted on in-school solutions that promoted the idea of training teachers in exceptional disabilities to meet the demands of behavior.[41]

In 1957, the bill H.R. 9591 was referred to the Committee on Education and Labor "to encourage and expand the training of teachers for the education of exceptional children."[42] Teacher training was a core goal of the educational disability rights movement, with more than $18 million committed to federal scholarships and $2 million in grants for colleges and universities. What proved impressive was not so much the federal money allotted to exceptional students at that time but the broad philosophy used to explain the new federal allocation. Immediately after the *Brown* decision, lawmakers applied equal educational opportunity discourse to other student constituencies:

> The Congress believes that the American promise of equality of opportunity extends to every child within our country, no matter what his gifts, his capacity or his handicaps, whether he is handicapped by defects of speech, of sight or of hearing, or crippling disease or condition, whether his adjustment to society is made difficult by emotional or mental disorders, or whether, on the other hand, he is endowed with outstandingly brilliant gifts of mind and spirit. All such exceptional children require special educational guidance for development of their total educational potential. The Congress finds that the educational problems presented by such exceptional children are of national concern, and that there is an acute national shortage of, and urgent national need for, individuals professionally qualified to teach such children, to supervise the teachers of such children, to train such teachers and supervisors, and to conduct research into the problems relating to the education of exceptional children.[43]

Training teachers to meet the needs of exceptional children meant "all children," including the "socially maladjusted" and the "juvenile delinquent." Though the social maladjusted and the "delinquent" were "otherized" and set apart in society and in the social science research, lawmakers recognized that students designated as such fell under the purview of special education disability:

> The term "exceptional children" means those children determined in accordance with regulations issued by the Commissioner to present special educational problems, such as (a) children who are unusually intelligent and gifted; (b) children who are mentally retarded; (c) children who are deaf or hard of hearing; (d) children who are blind or have serious visual impairments; (e) children who have serious health problems due to heart disease, epilepsy, or other debilitating conditions; (f) children who suffer from speech impediments; (g) children who are crippled (including those who have cerebral palsy); (h) children who are maladjusted emotionally and socially, including the institutionalized delinquent.[44]

Clearly, the "socially maladjusted" and the "institutionalized delinquent" were considered exceptional children, deserving of special education services. Equally clear, however, was the way the socially maladjusted and delinquent populations created problems for lawmakers. All manner of attention by Congress and the White House was given to the problems of troubled youth. Troubled youth, however, did not mean all youth, and certainly young people were "troubled" in different ways. Despite the language of equal educational opportunity, all children were not served equally. Some children were privileged over others. During this time, researchers and lawmakers clarified the definitions of delinquency, maladjustment, emotional and behavior disorder. This clarification led Congress to determine how best to address these students in policymaking, if at all. Congress took their cues from researchers and educators.

By the late 1950s and early 1960s, it was time to determine the bounds of emotional disturbance and social maladjustment in children. In a racialized educational system of winners and losers, color-blind language that invoked all children meant little in an environment where distinctions between life experiences and behaviors determined who was worthy of being covered by federal policy. Similar to the construction of LD, the educational disability rights movement needed to decide to whom these designations applied without specific references to race. Many experts in the field, however, still referred to emotional disturbance, social maladjustment, and delinquency in conflated disability terms, often using them interchangeably with racial undertones, as special education lecturer Barney Rabinow argued. The "emotionally disturbed" mostly included poor black and Latinx people who lived in cities supported by the social welfare system. Rabinow explained, "All we wish to state in this connection is that those families which parents or brothers or sisters have received attention from welfare, correction, police, or other social agencies, are likely to have emotionally disturbed children who will require the special attention of the school. While emotional disturbance is not a respecter of class, the larger incidence is a metropolitan phenomenon."[45] Even though Rabinow refused racial distinction here, the invocation of welfare, police, and social agencies served as what we would now call a racial dog whistle. By arguing that emotional disturbance is not class specific, he attempted to include white middle-class youth in his analysis of emotional disturbance but could not resist walking back his own statement by turning again to the problem of "metropolitan" areas where many people of color lived.

Examining the *implicit* racial conception of emotional disturbance like Rabinow's reveals the ways in which designations of social maladjustment and delinquency served *explicit* racial ends. Scholars continued to argue that the difference between ED and social maladjustment manifested in children's behavior. But since behavior is highly subjective, covering a wide range of actions and manners, scholars had to ground poor black behavior in conduct disorders, including maladjustment on one end of the bad behavior spectrum and delinquency on the other. Even though designations of delinquency and social maladjustment applied to poor whites, social scientists disproportionately fixed the labels to black and Latinx youth. Rabinow averred that social maladjustment "is manifest behavior—departure from the range of conformity norms or developmental norms or social growth norms, deviance from the variety of socially approvable and acceptable behavior. It is an external manifestation, the danger signal that warns 'stop and listen.'"[46] Rabinow and his contemporaries constructed a conception of black behavior rooted in deviant social maladjustment that portended criminal and delinquent implications.

It was for this reason that social and behavioral scientists, many of whom doubled as education specialists, made social maladjustment synonymous with black youth. Rabinow noted that unlike ED, "The term[s] socially maladjusted as well as delinquent have no clinical or educational value because they do not tell us about the nature of the child."[47] Race is revealed when one unpacks the word "nature" and its adjective, "natural." "Nature" had two applications: one for black and another for white students. Delinquency and maladjustment indicated the "nature" of black and brown students even though a few "progressive" thinkers at the time believed delinquency and maladjustment were "nurtured" by their environment. Delinquency and maladjustment had no clinical or educational value because they appeared "inherent" in blackness. Delinquent blackness not only described the state of a people "non-clinically" and "non-educationally," as psychologist Herbert Quay argued, blackness also described a subculture. "This child comes from a subculture in which aggressive behavior and 'conning' ability are valued and in which academic achievement and middle-class behavior standards are not highly esteemed," Quay claimed.[48] Though delinquency and maladjustment were included under the broad statutory definition of emotionally disturbed students, psychologists like Herbert Quay began to argue against its inclusion, writing: "There is a special point to be made about these children. It is probably inappropriate to consider them emotionally disturbed since in a very real sense they are only behaving in a way which is appropriate to their own world."[49]

By contrast, the "nature" of emotionally disturbed white students meant something altogether different. Rabinow wrote conclusively, "When we say a child is emotionally disturbed, we convey that the feelings of this child about himself and about others differ markedly from what we believe a child should feel at this age."[50] The value judgment of "what we believe a child should feel," is illustrative here, as no real evidence is needed by this claim. It is part of a complex construction designed to locate the source of white misbehavior in "congenital or the result of rearing experiences during early infancy," never white culture as a whole.[51] The misbehavior is an expression of inappropriate thinking and feeling created by induction into life where the "rearing experiences" were "excessive or deficient." The rearing experiences that created "white" emotional disturbance were localized to parents or perhaps an early negative school encounter, never the people, neighborhood, or culture from which the white child came (like in the cases of the black maladjusted

and delinquent). Thomas E. Stone captured this thinking when he out-
lined in his book:

> If one hypothesizes that the emotional disturbance is rooted in early dif-
> ficulties in development, *intrinsic in nature,* one must consider the impli-
> cation: parents are not to blame for the disturbance in the child. In the
> earlier literature, the responsibility of the disturbance was placed on the
> parents' shoulders. However, in the sixties, the focus shifted to an aware-
> ness of early inner developmental difficulties divorced from the way in
> which the parents handled the child. It has been fashionable through the
> years to put the onus on the parents while disregarding the variables that
> go into the personality configuration. The triangle of development, the
> "experiment in nature," is composed of ... milieu experiences and ... the
> unique way in which each child reacts to what is going on about him with
> his hereditary potentials ... and the way in which he perceives and defines
> the set of circumstances and experiences he undergoes.[52]

Rabinow never specifically defined emotional disturbance. "Part of the
problem ... of any attempt at an adequate description or definition of
the term," he claimed, "lies in the difficulty in cognitively describing the
complex affective state, called 'emotion.'"[53]

One would agree that a definition of emotion is hard to pin down. But
one could also surmise that no real pressure or stake existed to "properly"
define it until legislators demanded it in 1963. Therefore, if the socially maladjusted and delinquent were removed from the broad category of emotionally disturbed or handicapped, who would be left? Rabinow answered:

> We include mentally ill children, autistic, strange, fantasy ridden, the bizarre,
> out-of-touch, non-communicative, whose difficulties are congenital or
> the result of rearing experiences during very early infancy. These are the
> schizophrenic children. Next are the borderline cases which fuse into the
> personality patterns disorders—the inadequates, the schizoids, the impulse
> ridden; these are followed by the personality trait disturbances made up
> of the aggressive, the passive-aggressive—the rebellious, acting-out, tough
> children ... finally, we include the anxious, guilt-ridden, self-punishing
> children with psycho-neurotic reactions.[54]

Leo Kanner, the "founder of autism," confirmed these behavior patterns in 1962 when he wrote of three clinical types of emotional disturbances: (a) the pseudo-defective or autistic type; (b) the pseudo-neurotic or phobic, obsessive, compulsive, hypochondriac type; (c) and the pseudo-psychopathic or paranoid, acting-out, aggressive, antisocial type.[55] By the early 1960s, the three main vectors of emotional disturbance—autism, personality problems (ED), and social maladjustment—began to separate, referring to distinct student populations.

Eli M. Bower, a researcher who worked for the California State Department of Education in the late 1950s and early 1960s was a well-respected authority on ED who profoundly shaped our understanding of the disability. Eli Bower was for ED what Samuel Kirk was for LD. Bower did not advocate for a clean break between delinquent behavior and emotional disturbance (like Kirk advocated for LD from EMR), but he insisted on recognizing gradations "inherent in delineations of states of emotions," which created the context for an attempted separation. Bower advocated for the elimination of the word "disturbed" or "disturbance," as it was "indicative of the acting out, overtly aggressive problems" exhibited in some students—if read in another way, too close to what many referred to as "pre-delinquent" or the "institutionalized delinquent." Instead, he posited the "use of the phrase 'emotionally handicapped' . . . in place of emotionally disturbed, socially maladjusted, or other similar terms" so students designated as such can "be regarded as other handicapped children" without the stigma. Stigma is relative to the historical era, as the stigma associated with the term "disturbance" proved too burdensome for the newer appraisal of ED in the early 1960s. For Bower, the word "handicapped" meant "restriction of choice or alternatives of behavior." He pontificated that to "live is to make choices; when one's choices are severely limited by emotional lacks or injunctions, one's behavior can be regarded as handicapped."[56]

Distinguishing black and white behavior apparently created challenges for Bower and other ED theorists. But Bower identified a line of demarcation between prepathological and pathological, and suggested the "source" of one's behavior explained it all. He relied on the tried-and-true dichotomy of normal and deviant to explain why one set of behaviors denoted individual choices and another set of behaviors represented fate. Fate, or what Bower termed "necessity," constituted normalcy while choice signified pathology. "A major caution in the descriptive definition of children with emotional handicaps," noted Bower, "is the problem of differentiating incipient pathology from normal behavioral deviation." He went on:

> Marked differences in behavior are noted in children with emotional handicaps, but they are also noted in children who choose to behave somewhat idiosyncratically. Perhaps the key in differentiating the child whose behavioral deviation is caused by emotional problems and the child whose behavior is simply different is one of determining the source of the behavior. The behavior of the emotionally handicapped child is, to the extent of his handicap, *not a matter of choice, but necessity.* The degrees of behavioral freedom for the emotionally handicapped individual may be restricted by internal conflicts or by lack of inner controls.[57]

Key words and phrases are illustrative of racialized thinking that understood black and brown social maladjustment and delinquent behavior as "choices" African Americans and Latinx students made in contrast to the "lack of inner controls" exhibited by white students. Thus, black and brown students engaging in antisocial and delinquent acts revealed "natural" choices based on their race—whereas white student behavior was produced by the lack of emotional controls and "injunctions." This fate/choice model for socially maladjusted and delinquent black and brown student versus the fate/necessity paradigm assigned to white ED students by God speaks to what Shelley L. Tremain, and other feminist theorists of disability, refer to as the "politics of impairment" and the "apparatus of disability."[58]

Bower was not successful in replacing the word "disturbance" with "handicap" at the federal level but he did offer a definition of ED that stands today. His definition created a racialized special education category based on some of the most nebulous understandings of behavior in children. In an attempt to give ED scientific and clinical credibility, he started with a temporal lead-in to the definition "*To a marked extent and over a period of time,*" without actually specifying how much time a child needed to exhibit signs. Bower defined emotional disturbance (ED) as "*an inability to learn which cannot be explained by intellectual, sensory, or health factors.*"[59] He reasoned that "if all other possibilities have been

ruled out," like mental retardation, blindness, and other exclusionary disabilities, "emotional conflicts or resistances can be ruled in."[60]

The "*inability to build or maintain satisfactory interpersonal relationships with peers and teachers*" formed the second definition of ED:

> It isn't just getting along with others that is significant here. Satisfactory
> interpersonal relations refer to factors such as demonstrating sympathy
> and warmth toward others, ability to stand alone when necessary, ability
> to have close friends, ability to be aggressively constructive and to enjoy
> working and playing with others as well as enjoying working and play-
> ing by oneself. In most instances, children who are unable to build or
> maintain satisfactory interpersonal relationships are most visible to their
> peers. Teachers are also able to identify such children after a period of
> observation. [61]

Again, children at risk of being labeled ED, according to Bower's second definition, included loners, students who liked working and playing separately, or students who showed little sympathy or warm feelings
toward others. Bower's third definition, "*inappropriate types of behavior
or feelings under normal conditions,*"[62] begged the question, inappropriate for whom? It was difficult enough for trained psychologists or social
workers to answer this question. Bower and others left the answer solely
to the discretion of the teacher, shifting the power of identification from
the clinic to the classroom: "What is appropriate or inappropriate is best
judged by the teacher using her professional training, her daily observation of the child, and her experience working and interacting with the
appropriate behavior of large numbers of normal children." The other
components rounding out the definition included "*a general pervasive
mood of unhappiness or depression*" that could be discovered in "expressive play, art work, written composition . . . discussion periods . . . or social
relationships," and "*a tendency to develop illnesses, pains, or fears associated with personal or school problems.*"[63] Bower's definition of emotional
disturbance served as evidence of psychology's influence in redefining
disability categories. In many ways, emotional disturbance, maladjustment, and delinquency remained the property of mental health and the
clinical professions. During the legislative hearings between 1959 and 1963,
lawmakers, clinicians, and educators offered competing definitions of all

three categories, demonstrating how psychologists, educators, and lawmakers legislated around black and brown bodies.

Legislating around Black and Brown Students

In 1959 and 1960, the U.S. Congress held hearings in several cities on special education. The hearings revealed the state of play concerning disability nomenclature and definition. Public Law 85–926 had already passed in 1958, urging the expansion of teaching training for the intellectually disabled ("mentally retarded"). As a grant program to colleges and universities, PL 85–926 encouraged many clinical and educational professionals to support pending special education bills for students disabled in other ways. Joseph P. Phelan Jr., the executive director of Children's Village, was one of the first speakers to make his case in front of a House subcommittee in New York City, explaining that "our experiences to date indicate that we need a great deal more help from the Federal Government and from the State governments." [64] As the executive director to one of "the oldest and largest treatment institutions in the country dealing with disturbed children who are both delinquent and predelinquent," Phelan told members in the House of Representatives the most important issue for his organization was "special education for disturbed and delinquent youngsters."[65] Seeking help on Capitol Hill meant both justifying the need for congressional aid and clarifying the groups who need it. Taken aback by the interchangeable use of "disturbed" children and "delinquent" children, Representative Robert Giaimo of Connecticut asked Phelan if he meant to conflate the two terms. Giaimo queried, "You speak of disturbed and delinquent children. Are you restricting your definition of disturbed to include an element of delinquency in it?" Phelan replied, "My statement is based on the fact that legally the classification of delinquent is determined by an adjudication in a court." "From a treatment standpoint," Phelan continued, "we see no difference, in my own experience, between the disturbed child and a delinquent child. He is equally disturbed."[66]

When Dr. Melitta Schmideberg, one of the founders of the Association for Psychiatric Treatment of Offenders testified in front of the same congressional subcommittee, she reiterated Phelan's position regarding the equivalence of the disturbed and the delinquent but foregrounded her remarks in this student's inability to read. Again, Representative Giaimo's interest was piqued by the introduction of reading into the equation, asking: "Is it your contention that these people are emotionally disturbed not because of psychiatric disorders of some type or mental illness, but because of the fact that they do not know how to read?" Schmideberg did not answer Giaimo directly but hinted at a correlative association between compounded academic failure accumulated over the years and antisocial behavior. Schmideberg explained, "I think it is a vicious circle. It is a question of the hen and the egg. I think of somebody 3 months behind, but if it is not picked up until he is 3, 4, and 5 years behind ... he is utterly disinterested because he cannot follow."[67] Befuddled, Giaimo still wanted to know how academic challenges could create emotional disturbance. Schmideberg was more certain about this relationship for the student she considered "out of civilization," as she called it: "The other children look down on him. He feels like an outsider in the school. It makes him antisocial. He does not participate in normal activities. He feels different and he is different. The large proportion of them are likely to become delinquent, first, because they are different, and, second, because they are not likely to get a job or they will get a very, very poor job. Those who do not become delinquent I think become welfare cases. Those become emotionally disturbed."[68] According to Schmideberg, academic challenges coupled with peer perception is the road traveled by black and brown students to delinquency, welfare dependency, and emotional disturbance, a common assumption of many in the field of special education.

The special education hearings began on January 27 and 28, 1960, in Cullman, Alabama, a few days before the sit-ins in Greensboro, North Carolina. Ethel Gorman, from the Social Hygiene and Mental Health Association in Birmingham, told the subcommittee that "I am going to discuss a different type of handicap than most of the people here." Gorman immediately told the subcommittee that "delinquency is a handicap." If delinquency is a handicap most associated with African American behavior, then "his behavior is his handicap," Gorman stated. Thus, black behavior did not need "freedom," as articulated shortly by the sit-in movement that eventually spread to Montgomery and Birmingham but rather "rehabilitation" as defined in these special education hearings. For black delinquent students, educational rehabilitation in the South usually meant a short tenure in public schools and a long one in reform school. Gorman noted that Birmingham and Jefferson County public schools are "not meeting the needs of delinquent children" who have IQs in the 73 to 91 range. "In Alabama," Gorman continued, "there is no opportunity for a delinquent child to be taught new behavior on any consistent basis except perhaps at the Alabama Boys Industrial School, the State Training Schools for Girls, in Birmingham, and the Alabama Industrial School for Negro Children at Mount Meigs." Formerly known as the Alabama Reform School for Negro Law-Breakers, the Mount Meigs facility was described by Gorman as a way station, or some kind of pit stop for black "delinquents" on their way to a labor camp. Educational "rehabilitation" functioned as subterfuge for putting black youth to work in Alabama. Gorman proposed to the subcommittee a "residential work training and counseling facility" as the solution for Alabama's black delinquent disabled youth. The facility would exist under the auspices of the federal Vocational Rehabilitation Service, not Alabama school districts.[69] But there was more to this perspective.

Clay S. Sheffield, director for the Guidance Department in Birmingham Public Schools, supported his colleague's position. Like other areas in the South, Alabama was ordered to desegregate its public schools, which it staunchly resisted in the 1960s. When Sheffield testified before the subcommittee and argued that black students did not "deserve special thought and consideration," the conflation of black delinquency with disability became apparent. "I have not heard it mentioned here," Sheffield continued, "but I think it is very important that we need special physical facilities for dealing with these people"—something akin to a New Deal program. "I had an idea that perhaps the CCC—camp idea, a camp work situation for 14- and 15-year-olds might be a good one," he remarked. Sheffield's concern was not just with separate facilities for delinquent teenagers but also with "better coordination of the services of special education, vocational education, and vocational rehabilitation" for the purposes of identifying and removing predelinquent black students. He claimed, "These people would not be individuals who would be identified as delinquent. They are, however, potential delinquents. Frequently these young people constitute a major problem to the public schools and the community." Sheffield sought to create a pipeline from black segregated schools into vocational facilities, or out of newly integrated white schools into alternative settings that were not so much academic institutions but more like exploitative work camps.[70]

Lawmakers in the special education hearings were eager to understand definitions of maladjusted children in relation to emotionally disturbed children. Dr. R. N. Lowe, coordinator of school psychological services at the University of Oregon's School of Education told the Portland committee that "it is obvious that I used the terms interchangeably. If I shed some light on the one term, I am shedding equal light on the other. If a child is emotionally disturbed, he is maladjusted—if he is maladjusted, he is emotionally disturbed."[71] Asked to unravel the conflation with a definition for each, Lowe responded by saying, "Actually there is no uniformly accepted definition. Maladjustment is a broad term, commensurate in intent and scope to such earlier terms as insane and mentally ill and later to terms such as mental hygiene and mental health." Lacking the ability to provide clear definitions, Lowe placed both terms in the broad area of mental health, explaining that "all problems of maladjustment and emotional disturbance are problems of mental health."[72]

The working groups around the country appeared stymied by definitional challenges, leading some to merely provide descriptions of maladjusted and emotionally disturbed students. The Portland, Oregon working group exemplifies this challenge when it announced the following: "A socially maladjusted person is one who has failed to come to terms with his environment. These terms may be very broadly defined as applying to any person whose personal problems become too overwhelming for him to handle so that they interfere with his ability to function 'normally' in family, school, and community." Although sometimes confusing tautologically, the special education hearings, including the one in Portland, identified two kinds of emotionally disturbed students. First, social maladjustment is a manifestation of ED. "All social maladjustments or handicaps, therefore, spring from some basic emotional disturbance within the individual." And second, "Generally speaking and especially in the case of the delinquent—that emotional disturbance appears to stem from environmental causes."[73] A racial undercurrent to the special education hearings began emerging in the subcommittee deliberations. Questions arose about whether "emotional disturbance" was environmentally produced and for whom did the environment induce disturbance.

Lawmakers pressed every witness to explain themselves thoroughly if congressional aid was to be rendered on behalf of "emotionally disturbed" students. But disability experts described conditions more than they defined them. The longer the dialogue continued between professionals and public officials, the more racial signifiers emerged. Dr. Marion Langer, executive secretary of the American Orthopsychiatric Association told lawmakers, "Whatever the legal or social designation, whatever clinical diagnosis, the emotionally disturbed child can be described in the following terms":

> They are children who are frightened, fearful of human experience; children who have not had opportunity to discover the gratification of positive accomplishments necessary to their healthy growth. They may be impulsive, unable to tolerate anxiety, frustration, or competition, and may react with withdrawal, or aggression, or other defensive measures to protect them from their feelings of inadequacy and insecurity. They may be anxiety-ridden children who have never known the security of consistent living with people and control of their behavior. They are children who have experienced too little love or too much neglectful indulgence.[74]

As if the language above was not racially coded enough, the big reveal lay in Langer's discussion of the impact of the student's home environment on his or her emotional disturbance. But the home environment spoke of here is not "black" or "brown," but "white":

> Many come from homes not broken by poverty essentially, but more often by situations in which parents, either because of problems or other difficulties, are unable to cope with the demands of parenthood. Often the sheer weight of the child's problem and lack of adequate resources to help renders the parents unable to cope with the child. Many of these children have had brain damage, many have had little stability or continuity in their significant relationships with people, or they have been brought up by parents too upset themselves to permit normal identification to develop; or they may have had a combination of both.[75]

Splitting definitional hairs and descriptions led somewhere. That road led to the conceptualization of two distinct types of ED students.

Dr. David G. Salten, superintendent of schools in Long Beach, New York, chaired his working group for the "emotionally disturbed." Salten asked that if emotionally handicapped children "comprise the single largest group of exceptional pupils in our educational system," then his request to lawmakers was a simple one: "What we ask for today, Mr. Chairman, is a plea ... to the Congress to include the emotionally disturbed children among the categories of the handicapped." Not only did Salten make a request for legal recognition and inclusion of ED, he also asked for a provision to include support for teachers trained in special education, school psychologists, and social workers. Representative Graham Barden of North Carolina, who chaired the Committee on Education and Labor, asked Dr. Salten directly to "provide the best possible definition of what you mean by 'emotionally disturbed.'" Salten admitted that his working group spent a considerable amount of time trying to define ED and was left exasperated by the process: "Concerning the matter of definition, Mr. Barden, I say that the question of definition and incidence concerned the committee during the first 6 hours of its deliberation, and we decided at that point to move on to other matters." Salten revealed the dilemma posed by physical and sensory disabilities against cognitive, emotional, behavioral disabilities, or disabilities that are clear to the eye versus disabilities that were more subjective. "It is recognized that in the case of the blind, the deaf, the orthopedically handicapped," noted Salten, "the problem of definition is relatively simple." Physical and sensory disability definitions were not "simpler," rather, their meanings and characterizations could not be manipulated with esotery. The opposite of "blind" is sight; the opposite of "deaf" is hearing; and the opposite of "orthopedically handicapped" is full physical functionality. Chairman Barden remarked that emotional disturbance not only harbored confusion but also contained too much complexity, even beyond what lawmakers could understand. "You educated people just give me more trouble with these big combinations of words; but you never give me much light on the detailed definition. That is why I have been two or three times suggesting that when the term is used, the definition is terrifically important."[76]

Indeed, clear definitions are "terrifically" important, especially if unclear ones are utilized and politicized to exclude a particular student group. As part of his live testimony, Salten submitted a statement that included a section entitled, "The Problem of the Definition of the Emotionally Disturbed." Salten's workgroup created a definitional trail that began with descriptions of the emotionally disturbed under (a) "General Definitions," and ended on (b) "Proposed Definition for Use in Determining Federal

Legislation," of which Eli Bower's explanation of ED appeared at the bottom. Salten's group not only stated that the emotionally disturbed lived in "a chronic state of poor mental health," they described the manifestations of good mental health as "adequate personal strength to meet the trials and tribulations of living with responses that are acceptable to the social mores of the community at large." The group also described ED as "social adjustment that does not bring conflict with peers or authority." After providing general descriptions, the Salten group used McGraw-Hill's 1959 *Dictionary of Education* to add further support. The book's description of the "emotionally disturbed child" suggested however, a clinical understanding of deviance.[77]

Under the section, "Proposed Definition for Use in Determining Federal Legislation," McGraw-Hill's *Dictionary of Education* was compared to Eli Bower's definition, the former representing ED that was environmentally produced and the latter whose ED was not. Environmentally

Figure 3. Eli M. Bower (on the far left), was a pioneer researcher of emotional disturbance (ED) in the nation and helped establish many ED programs in California. Photograph courtesy of the University of Southern California (USC) Digital Library. *Los Angeles Examiner* Photographs Collection.

produced ED precludes participation in regular school activities. The student is unable to "benefit from the school situation because of deep psychological problems that bring about deviant behavior and resistance to learning, development, and growth." According to this definition, the ED student—his thinking, and behavior—is "deviant." The reason his thinking, manner, and behavior is "deviant" is that his neighborhood, family, and race is "deviant." In contrast, Eli Bower's definition of ED purposefully avoids using the language of deviancy, concealing that ED was ever associated with social maladjustment. Bower's ED definition had the *intended* consequence of distancing itself from what previous legislative language called the "socially maladjusted and institutionalized delinquent."[78]

By the time the issue appeared again during the Eighty-Eighth Congress in 1963, Bower's definition prevailed but with more handwringing about who would be covered by the legislation. More experts were ushered to the floor of the House of Representatives to make the case for the nonenvironmental emotionally disturbed. Dr. Gunnar Dybwad, executive director of the National Association for Retarded Children, the organization often credited as the "civil rights champion" of the intellectually disabled, provided the clearest picture between the two racialized definitions in an exchange with Representative Donald Brotzman of Colorado.

DR. DYBWAD: If I may interpolate here, Mr. Brotzman, as one who has worked for quite a few years in institutions for the delinquent child, I know personally of the need for specially trained teachers who deal with what is referred to as the social maladjustment problems on the delinquent child.

MR. BROTZMAN: Since you have kindly volunteered a little information on this term "socially maladjusted," define for me what a socially maladjusted child is.

DR. DYBWAD: I would define this ... within the provision of this bill which deals with ... special education.... It is a child so severely maladjusted socially that he does not fit into the normal classroom procedures ...

MR. BROTZMAN: *Now, let me ask you this question. Is this child that you are alluding to emotionally disturbed?*

DR. DYBWAD: *Not necessarily, because if this child comes from a thoroughly deteriorated neighborhood he is well adjusted to his neighborhood; he has no inner personal conflicts; he behaves like his father, mother, brothers do, and*

> he is not conflicted as another socially maladjusted child might be who comes
> from a family where his conduct is in conflict with that of the other members
> of the family and an outgrowth of emotional disturbance. As a matter of fact,
> we spoke in our training school . . . of the social type . . . they just lived outside
> of what you and I call society, following rules of behavior with some of their
> own and so they were not emotionally disturbed. They were merely living at
> best with themselves from their family but not at best with the rest of society.
> This is quite a different picture from the youngster who gets into delinquency
> because he has been subjected to emotional stress at home.[79]

Distinguishing environmental ED from nonenvironmental ED produced an explicit distinction between black ED versus white ED. To disconnect social maladjustment or environmental ED from nonenvironmental ED meant demonizing black students in the process. According to Dr. Dybwad and behavioral researchers, black students experienced no inner personal conflicts because they live comfortably with themselves. They behave the way their parents behave. They have made peace with their condition and station in U.S. society. The thinking went, they are not like us white people because they are "outside" of civilization. Hence, many educational disability advocates determined that black children should not be included in the pending legislation.

Daniel H. Cline's essay, "A Legal Analysis of Policy Initiatives to Exclude Handicapped/Disruptive Students from Special Education," has been one (if not the only) study that locates the social maladjustment exclusion debate before 1975. Cline's essay was paradigmatic in its ability to historically contextualize the social maladjustment exclusion debate, but he failed to show how race became a factor in the exclusion. Many special education scholars understood the issue as a post-1970s development, using P.L. 94–142 (Education for All Handicapped Children Act—EHA 1975) as a point of departure to examine the exclusion of the socially maladjusted and to conclude that the exclusion was an "accident of history."[80] Cline also noticed something that was not obvious during the legislative hearings in the late 1950s and early 1960s: the issue of comorbidity. Cline wrote, "Delinquent students whose *only* difficulties are antisocial were never meant to be included" in the legislation. Stated another way, a socially maladjusted student could *only* be included if their maladjustment was accompanied by one of Bower's five areas of nonenvironmental ED, meaning, a socially maladjusted student could be considered ED only after meeting one of Bower's five criteria.[81]

In a social milieu where emotional disturbance was synonymous with social maladjustment and delinquency until 1963, the educational disability rights movement closed ranks around the interests of white disabled students. The exclusion of the socially maladjusted ED proved purposeful as a racialized understanding of the socially maladjusted ED student emerged greater in the eyes of special educators as black. The attempt to exclude black and brown students from the legislation functioned as a way to prevent them from receiving federal disability services under ED. If the issue was one of cost, as many scholars suggest, then certainly the competition of limited resources provided an additional justification to exclude the socially maladjusted from ED based on race.[82] In one of the strangest ironies, black students would not only be increasingly labeled as ED or EBD at the state level; they would become overrepresented in many states in later decades. Despite the fine line drawn in policy between the maladjusted/delinquency and non-maladjusted ED, black students, with their so-called bad behavior, began attending white schools. White teachers, school psychologists, and social workers would be waiting, empowered to weaponize screening devices, instruments, and behavior rating scales that identified and placed black students in EBD.

Black Behavior Between Two Movements: Civil Rights and Educational Disability Rights

Despite the Supreme Court's *Brown v. Board of Education* decision in 1954, it was not until Congress passed the Civil Rights Act of 1964, threatening to withhold federal funds, that black students began attending white schools in droves. Carole Gupton, a former Milwaukee and Minneapolis teacher and administrator, remembered the common refrain of white teachers in the 1960s when black students began arriving in greater numbers: "They're coming! they're coming!" Black students were no longer excluded; they now took their constitutional place inside school buildings where they had been long denied. Attending white schools by the strong arm of federal law, black students now sat in front of white teachers culturally ill-prepared to teach them. But black students were not just the newly integrated, they sat in classrooms classified as "mildly mentally retarded," which stemmed from their supposed cultural deprivation. Now, their "bad behavior" placed them at risk of being labeled emotionally disordered or behaviorally disordered in greater numbers regardless of how researchers and lawmakers defined these disabilities. ED would not be able to hold black behavior outside its definitional boundaries, for in practice, ED classes became another vehicle to control black behavior. If the placement of black students in ED classes could be used as a form of social control, who cared what Eli Bower and other ED theorists thought about the finer points of a complex definition that could be associated with white bodies.

The fate of black students sat at the crossroads of the civil rights and educational disability rights. The civil rights movement insisted on a quality education, which included community control of schools, fighting de facto segregation, eliminating racist textbooks, changing the curriculum, and hiring black teachers. By contrast, educational disability rights focused on creating new disability categories like LD, or refining old ones like ED. The educational disability rights movement also became fixated with producing new diagnostic instruments and screening procedures to empower classroom teachers. Using the language of equal opportunity, the educational disability rights movement successfully transferred the "therapeutic milieu" from hospitals and clinics to schools, with much of the transfer coming at the expense of black and brown students whose behavior and intelligence psychologists and educators measured at every turn. If screening devices and approaches represented the cornerstone of educational disability rights, then the training of teachers was its complement. Representative Leonor K. Sullivan of Missouri stated clearly, "Special education does not always and invariably involve special classes, but it does involve specialized teaching."[83]

The civil rights movement, however, was in a race against time because many impediments to the black student experience needed addressing. The physical deterioration of urban schools, which black students attended in large numbers, was apparent. Carceral-like conditions with locked doors, high steel fences, "metal window bars and cages on basement and ground floor windows," defined the school as a security space more than a place of learning. Security guards and school personnel sat by the front door carefully quizzing visitors about their destinations in the building, and signatures were required in logbooks.[84] Once inside, one found ability-grouped classes arranged in such a way as to render a newly integrated school immediately resegregated:

> Those pupils who are ahead of schedule are classified as accelerated and placed in classes for the intellectually gifted; those who are on schedule are classified as average; those who are somewhat behind schedule are placed in classes for the slow; those who are far behind are designated as holdovers and may be placed in special classes ... ; older youth who are behind and have been truants or defined as potential truants may also be placed in special classes, sometimes referred to as "career guidance" (vocational) classes; other special classes may be found for the handicapped, the emotional disturbed, the non-English speaking, the mentally retarded.[85]

"Lower ability" classes principally dealt with untoward behavior. While classes for the emotionally disordered served children from "culturally deprived" backgrounds, teachers noticed students with "poor behavior" in gifted, average, slow, mentally retarded, and vocational classes. The further one "descended" into "lower-ability" classes, the blacker and browner the classes became, observed education anthropologist, G. Alexander Moore:

> This desirability of rating of the various classes is part of the segregation patterns in ghetto schools. It is here where the advantages of the observational method are clear, for the ghetto school is marked not only by the obvious segregation of class or ethnic group, but also by the formal, official segregation within each grade by ability; and further by an informal segregation in each grade according to behavior. Thus, many slum schools are divided into classes that are defined as teachable or non-teachable. The nonteachable or custodial classes are ranked at the bottom of each grade.[86]

Indeed, gifted and average-ability classes contained "unteachable" students; however, difficult students could always be placed into lower-ranked classes and isolated rooms. A result of ability grouping and the "ranking of children within the grade according to their academic worth is the use of the lower ranking groups as a 'dumping ground' for children who are behavioral problems so that they will not have a bad influence on those who are 'good' workers."[87] As white teachers and administrators targeted "unmanageable" black and brown behavior, these students would be placed in classes for the emotionally disturbed with greater frequency. In the 1960s, teachers and school administrators often referred to classes with so-called unteachable black and brown students as "discipline" classes even if they served special needs children or not.

School officials purported an association between black and brown students who underperformed academically and students who they identified as behaviorally problematic. To experience academic challenges in predominantly white schools proved a hard row to hoe; to be deemed habitually unruly on top of academic challenges was tantamount to an educational death sentence. Lacking the academic and social skills required to advance through the "normal" system, "black and brown children fell behind in all areas of measurement." School officials and educational authorities wrote them off even though the "school continues to have the responsibility for their custodial care during the legally required hours set aside for formal education." The perception of the "unteach-ables" and the classes they attended was devastating for students of color. "Informally, but quite openly," explained Elizabeth Eddy, director of research for Project TRUE, "schoolteachers and administrators refer to some classes for the slow child as 'discipline classes,' 'custodial classes,' 'jungle classes,' 'zoos,' and classes 'one can forget about as far as teaching is concerned.'"[88]

Recalling how a female teacher described the kind of student that sat in her classroom, G. Alexander Moore Jr., assistant professor of anthropology at Emory University, and part of the same research team as Elizabeth Eddy, wrote, "It must be remembered that it was Mrs. Auslander herself who defined this class as a discipline class. She went further and defined a 'discipline class,' saying it consisted of emotionally disturbed and mentally retarded pupils. The term *discipline class* is her own coinage and not official usage." Moore corroborated Mrs. Auslander's appraisal of her classroom. "The principal had also referred to [Mrs. Auslander's] classroom as a wild one, and the assistant principal spoke of it as being one of several 'jungle' classes," said Moore. Fieldnotes taken at the school revealed that "other teachers in casual conversation with our observers called it a 'zoo' or 'mental institution.'"[89] The attempt to constrict and limit ED from the socially maladjusted in definition and in policy made no difference in how education officials identified ED classes. As anthropologist

Elizabeth Eddy surmised, "Classes with the worst reputations are apt to be comprised of holdovers, truants, the emotionally disturbed, or others who share in common the fact that they have become defined as 'a discipline problem.'" "In the school in the slum area," Eddy concluded, "these classes are also likely to have at least some recent migrants and some who have been in trouble with law-enforcement agencies outside of the school."[90]

While the educational disability rights movement may have understood the increasing number of students identified as ED or LD as a benefit for the "handicapped," the civil rights movement took issue with how white teachers treated black students in classrooms. Black and Latinx students, with the assistance of civil rights organizations, staged boycotts in New York, Philadelphia, Los Angeles, and Boston, just to name a few. Many inequities, ranging from textbooks to the lack of educational resources, raised the ire of students and their parents. Nothing frustrated them more than racist white teachers and administrators whose blatant hostility and indifference made attending these schools unbearable. Author Jonathan Kozol, in *Death at an Early Age* expounded on the ways in which white teachers set the boundary between expectation and empathy, and how he, as a young volunteer teacher in a Boston public school, was dissuaded from connecting with black students. Kozol witnessed the amount of time a teacher spent working and caring for the dwindling number of white students at the school. "I did not once observe her having offered to do anything of that sort for any child who was Negro, unless it was prompted by a stark emergency," Kozol recalled. "I could not help noticing as well that when I took it on my own initiative to do something similar for a couple of the Negro children in my class, she heard about it immediately and came up to advise me that it was not at all a good idea."[91]

It was one thing for a white teacher to discourage another white teacher from connecting and showing genuine empathy to black and brown students. It was an entirely different situation when white teachers spoke negatively about students, parents, and other teachers who fought against racism and inequality in the schools. Communities of color responded with planned walk-outs and attendance boycotts with the hope that sympathetic teachers would support them in changing inequitable conditions. While a few white teachers joined student protests, most of them did not, preferring instead to offer pejorative comments about their students' actions. One teacher told Dr. Estelle Fuchs, a third researcher on the Project TRUE team: "If many of them are out, it's just that much less that I have problems with." This same teacher said the planned boycotts were "unethical" and "noneducational." With an air of dismissal that often accompanied white judgment, she concluded, "As far as I'm concerned, if they want to stay home and they believe in this, let them stay home. They'll lose a lot of work and it's ridiculous for them. They're so far behind anyway that they are going to stay out and miss more days of school! They're not going to benefit by it. If they want to stay home, let them stay home."[92] Never having to consider the experiences of students of color in hostile educational spaces, most white teachers refused to empathize with their plight even if one or two tried: "They talk about the Negroes being culturally deprived. I'm the one who's been goddamn culturally deprived," quipped a white teacher.[93]

The "cultural deprivation" of white teachers, as defined by a lack of knowledge about students of color, proved confessional. An entire body of research emerged from the civil rights and ethnic power movements to help train white teachers, assisting many to fill the knowledge gap and become better equipped to teach students outside of their experience. Black studies and ethnic studies,[94] anthropological perspectives on black culture and education,[95] cultural pluralism, and multicultural education[96] appeared on the educational landscape in the late 1960s. This body of research, however, would have a difficult time influencing the conversation on black student learning and behavior due to another body of literature in teacher training that privileged psychoeducational theories and practices. A profound difference existed between the two educational approaches. Culturally relevant practices placed the emphasis on what teachers needed to know about students of color. Psychoeducational practices placed emphasis on how students of color behaved. Psychoeducational practices proffered behavior management strategies in classrooms, allowing teachers greater agency in modifying troubled behavior. But it seemed impossible, however, to modify behavior without understanding the student of color's experience.

The educational disability rights movement merged the fields of mental health and education, creating the "therapeutic team" that placed trained special education teachers at the center of the intervention process. A key component of the movement was the development of a range of approaches to educate "emotionally disturbed" students, most involving deemphasizing the role of residential facilities and hospitals where many ED students learned. Eli Bower asked: "If such children were sick, they should be in hospitals. Some were—the seriously autistic and schizophrenic, but what of the others—the acting out, passive-aggressive, character disorders, personality problems, withdrawn, phobic and depressed children?"[97] Deinstitutionalization softened society's long-standing practice of confining people with mental health challenges in hospitals. Deinstitutionalization returned many to their families, placed them in community-based health programs, and ensured children with such difficulties attend public schools. The educational disability rights movement argued that the psychopathology of emotionally disturbed children could be aided by properly trained classroom teachers. Heretofore, teachers had the smallest influence in the intervention process and had little voice in strategizing how to educate/manage ED students.[98] "In the late 1950s, psychodynamic theories for explaining behavior and feelings were dominant in the mental health field," explained Frank Wood, professor of educational psychology at the University of Minnesota. "Psychiatrists, psychiatric social workers, and clinical psychologists dominated the discussion of related interventions," Wood continued. "Educators had a seat at the table but little opportunity to participate in the discussion."[99] If the "therapeutic milieu" was now the classroom, then teachers would not only teach content but also manage difficult behavior. But what constituted "difficult" and "unmanageable" behavior, particularly as it applied to black students? Black scholarship as well as the broader civil rights movement provided insight into this question; however, the black movement and its concomitant scholarship did not have the power to influence educational decisions over a majority of black children. Thus, privileging psychoeducational theories and practices based on the work of psychologist B. F. Skinner and other learning theorists while ignoring the important body of research on black identity and culture that would hurt black and brown students.[100] By the time culturally relevant teaching strategies were in vogue in the 1980s, the referral rates of black and brown students into EBD classes had skyrocketed. Overlooking the emerging body of research produced by black scholars about black education and black culture, the civil rights movement and the educational disability rights movement represented different learning and classroom management styles that worked at cross-purposes.

Throughout the 1960s, several white psychoeducational experts offered "solutions" to the ED "problem" through their research, including William Cruickshank's Montgomery County, Maryland study that focused on "routine, structure, and reduction of distracting stimuli"[101] and Dr. Nicholas Hobbs's Project Re-Ed, which promoted the teacher as counselor. Scholars implored teachers and administrators to focus on "teaching rather than on treatment."[102] Dr. William Morse of the University of Michigan agreed with this premise. He enhanced Dr. Fritz Redl's Life Space Intervention (LSI) model, which was used in group homes and camps in Detroit. Morse conceived of what he called the "crisis teacher," who would work alongside the regular classroom teacher. The crisis teacher served as an expert in the curriculum as well as remedial mental health techniques that she or he could employ in real time. The crisis teacher allowed emotionally disturbed students to remain in the classroom with their peers. Models like teacher as counselor, the teacher-therapist, and the crisis teacher offer evidence of the marriage between mental health and education. Child psychiatry had become a specialized field of study, carving out a space in the broad area of mental health and schooling. Since child psychiatry was an established field, it was only "natural" for clinicians to partner with teachers to create "conceptual models" to modify student behavior. "A conceptual model," wrote psychologist James M. Kauffman and special education professor Timothy J. Landrum, "provides the basic assumptions or ideas about how students learn, and an educational approach is the way those assumptions are put into practice in instruction."[103]

Conceptual models flourished in the mid-1960s and early 1970s with new teacher-training programs and screening techniques enhancing the "therapeutic milieu." The educational disability rights movement placed its faith in screening systems that assessed behavior. Assessing behavior required ad infinitum data collection for the purposes of rating. Names were given to instruments, such as the "School Self-Control Behavior Inventory (SCBI)"; variables were identified, like "classroom behavior," or "achievement pattern," or "self-concept as a learner"; the rater was either a teacher, a student rating him or herself, or a student rating another student. For such screening instruments to be effective, both administrative and the scoring time of the collected data should remain practicable. This process aimed to determine a student's "capacity to cope effectively in school," stated Nicholas Long, professor at American University. "For some pupils, success in schools seems questionable," Long reasoned, "and for a few others, it seems unlikely."[104]

Eli Bower's claim to fame was not just defining ED but also creating some of the earliest screening instruments that he believed empowered teachers working with ED students. He noted early on the "professional experience and the observational setting of the school give the teacher an unequaled opportunity to perceive and help the incipiently disturbed child."[105] Knowing a child's psychiatric nosology prior to the screening was unnecessary, Bower surmised, as the instrument used by the teacher "does not presume to go beyond what is observable in a school setting, and stays within the conceptual range of teachers, administrators, and pupil personnel workers."[106] The educator's proximity to clinicians reinforced the teacher's "observational" skill. "It is also noted that many teachers have access to special services such as remedial teachers, psychologists, counselors, speech correctionists, audiometrists, and school physicians," noted Bower.[107] However, the false belief in bias-free data gathering and assessing, especially of black students, proved problematic from the beginning. These assessments were tainted by the assumption that schools did not have to account for the racial experience of the students and the racism of the teachers. Furthermore, teachers may have perceived "disturbed" behavior differently as contexts changed. Ultimately, screening instruments did not measure emotional disturbance but rather accounted for whether students' behavior disturbed others. Bower admitted as much, conceding, "It accepts as a given that emotional disturbance is disturbing to others and may differ in quality and degree from one setting to another—as, for example, at home, in school, or with a peer group, as in play."[108] Screening devices and conceptual models did not give teachers more effective tools to help the disabled. Instead, they offered teachers more power to discriminate against students of color.

Esther Rothman enjoyed a long career as a clinician at Bellevue Psychiatric Hospital in New York City. She assumed the role of principal at the Livingston School for Girls, a day school for the emotionally disturbed and socially maladjusted students suspended from public schools.

According to Rothman, the female students at Livingston demonstrated the most profound disciplinary problems in the city, known as the "incorrigibles of the public school system." She noted that "over 85 percent of them were black." Lacking the foresight when she worked as principal, she reflected on her experience at Livingston years later with a moment of clarity: "I could not believe only black girls in New York City were the 'unmanageables.' What happened to the white incorrigible girls? The white girls, it turned out, found their way to the social agencies and the residential treatment centers. . . . The black girls were dumped in the school." Echoing Lloyd Dunn's cautionary tale in 1968 about the increasing number of black students forsaken in educable mentally retarded (EMR) classes, Rothman witnessed the proliferation of black students in classes for emotionally and behaviorally disordered. "The black girls at Livingston are labeled 'behavioral problems.' Undoubtedly, they all are. They are also labeled 'emotionally disturbed' and 'socially maladjusted.' Undoubtedly, many are not."[109] Rothman may have desired a stop to the over-identification of black students as emotionally disturbed and socially maladjusted, but she nevertheless framed black pupils as problematic.

If black students were not always emotionally disturbed or socially maladjusted, their teachers and schools certainly viewed them as disciplinary problems. Rothman's commentary reflected her years at the school, suggesting that black female students at Livingston saw the school and society as the source of their struggles. She reflected, "In many cases, their problems in school are related to their inability to see the school system in any light but an unjust one. In many cases, it is the system and/or society that needs to be changed, not the children; thus, I resent calling this group of children 'disturbed' or 'maladjusted.'" Rothman wondered if "teacher-training colleges throughout the country" and "special education departments" perpetuated the problem more than remedied it when these institutions labeled black children ED and socially maladjusted (SM). She believed greater discernibility was necessary, as she queried, "Should we talk of children who are discipline cases . . . in the same educational breath as we talk of schizophrenic or autistic children? I think not." Rothman's call for greater precision in the application of ED to black students represented a good faith reading of the dumping ground practice in ED. She admitted, "Thousands of children throughout the country find themselves in special programs and classes, labeled 'behavior problems' or 'disturbed' or 'maladjusted' . . . because they have not been able to conform to the practices of the school situation as it exists."[110] But Rothman's call for greater precision cut two ways. She admonished the practice of "dumping" black students in ED classes. However, she also advocated for a narrower definition of ED that would eliminate socially maladjusted/discipline students from ED classification. If Rothman had it her way, black students would still be "overrepresented" in the ED category from referrals in the 1960s. But so too were black students "underrepresented" in that "socially maladjusted" or "discipline" students received minimal or no services at all. Peter Stein, a director at a Community Action Agency Education Center confirmed both developments:

> They may not have been in school or were getting minimal services or inadequate services in school. . . . If they're not in school they'll probably be in the courts or be suspended or be put in special education programs that were like basement programs, watered-down programs. You have to realize that these were pre- 94–142 days (EHA). In addition, what was happening was that the community was just getting sensitive to the fact that a disproportionate number of kids who were minorities were being put in watered-down programs. . . . So the complaint was that a lot of our kids were being suspended, sent home, dropping out, being pushed out of school, whatever.[111]

When Stein refers to the pre- 94–142 days as an era of hodgepodge special education programs, he underscored how, prior to 1975, schools dealt with the educational needs of black and brown students with impunity. Because schools unceremoniously expelled and excluded students with special needs, special education and much of the legal apparatus of disability unfolded alongside in-class turbulence between black and brown students and their teachers.[112] UCLA education scholar Lawrence Vredevoe captured this trend in 1965 when he stated, "where secondary school attendance was a privilege instead of compulsory, administrators and teachers did not worry about the constant trouble maker. They just expelled him." [113] However, by 1975, according to Joseph Tropea, professor of sociology, "Expulsions of pupils from public school systems in the United States was largely precluded by law; American school authorities then had to resolve classroom problems within the organization of the school."[114] Legal cases, such as *Goss v. Lopez, Larry P., Diana, Lau v. Nichols* reflects this trend though in no way did expulsions disappear.[115]

Mills v. Board of Education became a foundational suspension and expulsion case that led to the creation of the Education for All Handicapped Children Act (EHA) in 1975. Seven black students and their families filed a lawsuit against the District of Columbia Public Schools, claiming that the district denied them a publicly supported education. Peter Mills was a twelve-year-old black boy, a dependent ward of the District of Columbia and a resident at Junior Village. The principal of Brent Elementary School excluded Mills in March of 1971 because he was a "behavior problem." Other students experienced similar treatment by D.C. public schools. Six other students joined Mills on the lawsuit:

Duane Blacksheare is thirteen years old, black, resident at Saint Elizabeth's Hospital, Washington, D.C., and a dependent committed child. He was excluded from the Giddings Elementary School in October, 1967, at which time he was in third grade. Duane allegedly was a "behavior problem." Defendants have not provided him with a full hearing or with a timely and adequate review of his status.

George Liddell, Jr., is eight years old, black, resident with his mother, Daisy Liddell at 601 Morton Street, N.W.... and is an AFDC recipient. George has never attended public school because of the denial of his application to the Maury Elementary School on the grounds that he required a Special Class. George allegedly was retarded. Defendants have not provided him with a full hearing or with a timely and adequate review of his status.

Steven Gaston is eight years old, black, resident with his mother, Ina Gaston, at 714 9th Street, N.E., Washington, D.C. and unable to afford private instruction. He has been excluded from the Taylor Elementary School since September, 1969, at which time he was in the first grade. Steven allegedly was slightly brain-damaged and hyperactive, and was excluded because he wandered around the classroom. Defendants have not provided him with a full hearing or with a timely and adequate review of his status.

Michael Williams is sixteen years old, black, resident at Saint Elizabeth's Hospital, Washington, D.C., and unable to afford private instruction. Michael is epileptic and allegedly slightly retarded. He has been excluded from the Sharpe Health School since October, 1969, at which time he was temporarily hospitalized. Defendants have not provided him with full hearing or with a timely and adequate review of his status.

Janice King is thirteen years old, black, resident with her father . . . at 233 Anacostia Avenue, N.E. . . . and unable to afford private instruction. She has been denied access to public schools since reaching compulsory age, and as a result of the rejection of her application, based on a lack of an appropriate educational program, Janice is brain-damaged and retarded, with right hemiplegia, resulting from childhood illness. Defendants have not provided her with a full hearing or with a timely and adequate review of her status.

Jerome James is twelve years old, black, resident with his mother . . . at 2512 Ontario Avenue, N.W., . . . and an AFDC recipient. Jerome is a retarded child and has been totally excluded from public school. Defendants have not given him a full hearing or a timely and adequate review of his status.[116]

The court ordered that the District of Columbia Public Schools provide the named plaintiffs with a publicly supported education and identify every child suspended, expelled, and excluded in district schools along with the reasons used to keep them out of the schools.

Mills is both a civil rights and a precedent-setting special education case, demonstrating how the civil rights and the educational disability rights movements overlapped in the 1970s. The judge on the case laid out the basic facts: "Although all of the named minor plaintiffs are identified as Negroes, the class they represent is not limited by their race. They sue on behalf of and represent all other District of Columbia residents of school age who are eligible for a free public education and who have been, or may be, excluded from such education or otherwise deprived by defendants of access to publicly supported education." [117] Thus, what ultimately leads to P.L.-94–142—the Education for All Handicapped Children Act (EHA) in 1975 is *Mills v. Board of Education.* Several cases led to *Mills,* including *Brown v. Board of Education, Bolling v. Sharpe,* and *Hobson v. Hansen. Brown* argued that education is the "very foundation of good citizenship," and that a child cannot be expected to "succeed in life if he is denied the opportunity of education. Such an opportunity . . . is a right which must be made available to all on equal terms."[118] *Bolling* reasoned that segregation in public education is not a government objective, and that racial separation "imposes on Negro children of the District of Columbia a burden that constitutes an arbitrary deprivation of their liberty in violation of the Due Process Clause."[119] *Hobson,* one of the first special education cases, concluded that the "doctrine of equal educational opportunity—the equal protection clause in its application to public school education—is in its full sweep a component of due process binding on the District."[120]

With *PARC v. Commonwealth of Pennsylvania, Mills v. District of Columbia,* and the passage of the Education for All Handicapped Children Act, the 1970s represented a triumphal era for civil and disability rights case law and legislation. One can argue that both movements converged at the point of educational justice for all children, or that the civil rights movement passed the baton to the educational disability rights movement. Though the educational disability rights movement was racially and ethnically diverse, it proved incapable of curtailing the discrimination black and brown students experienced inside schools. The suspension of students of color increased exponentially with their "behavior" as a scapegoat for a resegregation scheme. Teachers and school administrators continued to place students of color in special education classes and label them as EMR and ED despite the clear language of the law that required states to "prohibit racial or cultural discrimination in the classification and placement of handicapped children . . ."[121] T. H. Bell, the U.S. commissioner of education, communicated what he heard while testifying on behalf of the Education for All Handicapped Children Act: "The reports of widespread mislabeling of disadvantaged and bilingual children by identifying them as mentally retarded or emotionally disturbed, point to cultural bias found in commonly accepted and widely used screening instruments, and this must heighten our concern."[122]

Prior to 1975, court challenges from black and brown families relied on civil rights case law, now all subsequent challenges used the Education for All Handicapped Children Act. *Lora v. Board of Education of the City of New York* was a class action suit that began during the EHA legislative hearings. The case spoke principally to the growing problem of segregating black and Latinx youth who exhibited "bad" behavior. Prior to the flexibility afforded by the federal SED disability category and state-level EBD classes, misbehaved black and brown students were frequently placed in alternative schools as the case reiterated, "The underlying suit ... commenced on June 11, 1975, by seven Black and Hispanic New York City Public School students who were assigned to a 'special day school' for the education of the socially maladjusted and emotionally disturbed." The complaint relied primarily on the Fourth, Eighth, Thirteenth, and Fourteenth Amendments to the U.S. Constitution along with Title VI of the Civil Rights Act of 1964. By the time the trial started in 1977, a supplemental complaint was filed that withdrew the first three constitutional claims and substituted it with the Rehabilitation Act of 1973 and the Education for All Handicapped Children Act along with both laws' regulations.[123]

The Education for All Handicapped Children Act was signed into law in November 1975. It represented the culmination of educational disability rights and it acknowledged that parents bore the brunt of the struggle. While the law recognized the role played by parents, lawmakers responsible for passing the legislation may have overpromised what the law would do for families of color. Lawmakers presumed parents would no longer have to fight for their children's rights in court. Senator Jennings Randolph announced, "Over the past few years, parents of handicapped children have begun to recognize that their children are being denied services which are guaranteed under the Constitution. It should not, however, be necessary for parents throughout the country to continue utilizing the courts to assure themselves a remedy."[124] Despite the lofty rhetoric that frequently accompanies the signing of a new policy, the successful passage of EHA did not guarantee justice for *all* students and families as the name of the law implied. States grew skittish of the law's implementation and their compliance responsibilities as it pertained to federal entitlement and distribution formulas. Then there was the perennial problem of defining disability categories and the exclusion of the socially maladjusted from the federal definition of seriously emotionally disturbed (SED) that placed families and students of color at a legal disadvantage.

The attempt to exclude African Americans and Latinx students from the law proved far from accidental. The language that ultimately excluded most black and brown students from the "disabled" remained strong and clear. Senator Randolph wrote again: "The definition clearly refers only to children whose handicaps will require special education and related services, and not to children whose learning problems are caused by environmental, cultural or economic disadvantage."[125] Indeed, a host of white historical actors considered students of color "deprived" if they lacked a white middle-class upbringing and attendant social values that accompanied whiteness. Though educational authorities and researchers also considered working-poor white students disadvantaged, the language of "cultural deprivation" became constitutive of students of color and their educational ambitions. The second deliberate exclusion in the law prohibited it from extending services to the socially maladjusted. The law only covered students designated as seriously emotional disturbed (SED), a direct carry over from the 1963 policy.[126]

Special education scholars spent a considerable amount of effort debating questions of designation and inclusion, invariably called the social maladjustment exclusion clause in EHA. As aforementioned, education authorities and scholars used social maladjustment and emotional disturbance synonymously to describe black behavior. They referred to the terms interchangeably in clinical and educational settings for the greater part of the twentieth century. Due to its overwhelming association with African Americans, social maladjustment was excluded from the law. Social maladjustment and delinquency (court adjudicated social maladjustment) did not represent mere labels applied to black students like LD; social maladjustment and delinquent behavior were considered "normal" for African Americans. Scholars need only to examine the testimony of clinical professionals and school administrators who stood before Congress in the early 1960s; when pressed by lawmakers, these professionals split hairs when defining emotional disturbance and made distinctions between emotional disturbance and social maladjustment. The actions by well-respected professionals in the field were not inadvert, nor was Congress's acceptance of their views on the subject.

In addition, Eli Bower—the author of the federal definition—could not have it both ways. Bower's convincing research in the late 1950s and 1960s became the major contribution to our contemporary understanding of emotional disturbance. In Bower's 1982 essay, "Defining Emotional Disturbance: Public Policy and Research," he claimed ignorance of why Congress excluded the socially maladjusted category, citing "to differentiate between behaviors that are antisocial or active and the so-called neurotic or personality disabilities of a more passive kind as if they were indeed separate entities is unfortunate and misleading."[127] Bower contributed to the "misfortune" he invoked here. In his 1959 essay entitled "The Emotionally Handicapped Child and the School," Bower spent more time fleshing out the distinguishing characteristics of ED by first arguing for replacing the word "disturbed" with "handicapped." He affirmed, "The term 'handicap' has a more lasting and persistent quality; 'disturbances' are seen as transitory or temporary." To be sure, Bower's preference for the word "handicap" and its "more lasting and persistent quality" stemmed from his belief in the *persistence* of emotional disturbance and the *degrees* to which one may find emotions affecting a personality. For Bower, the term "disturbance" not only indicated socially maladjusted behavior that manifested in acting out and overly aggressive conduct but also emotions resulting in stealing, running away, and truancy. In other words, in Bower's mind, emotionally maladjusted "disturbance" was simple, straightforward, and predictably induced by environmental factors in contrast to emotionally nonmaladjusted "handicapped" persons whose emotions were defined by a breakdown in personality processes of the id, ego, and superego.[128]

Writing in the third person about himself in 1982, Bower provided a historical retrospective. He reflected, "The legal definition of 'emotional disturbance' proposed by the federal government under PL 94–142 is Bower's 1957 definition with some modifications. The modifications do serious damage to the integrity of the research and conceptual base from which the definition is drawn. The difficulties inherent in a definition of this type of handicap are delineated. It is suggested that where policymakers and researchers join together, such relationships are best enhanced when each respects the assumptions and concepts of the other."[129] Bower's statement proved disingenuous. Education and clinical researchers virtually camped out in the halls of Congress to advocate for new laws on behalf of the intellectually and emotionally disabled, which included the socially maladjusted and the "institutionalized delinquent." The quest for new legislation and federal funds to protect the rights of children was a constant process of give and take. Researchers often had to convince lawmakers, not the other way around. Researchers convinced lawmakers in the early 1960s after answering probing questions from them. In fact, the persistence of education and clinical researchers on Capitol Hill turned some public officials into advocates of the "emotionally disturbed" themselves. They championed the cause of educational disability rights through the passage of ESEA Title VI in 1969 and again in 1975 (EHA).

In 1982, Bower admitted that his conception of the emotionally disturbed child "had to be socially maladjusted in school."[130] Many experts believed the two categories were the same for the better part of the twentieth century. Bower also believed the conventional wisdom, although he purposely avoided defining ED with social maladjustment in the late 1950s. "The behavior of the emotionally handicapped child is, to the extent of his handicap, not a matter of choice, but necessity," averred Bower in 1959.[131] What appeared to be an obvious reason—the conflict over scarce resources—was actually about the attempt to racially exclude students from a federal definition of disability (though the two were not mutually exclusive) and an understanding of ED as a manifestation of "personality-derived" behavior problems. On the one hand, the exclusion tactics worked in that the socially maladjusted were separated from ED designations. On the other hand, the tactics failed, as teachers continued to place "maladjusted" black and brown students in ED classes across the states. The socially maladjusted student was, and still is, deemed the "conduct problem" student, now variously defined as "conduct disordered," "oppositional defiant disordered," or "antisocial disordered" if that student receives a clinical diagnosis. Some students who are placed in alternative settings like federal level four special education schools were and are considered "disruptive" students and are overdisciplined, suspended, expelled, and pushed out of general education classes. Many of these same students were and continue to be referred to as "delinquent" and "emotionally disturbed" students who have been court adjudicated. In too many states across the country, those students whose behavior does not conform to so-called norms and who exhibit the most "unsocialized" or "externalized" behaviors in school and society are disproportionately black.

Arguably, special education rested on a shaky foundation between 1975, when the Education for All Handicapped Children Act passed, and 1990, when it was reauthorized as the Individuals with Disabilities Education Act (IDEA). The slipperiness of disability definitions contributed to special education's faulty foundation. Definitions of disability categories, particularly ED, were debated repeatedly as well as redefined from the 1970s through the early 1990s. Tied to the definitional conundrum were the projected prevalence rates of all disabled students. According to the Bureau of Education for the Handicapped (BEH) in the U.S. Office of Education, 230,000 ED students were served in 1974–1975, while it was projected that slightly over one million more were unidentified and unserved. The BEH reported that of the more than "8 million children (between birth and twenty-one years of age) with handicapping conditions requiring special education and related services, only 3.9 million such children are receiving an appropriate education."[132] Congress appeared concerned about the projections of the unserved and the cost as it pertained to "mild" disability categories. "Because of the 6 years that I served on the Dade County School Board," began Representative William Lehman of Florida, "one of the problems . . . is the appearance of these borderline cases of so-called handicapped. I know there is an area of autistic kids that don't seem to fit in anything in the public school program that I have seen. Then, we also get these kids with what the parents call 'leaning difficulties,' and they don't want to call them mentally retarded . . ." Representative Lehman asked James A. Harris, president of the National Education Association, directly: "I just wonder if you had in mind anything that we could put in this bill that would take care of this problem?"[133]

Lawmakers in Congress demanded definitional clarity to avoid wasting taxpayer funds on a system of categories broadly or abstractly defined. The categories in the 1970s included the "mentally retarded," "hard of hearing," "deaf," "speech impaired," "visually handicapped," "seriously emotionally disturbed," "crippled," or "other health impaired" children, who by reason thereof required special education and related services. Some lawmakers remained uncomfortable with the vagueness of the categories. Representative John Brademas of Indiana asked Frederick J. Weintraub, assistant executive director of governmental relations with the Council for Exceptional Children, for his professional opinion. Taking issue with ED and "other health impaired" persons, Brademas remarked before allowing Weintraub to answer, "Now, I have two problems. One is, a couple of those phrases are fairly open-ended. . . . It would seem to me that emotionally disturbed, as the phrase, 'other health impaired children,' that we have . . . a moral problem, and a fiscal problem as well as an educational problem. What is the universe? What do you think . . . we should mean when we say 'handicapped' for the purposes of providing Federal tax dollars to support their education?"[134] Weintraub responded:

Mr. Chairman, we would concur and support the retaining of the existing definition as you have read it. The definition in the legislative history is the definition that has gone back, I believe, since 1963, other than the more recent inclusion of the terminology "learning disability," which has been added. In addition to that definition, our Federal Government, and the history of the Government on terms like, "emotionally disturbed," we have long talked about seriously emotionally disturbed children. There are Federal regulations and guidelines which lay out the parameters of what the term "seriously emotionally disturbed" means. The term "health impaired" has been a problem.[135]

The dilemma of disability definitions—their meaning and their application—seemed unresolvable. Emotional disturbance became the greatest example of this intractable problem, as added explanations and exclusionary language in the federal definition created more confusion than clarification. A congressional subcommittee hearing captured this enigma: the "term includes children who are schizophrenic or autistic. The term does not include children who are socially maladjusted, unless it is determined that they are seriously emotionally disturbed."[136]

Between the late 1970s and the early 1990s, the broad understanding of ED experienced challenges, particularly the reconceptualization of autism (as originally defined by Leo Kanner and its severing from ED). Like social maladjustment and delinquency, autism was also understood by social scientists as an emotional disturbance. But Kanner, a child psychiatrist, had differentiated "children who were born with or developed psychotic behavior very early in their lives from the schizophrenic child who evidenced some early normal development and then became sick." Kanner believed autistic children were neither psychotic nor schizophrenic but nonetheless suffered from emotional disturbance. The Federal Register reported that when the implementation regulations for the Education for All Handicapped Children Act were published in 1977, "Autism was placed under the category of seriously emotionally disturbed, based on the knowledge available to the agency at the time. This original classification is now inappropriate, because it has been found that not all autistic children are seriously emotionally disturbed."[137] Even in the early research of Kanner, autistic behavior was believed to be nondeviant, which signified nonblack behavior. According to Kanner, though

autistic behavior resembles neurosis and psychosis, it is more associated
with children who experience difficulties with social interaction as well
as speaking, walking, and eating. Because of this modification of emotional disturbance, "Autism is now defined under Federal Regulations as
a condition manifested by severe communication and other developmental and educational problems, or having limited strength, vitality, or alert-
ness due to chronic or acute health problems."[138] Thus, on "January 16,
1981, the Department of Education recommended the deletion of childhood autism from the classification of 'severely emotionally disturbed'
and its placement in the category of 'other health impaired.'"[139] As the
author of ED, Bower disagreed with this turn, citing that "there is, however, no significant research that would suggest that childhood autism is
a product of other childhood diseases or a communicative disorder as
the term is understood."[140]

What seem like arbitrary changes in definitions, with or without supportive research, spoke more to the power of organizations and the politicization of disability. The National Society for Autistic Children and the
National Institute for Neurological and Communicative Disorders positioned themselves at the forefront of the struggle to wrestle autism from
ED. Then in the late 1980s, the Mental Health and Special Education
Coalition, a group of twenty organizations, and the Council for Children
with Behavioral Disorders (CCBD) led an effort to completely redefine
emotional disturbance and reverse the overrepresentation of black students in ED. The NAACP and La Raza participated in this endeavor, and
both organizations saw the uncoupling of autism from ED as a different
fight from theirs. The struggle for civil rights sought to curtail the disproportional placement of black and brown students in EBD. The disability
rights front, however, wanted to ensure the protection of white underrepresented students who needed services. But in the way the EHA defined
disability, black and brown students proved equally "underrepresented"
due to the exclusionary criteria in the SED federal definition while civil
rights groups fought against black and brown "overrepresentation" in EBD
across states and districts. A story in *Education Week* understood the
quandary well in 1992: "Sometimes perceived simply as bad kids, many
emotionally disturbed children fall through the cracks because they do
not meet the criteria of the current federal special education definition
(SED). At the same time ... the existing definition may also be causing

large groups of children to be mislabeled as emotionally disturbed when their problems may be less severe in nature or have more to do with cultural differences or their home environments."[141]

The struggle led by the civil and disability rights coalition brought the history of ED full circle. Again, "socially maladjusted" African American and Latinx students, along with perspectives about their behavior and culture, were at the center of the policy debate. The effort to recognize the "socially maladjusted" required the merging of two seemingly distinct but related categories, ED and BD.[142] The use of the term E/BD to underscore the behavioral component "is meant to signal that children who have conduct disorders—a condition characterized by a consistent pattern of rule-breaking and social aggression toward peers—would also be included," wrote Debra Viadero of *Education Week*.[143] This time, however, research on behavior, culture, and learning styles published primarily by black and Latinx scholars was brought to bear in the attempt to change the federal definition on behalf of students of color.[144] While historically excluded from the federal definition of seriously emotionally disturbed (SED), the so-called socially maladjusted had been designated as behavioral disordered (BD) in many states and districts across the country. Black and Latinx student placement under state E/BD criteria reflected the national trend of managing students with social maladjustment problems. The proposed change in the federal SED definition not only reflected this population, but the use of BD as a state category:

The term "emotional or behavioral disorder" means a disability that is characterized by behavioral or emotional responses in school programs so different from appropriate age, cultural, or ethnic norms that the responses adversely affect educational performance, including academic, social, vocational or personal skills; more than a temporary, expected response to stressful events in the environment; consistently exhibited in two different settings, at least one of which is school-related; and unresponsive to direct intervention applied in general education, or the condition of a child is such that general education interventions would be insufficient.

The term includes such a disability that co-exists with other disabilities. The term includes a schizophrenic disorder, affective disorder, anxiety disorder, or other sustained disorder of conduct or adjustment, affecting a child if the disorder affects educational performance as described in paragraph 1.[145]

This proposed statement moved beyond Bower's false dichotomy in his original definition that an "inability to learn which could not be explained by intellectual, sensory, or other health factors" indicated an emotional disturbance.[146] It also deemphasized Bower's "inability to build or maintain satisfactory interpersonal relationships with peers and teachers" as determinative of ED.[147] Further, the proposed definition accounted for the impact of a student's out-of-school environment instead of positing its normality. The proposed definition required a heightened level of teacher vigilance in distinguishing the differences between "bad" black behavior and black cultural practices.

Participating in the Ad Hoc Committee on Ethnic and Multicultural Concerns in the CCBD, Dr. Thomas McIntyre provided professionals in the field of special education with the blueprint. Synthesizing the research published by black, brown, and several progressive white scholars in fields like anthropology, linguistics, sociology, history, and education since the 1970s, McIntyre confessed:

> Ethnicity, culture, and heritage play an important role in the psychological and educational development of our pupils. Sadly, culturally determined behaviors are commonly misinterpreted or viewed negatively by educators not from those cultures. Given that many educational professionals lack knowledge of cultural influences and differences, and assessment instruments commonly contain cultural bias, culturally different youngsters are at risk for being identified as having an emotional or behavioral disorder when they do not.[148]

McIntyre, the CCBD, and the task force sought to include the cultural background of the student as part of all identification, assessment, and placement practices in E/BD. They also insisted that "valid cultural differences in behavior not be viewed as disordered."[149] The CCBD sent the following guidelines and recommendations to the federal government:[150]

1. Removal from special programs all culturally different students who are not truly exhibiting emotional and/or behavioral disorders, but rather are displaying culturally based behavior.
2. Provision of respectful and culturally appropriate educational and treatment services to culturally different students who do possess emotional and/or behavioral disorders.

3. Implementation of culturally and linguistically competent assessment procedures.
4. Recruitment of culturally different professionals.
5. Provision of preservice and inservice training in modifications of practice that better address the characteristics of culturally different students with emotional and/or behavioral disorders.
6. Creation of welcoming institutional atmospheres in which culturally different students with EBD feel valued, respected, and physically and psychologically safe.
7. Enhancement of the cultural knowledge base of professionals, clients/students, and the public at large.

The initiative to change the federal definition of SED, prohibit future misplacement by altering identification and assessment, and reverse old placement abuses lasted five years. The coalition began waging its fight in 1987, culminating in a vote as part of a scheduled reauthorization of the Rehabilitation Act of 1973 in the summer of 1992. Many believed the struggle to change the definition would pass easily since the coalition wrote position papers and lobbied school districts, civil rights groups, special education experts, and mental health organizations, all of whom threw their collective weight behind the SED/EBD issue. But the vote failed. The National Schools Boards Association (NSBA) objected to the coverage of the "socially maladjusted" in the reauthorization. Thus, as the status quo continued, so too did the politics of black behavior in schools and society.[151]

The failure to include the socially maladjusted in the reauthorization of the law meant that black students and families found themselves in a race against time to avoid suspensions and expulsions without legal due process. Black behavior was not only theoretical—it was a lived experience, manifesting in hallways and classrooms. School authorities responded to variations in behavior of black children with invariable punitive measures. In 1975, the U.S. Supreme Court "established due process as a prerequisite to suspension and expulsion" in the precedent-setting case, *Goss v. Lopez*.[152] The court held that school officials must give "an explanation of the evidence" against a student and provide "an opportunity" for that student "to present his side of the story."[153] In *Goss v. Lopez*, the principals at Marion-Franklin High School, Central High School, and McGuffey Junior High School in Columbus, Ohio, failed to do so. Ohio law empowered administrators to "suspend a pupil for misconduct for up to 10 days or to expel him. A pupil who is expelled, or his parents, may appeal the decision to the Board of Education and in connection therewith shall be permitted to be heard at the board meeting."[154] Instead of placing the burden onto students and their parents through the appeal process, the Supreme Court forced schools to provide a hearing for students prior to the act of suspension or expulsion.

In the *Goss* case, the pattern of discipline by schools must be seen in the larger context of student unrest and political grievances. The marginalization of black life in Ohio mirrored other states, boiling over into public disturbances on school grounds and in neighborhoods. Protests at Kent State University and Ohio State University in 1969 and 1970, respectively, provided a backdrop for what manifested in public schools and in the streets. A sixty-nine-year-old white dry cleaner owner named David E. Chestnut shot and killed twenty-seven-year-old Roy Beasley, a black city sanitation worker, over the issue of children playing in Chestnut's backyard. The unrest began on E. Main Street on the Near East Side of Columbus after Beasley's murder. But when Chestnut, claiming self-defense, was acquitted of second-degree murder by eleven white jurors and one black juror, the rebellions commenced again in June of 1970. In February 1971, Dwight Lopez, the named defendant in the case, remarked on the conflict at Central High School during Black History Week. He explained that black students entered the lunchroom and began overturning tables. Tensions continued throughout February and March, resulting in seventy-five students suspended at Central, of which Lopez was one. The protest spilled over to Marion-Franklin High School, where Tyrone Washington, Clarence Byars, Rudolph Sutton, and Bruce Harris were suspended for being party to the conflict. Disturbances occurred at the same time at McGuffey Junior High School where students were dismissed for the day after breaking lightbulbs and throwing objects in the school cafeteria. On their way home, thirteen-year-old Betty Chrome and several other students from McGuffey were arrested after stopping at Linden McKinley High School to observe that school's racial hostilities. Chrome was not charged with a crime, but her school suspended her, nevertheless. Like the others above, she too would be one of the named plaintiffs in the *Goss v. Lopez* case.

The rate at which black and Latinx students integrated white schools created a sense of moral panic across the United States.[155] Court-ordered desegregation plans attempted to fulfill the promise of *Brown v. Board* and break the back of white resistance in the 1970s and 1980s. When black students appeared, not only did conflicts erupt over Black History Week, but white teachers and administrators scrutinized black intelligence and behavior and applied a host of labels. "Black students had been regarded by staff as having low ability," wrote Judith Preissle Goetz and E. Anne Rowley Breneman in reference to schools in the South. "When the district was desegregated, they were placed in separate classrooms and labeled educable mentally retarded, learning disabled, or behavior disordered."[156] Undoubtedly, misconduct and unacceptable behavior occurred in a number of schools, causing school officials to meet the challenge with disciplinary punishment. Students of color proved to be particularly vulnerable, but those with disabilities were even more susceptible to school discipline policies. Though the *Goss* case restored due process rights to educational decision-making, it did not slow the practice of suspensions and expulsions stemming from "untoward" behavior and misconduct. Black students with emotional and behavior disorders or those deemed socially maladjusted were not spared from punitive disciplinary practices. In fact, those practices increased. Public Law 94–142 along with the court decisions in *Stuart v. Nappi* (1978) and *Doe v. Koger* (1979) attempted to curtail harsh school disciplinary practices by establishing that disruptive and ill-behaved students could not be expelled from schools if said misconduct was linked to their disability.[157]

Students with histories of "repeated maladaptive, disruptive or aggressive behavior, extensive in scope and serious in nature" often became targets of teachers and administrators as the case *Lora v. Board of Education of the City of New York* documented.[158] A common practice in managing emotionally disturbed black and Latinx students included placing them in special day schools for egregious behavior, and if that behavior proved unacceptable but tolerable, placing them in classes for the emotionally disturbed in integrated schools. Plaintiffs in the *Lora* case alleged that placing black and brown students in either day schools or ED classes functioned as a way for schools to keep "regular" or "mainstream" classes as white as possible:

> They contend that the special day schools are intentionally segregated "dumping grounds" for minorities forced into inadequate facilities without

due process. Racial composition ... in these special day schools is 68% Black; 27% Hispanic; and 5% Other, primarily White (figures as of October 31, 1977). The higher percentage of "minorities" in these schools is not a recent phenomenon; rather, a disparate racial composition has remained constant for nearly 15 years. The other major services for children with emotional disturbance, "classes for emotionally handicapped" (CEH classes) have a higher proportion, 20% of non-minority students. Still higher is the proportion of Whites in the New York City public school ... 36% Black, 23% Hispanic and 41% Other.[159]

New York City reported that over 90 percent of its special day school for students with emotional disturbance were students of color; its ED classes were 80 percent students of color; and its general education classrooms were 56 percent students of color. Thus, the ED school, the ED class, and the ED label served as proof of the immediate resegregation of black and brown students during the era of integration. To add insult to injury, administrators further divided classes for the emotionally handicapped (CEH as New York City called them) with the use of racial signifiers created by the likes of Eli Bower and others who promoted two types of ED:

There are, in addition to the special day schools, classes for the emotionally handicapped of two types: 1) CEH (A) classes ... and 2) CEH (B) classes. The behavior of those in the (A) classes may be termed bizarre in that it reflects a lack of touch with reality, caused by severe emotional crises. Many of these children may be schizophrenic, autistic, or psychotic. ... The CEH (B) children, on the other hand, have difficulty handling themselves in the regular learning situation and in relating to peers and authority figures. Their problems are closest to those of the pupils referred to special day schools.[160]

The final point to be made about black behavior is not exclusively about where this constructed behavior emerges and where it appears—special day schools, EBD classes at one level or another, or the juvenile justice system—but how black student behavior arrived at those sites in the first place. Black overrepresentation in EBD, just like LD and EMR, is a known phenomenon contemporarily, if not historically. Black overrepresentation is not a 1990s educational practice; it is as old as the system of special education itself. "The youngsters in deprived groups—that is, the youngsters who are from socioeconomic, ethnic, or racially disadvantaged groups—are almost always overrepresented in various kinds of statistics describing non-adaptive behavior," explained black educational psychologist Frank Wilderson Jr. "In delinquency, dropping out, mental illness, and the like," Wilderson observed, "this type of youngster contributes disproportionately to the incidence of the problem under consideration."[161] Black disproportional presence in EBD, LD, EMR specifically, and in special education in general, became a fait accompli based on discourses about black children and attendant labels that followed them from throughout the twentieth century: "emotionally disturbed," "disruptive," "behaviorally disordered," "behavior problem," "delinquent/offender," "aggressive," "pre-delinquent," "conduct problem," "maladapting," "noncompliant," "behaviorally disabled," "behaviorally disturbed," "moderately disturbed," "emotionally handicapped," and "conduct disordered."[162] Our understanding of contemporary black behavior, however, can become unmoored from these labels and their histories. Psychologists Leonard Ullmann and Len Krasner provided the most comprehensive understanding of how "bad" behavior rarely involves the actions of single individuals but is contextually produced by:

> The behavior itself, its social context, and an observer who is in a position of power. No specific behavior is abnormal in itself. Rather an individual may do something (e.g., verbalize hallucinations . . . stare into space, dress sloppily) under a set of circumstances (e.g., during a school class . . .) which upsets, annoys, angers, or strongly disturbs somebody (e.g., . . . teacher, parent, or the individual himself) sufficiently that some action results (e.g., a policeman is called, seeing a psychiatrist is recommended, commitment proceedings are started) so that society's professional labelers (e.g., physicians, psychiatrists, psychologists, judges, social workers) come into contact with the individual and determine which of the current set of labels (e.g., schizophrenic reaction, sociopathic personality, anxiety reaction) is most appropriate. Finally, there follow attempts to change the emission of the offending behavior (e.g., institutionalization, psychotherapy, medication).[163]

The labels we use to describe behavior as well as intelligence are fungible. "Moron," "mentally retarded," and now "intellectually disabled" are three examples of "subaverage" intelligence applied overwhelmingly to black and brown youth over the past century. Though the labels have changed, educational authorities continue to use outdated and harmful courses of action when identifying, placing, and segregating "unteachable" students in special education classes. This history demonstrates the power of psychiatrists, psychologists and educators in racializing EBD, LD, and EMR. It might be tempting to perceive the system of special education as broken (which it is), but this passive reading elides the ways in which white psychiatrists, social scientists, school administrators, and teachers conspired to create a separate and under-resourced system for students of color, and a sympathetic and financially generous one for white disabled students.

6

The Implications of Unteachability

Special Education into the Twenty-First Century

Segregation, particularly of Black and brown students labeled with a dis/ability, would be illegal if based upon race, but is allowed because dis/ability is seen as a "real" rather than a constructed difference.

—DAVID J. CONNOR, BETH A. FERRI, and SUBINI A. ANNAMMA,
DisCrit: Disability Studies and Critical Race Theory in Education

A student can be labeled in one school and then move to another teacher, grade level, school, district, or state and that label can be changed or removed altogether.

—SUBINI ANCY ANNAMMA, *The Pedagogy of Pathologization*
Dis/abled Girls of Color in the School-Prison Nexus

Throughout the twentieth century, cadres of white education stakeholders framed black and brown learners as unteachable. The invention of unteachability, mediated through racialized disability labels, served powerful ideological and material functions. Numerous white researchers, lawmakers, teachers, and administrators wielded the fiction of unteachability to marginalize and malign students of color. Especially after *Brown*, they relied on old tropes of black debility to mount new schemes of resegregation. The exclusion of "disabled" students of color from white classrooms protected white learners, teachers, schools, and parents from notions of educational risk. Fully integrated classrooms, with black and brown students of varying abilities, threatened ideas of white academic achievement, ability, and space. White educators feared the "risk" that black and brown students posed to these cherished privileges. It is no wonder that at the end of the twentieth century, many students of color were referred to as "at-risk."[1] The history of special education reveals how racialized fears of "risk" continue to shape who is deemed educationally disabled. "Underachieving" and so-called bad black students are not "at-risk": they pose risk.

Racialized fears of risk must be understood within the polarity of "us" versus "them," white "privileged" students versus black and brown "underprivileged" students. To comprehend the history of "us" and "them" in special education, one must place it in its original context as a form of differential education. In a stratified society like the United States, "us" and "them" pivot around dominant and marginal subjectivities. And though "us" and "them" are objective personal pronouns, they describe relationships in oppositional contexts: rich versus poor; white versus black; male versus female; straight versus gay; able versus disabled.[2] As a result of the passage and enforcement of compulsory attendance laws in the early twentieth century, differential education arose to serve as a system to protect the dominant subject positions in these binaries. The guidance of education and clinical professionals guarded the interests of white wealthy and middle-class children against the interests of poor black and brown children compelled into the system by law and policy. That protection manifested itself in new disciplines (special education and educational psychology); new professions (special education teachers); new measuring techniques (IQ, aptitude, and achievement tests); and new disabilities (mental retardation, emotional behavior disorders, learning disabled). In capturing the history of "us" versus "them" that persisted into the twenty-first century, this chapter argues the politics of risk, unteachability, and disproportionality allowed for both the proliferation of disciplinary practices and psychiatric diagnoses of black behavior to flourish, forcing black disabled and nondisabled students into alternative schools and juvenile justice settings.

Race, Risk, and Dis/Ability

Special education categories have become self-evident disabilities. We hold these disabilities to be self-evident because they have been around for the better part of a century; self-evident because of technical terms like "high-incidence," which we apply to the most populated disability categories; self-evident because ever more "disabled" students are claimed to be yet identified; self-evident because each disability has generated a large body of research; self-evident because the disabilities need not be explained anymore; self-evident because segregating students based on disability is seen as natural if not legal. "Scientifically 'correct' and objectively determined," self-evident disability categories like EMR, LD, and EBD, makes them "impervious to criticism."[3] Noumena-like, to borrow a Kantian concept, special education categories exist as things in themselves, having become presumed things or unknowable realities.[4] Special education and its disabilities have reached a stage of *presumability* because we think we know what they are when we hear the names of the categories and *unknowability* because they mean different things to different people.[5]

But what no longer seems evident is what EMR, LD, and EBD originally described and explained: underachievement, academic failure, and unruly behavior, not any disabling condition. Categorical disabilities like EMR, LD, and EBD are ex post facto, created and elaborated on by psychologists after the apparatus of differential/special education was created. They protected what became the most important common noun and adjective in the educational landscape: "normal," which is translated as white middle-class children in public education, against the rise of the second most important common noun and adjective, the "subnormal," described as black and brown working-class and poverty-stricken children in cities and in rural counties in the North and South. Though newly arrived European immigrants were classified as "subnormal," their whiteness allowed them to shift their positions upward in the racial hierarchy over time, affording them a different experience in general and special education. "Not all white people profit equally from their whiteness," wrote George Lipsitz, "but all whites benefit from the association of whiteness with privilege."[6] Protecting "normal" whiteness in education meant creating separate and privileged geographies in schools as well as an entire separate system called "special education." Self-evident disabilities required a separate self-evident system. As sociologist James Carrier observed, "Only with mass schooling did the schools need to develop internal sorting mechanisms and thus ... mass schooling is a necessary condition for the development of special education."[7]

In their 2006 book, Beth Harry and Janette Klingner posed the question, why are so many minority students in special education?[8] As the first book in the broad field of special education I read, I was struck by the language of containment Harry and Klingner used: "Special education became the corner of the system that could contain those whose differences were perceived to be too extreme to serve in the mainstream?"[9] Harry and Klingner's language of containment described not so much a system that merely boxed black and Latinx children in but one that institutionalized the concept of pathological deficits through medical language. Their argument built on Thomas Skrtic's 1991 essay in the *Harvard Educational Review* entitled, "The Special Education Paradox: Equity as the Way to Excellence."[10] Just as I was struck by Harry and Klingner's perspective, they seemed to be equally taken aback by Skrtic's language of containment, which described special education as "the institutional practice that emerged in the 20th century to contain the failure of public education to realize its democratic ideals."[11] Building off Skrtic, Harry and Klingner concluded: "Thus, sometime in the early 1970s, the special education movement and the desegregation movement officially collided. Those whom the society had rejected, and had excluded from its public schools, would meet in the special education system. The concept of deficit, by then an ingrained part of the educational belief system, would become the chief metaphor to encompass difference."[12] As a historian of the African American experience, I too wondered why so many students of color were placed in special education.

To make sense of why so many black students were and still are in special education, one must center "race" and "dis/ability" and reevaluate what "risk" means. Racial disproportionality in special education protects the property status of "whiteness and ability" from notions of educational risk.[13] Black, brown, working-class, and poor children have and continue to be treated as "risky" learners.[14] Tellingly, McDermott, Raley, and Seyer-Ochi affirm that "the diagnosis of risk is embedded in cultural preoccupations and circumstance that, because rarely specified, invite general bias: White, middle-class lives offer children the best of all worlds."[15] But there are two sides to risk. Historically, education stakeholders conceived of white middle-class children as advantage-rich students who needed protection. In a peculiarized way, these students were also "at-risk" of losing status, resources, or attention, amid encroaching blackness.

Centering race and dis/ability is the hallmark of DisCrit, the intersection of disability studies and critical race theory. "A DisCrit theory in education," Connor, Ferri, and Annamma write, "is a framework that theorizes about ways in which race, racism, dis/ability and ableism are built into the interactions, procedures, discourses, and institutions of education, which affect students of color with dis/abilities qualitatively differently than White students with dis/abilities."[16] DisCrit flips, overturns, splits, and curves units of analyses so that dominant subjectivities inside binaries can be interrogated equally, if not more, than marginal ones. "Discrit problematizes the ways that binaries between normal/abnormal and abled/disabled play out in a range of contexts,"[17] spotlighting "quarantined spaces" where dominant subject positions hang out undetected, secluded, isolated, and separated. As a generic noun for "debility" or "ill-health," disability underscores the impaired body as nonnormative. Disability names and identifies the "impaired body" while concealing its opposite, "ability" or the "healthy body." Disability obscures ability, the power behind ableism, that make bodies and people impaired and nonnormative in the first place. Dis/ability, on the other hand, decouples ability from disability, exposing ableism as an oppressive force. Scholars, like Sami Schalk, use (dis)ability to reveal a similar decoupling, positing: "I use (dis)ability because unlike other terms such as *gender*, which references man, woman, genderqueer, transgender, and other gender identities, disability without the parenthetical adjustment merely references disability and impairment. The term *(dis)ability* also highlights the mutual dependency of disability and ability that define one another. While other scholars use *dis/ability* or *ability/disability* to similar effect, I believe the parenthetical curve as opposed to the backslash better visually suggests the shifting, contentious, and contextual boundaries between disability and ability."[18]

DisCrit not only decouples ability from disability, it also names ableism and racism as mutually normalizing forces that work in tandem. "We believe, for instance, that racism and ableism are normalizing processes that are interconnected and collusive," said Connor, Ferri, and Annamma. "Racism and ableism often work in ways that are unspoken, yet racism validates and reinforces ableism, and ableism validates and reinforces racism."[19] I use DisCrit to help me think about other binaries, asking, who is on the other side of them? If special education is what disability focuses our attention on, then who is over in general education? If there are some people who are "subnormal," then who are the "normal"?

If there are students who are "educable mentally retarded," then who are the "cognitively" ordinary or superior? If there are children labeled "emotional behavior disordered" or "socially maladjusted," then who are the "adjusted?" If the preponderance of the people on the unspoken and invisible side of the ability-divide are white, and there exists an over-representation of black and brown children on the disability side, then those systems, discourses, classes, and programs are not only segregated, but they are also patently racist and ableist, full stop.

The tenets of DisCrit posit that dis/ability and race are socially constructed as a "response to 'differences' from the norm"; the "property status" of whiteness and ableness has the greatest value in society; dis/ability and race "became equated and molded through pseudo-sciences" validated with "objective clinical assessment practices"; dis/ability and race were "reified through laws, policies, and programs until these concepts became uncritically conflated and viewed as the natural order of things"; and the converging interests of white people with people of color is the only action that will bring about changes in policies, practices, and programs.[20] Interest convergence, a concept first articulated by Derrick Bell in 1980,[21] and repurposed by DisCrit, has haunted me throughout the writing of this book, leaving me with a nagging conclusion: racial over-representation in special education will never end until it no longer serves white people attempting to keep unwanted black learners from accessing general education.

Psychologists baked whiteness and ability inside the system of special education when they first created it at the beginning of the twentieth century. The statement from a 1912 educational psychology editorial is worth repeating here, as it reminds us of who endured as the hallmark of our educational system: "The normal child is the future torchbearer of our civilization. Is his education receiving the careful, individualized study which his capacity for improvement warrants? Admittedly it has not in the past."[22] As a modern-day expression of whiteness, the gender explicit "male" and implicit "white middle-class" sets the subject apart from the "other" who is *not* society's future torchbearer. But what are working-class and poor black and brown children if they are not also society's future torchbearers? Are educational "others," "laggards," as one author called them in 1909?[23] Ableists psychologists suggested the potential investment in "others" placed society's "normal" in peril, as it reduced, if not precluded, any capacity for greater improvement, investment, and advantage of white middle-class children. Not only was ableist thinking zero-sum in its spirit, an "us against them" mentality was also at play. Inasmuch as at-risk discourses focused on black and brown debility, the dawning of special education in the United States was an early form of risk assessment and management on behalf of white middle-class children in public education.

Proponents of special education played the critical role of risk assessor and mitigant. To mismanage and exacerbate white middle-class risk and not engage in risk mitigation would have allowed all students to access general education irrespective of race and class. For privileged families and professionals, the thought of permitting students from every walk of life to attend public schools did not cross their collective minds until the enforcement of compulsory attendance. Risk assessors identified compulsory education as potentially harmful to so-called normal students. To recall Edgar A. Doll's words, "Compulsory education sends all children to school regardless of their mental limitations. This condition is rapidly forcing a fundamental reorganization of educational practice."[24] The reorganization Doll invoked led to a risk management plan called "special education." Special education functioned as a way to mitigate the probability of risk to putatively normal students by creating special classes for the "mentally retarded," the "emotionally disturbed," the "borderline subnormal" (i.e., the reading and learning disabled), the "blind," the "deaf," the "crippled," the "truant," the "delinquent," and the "defective" student, as they have been variously called throughout history. Educational assessors were equally concerned with the risk posed by students with physical and sensory challenges even though the numbers in special education rarely exceeded their numbers in the school-age population.[25]

By contrast, risk assessors did not hide their intentions regarding academically struggling black and brown students. Ableists could no longer count on the naturally occurring reality of black and brown students starting school at later ages and leaving school earlier than their white counterparts. When compulsory education began, ableists added greater numbers of students of color to the category, "mentally retarded," which kept them from accessing general education.[26] Risk managers of America's public schools, like Doll, couched their risk mitigation practice in the language of progressive reform: "No school system can today be rated progressive which does not provide special education for its mentally subnormal."[27] Placing so-called mental subnormals in classes for the educable mentally retarded inevitably produced a system that grew disproportionately out of control with other disability classes, such as LD and EBD.

Racial Disproportionality along the Behavior Continuum

By the time the Office of Civil Rights (OCR) began collecting federal data on the overrepresentation of black students in EMR, LD, and SED/EBD in the late 1960s and 1970s, schools had pigeonholed the black student as the "poor learner," "juvenile delinquent," "socially maladjusted," and the "truant" pupil. Though not all the terms represented diagnostic labels, they primarily identified two kinds of students, the so-called underachiever and the disrupter. The disciplines of special education and psychology transformed these labels into various diagnostic and administrative identities. Many of these characteristics were captured in the categories EMR, LD, and SED/EBD, and undoubtedly some black EMR, LD, and SED/EBD students emerged among the "truant," the "dropout," and the "delinquent." In addition to SED/EBD, disruptive behavior ranged from conduct disorder (CD) to oppositional defiant disorder (ODD). If black students were already overrepresented in EMR by the 1960s,[28] then they would inevitably become overrepresented in LD and SED/EBD over the ensuing decades in spite of the institutional tendency to keep LD and SED/EBD white. By the 1970s, black students were well on their way to becoming overrepresented in LD and SED/EBD. As Marleen Pugach, professor of teacher education noted, "Once the referral process is initiated the probability that a student will receive special education services is high."[29] Indeed, referral for underachievement and/or disruptive behavior nearly guaranteed black placement in special education.

From the 1970s through the first decade of the twenty-first century, racial disproportionality worsened with placements increasing exponentially during the mainstreaming and regular education movements.[30] In the era of zero tolerance policies, the growth of black special education expanded the use of harsh discipline practices like suspensions and expulsions against students with disabilities across the country. School disciplinary practices and the use of IQ tests to "dump" black students into EMR and LD categories created another backlash, triggering changes to the Individual with Disabilities Education Act (IDEA) in 1997 and 2004. Again, black behavior and schools' punitive action against that behavior were at the center of the conversation. Debates about social maladjustment and emotional behavior disorder resurfaced at the turn of the twenty-first century, with black behavior now measured along a continuum that included EBD, conduct disorder, oppositional defiant disorder, and juvenile delinquency.

If the politics of black behavior and school disciplinary practices triggered the IDEA amendments of 1997, then the IQ/achievement discrepancy criteria that placed many black students in LD prompted the IDEA amendments of 2004, allowing districts to employ a response-to-intervention (RTI) model instead of IQ measurements. Like the compulsory attendance era, special education's growth at the turn of the twenty-first century reflected the increasing presence of "unruly" black and brown bodies in general education. Thus, federal special education law had to acknowledge the problem of racial disproportionality even if it failed to prohibit it. The 2004 amendment to IDEA stated as much:

> More minority children continue to be served in special education than would be expected from the percentage of minority students in the general school population. African-American children are identified as having mental retardation and emotional disturbance at rates greater than their White counterparts. In the 1998–1999 school year, African-American children represented just 14.8 percent of the population aged 6 through 21, but comprised 20.2 percent of all children with disabilities. Studies have found that schools with predominately White students and teachers have placed disproportionately high numbers of their minority students into special education.[31]

The federal government acknowledged racial bias in the language of its special education policy, invoking disproportionality studies that showed white teachers were the most responsible for the referral to placement process. The 1997 amendment to IDEA was the first time federal legislation directed the states to confront the issue of racism in special education.[32]

Growing racial disparities in high-incidence disabilities must be partly understood as a failure of the federal and state governments to curtail placement practices even while they provide oversight responsibilities.

Special education served more as a political battlefield than a means of rehabilitation and learning. Federal agencies responsible for the enforcement of special education have been and continue to be unwilling to dictate how its policies must be adhered to at local levels. Instead, teachers determine the procedural aspects of special education through identification and referral practices.[33] Situational differences in identifying special education students also add to the trouble of local practices. For example, in a mental health clinic, a student exhibiting certain behavior characteristics might be considered "conduct disordered." That same student exhibiting similar characteristics inside a school may be deemed "behavior disordered." Mental health professionals *diagnose* students as conduct disordered but assign the administrative label EBD when students meet the criteria in schools.[34] This parsing is confusing and illogical. While splitting hairs in special education may serve clarification purposes for the professions of medicine and teaching, it also reifies black students as "problematic" along the entire behavior continuum. If students are "psychiatrically" conduct disordered in one space and "administratively" emotional behavior disordered in another, they come to embody both labels politically. Thus, special education and the disproportionality it produced is only one half of the story. The other half is the implications of unteachability in the early twenty-first century that placed psychiatric diagnoses on black students, forcing many of them into alternative schools, mental health, and juvenile justice settings.

The Office of Civil Rights (OCR) commissioned the National Research Council (NRC) to study the phenomenon of racial disproportionality in the 1970s. Starting with the premise that there were discernable "causes" of disproportionality, the NRC panel stated that the more important research question was not "what are the causes of disproportionate representation of minorities and males in special education," but rather *"why* is disproportionate representation of minorities and males a problem?"[35] Framed in this way, the NRC explained, "our reformulated question is premised on the belief that disproportion per se is not a problem: unequal numbers do not by themselves constitute an inequity. Instead, disproportion signals that certain underlying conditions *may* be problematic, and the task becomes one of identifying these conditions." Hesitating on "who" and "what," the NRC recast its questions as "why" and "how": "The reformulated questions also changed the outcome of our study.

Rather than suggest procedures that eliminate or reduce disproportion, we recommend practices that directly redress the inequitable conditions underlying it." The NRC argued that the assessment of black students for placement in EMR classes was invalid and that the instruction they received in EMR programs lacked quality. Changing practices to better assess and place students as well as using better curriculum materials and pedagogical approaches in EMR classes represented an earnest beginning; however, the NRC's obfuscating of the "who" and "what" questions allowed people, politics, and power to remain uninterrogated in its study of disproportionality.[36]

While the NRC's identification of bad assessments placed emphasis on the instruments used to perform the assessment, the NRC's identification of practice laid emphasis on pedagogy isolated from the persons delivering the instruction. "Teachers" are the answer to the NRC's original "who" question, but the NRC's reformulated question shifted attention away from teachers as the main causes of racial disproportionality, focusing the reader's attention on the curriculum materials teachers may deploy, or the instruments they may use to assess, or the instructional practices they may utilize in classrooms. As if time stood still, the NRC conducted another study in 1998: "Twenty years later, concern about the disproportionate representation of minority children in special education persists, and the NRC has been asked to revisit the issue."[37] The turn of the twenty-first century witnessed an explosion of racial disproportionality research that revisited questions as diverse as teacher bias, socioeconomic risk factors, poor assessments, pedagogy, and behavior.[38]

Racial disproportionality in special education perpetuates inequality because black behavior and academic underachievement have either perplexed or engendered resistance from schools, districts, states, and the federal government as an intractable problem. Compartmentalizing an understanding of black behavior within disproportionality research misses how one set of learning and behavioral attributes overlaps with others. Like all behavior, black behavior exists along a continuum. Discourses on "bad" black behavior overlap along a spectrum of "black" social deviance, ranging from disruptive conduct that is either "emotionally disturbed," or disruptive behavior that is considered "behavior disordered." These categories of "bad" behavior could be considered "socially maladjusted," which, if they violate a statute and is adjudicated in a court, could then be deemed a form of "delinquency," and if that delinquency can be interpreted as psychopathological, it could be considered "mentally ill."

Though the Diagnostic and Statistical Manual (DSM) delineates mental disorders in society and behavioral disabilities in school, the overlapping nature of the classifications bear themselves out in the punitive structures of alternative placement settings and the juvenile justice system.[39] The dynamism of black behavior, often understood as emotionally disturbed and socially maladjusted in schools is supplanted by conduct disorder, delinquent, and psychopathic perspectives in society. Writing in 1966, behavioral researcher Richard L. Jenkins connected psychiatric syndromes and family background with an implicit understanding of race, stating, "I do not believe that [juvenile delinquency] represents psychopathology so much as social pathology."[40] Jenkins's beliefs have been reinforced in the social science and psychiatric literature throughout the late twentieth and twenty-first centuries. The long history of classifying black people as emotional behavior disordered (educationally disabled), psychopathic (mentally disordered), and sociopathic (deviant) has set the stage for contemporary black segregation and marginalization in alternative spaces in schools, mental health institutions, and prisons. Thus, the line between psychiatric syndromes and behavioral taxonomies, between mental health nosology and educational classifications have grown increasingly indistinguishable when it comes to black youth.

Just as President Dwight D. Eisenhower cautioned about the buildup of an American military industrial complex to close the so-called missile gap with the Soviet Union, and just as the prison industrial complex responded to a so-called increase in crime beginning in the 1960s, a behavior industrial complex has arisen in response to black behavior in schools.[41] Like the other "complexes," the increase in "bad" black behavior was exaggerated at best and at worst invented to describe schools under siege. If black behavior posed a problem, then the multiinstitutional actions taken against it became the crisis/complex.[42] The behavior industrial complex brought the clinical forces of psychiatry, psychology, and law enforcement to bear inside schools. This behavior industrial complex did not recognize the diagnostic separation of different kinds of comportment defined by clinical and nonclinical fields of study. It took the action against black learners that resulted in a "punitive whirlwind."[43]

The behavior industrial complex was created by psychiatrists and represented by the DSM.[44] The scientific handbook of mental disorders constructed "illnesses" out of every human trait and characteristic, breaking up what used to epitomize broad categories of psychosis and neurosis into distinct symptom profiles, types, and sub-types. The DSM no longer required etiology for a classification, only observable symptoms. "The framers of the DSM," wrote Allan Horowitz, "took the problems that dynamic psychiatry had so successfully defined as psychological disturbances and reformulated them in the language of categorical illnesses." "Deviant behaviors," he continued, "had to be transformed into disease entities that could be properly formulated and treated within the diagnostic framework of the DSM-III."[45] As an ascendant product of diagnostic psychiatry, the DSM-III in 1980, with DSM-IV and DSM-5 following in later decades, redefined psychopathology out of the broad spectrum of behavior. The DSM did not define black misbehavior so much as it further pathologized and criminalized it.

The manual completed the demonization of black behavior by picking up where schools left off, extending emotional behavior disorder (EBD) into behavioral mental disorders known variously as oppositional defiant disorders, conduct disorders, and antisocial personality disorders.[46] Defining the range of behavior was important because it initiated a process that proved critical in controlling black misbehavior in a variety of institutional settings. Within the behavior industrial complex, the multi-institutional response to black misbehavior allowed for a synergy in responsibilities and professional coordination between school administrators, teachers, resource officers (school police), city police, mental health practitioners, and the courts. School officials monitored "tolerant" black misbehavior within the confines of special education and the therapeutic milieu of positive behavior interventions and supports (PBIS).[47] So-called intolerant black behavior experienced surveillance and discipline practices enforced by zero tolerance policies, thereby removing students from schools and placing them into residential facilities and the juvenile justice system.

The behavior industrial complex demonstrates how the fields of psychology and psychiatry treated black behavior as a fungible object. Early social scientists and clinicians classified black behavior as a disability (an impairment), a disorder (an internal dysfunction), and deviance (expected behavior of a group) at different times in U.S. history, and all three co-exist today. Though black behavior is represented in all three, some scholars have worked hard to project deviance onto black children in each case. Alan Horowitz noted that the field of psychology separated deviance and mental disorders for much of the twentieth century, explaining, "Deviant behaviors are not mental disorders unless they stem from some dysfunction of an internal psychology mechanism. The distinction between mental disorders and deviant behavior is the distinction between people who *can't* conform and those who *won't* conform."[48] Horowitz affirmed that "a valid definition of mental disorder does not encompass deviant behaviors unless they are also internal dysfunctions."[49] The distinction between people who *can't* conform and who *won't* conform was how psychological and psychiatric behavior discourses became racialized in the first place. Much of this distinction centered around the cluster of behaviors defined interchangeably as social maladjustment and conduct disorder, what psychologists like Herbert Quay long associated with the "acting-out child":

> One major category of the conduct problem child, and the group which tends to be perhaps the most persistently troublesome, is that group of children referred to as unsocialized aggressive or psychopathic. The second major category of the acting-out child seems to be primarily a phenomenon of the urban socially deteriorated area. This child comes from a subculture in which aggressive behavior and "conning" ability are valued and in which academic achievement and middle class behavior standards are not highly esteemed. There is a special point to be made about these children. It is probably inappropriate to consider them emotionally disturbed since in a very real sense they are only behaving in a way which is appropriate to their own world.[50]

The historical irony here is that black students, as the main behavior "problem" inside schools, were disproportionately placed in SED/EBD despite the attempt in the early twentieth century by behavior scientists to keep these designations reserved for white students. As an administrative label given by schools rather than a diagnostic one given by mental health professionals outside of schools, researchers still theoretically saw SED/EBD, despite its disproportionate blackness, as a white preserve.

In contrast to SED/EBD, hard-core social deviancy became synonymous with social maladjustment, conduct disorder, delinquency, and psychopathology in theory and practice. Psychiatrist Richard L. Jenkins and psychologist Herbert C. Quay spent the better part of their careers fleshing out the characteristics of socialized and unsocialized delinquents, distinguishing "types" of behavior, and racializing "clusters" of children not only as emotional behavior disorder but also as psychopathic.[51] Quay, Morse, and Cutler suggested that although EBD represents a form of deviancy, black behavior that is "aggressive, hostile, and contentious" falls outside the purview of EBD:

> There has frequently appeared a constellation of behavior traits which has been labeled subcultural or socialized delinquency. The failure of this syndrome to emerge in this study is likely due both to the fact that few items in the rating scale tap this factor, and to the fact that children representative of this syndrome are not quite so likely to be found in classes for the emotionally disturbed. As one of us have indicated elsewhere (Quay 1963), these children are not truly emotionally disturbed and represent a quite different educational problem.[52]

Psychodynamic theory racialized behavior throughout the behavior continuum of EBD and SM, recognizing the connection between EBD and delinquency, and acknowledging they both spring from the same behavior well, but designating and ascribing their psychopathology accordingly. The main takeaway from behavior scientists from the 1960s is that the psychological development of black children was fixed at a pathological delinquent stage rooted in antisocial or criminal behavior that have always seemed to represent more than the run-of-the mill EBD label in schools. One can make an argument that EBD was the better behavior designation given how psychiatrists understood and "treated" deviant behavior over time.

Despite the relative "mildness" of EBD on the behavior continuum, disruptive black children raised the ire of teachers and administrators alike and represented the same educational problem for schools in the mid-twentieth century as they do presently. Though disruptive behavior is relative, "bad" black behavior increased the rancor of the social maladjustment exclusion debate in the 1990s and into the twenty-first century.[53] Black behavior created an impasse in the scholarly SM exclusion debate and unleashed harsher punitive measures in schools and the courts. Like the 1970s, racialized notions of behavior at the turn of the twenty-first century continued to shape special education policy and practice as educational psychologists Amanda Sullivan and Shanna Sadeh captured. "Socialized delinquency" in the form of drug use, gang violence, and antisocial behavior highlights "predatory behavior and [social maladjustment's] imperviousness to treatment," and thus, continued Sullivan and Sadeh, "excluding it from special education to conserve resources and limit exposing antisocial students to vulnerable students with internalizing disorders." Protecting "internalizing" behavior served to protect white students who "could not" conform as well, but "diagnostically," these white students possessed personality disorders, as opposed to black children with conduct disorders. Like EMR, LD, and EBD, the irony is that "social maladjusted," "conduct disordered," and "antisocial personality disordered" are predominantly white because of white people's total numbers in the U.S. population.[54]

Daniel Olympia and colleagues at the University of Utah listed seven basic assumptions about social maladjustment they believed previous researchers wrongly concluded and reported in their findings. But even if we are to accept that long-standing assumptions "wrongly" defined social maladjustment, the suppositions proved how this research racially defined black behavior and shaped the way we think about a people.

1. Social maladjustment is equivalent to the psychiatric diagnoses of Conduct Disorder and Oppositional Defiant Disorder.
2. The socially maladjusted child makes a *conscious decision* to behave negatively, whereas the child with serious emotional disturbance acts without forethought.
3. The socially maladjusted child *understands* the consequences or impact of his/her behavior, while the child with serious emotional disturbance fails to appreciate the consequences of their behavior.
4. The socially maladjusted child has the ability to *control* his/her behavior, while the child with serious emotional disturbance lacks the ability to regulate or inhibit behavior.
5. The socially maladjusted child exhibits *no guilt or remorse* for his/her negative behavior.

6. The socially maladjusted child exhibits *externalizing* behaviors while the seriously emotionally disturbed child exhibits internalizing behaviors.

7. The socially maladjusted child is *nondisabled* while the seriously emotionally disturbed child is disabled.[55]

Despite more whites being defined as socially maladjusted, conduct disordered, or antisocial personality disordered, black and brown racialization occurs in how certain behaviors are projected onto the body. "A 'symptom' is a behavior, anything that can be observed by others . . . such as arguing, starting fights," explained psychologist Ralph Dreger.[56] "A 'syndrome,' sometimes called a 'characteristic,' is a group of such behaviors, that tend to occur together in the same child . . . [and] in this sense, 'aggressiveness' is a syndrome consisting of aggressive acts, hitting, kicking, pinching, teasing, arguing, etc. which tend to go together in the same child, . . . [and] a 'type' is a group of children whose 'syndromes' tend to go together."[57] This typing and subtyping of children led to a host of conclusions about the kinds of racial bodies that "practice" certain behaviors. Often, the behavior is implied in its definitional characteristics as well as in its group attributes. Sometimes, the behavior is explicitly stated by naming the group it applies to. Authors of a national comorbidity survey on the DSM-IV wrote, "Membership in the Aggressive subtype is associated with younger age cohort [and] black ethnicity."[58] The social science and clinical literature is replete with racial and ethnic references of this sort.

"Syndroming" (identifying a group of behaviors) and "typing" (identifying a group of children whose syndromes go together) tend to follow black learners throughout their schooling. Carl Gacono and Tammy Hughes presented traits comparing conduct disorders (CD), antisocial personality disorders (ASPD), Cleckley's Characteristics of Psychopathy, and Hare's Psychopathy Trait Behaviors. Not only are some of the traits similar, populations already considered deviant would meet many of the behavior characteristics in all four categories. Gacono and Hughes note that, in terms of psychopathology, "Conduct Disorder and Antisocial Personality Disorder are based largely on a social deviance model defined predominantly in terms of antisocial and criminal behaviors."[59] The full range behavior patterns do not start with CD or ASPD. "Numerous studies have shown that teacher referral for special education is related to the level of student disruption in the classroom," Tara Raines and her colleagues argued persuasively. "Students with more disruptive behaviors, despite the cause or nature of the disruption, are more likely to be referred to special education."[60] Early forms of disruptive behavior can make "deviant-defined" groups like African Americans "pre-pathological" or understood as fledgling "psycho-paths" in schools.[61]

Schools often view African American behavior as an *inability* to comply with teachers and an *unwillingness* to have positive interpersonal relationships with them. How black students "behave" or "misbehave" could be the difference between receiving an EBD placement (a disability), or an SM profile (a deviancy), or any of the rule-defiant behaviors under the umbrella disruptive behavior disorders (DBD) triggered by a mental health referral (a diagnosis).[62] The research literature posits that pathological disruptive behavior identifies "at-risk" black students, but I contend this directionality is not quite correct. The growing body of behavior research exacerbates black "at-riskness," creating more opportunities to place black students on the behavior continuum that leads to increased "risk" of black student push-out of general education schools. For too many black students, the result is placement into federal level four alternative special education schools, a mental health clinic, or the juvenile justice system.

Black Dis/Ability as Discipline and Punishment

Racist academic research continues to play a role in perpetuating racialized assumptions in studies on disproportional referrals, disciplinary actions, and mental diagnoses, particularly in describing the prevalence of these practices in children from "depressed" neighborhoods and "poorly bred" families. Though ecological perspectives characterize many modern-day interpretations, genetic explanations returned in the twenty-first century to describe black behavior. The academy continues to produce research that racializes untoward school behavior as black. Synthesizing the various findings of himself and other scientific racialists, English psychologist Richard Lynn, concluded that "conduct disorders of aggression and anti-social behaviour were both significantly greater among blacks ... [and] the broad heritability of hyperactivity-conduct disorder" and psychopathic personality disorder "have a genetic basis."[63] With no evidence to suggest a genetic connection to various disorders based

on race, scholars of psychiatric syndromes and types have produced a discourse on "risk factors" that is thoroughly racialized and patently racist,
moving from genetic explanations to ecological ones.[64] As Joseph Murray and David P. Farrington, two criminologists from the University of
Cambridge put it, "The most important risk factors that predict CD and
delinquency include impulsiveness, low IQ and low school achievement,
poor parental supervision, punitive or erratic parental discipline, cold
parental attitude, child physical abuse, parental conflict, disrupted families, antisocial parents, large family size, low family income, antisocial
peers, high delinquency rate schools, and high crime neighborhoods."[65]

Two facts about school discipline and crime warrant explanation.
Between 1991 and 2005, the rate of discipline practices increased for
black students while the overall rate of juvenile crimes decreased. "The
nexus between criminalization of school discipline and the increasing
rate of public students' contact with the criminal justice system," noted
Abiodun Raufu, is "not supported by any evidence that there is an up-
surge in juvenile delinquency."[66] If that is the case, why does the disciplining, criminalization, and removal of students from schools often
result in these students' eventual incarceration? Incarcerating disability
accounts for some of this result—black EMR, LD, and EBD students often
end up in the "pipeline."[67] But to say black EMR, LD, and EBD students
are overdisciplined and pushed out of schools is to lose sight of the big-
ger picture. All black students who "act-out" and disrupt are potential
targets of school pushout practices. This not only includes black students
with individualized education plans (IEPs), and black students who are
"socially maladjusted" and "conduct disordered" but also black students
who "act-out" in general education. The result for many of these students
is suspension, expulsion, and referral to law enforcement and the juvenile
justice system for arrest, conviction, and imprisonment. However, many
black students in general education experience other forms of punitive
actions while remaining in schools.

Some scholars believe "predispositions," such as low academic achievement and poor school attendance serve as suitable explanations for why
black students are overly disciplined. Predispositions or "risk factors"
are constructed variables that allow schools to accrue justifications to
invest less in black student advancement. To be sure, predispositional
risk factors are provided as the justification behind punitive practices.

The boundless interpretations of black lives, however, has the effect of stacking the deck, rendering black students less deserving of educational resources. The more that risk factors are introduced into the equation, the greater the marginalization in the educational space. Arguably, predisposing factors lead to the invention of other risk factors. When increasing numbers of black students attended white schools at the turn of the twentieth century, their below-grade-level status functioned as a constructed risk factor that marginalized black students in public schools and justified the invention of "mental retardation" and the creation of special education. Thus, the founders of special education, white psychologists and educators, responded to the growing presence of black students by developing a differential form of education, and by doing so, simultaneously created malleability in the special education system that could identify levels of unacceptable and unwarranted underachievement and bad behavior for future teachers, administrators, and psychologists to respond how they saw fit. As more black students enter the system, the predispositional lever can be pulled at will to invent and/or elaborate on risk factors for placement purposes. But more identification and placement in special education does not necessarily lead to more resources. Black students in special education often receive fewer resources as disabled students. Special education resources tend to work against them. Subini Ancy Annamma of Stanford University described this incongruity as a kind of "creative destruction" that divests resources from black students while investing in policies that criminalized them.[68]

As general education excluded and prohibited black student access, special education differentiated and set black students apart. The Individuals with Disabilities Education Act (IDEA) emphasized that "special education is not a place," asserted Daniel Losen and Kevin Welner, "rather, it consists of supports and services."[69] For many black children, however, special education functioned as a racialized place to "warehouse" underachieving and "disruptive" students.[70] Losen and Orfield, of the Harvard University Civil Rights Project, admitted that "minority students deemed eligible for special education are significantly more likely than their white counterparts to wind up in substantially separate settings with a watered-down curriculum. They are in double jeopardy of experiencing a denial of educational opportunity, first on account of racial discrimination and again on account of their disability status."[71]

Thus, being "disabled" and "black" has intended rather than unintended consequences. Those intended consequences resulted from the intended practices of separation and underachievement embedded in a public education system based on rewards and punishments and winners and losers.

Marian Wright Edelman raised the question of intentionality regarding the disciplinary actions taken by schools. One can draw a direct line from Edelman's critique of special education in the 1970s to today's opponents of zero tolerance practices who regard the hyperdisciplinary actions and exclusionary measures against students of color as purposeful. Edelman was struck by the nonenrollment of black and Puerto Rican children across the country, almost as if they never attended school. "I knew it was a problem in Mississippi and in Boston," she noted, "but had no sense it was an epidemic of national proportions." The nonenrollment of students of color was not a new phenomenon in the 1970s. Public education in the early twentieth century was consumed with the problem called "elimination": the inability of students of color and white students from immigrant families to stay consistently enrolled in schools. Put differently, elimination allowed schools to push its least-desired students out of the system altogether. Dedicating her early career to addressing the exclusion of children from schools, Edelman was concerned with the placement of black and brown children disproportionately in special education as well as the incarceration of juveniles. As a result, Edelman was forced to speak out. She remarked, "Many discipline problems seem to me to be education problems." She noticed schools were quick to act against students of color for the slightest of infractions: "It's as if schools get rid of children as a first, not last, resort." Schools operated in insidious ways to "encourage children to leave," through "disciplinary transfers" and "in-house suspensions."[72]

Disciplinary actions are contextual, meaning that the governing principles of discipline protocols—the school policy handbook or some other written (or unwritten) procedures—is not how disciplinary actions actually manifest inside schools. Frances Vavrus, professor in the College of Education and Human Development at the University of Minnesota, and KimMarie Cole, professor at the State University of New York–Fredonia, suggest that education scholars should take a discursive approach in exploring "patterns of classroom interactions," what they call "*disciplinary moments* . . . [the] moment-by-moment interactions among teachers and students in specific classrooms contexts."[73] Author Jawanza Kunjufu referred to classroom interactions between black students and white teachers as "the showdown."[74] To take seriously the discursive or multiple and competing discourses inside classrooms allows us to transcend myths perpetuated by teachers and schools: that harsh disciplinary measures, like suspension and expulsion, are meted out against the most "disruptive" students who engage in the most unruly and violent-prone behaviors.

According to Vavrus and Cole, an ethnographic understanding will allow schools to "treat the activity preceding suspensions as negotiated social practice rather than as a series of events that can be specified in school discipline policy without regard to the sociocultural context of the classroom." Vavrus and Cole go on to argue that "by foregrounding the study of classroom discourse and discourses about urban schools, we can then question certain assumptions about the presumed link between suspension and violence in contemporary debates about school safety." Indeed, the "commonsense" ways in which we understand school discipline "may not hold up under critical scrutiny and may need to be revised in light of these findings."[75] Ethnographic renderings of classroom interactions that privilege black student voices would reveal a war of attrition. Although both teachers and students are emotionally exasperated, the unequal distribution of power inside classrooms allows teachers and administrators to maintain educational power and to wield it at will. To maintain the balance of power, teachers and administrators instead employ harsher penalties for minor infractions to preserve order. When the moral panic of integration gripped white schools in the 1970s, constitutional scholar Mark Yudof observed that school authorities often dealt "with relatively minor infractions with the heavy-handed sanction of exclusion."[76] Agreeing with this premise, education scholar Pedro Noguera asserts that "throughout the United States, schools most frequently punish the students who have the greatest academic, social, economic, and emotional needs."[77]

Part ethnographic survey of students inside schools and part data-driven portrait of national suspension rates, Edelman's report not only shows how schools resisted integration and used behavior as a pretext to suspend black students in the 1960s and 1970s but also demonstrated that suspension and other disciplinary practices served as a forerunner to zero tolerance policies of the 1990s and early 2000s:

While the largest numbers of suspended children are white, proportionately suspensions hurt more children who are black, poor, older and male.
Most striking is the disparate suspension of black school children; they are
suspended at twice the rate of any other group. Twenty school districts
reported suspending one-third to one-half of their black students; one
district suspended 64 percent of its black students; another district suspended 53 percent. Although black suspension rates stand out, our survey
data and interviews make plain that they are part and parcel of a pervasive
intolerance by school officials for children who are *different* in any number
of ways.[78]

The report issued another reality check about long-held myths regarding school suspensions. Wholesale suspensions go unquestioned because
"many people assume that school suspensions affect a few patently unruly troublemakers who are mostly black and in large inner-city school
districts." With blackness and belligerent appearing synonymous, the over-
disciplining of such students remains incontrovertible. The report dis-
pelled additional myths that are still with us today, such as "suspensions
are an effective educational tool, evenhandedly administered, used only
after other alternatives have been tried and failed, and are an essential
deterrent to growing reports of school violence and disruption. None of
these assumptions are true," decried Edelman.[79]

The "pedagogy of pathologization"—the way in which teachers, administrators, and schools respond to black comportment with harsher
punishment—challenges assumptions that black students have become
increasingly unruly and violent since the 1970s. The behaviors flagged
by schools in the twenty-first century are remarkably similar in simplicity to the ones identified in the 1970s. The Edelman report stated that
"of all the suspensions recorded in our survey, 63.4 percent were for
infractions of school rules, not for dangerous violent acts." What the
report termed "victimless offenses" referred to students suspended for
truancy and tardiness. As if suspending students from school for truancy
and tardiness were not egregious enough, the report noticed a more trou-
bling trend:

A range of personal conditions—pregnancy, marriage, parenthood, "handicap," or poverty-related problems—were also grounds for suspension. We

found one child suspended for having lice, another because he was a bed-wetter at night, and another because he could not afford to pay for a ruler he had accidently broken in shop class. Numerous districts resort to suspension to correct dress or other personal habits of children. Four black children were suspended for not having their gym suits. Almost 6 percent of the suspensions . . . were for smoking.[80]

The arbitrariness of suspensions for "personal conditions" formed the basis of the school discipline and suspension crisis in the 1970s and represents a continuation of the way in which black students are singled out.

This singling out is still a phenomenon in public education and constitutes an enduring example of resistance in schools across the country. In a report titled, *Black Girls Matter: Pushed Out, Overpoliced and Underprotected,* Kimberlé Williams Crenshaw and the African American Policy Forum presented a series of powerful yet disturbing instances of over-policing and punitive actions against black girls. A few of these examples read:

In 2014, a 12-year-old girl faced expulsion and criminal charges after writing "hi" on a locker room wall of her Georgia middle school. . . . In 2013, an 8-year-old girl in Illinois was arrested for acting out, and a 16-year-old girl in Alabama who suffers from diabetes, asthma, and sleep apnea was hit with a book by her teacher after she fell asleep in class. In 2007, a 6-year-old girl was arrested in a Florida classroom for having a tantrum. Later that year, a 16-year-old girl was arrested in a California school for dropping cake on the floor and failing to pick it up to a school officer's satisfaction.[81]

The randomness of victimless offenses from truancy and smoking in the 1970s has exposed the myth of the black "troublemaker" in the 2000s. The actions taken by schools have become more punitive for less serious transgressions. Professor of anthropology of education Frederick Erickson and Stanford University professor of education Subini Annamma remind us that students do not construct their own concept of bad behavior. The way a student feels about his or her behavioral worth is partially, if not wholly, influenced by the demonization of their perceived misbehavior at school.[82]

Filmmaker and author Monique Morris and Subini Annamma illustrate how schools expanded the "bad" black behavior continuum, allowing for the creation of more predispositional risk factors that led to the punishment of black disabled, conduct disordered, and delinquent students. Morris and Annamma identify the school-to-prison nexus as a racial contract that, to paraphrase Charles Mills, demarcates general educational spaces from special education and juvenile justice education as "wild spaces."[83] Morris and Annamma additionally challenge gendered assumptions that the victims of white school discipline are black males, supplementing the research of Ann Ferguson, *Bad Boys: Public Schools in the Making of Black Masculinity* (2001) and Pedro Noguera, *The Trouble with Black Boys* (2008).[84] While scholars have rightly focused on the disproportionate placement and punishment on black male students, black female students have been penalized at an alarming rate in the past thirty years. Schools have constructed images of the "bad" black girl, punishing black girls in the twenty-first century with greater frequency.[85] The "norming" of schools as penal spaces stems from racial and gendered notions of educational deficiency and "risky" behavior for both black girls and black boys.

Indeed, the historical placement of black students in high incidence disabilities like EMR, LD, and EBD have been gendered male. Much of that understanding speaks to the difficulty of all males, and particularly black males' experience adjusting to learning environments and behavior expectations. Though the school adjustment problems of black males have been disproportionate, black girls have always experienced difficulty inside classrooms. The fixation with the higher numbers of black males disproportionately placed and punished has falsely promoted the discourse of the "bad boy" as education's greatest challenge. Black girls have also struggled to be treated as valuable learners. Racism, sexism, and adultification often shapes how their peers, teachers, and administrators regard black female students. As Morris argues, "The question of survival among Black girls has always been about *whether* they are seen, and if so, *how* they are seen, particularly in economically and socially isolated spaces."[86]

Black girls occupy, perform, and are punished in the same space, engaged in "showdowns" with whom Gloria Ladson-Billings called custodian teachers and referral agents.[87] Custodian teachers and referral agents

portray classrooms not only as spaces "imprinted with certain characteristics," but as "spaces that need taming." In an "active spatial struggle,"
teachers claim "bad" black girls and boys have made schools and classrooms "strange landscapes" that "must be . . . subordinated." Charles Mills's
interpretation of the "social contract" as a "racial contract" demonstrates
how macro and micro spaces are racially defined and set apart:

> The battle against this savagery is in a sense permanent as long as the
> savages continue to exist, contaminating (and being contaminated by) the
> non-Europeanized space around them. So it is not merely that space is
> normatively characterized on the macrolevel *before* conquest and colonial
> settlement, but that even *afterward,* on the local level, there are divisions,
> the European city and the Native Quarter, Whitetown and Niggertown/
> Darktown, suburb and inner city.[88]

Spatial binaries are not limited to continents, countries, cities, and neighborhoods but also schools (white and "colored"), educational systems
(general and special education), special education classrooms (EMR,
LD, EBD, autism, etc.) and academic programs (Gifted and Talented and
Young Scholars at the primary level and Advanced Placement and AVID
at the secondary level). Charles Mills concludes: "Part of the purpose
of the color bar/the color line/apartheid/Jim Crow is to maintain these
spaces *in their place,* to have the checkerboard of virtue and vice, light
and dark space, *ours* and *theirs,* clearly demarcated so that the human
geography prescribed by the Racial Contract can be preserved."[89]

Racializing bad behavior allows teachers and administrators to fit black
conduct into existing criminal categories. Sometimes poor conduct is
deemed "willful defiance." States passed willful defiance laws that dove-
tailed with school zero-tolerance policies in the 1990s. "Zero-tolerance
policies ignited a consciousness and school discipline ethos that supported the removal of students from the classroom if their actions were
perceived as defiant in any way," noted Morris.[90] While zero-tolerance
directed its focus against school violence and mass shootings, "willful
defiance" laws targeted socially maladjusted, conduct disordered, "un-
adjustable or incorrigible" children. Louisiana's law is illustrative of conduct that would make suspension mandatory:

A school principal may suspend from school or suspend from riding on any school bus any student who: (i) is guilty of willful disobedience, (ii) treats a teacher, principal, superintendent, member, or employee of the local school board with intentional disrespect, (iii) makes against any one of them an unfounded charge, (iv) uses unchaste or profane language, (xiv) leaves the school premises without permission, (xv) leaves his classroom during class hours or detention without permission, (xvi) is habitually tardy or absent.[91]

California's education code also enumerated infractions that precipitated mandatory suspensions, including violent acts, firearm possession, and controlled substances. But like Louisiana, it also included a "willful defiance" provision in the law: "disrupted school activities or otherwise willfully defied the valid authority of supervisors, teachers, administrators, school officials, or other school personnel engaged in the performance of their duties." Violating willful defiance policies did not merely represent transgressions against "internal" school policy; rather, willful defiance was akin to disturbing the peace, which called for criminal sanction. Again, Louisiana law compelled teachers to act: "Every teacher is authorized to hold every pupil to a strict accountability for any disorderly conduct in school ... playground of the school ... school bus ... or during intermission or recess."[92] Schools have instituted a "law and order" mindset that funnels black students out of school and into the juvenile justice system through arrests and court referrals.[93] In the last thirty years, black girls have become the face of willful defiance, prompting Subini Annamma to conclude: "Thus, many became constructed as criminals before they had even committed a crime. Once they were catapulted into the legal system, this identity was cemented."[94]

Schools added "criminal" disrupter to black students' identity, with the word "criminal" stretched beyond its definitional boundaries. What changed from the 1970s through the 2000s is not black behavior, but rather, white responses to it. Young black people "behave" the same way now as many have in the past. The response of some teachers and administrators, who have invited school resource officers and city law enforcement inside schools, has changed. Indeed, schools transformed black behavior into criminal offenses in the era of willful defiance, whereas "willful" white behavior is overlooked or excused. "Willfully defiant" black girls represent preschoolers, primary grade students, and secondary middle and high school students. At any moment during the school day, black students can be deemed a threat to public safety. Desre'e Watson and Salecia Johnson, both six years old, engaged in what amounted to tantrums: they threw toys and books while in class. Both were arrested in Florida and Georgia, respectively. Black middle and high school girls were also suspended for willful defiance by "standing up for themselves, asking questions, wearing natural hair, wearing revealing clothing," rolling their necks, snapping their fingers, and communicating in a style considered "biting and provocative," feisty, sassy, ratchet as artistically captured by rapper Megan Thee Stallion.[95] The disciplining of verbal and nonverbal black communication styles and appearances is explicitly gendered, with black girls, according to Ann Ferguson, cited more frequently for "being sassy, demanding everyone's attention, constantly talking," while the disruptive actions of black boys included making "constant noise, Indian whoops," rapping and joking incessantly.[96] Black hair has also served as a target for discipline. Teachers have used black children's hair to argue for black students' disruptive or provocative behavior. While black girls are targeted today for their hair, both black girls and boys were targeted in the 1970s for wearing picks in their Afros, leading to repeated confrontations, as Edelman's Children's Defense Fund reported.[97] Monique Morris observed: "The politicization (and vilification) of thick, curly, and kinky hair is an old one. Characterizations of kinky hair as unmanageable, wild, and ultimately 'bad hair' are all signals (spoken and unspoken) that Black girls are inferior and unkempt when left in their natural state."[98]

The classroom has become a space in which teachers and administrators serve as legal arbiters of student behavior. Although policy (federal, state, local, and school) abounds, teachers and administrators decide when and how to apply policy. Harvard University's Civil Rights Project found that "schools often have one strict written policy but may apply the policy in a lax fashion to whites and in strict fashion to students of color. The schools have, in effect, adopted a 'dual' disciplinary code."[99] The racialization of educational disability allows for the lopsided application of disciplinary codes. School officials keep disability and nondisability categories "open" so that they may place children where they deem appropriate in order to control their present and future behavior. This dynamic process

represents the misalignment of policy and practice in how school officials treat students, contrary to what is stated in the letter of the law, the
school code, and the IEP. Misalignment also occurs when concepts of
disability in some students is perceived differently in others. Ideas of
racial difference often accounts for this misalignment. Annamma reiter-
ates: "Dis/ability is not something that is static no matter the place, time,
or space. Instead, dis/ability is something socially constructed based on
race and other identity markers." She notes that "a student can be labeled
in one school and then move to another teacher, grade level, school, district, or state and that label can be changed or removed altogether."[100]
Annamma's subjects revealed that disability labels were mutable and
applied capriciously by schools.

In their attempt to explain these paradoxes and inconsistencies, education officials argue that positive intent should always be assumed even
when disability labels are messily applied. Education legal observers argue
that policy and procedures prohibit this kind of slippage, preventing
students from being mislabeled or punished because of their disability. Many point to IDEA's stay-put provision that prohibits disabled students from being suspended from school due to their disability. But that
was not the case in the 1970s and early 1980s as researchers found black
EMR, LD, and EBD students were suspended and incarcerated at higher
rates along with other black juveniles who were socially maladjusted,
conduct disordered, and delinquent. If conduct disordered black youth
seemed destined for juvenile courts and prisons, suspending, expelling,
and prosecuting students was also a fait accompli for many black disabled students, demonstrating the fine line between disabled and nondisabled black students when it came to punitive action. "If retardation
and criminality are not synonymous and if there is no clear cause-and-
effect relationship between the two," Miles Santamour wondered, "then
why is there a disproportionate number of offenders with retardation
in prison today?"[101] Santamour, an expert in the field of intellectual disability and juvenile justice, posed that question about the 1970s and early
1980s, not about 2020. Schools and law enforcement officials identified a
cause-and-effect relationship that explained the high rates of students in
prisons with LD and EBD. James E Gilliam and Brenda Scott reported
that "professionals working in the area of corrections believe that many of
their students are behaviorally disordered, . . . that many of their students

engage in delinquent behavior and are potential candidates for incarceration."[102] Ingo Keilitz and Noel Dunivant advanced a susceptibility thesis for LD and imprisonment, arguing that "children with LD possess certain cognitive and personality characteristics that predispose them to commit crimes. Such characteristics—which are components of or are caused by LD—may include lack of impulse control, inability to anticipate the future consequences of actions, poor perception of social cues, irritability, suggestibility, and a tendency to act out ... these disorders, which are frequently associated with LD, directly contribute to the development of delinquent behavior."[103]

Official government studies promoted the idea that black students with disabilities in schools share a self-fulfilling prophesy with incarcerated youth with disabilities in correctional facilities. Mid- to late twentieth-century psychologists believed that black overrepresentation in EMR, LD, and EBD was a "natural" consequence of black cognitive, learning, and behavior disorders. By extension, studies on incarcerated youth with high incidence disabilities have suggested disabled children are predisposed to commit criminal offenses. Nelson, Rutherford, and Wolford noted that "school failure theory suggests that learning disabilities produce academic failure that, in turn, results in delinquent behavior. The theory implies a causal chain linking the learning and social characteristics of LD youth to school failure, dropout, and juvenile delinquency. Such negative labeling and association with delinquency-prone children may prompt LD youths to engage in socially troublesome behavior."[104] This self-fulfilling discourse includes both disabilities and "disorders." Disabled populations are often perceived as disordered, garnering clinical interpretations about their incarcerated-disabledness: "Some researchers ... have found evidence to suggest a correlation between certain behavioral patterns and what they term a 'clinical delinquent personality sub-type.'" "Emotional disturbances in juvenile corrections," Peter Leone and his colleagues reported in another study, "found that this subgroup had diagnoses that mirror those found in a psychiatric institution, both in type and in prevalence."[105] A General Accounting Office report about Washington, D.C., claimed that "approximately 46 percent, or about 595 of the 1,287 juvenile delinquents studied were identified as handicapped in 1983. Almost all the delinquents identified as handicapped were learning disabled or emotionally disturbed." From one reality (black disabled) to another (incarcerated disabled), a third materializes in spite of the language in the Education for All Handicapped Children Act (P.L. 94–142), that all children have a right to a free and appropriate education. Though the law says incarcerated disabled youth must receive an education, many black disabled youth were not receiving such an education, according to Nelson, Rutherford, and Wolford: "Despite the fact that almost half of the District of Columbia's juvenile delinquents have been identified as handicapped, most are not receiving special education services, according to testimony given before a House panel this month."[106] Nelson, Rutherford, and Wolford confronted this problem in the 1980s. According to the Office of Special Education and Rehabilitative Services in 2017, "Incarcerated youth with disabilities range from 30 percent to 60 percent, with some estimates as high as 85 percent."[107] Children with conduct disorder ranged as low as 50 percent and as high as 90 percent; 36 percent of incarcerated youth are learning disabled; and 13 percent are intellectual disabled.[108] What is tragic about this phenomenon is that according to another federal government study conducted by the Office of Juvenile Justice and Delinquency Prevention (OJJDP), "the percentage of youth in juvenile correctional facilities who were previously identified and served in special education programs prior to their incarceration is at least three to five times the percentage of the public school population identified as disabled."[109] Only a fraction of the students with disabilities and mental diagnoses are receiving an education required by law.

Hyperlabeled, hypersurveilled, and hyperpunished, the criminalization of black students in schools produced more risk discourses as both "disabled," and "incarcerated." These ill-fated discourses have been used to justify why marginal experiences and oppressive conditions do not improve among black students in schools. As twin pillars of special education, black disability and delinquency emerged as enduring juggernauts well into the twenty-first century with no signs of abatement despite calls to decriminalize students with disabilities.[110] What we are witnessing today has come full circle or perhaps it is a changing same in how white people hyper-watch, hyper-label, and over-criminalize black student bodies. Mental retardation as a discourse and special education as a system appeared to explain black student underperformance 100 years ago. Labels of "mental retardation" and "subnormal" intelligence led to the disproportionate and unnecessary placement of black students in special education. In turn, the disproportionate numbers of black students seemed to "validate" long-standing ideas about black mental and cognitive disabilities in a reinforcing, self-fulfilling, and racist feedback loop. The creators of special education and disability discourses have been shrewd in concealing intentionality as part of a larger strategy of containment that structurally and programmatically keep black and brown students from accessing the benefits of general education and the most-resourced parts of special education. That was true in the 1920s as much as it is true in the 2020s.

Special education as a form of differential education was sold to the public in the early twentieth century by psychologists, promising efficient and progressive educational reform. In the post–World War II period, special education was repackaged and presented as a social justice and equity measure for "handicapped" children, with the proclamation by 1975 that all children had a right to a free and appropriate education. For many black and brown students, the opposite proved true. When special education is touted as a positive good, students of color rarely experience its benefits. Subini Annamma recalled the words of one of her students: "Rivera recognized that special education was supposed to provide individual help in theory, but she did not receive that academic support in practice. She thought her schools must not have had special education because of the lack of support she found."[111] Arthur Hill made a similar point sixty-five years ago in the 1950s: "As special educators we often declare our belief in 'education for all the children of all the people,' but in practice we are prone to delimit our interests and erect barriers which exclude many children from educational services."[112] Special education not only manifested policy and practice gaps; special education was/is also weighed down by paradoxes. One the most significant paradoxes recognized by education professor Alfredo Artiles was a *purported* system based on inclusion and a *manifested* reality based on overrepresentation.[113] Unable to reconcile the civil rights of some, and the educational disability rights of others, special education reflects the racial divisions in U.S. society. Burton Blatt's reflection more than forty years ago is a fitting final observation: "In this field we call special education, history has not served us well. We have not learned from it."[114]

Acknowledgments

The *Unteachables* was ten plus years in the making. Like most book projects, it was marked by ebbs and flows, fits and starts, pauses, and full stops. My desire to write this book, however, never waned, and I spent a decade determined to chronicle a long-overdue history of race, education, and disability. During that time, numerous colleagues, interlocutors, and loved ones enthusiastically championed this project, and it would have been impossible to complete it without them.

Though long, this acknowledgment section is shorter than it should be, as I am unable to remember every individual who helped me along the way. For that omission, please accept my sincerest apologies. Danielle Kasprzak acquired the manuscript and handed it to Pieter Martin at the University of Minnesota Press. I would like to thank the acquisition and production staff at the Press who made the project seamless throughout its various stages. I thank those who read the manuscript fully or partially, including Scot Danforth, Adam Nelson, Christine Sleeter, Peter Demerath, Brian Lozenski, Pero Dagbovie, Jen Gilbert, Jennifer Jones, Joyce Bell, Lula Nur, and the anonymous reviewers. Ava Purkiss meticulously read the entire manuscript and provided extraordinarily helpful feedback. I am grateful for her intellectual generosity, encouragement, and love. I also want to thank the research assistants and former students that found documents in archives and worked on portions of chapters in directed studies and research programs: Jacob (Coby) Oertel, Samantha Weiman, Yahsmene Butler, Hawi Teizazu, Calvin Hylton, Chaltu Muse, Anna Freyburg, Bruno Indig, Nautica Flowers, Hanan Karia, Devona Thomas, and

Christopher Armstrong. A special thank you to Coby Oertel. His tireless effort in tracking down hard-to-find books, articles, primary sources, and reports at a moment's request, proved critical to the writing of this book. His research acumen is unmatched, and I am forever grateful for his hard work, dedication to the project, and unyielding support. I would also like to thank the librarians and archivists at the University of Illinois at Urbana-Champaign (Samuel A. Kirk Papers); Harold Washington Library Center (Chicago Public Library), Chicago History Museum Research Collections, the Minnesota Historical Society, Manuscript Division, Wilson Library at the University of Minnesota, and the Pritzker Legal Research Center at Northwestern University.

My colleagues at the University of Minnesota in the College of Liberal Arts (CLA) and the College of Education and Human Development (CEHD) have offered praise and unending support, including Yuichiro Onishi, Tade Okediji, Rose Brewer, Terrion Williamson (now at the University of Illinois at Chicago), Josef Waldense, Vicki Coifman, Njeri Githire, Bula Waylessa, Said Ahmed, Angalika Muaka, Christine Powell, Vanessa Steele, Agnes Mrutu, Peter Demerath, Timothy Lensmire, Muhammad Khalifa (now at The Ohio State University), Nicola Alexander, Tania Mitchell, Katie Pekel, J. B. Mayo, Vichet Chhuon, Annie Mason, Malinda Lindquist, Jimmy Patino, Katharine Gerbner, Brian Lozenski (Macalester College) and Jonathan Hamilton (Macalester College). Former graduate students that asked me to serve on their dissertation committees like Courtney Bell, Bodunrin Banwo, Corey Yeager, Michael Walker, Molly Siebert, Leah Fulton, and Kidiocus Carroll, now all PhDs and/or assistant professors, never missed an opportunity to compliment the progress of the book's writing and its future publication. The Center for Race, Indigeneity, Disability, Gender & Sexuality Studies (RIDGS) in the College of Liberal Arts coalesces the critical work from the departments of African American and African Studies, American Indian Studies, Chicano and Latino Studies, Gender, Women, and Sexuality Studies, American Studies, the Asian American Studies program and the Critical Disability Studies Collective, making our scholarship visible to the larger university and the public at large. I am honored to be RIDGS current director. A half-year sabbatical from CLA in late 2020 allowed me to complete the manuscript.

Critical to my understanding of special education practice were Carole Gupton, Alexis Mann, Tatiana Gary, and Tanaiah Mitchell: four current or former special education teachers who engaged me in extensive

cknoledgments

conversations about their knowledge of disabilities and practical experiences in the classroom. Additionally, I express gratitude to the special education teachers and administrators at federal level-IV institutions—Transition Plus, RiverEast, and the Harrison School, particularly principal Nate Hampton, who allowed me to talk to his staff at Harrison on multiple occasions about the history of special education and constructions of black disability. Nothing has been more professionally rewarding than working directly with teachers and administrators on special education, ethnic studies, and social studies curricula at Minneapolis Public Schools, St. Paul Public Schools, South Washington County Schools, Anoka-Hennepin Schools, Stillwater Area Public Schools, and Mankato Area Public Schools.

My family has served as a constant source of encouragement, reassurance, and praise throughout the book writing process. My two sons, Myles Mayes and Marcus Mayes, lived with the writing of this book up close and for a large portion of their lives; I thank them for their enduring love and support as well as their curiosity about the subject. Kiesha Mayes provided love and support as I conceived of, drafted, and shaped the manuscript into a book. The frequent requests for legal cases and a listening ear are only a few of her invaluable contributions. From a distance, thank you to those who asked about the book's progress and cheered me to the finish line: Keith Mayes Sr., Daphne Hinkson, Carolyn Bowman, Steven Belcher, Karen Spearman-Harris, Damion Grissom, Sharay Ebony Harris, Rhonda Campbell, Debra, Donna, Kim, and Kevin Spearman. For decades, and especially during the writing of this book, California has been a refuge and a second home. I want to thank Michael and Edith Mayes and the entire Los Angeles Mayes family, including Kia, Jason, Jared, Marissa, Aleia, Jai, Jamon, Joshua, and their spouses and children. Great friends Will Tompkins, Eric Stewart, Adrian Mack, Wynfred Russell, and Jamal Harraut checked in not only about the progress of the book but equally about life and my well-being. For their unwavering emotional support, I am forever indebted.

This book is dedicated to my grandmother Marion Mayes, who passed away at the age of ninety-seven before its completion, and two members of the family who left us before the age of forty: Marissa Mayes and Shaquana Anderson. Lastly, I would be remiss not acknowledging the thousands of black and brown students misdiagnosed with a disability who did not have one and the thousands of children never diagnosed who did.

Appendix

Policy Summaries

P.L. 83–531: The Cooperative Research Act (1954, 1957): One million dollars of which $675,000 was appropriated for research related to the education of the "mentally retarded."

P.L. 85–926: Grants for Teaching in the Education of Mentally Retarded Children (1958): Encouraged the expansion of teaching in the education of mentally retarded children through grants to institutions of higher learning and to state educational agencies.

P.L. 88–164: Section 301—Professional Personnel/Community Mental Health Act (1963): Began the process of deinstitutionalization from residential facilities. In addition to the "mentally retarded," and the "deaf," the law authorized the training of professionals for the "hard of hearing," "speech impaired," "visually impaired," "seriously emotionally disturbed," "crippled," or "other health impaired."

P.L. 88–452: Economic Opportunity Act (EOA) (1964)—Title II ("Community Action Program"): Head Start was the major community action program that focused on the needs of low-income individuals and families, particularly those children that evidence low educational attainment, with incidences of disease, disability, crime, and juvenile delinquency.

P.L. 89–10: Elementary and Secondary Education Act (ESEA) (April 1965)—Title I: Authorized states and local school districts to use federal funds to educate poor and low-achieving children called "culturally deprived" and "educationally disadvantaged."

Title III: Funded supplemental education centers, exemplary projects, and provided remedial aid to children, including the "handicapped."

P.L. 89–313: (ESEA) (November 1965): Amended Title I to provide grants to states for children in state-operated or supported schools for the "handicapped."

P.L. 89–750: Education of Handicapped Children (ESEA) (November 1966)—Title VI: First stand-alone title in ESEA for disabled students. Funds earmarked to provide grants to states to assist in the initiation, expansion, and improvement of special education services to preschool, elementary, and secondary "handicapped" students.

P.L. 90–538: Handicapped Early Education Assistance Act (ESEA) (1968): Funded the development of preschool educational programs for "handicapped" children.

P.L. 91–230: Children with Specific Learning Disabilities Act (ESEA) (1969/1970): Amended Title VI (Education of Handicapped Children) to provide a new program for children with learning disabilities. Grants to states for (1) research, (2) professional training, and (3) creating model (demonstration/pilot) programs.

P.L. 93–112: The Rehabilitation Act, Section 504 (1973): Prohibits discrimination on the basis of disability in programs that receive federal financial assistance.

P.L. 94–142: Education for All Handicapped Children Act (1975): First stand-alone law in special education. It mandated a free appropriate public education (FAPE) for all "handicapped" children, ensuring due process, plus instituting individual education plans (IEPs) and the least restrictive environments (LREs).

P.L. 101–476: Individuals with Disabilities Education Act (IDEA) (1990): Reauthorized the Education for All Handicapped Children Act requiring FAPE, IEPs, LREs, due process, and parent and teacher participation. Included autism and traumatic brain injury to the list of disability categories.

P.L. 105–17: Individuals with Disabilities Education Act (IDEA) Amendments of 1997: Established adjudication protocols and procedures for disabled students in violation of school disciplinary and behavior policies.

P.L. 108–446: Individuals with Disabilities Education Act (IDEA) Amendments of 2004: Eliminated the "severe discrepancy" criteria between intellectual ability and academic achievement that previously "proved" a student had a learning disability. Instituted instead a process known as Response-to-Intervention (RTI) to determine if a student in general education could have a specific learning disability and acted to prevent said student from being placed in special education.

.

Notes

Note on Terminology

1. Chris Bell, "Introduction: Doing Representational Detective Work," in *Blackness and Disability: Critical Examinations and Cultural Interventions,* ed. Christopher M. Bell (East Lansing: Michigan State University Press, 2011), 3–4.

Introduction

1. Michael J. Herrick, "Developing Individualized Instruction is the Difference," *Journal of Special Education,* 7, no. 4 (December 1973): 417. This essay was in response to a full debate beginning with Michael J. Herrick, "Disabled or Disadvantaged: What's the Difference?," *Journal of Special Education* 7, no. 4 (December 1973): 381–86; Ronald Bassman, "Label Jars Not People," *Journal of Humanistic Psychology* 59, no. 3 (May 2019): 339–45.

2. W. C. Martindale, "How Detroit Cares for Her Backward Children," *Psychological Clinic* 6, no. 5 (October 15, 1912): 128.

3. G. Alexander Moore Jr., *Realities of the Urban Classroom: Observations in Elementary Schools* (Garden City, NY: Anchor, 1967), 6–7.

4. Carole Gupton was an elementary school principal at Minneapolis Public Schools for over thirty years. After retiring, she worked at the University of Minnesota, College of Education and Human Development (CEHD) as the director for the Preparation-to-Practice Group in special education disproportionality. Gupton began her career as a special education teacher in Milwaukee.

5. Kenneth J. Meier, Joseph Steward Jr., and Robert E. England, *Race, Class, and Education: The Politics of Second Generation Discrimination* (Madison: University of Wisconsin Press, 1989).

6. "The Normal and the Subnormal Child," *Journal of Educational Psychology* 3, no. 9 (November 1912): 535.

7. Kirby A. Heller, Wayne H. Holtzman, and Samuel Messick, eds., *Placing Children in Special Education: A Strategy for Equity* (Washington, D.C.: National Academy Press, 1982).

8. Venus E. Evans-Winters, "Schooling at the Liminal: Black Girls and Special Education," *Wisconsin English Journal* 58, no. 2 (Fall 2016): 140–53; Susan Burch and Lindsey Patterson, "Not Just Any Body: Disability, Gender, and History," *Journal of Women's History* 25, no. 4 (Winter 2013): 122–37; Nirmala Erevelles and Andrea Minear, "Unspeakable Offenses: Untangling and Race and Disability in Discourses of Intersectionality," *Disability Studies Reader*, ed. Lennard J. Davis (New York: Routledge, 2017).

9. Monique W. Morris, *Pushout: The Criminalization of Black Girls in Schools* (New York: New Press, 2016); Subini Ancy Annamma, *The Pedagogy of Pathologization* (New York: Routledge, 2018); Erica Young, "#BlackGirlMagic: Due Process and the Disappearance of Black Girls in Public Education," *Social Justice & Equity Journal* 3, no. 2 (2020): 209–32.

10. For an early article that shows how schools, the courts, and welfare agencies were disability-making systems, see Thomas D. Eliot, "Welfare Agencies, Special Education, and the Courts," *American Journal of Sociology* 31, no. 1 (July 1925): 58–78. The graphics of the typological visual are unsophisticated but highly informative about how social agencies constructed children's identity and "managed" them.

11. Sociologist and anthropologist James Carrier put it bluntly when he said, "Education handicaps and the fields of educational psychology, which studies them, and special education, which treats them, are social products that are affected by social forces, reflecting social interests, and amenable to sociological analysis. I need to stress this point. It is not enough to say that there are such things as educational handicaps and that certain children have them. Such a view is questionable even for so self-evident a condition as blindness, which . . . is not fixed and absolute but profoundly social. And if this is so for an apparently objective condition like blindness, it will be much more so for the sorts of mild disabilities that Sally Tomlinson has called the nonnormative conditions, those for which there is little normative agreement about signs, symptoms, and diagnosis, conditions that characterize the bulk of children in special education: learning disability, mild retardation, and emotional disturbance." James G. Carrier, "Sociology and Special Education: Differentiation and Allocation in Mass Education," *American Journal of Education* 94, no. 3 (May 1986): 283.

12. Bernadette Baker, "The Hunt for Disability: The New Eugenics and the Normalization of School Children," *Teachers College Record* 104, no. 4 (June 2002): 663–703.

13. Christine Sleeter was the first scholar I encountered who wrote about the "whiteness" of LD as a racialized category. See Christine E. Sleeter, "Learning Disabilities: The Social Construction of a Special Education Category," *Exceptional Children* 53, no. 1 (September 1986): 46–64. Her essay is also in *Critical Voices on Special Education: Problems and Progress Concerning the Mildly Handicapped*, ed. Scott B. Sigmon (Albany: State University of New York Press, 1990). See also, Christine Sleeter, "Why Is There Learning Disabilities? A Critical Analysis of the

Birth of the Field in Its Social Context," *The Formation of School Subjects: The Struggle for Creating an American Institution*, ed. Thomas S. Popkewitz (Abingdon, Oxon, UK: Routledge, 2019, 1987). Kenneth Kavale and Steven Forness disagreed with Sleeter's assessment, stating, "It is difficult to see why Sleeter is distressed by the racial composition of LD programs during its early stages. Might we not be equally distressed that the composition of compensatory education programs was predominantly lower SES and minority children?" The irony that disability categories were either predominantly one racial group or another as a function of racism and historical racialization is lost on Kavale and Forness. See Kenneth A. Kavale and Steven R. Forness, "History, Politics, and the General Education Initiative: Sleeter's Reinterpretation of Learning Disabilities as a Case Study," *Remedial and Special Education* 8, no. 5 (September/October 1987): 10.

14. The educational disability rights movement functions more like an advocacy group of privileged parents, social scientists, educational professionals, lawmakers in Congress and politicians in presidential administrations. It begs the question whether they can be called a movement at all. Though the parents and the organizations they created on behalf of their children can be considered movement oriented, the educational disability rights movement of the 1940s through the 1960s was not the grassroots disability rights movement of the 1970s through the 1990s, though they shared some common concerns about a variety of disabilities in the United States.

15. Ableist placement practices of black and brown students over the last one hundred years forces us to think about how dismantling overrepresentation in special education should be both a form of racial justice and disability justice.

16. Diane Driedger, *The Last Civil Rights Movement* (New York: St. Martin's Press, 1989); Joseph P. Shapiro, *No Pity: People with Disabilities Forging a New Civil Rights Movement* (New York: Three Rivers Press, 1994); James I. Charlton, *Nothing about Us without Us: Disability Oppression and Empowerment* (Berkeley: University of California Press, 2000); Doris Z. Fleischer and Frieda Zames, *From Charity to Confrontation* (Philadelphia: Temple University Press, 2000); Linda Hamilton Krieger, ed. *Backlash Against the ADA: Reinterpreting Disability Rights* (Ann Arbor: University of Michigan, 2003); Fred Pelka, *An Oral History of the Disability Rights Movement* (Amherst: University of Massachusetts Press, 2012); Nancy J. Hirschman and Beth Linker, eds., *Civil Disabilities: Citizenship, Membership, and Belonging* (Philadelphia: University of Pennsylvania Press, 2015); Bruce J. Dierenfield and David A. Gerber, *Disability Rights and Religious Liberty in Education: The Story behind Zobrest v. Catalina Foothills School District* (Urbana: University of Illinois Press, 2020). A newer generation of feminist, queer, and disabled activists of color have called the movement for "disability rights" into question, arguing and advocating instead for a "disability justice" vision of liberation that not only centers the voices and experiences of disabled queer, trans, black, and brown people but also calls for the abolition of capitalist and gender normativity, able-bodied supremacy, and white supremacy. See Leah Lakshmi

Piepzna-Samarasinha, *Care Work: Dreaming Disability Justice* (Vancouver: Arsenal Pulp, 2018). See also, Liat Ben-Moshe, *Decarcerating Disability: Deinstutionalization and Prison Abolition* (Minneapolis: University of Minnesota Press, 2020).

17. Sally Tomlinson, *The Politics of Race, Class and Special Education: The Selected Works of Sally Tomlinson* (London: Routledge, 2014); Sally Tomlinson, *Educational Subnormality: A Study in Decision-Making* (Abingdon, Oxon, UK: Routledge, 2019, 1981); Sally Tomlinson, *A Sociology of Special and Inclusive Education: Exploring the Manufacture of Inability* (Abingdon, Oxon, UK: Routledge, 2017); John A. Richardson and Justin J. W. Powell, *Comparing Special Education: Origins to Contemporary Paradoxes* (Stanford: Stanford University Press, 2011).

18. Robert L. Osgood, *The History of Special Education: A Struggle for Equality in American Public Schools* (Westport, Conn.: Praeger, 2008); Margret A. Winzer, *From Integration to Inclusion: A History of Special Education in the 20th Century* (Washington, D.C.: Gallaudet University Press, 2009).

19. Robert L. Osgood, *For 'Children Who Vary from the Normal Type:' Special Education in Boston, 1838–1930* (Washington, D.C.: Gallaudet University Press, 2000); Jason Ellis, *A Class by Themselves? The Origins of Special Education in Toronto and Beyond* (Toronto: University of Toronto Press, 2019). Osgood and Ellis give the reader a detailed overview of early special education classes and the ideas that produced them in Boston and Toronto. Osgood and Ellis not only introduce the reader to the larger intellectual currents impacting public policy (i.e., eugenics) but both authors establish what principal organizations and influential people in the United States and Canada created the system of special education. Two other books, Adam R. Nelson, *The Elusive Ideal: Equal Educational Opportunity and the Federal Role in Boston's Public School, 1950–1985* (Chicago: University of Chicago Press, 2005), and Allison C. Carey, *On the Margin of Citizenship: Intellectual Disability and Civil Rights in Twentieth Century America* (Philadelphia: Temple University Press, 2009), addressed the history of disability through the discourse on political rights and equal educational opportunity, moving back and forth between a rights discourse and the lived realities of children inside schools and in society. Carey demonstrates how disability rights advocates borrowed ideologies from grassroots movements for their specialized agendas, while Nelson explores how the federal government used Massachusetts state education policies to create their own compensatory program for "disadvantaged" and "disabled" youth. *The Unteachables* combines the strengths of all four monographs but charts a new course by looking closely at the evolution of disability categories and the genealogy of discourses that produced a racially disproportionate special education system with direct assistance from the federal government.

In addition to the work of Osgood, Ellis, Carey, and Nelson, the cognitive disability that has received the most scholarly attention is "mental retardation." Mark Ripley, *The Social Construction of Intellectual Disability* (Cambridge: Cambridge University Press, 2004), Michael L. Wehmeyer, ed., *The Story of Intellectual*

Disability: An Evolution of Meaning, Understanding, and Public Perception (Baltimore: Paul H. Brookes, 2013), and Patrick McDonagh, *Idiocy: A Cultural History* (Liverpool: Liverpool University Press, 2008), are other examples. James W. Trent Jr.'s classic, *Inventing the Feeble Mind: A History of Mental Retardation in the United States* (New York: Oxford University Press, 1994), Steven Noll, *Feeble-Minded in Our Midst: Institutions for the Mentally Retarded in the South, 1900–1940* (Chapel Hill: University of North Carolina Press, 1995), and Steven Noll and James W. Trent Jr., eds., *Mental Retardation in America* (New York: New York University Press, 2004) pioneered the historical study of intellectual disability as both a product of medical discourses and the hospitals and residential facilities that institutionalized the "mentally retarded" to great detriment. Equally, Scot Danforth, in *The Incomplete Child: An Intellectual History of Learning Disabilities* (New York: Peter Lang, 2009), has written a comprehensive history of learning disabilities, examining work of LD's intellectual progenitors from the early twentieth century to the 1960s. James G. Carrier provided an excellent historical-theoretical framework of learning disability in his book, *Learning Disability: Social Class and the Construction of Inequality in American Education* (New York: Greenwood, 1996). Two books that cover all things factual about learning disabilities are Kenneth A. Kavale and Steven R. Forness, *The Nature of Learning Disabilities: Critical Elements of Diagnosis and Classification* (Mahwah, N.J.: Lawrence Erlbaum Associates, 1995) and Renee Bradley, Louis Danielson, and Daniel P. Hallahan, eds., *Identification of Learning Disabilities: Research to Practice* (Mahwah, N.J.: Lawrence Erlbaum Associates, 2002). David J. Connor produced an interdisciplinary work of vignettes by LD students marginalized by race and class, *Urban Narratives, Portraits in Progress: Life at the Intersection of Learning Disability, Race, and Social Class* (New York: Peter Lang, 2008).

20. Many disciplinary fields exist along racial fault lines with the adjective "black" (as in "black" disability studies/history) often filling in the silences and erasures created by the invisible and unnamed modifier ("white" disability studies/history) though the racial identity of scholars may cross disciplinary fields. Simi Linton, *Claiming Disability: Knowledge and Identity* (New York: New York University Press, 1998); Lennard J. Davis, ed., *The Disability Studies Reader* (New York: Routledge, 2017, 1997); Paul Longmore and Lauri Umansky's *The New Disability History: American Perspectives* (New York: New York University Press, 2001); Kim E. Nielsen, *A Disability History of the United States* (Boston: Beacon, 2012); Susan L. Gabel and Scot Danforth, eds., *Disability and the Politics of Education: An International Reader* (New York: Peter Lang, 2008); Susan Burch and Michael Rembis, eds., *Disability Histories* (Urbana: University of Illinois Press, 2014); Tobin Siebers, *Disability Theory* (Ann Arbor: University of Michigan Press, 2008); Ellen Samuels, *Fantasies of Identification: Disability, Gender, Race* (New York: New York University Press, 2014); Margaret Price, *Mad at School: Rhetorics of Mental Disability and Academic Life* (Ann Arbor: University of Michigan Press, 2011); Christopher M. Bell, *Blackness and Disability: Critical Examinations and*

Cultural Interventions (East Lansing: Michigan State University Press, 2011); Therí A. Pickens, *Black Madness:Mad Blackness* (Durham, N.C.: Duke University Press, 2019); also see the Therí Pickens–curated special issue of *African American Review* on Blackness and Disability, 50, no. 2 (Summer 2017); Nirmala Erevelles, "Becoming Disabled/Becoming Black: Crippin' Critical Ethnic Studies from the Periphery," in *Critical Ethnic Studies: A Reader,* ed., Nada Elia, David M. Hernández, Jodi Kim, Shana L. Redmond, Dylan Rodríguez, and Sarita Echavez See (Durham, N.C.: Duke University Press, 2016); Moya Bailey, "A Black Feminist Disability Framework," *Gender & Society,* 33, no. 1 (February 2019): 19–40; David J. Connor, Beth A. Ferri, and Subini A. Annamma, eds., *DisCrit: Disability Studies and Critical Race Theory in Education* (New York: Teachers College Press, 2016); Sami Schalk, *Bodyminds Reimagined: (Dis)ability, Race, Gender in Black Women's Speculative Fiction* (Durham, N.C.: Duke University Press, 2018); Susan Burch and Hannah Joyner, *Unspeakable: The Story of Junius Wilson* (Chapel Hill: University of North Carolina Press, 2007); Dea H. Boster, *African American Slavery and Disability* (New York: Routledge, 2013). Stefanie Hunt-Kennedy, *Between Fitness and Death: Disability and Slavery in the Caribbean* (Urbana: University of Illinois Press, 2020); Jennifer L. Barclay, *The Mark of Slavery: Disability, Race, and Gender in Antebellum America* (Urbana: University of Illinois Press, 2021).

21. James D. Anderson, *The Education of Blacks in the South, 1860–1935* (Chapel Hill: University of North Carolina Press, 1988); V. P. Franklin, *The Education of Black Philadelphia: The Social and Educational History of a Minority Community, 1900–1950* (Philadelphia: University of Pennsylvania Press, 1979); Louis R. Harlan, *Separate and Unequal: Public School Campaigns and Racism in the Southern Seaboard States, 1901–1915* (Chapel Hill: University of North Carolina Press, 1958); Mary Niall Mitchell, *Raising Freedom's Child: Black Children and Visions of Future After Slavery* (New York: New York University Press, 2008); Ronald E. Butchart, *Schooling the Freed People: Teaching, Learning, and the Struggle for Black Freedom, 1861–1876* (Chapel Hill: University of North Carolina Press, 2010); "African American Children with Special Needs," *Journal of Negro Education* 70, no. 4 (Autumn 2001), special series.

22. Vanessa Siddle Walker, *Their Highest Potential: An African American School Community in the Segregated South* (Chapel Hill: University of North Carolina Press, 1996); Vanessa Siddle Walker, *The Lost Education of Horace Tate: Uncovering the Hidden Heroes Who Fought for Justice in Schools* (New York: New Press, 2018); John L. Rury and Shirley A. Hill, *The African American Struggle for Secondary Schooling, 1940–1980* (New York: Teachers College Press, 2012). See also, David G. Garcia, *Strategies of Segregation: Race, Resistance, and the Struggle for Educational Equality* (Oakland: University of California Press, 2018).

23. Crystal R. Sanders, *A Chance for Change: Head Start and Mississippi's Black Freedom Struggle* (Chapel Hill: University of North Carolina Press, 2016); Russell Rickford, *We Are an African People: Independent Education, Black Power, and the*

Radical Imagination (New York: Oxford University Press, 2016); Kabria Baumgartner, *In Pursuit of Knowledge: Black Women and Educational Activism in Antebellum America* (New York: New York University Press, 2019); Jarvis R. Givens, *Fugitive Pedagogy: Carter G. Woodson and the Art of Black Teaching* (Cambridge, Mass.: Harvard University Press, 2021).

24. Zoë Burkholder, *An African American Dilemma: A History of School Integration and Civil Rights in the North* (New York: Oxford University Press, 2021); Clarence Taylor, *Knocking At Our Own Door: Milton A. Galamison and the Struggle to Integrate New York City Schools* (Lanham, MD: Lexington, 2001); Davison M. Douglas, *Reading, Writing & Race: The Desegregation of the Charlotte Schools* (Chapel Hill: University of North Carolina Press, 1995); Jack Dougherty, *More Than One Struggle: The Evolution of Black School Reform in Milwaukee* (Chapel Hill: University of North Carolina Press, 2004); Elizabeth Todd-Breland, *A Political Education: Black Politics and Education Reform in Chicago Since the 1960s* (Chapel Hill: University of North Carolina Press, 2018); Dionne Danns, *Desegregating Chicago Public Schools: Policy Implementation, Politics, and Protest, 1965–1985* (New York: Palgrave Macmillan, 2014); Barbara J. Shircliffe, *Desegregating Teachers: Contesting the Meaning of Equality of Educational Opportunity in the South Post Brown* (New York: Peter Lang, 2012).

25. John Charles Boger and Gary Orfield, eds., *School Resegregation: Must the South Turn Back?* (Chapel Hill: University of North Carolina Press, 2005); Gary Orfield, Susan E. Eaton, and the Harvard Education Project on School Desegregation, *Dismantling Desegregation: The Quiet Reversal of Brown v. Board of Education* (1996).

26. James D. Anderson, "Crosses to Bear and Promises to Keep: The Jubilee Anniversary of *Brown v. Board of Education*," *Urban Education* 39, no. 4 (July 2004): 359–73; Dionne Danns, *Crossing Segregated Boundaries: Remembering Chicago School Desegregation* (New Brunswick, N.J.: Rutgers University Press, 2021).

27. Wanda J. Blanchett, Vincent Mumford, and Floyd Beachum, "Urban School Failure and Disproportionality in a Post-*Brown* Era: Benign Neglect of the Constitutional Rights of Students of Color," *Remedial and Special Education* 26, no. 2 (March/April 2005): 70–81; Wanda J. Blanchett, "A Retrospective Examination of Urban Education: From *Brown* to the Resegregation of African Americans in Special Education—It Is Time to 'Go for Broke,'" *Urban Education* 44, no. 4 (July 2009): 370–88; Monika Williams Shealey, Martha Scott Lue, Michael Brooks, and Erica McCray, "Examining the Legacy of *Brown*: The Impact on Special Education and Teacher Practice," *Remedial and Special Education* 26, no. 2 (March/April 2005): 113–21; Thomas V. O'Brien, "What Happened to the Promise of *Brown*? An Organizational Explanation and an Outline for Change," *Teachers College Record* 109, no. 8 (August 2007): 1875–1901; Thomas S. Serwatka, Sharian Deering, and Patrick Grant, "Disproportionate Representation of African Americans in Emotionally Handicapped Classes," *Journal of Black Studies* 25, no. 4 (March 1995): 492–506; Kathy-Anne Jordan, "Discourses of Difference and the

Overrepresentation of Black Students in Special Education," *Journal of African American History: Brown v. Board of Education: Fifty Years of Educational Change in the United States, 1954–2004* 90, no. 1/2 (Winter 2005): 128–49; Tori Kearns, Laurie Ford, and Jean Ann Linney, "African American Student Representation in Special Education Programs," *Journal of Negro Education* 74, no. 4 (Fall 2005): 297–310; James M. Patton, "The Disproportionate Representation of African Americans in Special Education: Looking Behind the Curtain for Understanding and Solutions," *Journal of Special Education* 32, no. 1 (April 1998): 25–31.

28. Derrick Darby and John L, Rury, *The Color of Mind: Why the Origins of the Achievement Gap Matter for Justice* (Chicago: University of Chicago Press, 2018).

29. Black scholars like W. E. B. DuBois and Doxey Wilkerson, and several white commentators, such as Walter Lippman and John Dewey, vehemently questioned and spoke out against the use of IQ tests to place black students in special classes in the 1920s.

30. Russell Skiba and Kenneth Grizzle, "The Social Maladjustment Exclusion: Issues of Definition and Assessment," *School Psychology Review* 20, no. 4 (1991): 580–98.

1. Who Are the Unteachables?

1. Stephen Jay Gould, *The Mismeasure of Man* (New York: W.W. Norton, 1996, 1981).

2. Tracy L. Steffes, *School, Society, & State: A New Education to Govern Modern America, 1890–1940* (Chicago: University of Chicago Press, 2012).

3. Edgar A. Doll, "Mental Hygiene Aspects of Special Education," *Journal of Psycho-Asthenics* 35 (June 1929–June 1930): 73.

4. Doll, "Mental Hygiene Aspects of Special Education," 74.

5. Doll, "Mental Hygiene Aspects of Special Education," 74.

6. James H. Van Sickle, "Provision for Exceptional Children in the Public Schools," *Psychological Clinic* 2, no. 4 (June 15, 1908): 103.

7. Van Sickle, "Provision for Exceptional Children in the Public Schools," 103.

8. Van Sickle, "Provision for Exceptional Children in the Public Schools," 103.

9. The early 1900s obsession with efficient classrooms, like smooth-running machines, created a strong argument for weeding out the students who gummed up the public school system and slowed things down for the conforming rest. See Raymond Callahan, *Education and the Cult of Efficiency: A Study of the Social Forces That Have Shaped the Administration of the Public Schools* (Chicago: University of Chicago Press, 1962).

10. Ian Hacking, "Making Up People," in *Forms of Desire: Sexual Orientation and the Social Constructionist Controversy,* ed. Edward Stein (New York: Routledge, 1992), 69–88.

11. Quoted in L. Rauscher and J. McClintock, "Ableism Curriculum Design," in *Teaching for Diversity and Social Justice,* eds. M. Adams, L. A. Bell, and P. Griffin (New York: Routledge, 1997), 198–229; Susan Baglieri and Priya Lalvani, *Undoing*

Ableism: Teaching About Disability in K-12 Classrooms (New York: Routledge, 2020), 2.

12. Baglieri and Lalvani, *Undoing Ableism,* 2.

13. Hacking, "Making Up People," 69–88.

14. Ian Hacking, "Biopower and the Avalanche of Printed Numbers," *Humanities in Society* 5 (1982): 280.

15. Tukufu Zuberi, *Thicker Than Blood: How Racial Statistics Lie* (Minneapolis: University of Minnesota Press, 2001); Theodore M. Porter, *Trust in Numbers: The Pursuit of Objectivity in Science and Public Life* (Princeton, N.J.: Princeton University Press, 1995).

16. Quoted in Tremain, *Foucault and Feminist Philosophy of Disability,* 53.

17. Tremain, *Foucault and Feminist Philosophy of Disability,* 97.

18. Tremain, *Foucault and Feminist Philosophy of Disability,* 49.

19. Roland P. Falkner, "The Fundamental Expression of Retardation," *Psychological Clinic* 4, no. 8 (January 15, 1911): 217.

20. Hilda Volkmor and Isabel Noble, "Retardation as Indicated By One Hundred City School Reports," *Psychological Clinic* 8, no. 3 (May 15, 1914): 77.

21. Barbara D. Bateman, "An Educator's View of a Diagnostic Approach to Learning Disorders," in *Learning Disorders* 1, ed. J. Hellmuth (Seattle: Special Child, 1965), 219–39.

22. Marion Monroe, *Children Who Cannot Read: The Analysis of Reading Disabilities and the Use of Diagnostic Tests in the Instruction of Retarded Readers* (Chicago: University of Chicago Press, 1932).

23. Ray McDermott, Shelley Goldman, and Herve Varenne, "The Cultural Work of Learning Disabilities," *Educational Researcher* 35, no. 6 (August–September 2006), 13.

24. William Sloan and Harvey A. Stevens, *A Century of Concern: A History of American Association on Mental Deficiency, 1876–1976* (Washington, D.C.: American Association on Mental Deficiency, 1976), 209.

25. James E. Bryan, "A Method for Determining the Extent and Causes of Retardation in a City School System," *Psychological Clinic* 1, no. 2 (April 15, 1907): 42.

26. Horace Mann Bond, "The Extent and Character of Separate Schools in the United States," *Journal of Negro Education* 4, no. 3 (July 1935): 324.

27. Lightner Witmer, "What is Meant by Retardation?," *Psychological Clinic* 4, no. 5, (October 15, 1910): 124.

28. Witmer, "What Is Meant by Retardation?"

29. G. E. Johnson, "Contribution to the Psychology and Pedagogy of Feebleminded Children," *Journal of Psycho-Asthenics* 1 (1896–1897): 91, 97.

30. Edward Ellis Allen, "Education of Defectives," in *Monographs on Education in the United States,* Vol. 2, ed. Nicholas Murray Butler (Albany, N.Y.: J. B. Lyon & Co., 1900), 508. Dr. Edward Ellis Allen was principal of the Pennsylvania Institution for the Instruction of the Blind, now named Overbrook School for the Blind.

31. Samuel G. Howe, "On the Causes of Idiocy," in Vol. 1 of *The History of Mental Retardation, Collected Papers*, eds. Marvin Rosen, Gerald R. Clark, and Marvin S. Kivitz (Baltimore: University Park Press, 1976), 37. For a myriad of explanations put forth about feeblemindedness and mental retardation in annual conference proceedings, see William Sloan and Harvey A. Stevens, eds., *A Century of Concern: A History of American Association on Mental Deficiency, 1876–1976* (Washington, D.C.: American Association of Mental Deficiency, Inc., 1976).

32. Quoted in Thomas S. Ball, *Itard, Seguin and Kephart: Sensory Education— A Learning Interpretation* (Columbus, Ohio: Charles E. Merrill. 1971), 6–7.

33. Ball, *Itard, Seguin and Kephart.*

34. For a history of political theory and intellectual disability, see Stacy Clifford Simplican, *The Capacity Contract: Intellectual Disability and the Question of Citizenship* (Minneapolis: University of Minnesota Press, 2015).

35. J. Langdon H. Down and M. D. London, "Observations on an Ethnic Classification of Idiots," *London Hospital Reports* 3 (1866): 259–62, www.neonatology .org/classics/down; Norman Howard-Jones, "On the Diagnostic Term 'Down's Disease,'" *Medical History* 23 (1979): 102–4. For a comprehensive history of Down syndrome, see David Wright, *Downs: The History of a Disability* (New York: Oxford University Press, 2011); for a history of racism and Down syndrome see W. H. Thompson, "A Study of the Frequency of Mongolianism in Negro Children in the United States," *Journal of Psycho-Asthenics* 44 (June 1939): 91–94 and Chris Borthwick, "Racism, IQ and Down's Syndrome," *Disability & Society* 11, no. 3 (1996): 403–10.

36. Steven Selden, *Inheriting Shame: The Story of Eugenics and Racism in America* (New York: Teachers College Press, 1999), 136.

37. Quoted in Norman Howard-Jones, "On the Diagnostic Term 'Down's Disease,'" *Medical History* 23 (1979): 102–4.

38. Licia Carlson, "Cognitive Ableism and Disability Studies: Feminist Reflections on the History of Mental Retardation," *Hypatia* 16, no. 4 (Autumn 2001): 126.

39. Quotes taken from *A Century of Concern*, 14–15, 22.

40. The early fleshing out of psychological and psychiatric discourses was evident in state commitment laws in which different kinds of people whom society considered untoward were institutionalized in the same place. A paper read at the Sixth Annual Meeting of Alienists and Neurologists of America in July 1917 about the Illinois law reveals the making of early inventories of "diseases" and "disorders" and the arbitrary nature of classification and placement. "Under this law there have been committed 1,201 persons within a two-year period beginning July 1, 1915. Of these, twenty were found to be insane, eight were classified as 'constitutional inferiors' or 'control defectives,' and fifty-eight as borderland or backward children. Classified as 'control defectives' or 'constitutional inferiors' are adults who reach the institutions because of their very striking non-conformity to social order. They form the 'psychopathic personalities' of Kraepelin, and are

frequently reported to the institution by the medical commissioners as 'slightly feeble-minded,' 'nymphomaniacs,' 'dipsomaniacs,' or 'moral imbeciles.' In other words, the method of commitment from a professional standpoint failed in but eighty-six cases at an accurate diagnosis. When one understands the perplexities surrounding a problematic case of arrested mental development, one is not surprised that eighty-six cases were sent to the institution that were not feeble-minded, for, notwithstanding the fact that they do not classify as feeble-minded, there was in every instance some defect of character or of self-control or some mental aberration which made commitment imperative. Thus, 7 per cent of the commitments proved not to be feeble-minded." Harrison L. Harley, "Observations on the Operation of the Illinois Commitment Law for the Feeble-Minded," *Journal of Psycho-Asthenics* 22, no. 2 (December 1917): 95. For a similar arbitrariness in commitments, see Steven Noll, "Southern Strategies for Handling the Black Feeble-Minded: From Social Control to Profound Indifference," *Journal of Policy History* 3, no. 2 (April 1991): 130–51. For an understanding of overlapping trajectories in the disciplines of psychiatry and psychology see John Chynoweth Burnham, "Psychiatry, Psychology and the Progressive Movement," *American Quarterly* 12, no. 4 (Winter 1960): 457–65. For a gendered history of eugenics and sterilization, see, Wendy Kline, *Building a Better Race: Gender, Sexuality, and Eugenics from the Turn of the Century to the Baby Boom* (Berkeley: University of California Press, 2001).

41. Byron A. Phillips, "Retardation in the Elementary Schools of Philadelphia," *Psychological Clinic* 6, no. 3 (May 15, 1912): 79.

42. In 1896 school administrators in Providence, Rhode Island, opened the first public special education class in the United States. Beginning with fifteen higher-grade pupils, the class opened in a fire station (Providence School Committee 1896–97). Soon one city after another followed with classes in Springfield, Massachusetts, in 1897; Chicago in 1898; Boston in 1899; New York in 1900; Philadelphia in 1901; Los Angeles in 1902; Detroit in 1903; and Washington, D.C.; Bridgeport, Connecticut; and Rochester in 1906. By 1913, 108 cities had special classes and special schools; ten years later more than sixty additional cities had added classes and schools. In 1923, 33,971 students were in the nation's various special education programs. James W. Trent Jr., *Inventing the Feeble Mind: A History of Mental Retardation in the United States* (Berkeley: University of California Press, 1994), 147. For a fuller treatment specifically on the early history of special education see, Robert L. Osgood, *For 'Children Who Vary from the Normal Type:' Special Education in Boston, 1838–1930* (Washington, D.C.: Gallaudet University Press, 2000) and Jason Ellis, *A Class by Themselves? The Origins of Special Education in Toronto and Beyond* (Toronto: University of Toronto Press, 2019). In addition, see Jason Ellis, "'Inequalities of Children in Original Endowment': How Intelligence Testing Transformed Early Special Education in a North American City School System," *History of Education Quarterly* 53, no. 4 (November 2013): 401–29.

43. Quote taken from *A Century of Concern,* 67.

44. Ada M. Fitts, "The Function of Special Classes for Mentally Defective Children in the Public Schools," *Journal of Psycho-Asthenics* 21, no. 3–4 (March and June 1917): 94-98.

45. Charles Scott Berry, "The Aims and Methods of Education as Applied to Mental Defectives," *Journal of Psycho-Asthenics* 35 (June 1929–June 1930), 69.

46. George W. Twitmyer, "Clinical Studies of Retarded Children," *Psychological Clinic* 1, no. 4 (June 15, 1907): 97.

47. Twitmyer, "Clinical Studies of Retarded Children," 98.

48. Twitmyer, "Clinical Studies of Retarded Children," 98–99.

49. Hilda Volkamor and Isabel Noble, "Retardation as Indicated by One Hundred City Reports," *Psychological Clinic* 8, no. 3 (May 15, 1914): 80–81.

50. Leonard Porter Ayes, *Laggards in Our Schools: A Study of Retardation and Elimination in City School Systems* (New York: Russell Sage Foundation, 1909), xiii.

51. Byron A. Phillips, "Retardation in the Elementary Schools of Philadelphia," *Psychological Clinic* 6, no. 3 (May 15, 1912): 84.

52. Phillips, "Retardation in the Elementary Schools of Philadelphia," 85.

53. Phillips, "Retardation in the Elementary Schools of Philadelphia," 85

54. Phillips, "Retardation in the Elementary Schools of Philadelphia," 89.

55. Byron A. Phillips, "Retardation in the Elementary Schools of Philadelphia," *Psychological Clinic* 6, no. 4 (June 15, 1912): 107.

56. W. E. B. Du Bois, *The Philadelphia Negro: A Social Study* (Philadelphia, Printed for the University, 1899), 92, 94.

57. Byron A. Phillips, "Retardation in the Elementary Schools of Philadelphia," *Psychological Clinic* 6, no. 3 (May 15, 1912): 90.

58. August Meier and Elliot Rudwick, "Early Boycotts of Segregated Schools: The East Orange, New Jersey, Experience, 1899–1906," *History of Education Quarterly* 7, no. 1 (Spring 1967): 23–25.

59. Joe L. Kincheloe, *Knowledge and Critical Pedagogy: An Introduction* (Springer Science + Business Media B.V., 2008, 2010), 54.

60. Aristotle, *Metaphysics,* trans. John H. McMahon (Buffalo, NY: Prometheus, 1991), 86–89.

61. William James, "Pragmatism's Conception of Truth," in *Pragmatism: The Classic Writings,* ed. H. S. Thayer (Indianapolis, IN: Hackett), 229.

62. Kincheloe, *Knowledge and Critical Pedagogy,* 73.

63. Kincheloe, *Knowledge and Critical Pedagogy,* 51.

64. William James, "A Plea for Psychology as a 'Natural Science,'" *Philosophical Review* 1, no. 2 (March 1892): 146.

65. Quoted in Morton Hunt, *The Story of Psychology* (New York: Anchor, 1993, 2007), 175.

66. William James, "A Plea for Psychology as a 'Natural Science,'" 151. William James and John Dewey were pragmatists, not positivists. Though James opposed

the authority and certainty of psychology even if he wished it to be a natural science, he still advanced global racist notions of the will. "There will be two types of will, in one of which impulsions will predominate, in the other inhibitions. We may speak of them, if you like, as the precipitate and the obstructed will, respectively. When fully pronounced, they are familiar to everybody. The extreme example of the precipitate will is the maniac: his ideas discharge into action so rapidly, his associative processes are so extravagantly lively, that inhibitions have no time to arrive, and he says and does whatever pops into his head without a moment of hesitation. Certain melancholics furnish the extreme example of the over-inhibited type. Their minds are cramped in a fixed emotion of fear and helplessness, their ideas confined to the one thought that for them life is impossible. So they show a condition of perfect 'abulia,' or inability to will or act. They cannot change their posture or speech or execute the simplest command. The different races of men show different temperaments in this regard. The Southern (global) races are commonly accounted the more impulsive and precipitate: the English race, especially our New England branch of it, is supposed to be all sicklied over with repressive forms of self-consciousness, and condemned to express itself through a jungle of scruples and checks. The highest form of character ... must be full of scruples and inhibitions. ... I say ... such a mind [is] the ideal sort of mind that we should seek to reproduce in our pupils. Purely impulsive action ... is ... the lowest type." William James, *Talks to Teachers on Psychology* (New York: Henry Holt, 1899), 77–78.

67. George Trumbull Ladd, *The Philosophical Review* 1, no. 1 (January 1892): 30. Ladd's essay is a review of William James's two-volume book, *The Principles of Psychology* (New York: Henry Holt, 1890). James's essay in the same *Philosophical Review* is a counter-response to Ladd.

68. Lisa Feldman Barrett, "The Future of Psychology: Connecting Mind to Brain," *Perspective Psychology Science,* 4, no. 4, (July 2009): 326.

69. Ladd, "Psychology as So-Called 'Natural Science,'" 33.

70. William James, "Pragmatism's Conception of Truth," 228.

71. Freud's work was becoming influential. See Freud, *The Interpretation of Dreams.*

72. Ladd, "Psychology as So-Called 'Natural Science,'" 34.

73. Ladd, "Psychology as So-Called 'Natural Science,'" 37.

74. Edward L. Thorndike, "The Contribution of Psychology to Education," *Journal of Education Psychology* 1, no. 1 (1910): 6; For the founding era in the field of educational psychology, 1890 to 1920, see, Barry J. Zimmerman and Dale H. Schunk, eds., *Educational Psychology: A Century of Contributions* (New York: Routledge, 2009). Robert I. Watson, "A Brief History of Educational Psychology," *Psychological Record* 11 (1961): 209–242.

75. Thorndike, "The Contribution of Psychology to Education," 8.

76. Thorndike, "The Contribution of Psychology to Education," 8.

77. Thorndike, "The Contribution of Psychology to Education," 9.

78. Lightner Witmer, "The Study and Treatment of Retardation: A Field of Applied Psychology," *Psychological Bulletin* 6, no. 4 (April 15, 1909): 121–26. There was some criticism in psychology about the rush to use mental testing. "With very few exceptions, clinical psychologists must plead guilty to the charge of over-emphasizing mental tests. Much effort is being directed toward devising, refining, and standardizing testing devices with the apparent purpose of making them automatically measure intelligence in finely calibrated units. The futility of attempting this beyond certain limits is obvious when one remembers that psychology has not yet worked out all of the principles underlying the tests, and that standards of normal mentality are vague and indefinite." Quote from R. H. Sylvester, "Clinical Psychology Adversely Criticized," *Psychological Clinic* 7, no. 7 (December 15, 1913): 182.

79. The real battle in the field of educational psychology was between Dewey's holism and James's humble and experiential epistemology versus Thorndike's atomism and strong epistemology. Thorndike's ideas prevailed. I thank professor Scot Danforth for this observation. Edward Lee Thorndike wrote, "If there existed a perfect and complete knowledge of human nature—a complete science of psychology—it would tell the effect of every possible stimulus and the cause of every possible response in every possible human being." Edward Lee Thorndike, *The Principles of Teaching Based on Psychology* (New York: A.G. Seller, 1906), 9.

80. John T. Morgan, "The Race Question in the United States: An Overview in 1890," *The Development of Segregationist Thought,* ed. I. A. Newby (Homewood, IL: Dorsey, 1968), 22.

81. Howard Odum, *Social and Mental Traits of the Negro* (New York: Columbia University Press, 1910), 44–45; also quoted in *The Development of Segregationist Thought,* 66; for an overview of the late nineteenth and early twentieth century see, Robert Wiebe, *A Search for Order, 1877–1920* (New York: Hill and Wang, 1967); Nell I. Painter, *Standing at Armageddon: The United States, 1877–1919* (New York: W.W. Norton, 1987); Gary Gerstle, *American Crucible: Race and Nation in the Twentieth Century* (Princeton, N.J.: Princeton University Press, 2001).

82. Rayford Logan, *The Negro in American Life and Thought: The Nadir, 1877–1901* (New York: Dial, 1954).

83. Anna Julia Cooper, "The Ethics of the Negro Question," in *The Voice of Anna Julia Cooper,* eds. Charles Lemert and Esme Bhan (Lanham, MD: Rowman & Littlefield, 1998), 207–8.

84. John W. Cell, *The Highest Stage of White Supremacy: The Origins of Segregation in South Africa and the American South* (New York: Cambridge University Press, 1982, 1992), x.

85. Cell, *The Highest Stage of White Supremacy,* 2.

86. George Lipsitz, "The Possessive Investment in Whiteness: Racialized Social Democracy and the 'White' Problem in American Studies," *American Quarterly* 47,

no. 3 (September 1995): 381. See also George Lipsitz, *The Possessive Investment in Whiteness: How White People Profit from Identity Politics* (Philadelphia: Temple University Press, 2006). On sociology's role in the construction of whiteness, see Teresa J. Guess, "The Social Construction of Whiteness: Racism by Intent, Racism by Consequence," *Critical Sociology* 32, no. 4 (2006).

87. Karen E. Fields and Barbara J. Fields, *Racecraft: The Soul of Inequality in American Life* (London: Verso, 2014), 18, 25.

88. W. H. Pyle, "The Learning Capacity of Negro Children," *Psychological Bulletin* 13, no 2 (February 1916): 82–83.

89. R. S. Woodworth, "Comparative Psychology of Races," *Psychological Bulletin* 13, no. 10 (October 1916): 391–92; George Oscar Ferguson Jr., *The Psychology of the Negro: An Experimental Study* (New York: Science Press, 1916, repr. Forgotten Books, 2015). Franz Samelson, "From 'Race Psychology' to 'Studies in Prejudice': Some Observations on the Thematic Reversal in Social Psychology," *Journal of the History of the Behavioral Sciences* 14 (1978): 265–78.

90. One of the best histories of race and psychology, from racial differences and psychometric testing to the development of black psychology as a field see Robert V. Guthrie, *Even the Rat Was White: A Historical View of Psychology* (Boston: Pearson, 2004). See also, Reginald L. Jones, ed. *Black Psychology* (New York: Harper & Row, 1980).

91. Douglas C. Baynton, *Defectives in the Land: Disability and Immigration in the Age of Eugenics* (Chicago: University of Chicago Press, 2016), 61–62.

92. Marvin Rosen, Gerald R. Clark, and Marvin S. Kivitz, eds., *The History of Mental Retardation: Collected Papers,* Vol. 1 (Baltimore; University Park Press, 1976), 342.

93. Rosen, Clark, and Kivitz, *History of Mental Retardation.*

94. Leila Zenderland, *Measuring Minds: Henry Herbert Goddard and the Origins of American Intelligence Testing* (Cambridge: Cambridge University Press, 1998), 95.

95. Gould, *The Mismeasure of Man,* chap. 5.

96. Zenderland, *Measuring Minds*, 99–103.

97. Rosen, Clark, and Kivitz, *A History of Mental Retardation, Collected Papers*, 364

98. Henry Herbert Goddard, *School Training of Defective Children* (Yonkers-on-Hudson, New York: World Book Company, 1914), xvii.

99. J. D. Heilman, "Psychology in the School Room," *Journal of Educational Psychology* 7, no. 6 (June 1916): 341. Special education as differential education as segregated education was carried out by school districts across the country. The Survey Committee of the Cleveland Foundation conducted a study of mental retardation in Cleveland schools making the distinction between the socially competent, those with physical and sensory disabilities, and the socially incompetent, those considered feebleminded. "The training of the socially incompetent should take place in separate classrooms, and, if possible, in separate buildings.

To meet the needs of these children different programs of instruction must be provided. The abnormally slow and the seriously handicapped must be sent to special classes." David Mitchell, *Cleveland Education Survey, Schools and Classes for Exceptional Children* (Cleveland, OH: The Survey Committee of the Cleveland Foundation, 1916, repr. Leopold Classic Library, 2020), 23–24. See also, Arthur Holmes, *Backward Children* (Indianapolis: Bobbs-Merrill, 1915, repr. Alpha Editions, 2019) and Herbert Hollingsworth Woodrow, *Brightness and Dullness in Children* (Philadelphia: J. B. Lippincott and Co., 1919).

100. Alfred Binet and Theophile Simon, "Upon the Necessity of Establishing a Scientific Diagnosis of Inferior States of Intelligence," 1905, in Marvin Rosen, Gerald R. Clark, and Marvin S. Kivitz, Vol. 1 of *The History of Mental Retardation, Collected Papers* (Baltimore: University Park Press, 1976), 332–33.

101. This range over time including the moron extended to 75 then back to 70 later in the twentieth century.

102. Quote taken from *A Century of Concern*, 96.

103. Lewis M. Terman, *The Measurement of Intelligence: An Explanation of and a Complete Guide for the Use of the Stanford Revision and Extension of the Binet-Simon Intelligence Scale* (1916, repr. on demand, 2020), 43. Lewis M. Terman, "The Binet Scale and the Diagnosis of Feeblemindedness," *Journal of the National Education Association* 1 (1916–1917): 874–79.

104. Lewis Terman is one of the first to promote the prevalence figure of 2 percent. "Wherever intelligence tests have been made in any considerable number in the schools, they have shown that not far from 2 percent of the children enrolled have a grade of intelligence which, however long they live, will never develop beyond the level which is normal to the average child of 11 or 12 years. The large majority of these belong to the moron grade; that is, their mental development will stop somewhere between the 7-year and 12-year level of intelligence, more often between 9 and 12." Terman, *The Measurement of Intelligence*, 4. James G. Riggs, a principal at the state normal and training school in Oswego, New York, wrote, "Some statisticians say 4 percent are feebleminded, the more conservative assert 2 per cent, while the number depends entirely upon the classes or degrees of abnormality one establishes among the children whose minds have not developt [*sic*] normally. Some localities have a larger number of such children than others, but the average seems to be about 2 per cent, so we would expect to find among 5000 children 100 who would come safely within the category of defectives." James G. Riggs, "Training of Teachers in Special Classes," *Journal of the National Education Association* 1 (1916–1917): 880.

105. David L. Kirp, "Schools as Sorters: The Constitutional and Policy Implications of Student Classifications," *University of Pennsylvania Law Review* 121 (1975): 712.

106. W. C. Martindale, "How Detroit Cares for Her Backward Children," *Psychological Clinic* 6, no. 5 (October 15, 1912): 126.

107. Martindale, "How Detroit Cares for Her Backward Children," 128, 126.

108. Byron A. Phillips, "The Binet Tests Applied to Colored Children," *Psychological Clinic* 8, no. 7 (December 15, 1914): 196. As soon as the Binet-Simon revision and Terman's Stanford-Binet revision were complete, several comparative intelligence studies of white and black children were conducted between 1910 and 1920. For a study in Columbia, South Carolina, see Alice C. Strong, "Three Hundred Fifty White and Colored Children Measured by the Binet-Simon Measuring Scale of Intelligence: A Comparative Study," *Pedagogical Seminary*, 20, no. 4 (1913): 485–514. In Lawrence, Kansas, see, R. A. Schwegler and Edith Winn, "A Comparative Study of the Intelligence of White and Colored Children," *Journal of Educational Research* 2, no. 5 (December 1920). In Evanston, Illinois, William I. Lacy, "A Study of 100 Retarded Fourth Grade Pupils Tested By the Binet Scale," *Psychological Clinic* 12, no. 1 (March 15, 1918). These studies had one thing in common, to prove "that on the whole, the intelligence of the colored children is inferior to that of the whites." Lacy was blunt when referring to black students in the Evanston, Illinois school system, answering his own question, "What is to be done with such children? It is evident that there are in the school system certain children who are being carried on from year to year, who, from the tests given, are of such low stages of intelligence that they are incapable of doing regular school work. The Binet test will bring to light these cases of feeblemindedness. All such cases should be removed to special institutions, schools or rooms, according to local institutions, where special provision is made to take care of them. This will be far better not only for the children themselves, but also for the progress of the other children with whom they are now associated. In conclusion, we think, on the evidence from this study, that: *First:* The systems of promotion generally in vogue in this country are unfair to the child, uneconomic and unscientific; and the use of intelligence tests for promotion should be adopted. *Second:* Having white and colored children together in the same school is educationally and socially unwise; separate schools for colored children should therefore be established. *Third:* Feeblemindedness should be detected through the use of intelligence tests, and children found to be feebleminded or very nearly so, should be placed in regular institutions, schools, or rooms equipped to take care of them. *Fourth:* The Intelligence Quotient should be found for all children, and the subject matter and methods of instruction adapted to the intellectual capacity, rather than the chronological age."

109. Lewis Terman, "Mentality Tests: A Symposium," *Journal of Educational Psychology* 7, no. 6 (June 1916): 349–50.

110. George F. Arps, "The Army Intelligence Tests," *Natural History* 19, no. 6 (December 1919): 671; Major Robert M. Yerkes, "Psychology in Relation to the War," *Psychological Review* 25, no. 2 (March 1918).

111. George F. Arps, "The Army Intelligence Tests," *Natural History* 19, no. 6 (December 1919): 671; for a comprehensive history of African Americans in World War I, see Chad Williams, *Torchbearers of Democracy: African American Soldiers in the World War I Era* (Chapel Hill: University of North Carolina Press, 2010);

for a history of measuring black people for the war effort, see Paul R. D. Lawrie, *Forging a Laboring Race: The African American Worker in the Progressive Imagination* (New York: New York University Press, 2016) chapter 3.

112. Edgar A. Schuler, "Race Riots During and After the First World War," *Negro History Bulletin* 7, no. 7 (April 1944): 155–56, 158–60, 166.

113. M. R. Trabue, "The Intelligence of Negro Recruits," *Natural History* 19, no. 6 (December 1919): 680.

114. Joel H. Spring, "Psychologists and the War: The Meaning of Intelligence in the Alpha and Beta Tests," *History of Education Quarterly* 12, no. 1 (Spring 1972): 3–15. See also James H. Capshew, *Psychologists on the March: Science, Practice, and Professional Identity in America, 1929–1969* (Cambridge: Cambridge University Press, 1999).

115. Capshew, *Psychologists on the March*, 685. For an account on the intelligence of black recruits at a single camp, see George Oscar Ferguson, "The Intelligence of Negroes at Camp Lee, Virginia," *School and Society* 9, no. 234 (June 14, 1919). For the influence of psychologists during World War I, see Franz Samelson, "World War I Intelligence Testing and the Development of Psychology," *Journal of the History of Behavioral Sciences,* 13 (1977): 274–82; Michael M. Sokal, *Psychological Testing and American Society, 1890-1930* (New Brunswick: Rutgers University Press, 1987).

116. Doxey Wilkerson, "Racial Differences in Scholastic Achievement," *Journal of Negro Education* 3, no. 3 (July 1934): 453–77.

117. For earlier histories of disability, see Sarah F. Rose, *No Right to Be Idle: The Invention of Disability, 1840s-1930s* (Chapel Hill: University of North Carolina Press, 2017); Douglas C. Baynton, "Disability and the Justification of Inequality in American History," in *New Disability History: American Perspectives,* eds. Paul Longmore and Lauri Umansky (New York: New York University Press, 2001); Stefanie Hunt-Kennedy, *Between Fitness and Death: Disability and Slavery in the Caribbean* (Urbana: University of Illinois Press, 2020); Jennifer L. Barclay, *The Mark of Slavery: Disability, Race, and Gender in Antebellum America* (Urbana: University of Illinois Press, 2021).

118. A discourse on normal, subnormal, and supernormal children evolved into an apparatus or framework of future disability. One can see this in how a psychological clinic functioned. "The psychological clinic is a clearing-house whose function it is to help in the solution of all kinds of problem cases. It is to the teacher what the specialist is to the general physician. To it are brought the exceptional or atypical children, the misfits in the school system. It is the duty of the staff of the clinic—clinical psychologists, physicians, social workers—to discover the cause of the child's retardation and prescribe the proper remedial treatment, whether the treatment be educational, medical, or social. Its practical value to a school system may perhaps be best shown by describing the types of cases it investigates, thus giving an idea of the scope of its work." The types of children (and later disabilities) were *feebleminded or permanently retarded children*

(the moron, later the educable mentally retarded), *restorable cases* (later the learning disabled), *the normal child with certain specific mental defects which do not exclude the possibility of normal progress but require special treatment* (later the learning disabled), *disciplinary cases* (the juvenile delinquent, the socially maladjusted, and later the emotional/behavior disordered), *the child with physical defects that interfere with normal progress,* and *the supernormal child* (the talented and gifted). Frank Cody, "The Practical Value of Psychological Tests—Do They Find the Bright and Dull Pupils?," *Journal of the National Education Association* 3 (1918–1919): 392–93.

119. "The Normal and the Subnormal Child," *Journal of Educational Psychology* 3, no. 9 (November 1912): 535.

120. Jennifer Scuro, *Addressing Ableism: Philosophical Questions Via Disability Studies* (Lanham, MD: Lexington, 2018).

121. J. E. Wallace Wallin, *The Education of Handicapped Children* (Boston: Houghton Mifflin, Co., 1924), 93.

122. Fiona Kumari Campbell, "Legislating Disability: Negative Ontologies and the Government of Legal Identities," in *Foucault and the Government of Disability,* ed. Shelley Tremain (Ann Arbor: University of Michigan Press, 2018), 113, 115.

123. Wallin, *The Education of Handicapped Children,* 157.

124. Frank J. O'Brien, "Psychometric Testing," *Opportunity* (November 1923): 335.

125. Lewis M. Terman, "The Possibilities and Limitations of Training," *Journal of Educational Research* 10, no. 5, (December 1924): 337.

126. Quote taken from Russell Marks, "Lewis M. Terman: Individual Differences and the Construction of Social Reality," *Educational Theory* 24 (Fall 1974): 337.

127. *"Blind:* One who cannot see at all. *Partially Blind:* One who is not totally blind, but whose sight is so impaired that he cannot use advantageously the facilities provided for the normally seeing child. *Deaf:* One who cannot hear at all. *Partially Deaf:* One who is not totally deaf, but whose hearing is so defective that he cannot hear ordinary conversation without the aid of some amplifying device, or at an unusually short distance from the source of sound. *Crippled:* One whose body is so impaired that he cannot use advantageously the facilities provided for the normal child." Quoted in Eva T. Honesty, "The Handicapped Child," *Journal of Negro Education* 1, no 2 (July 1932): 306; For the federal government definitions of disability, see United States Department of the Interior, Harold L. Ickes, Secretary, Office of Education, George F. Zook, Commissioner, *The Education of Exceptional Children: Being Chapter VI of the Biennial Survey of Education in the United States: 1930-1932,* p. 12.

128. J. E. Wallace Wallin, "Classification of Mentally Deficient and Retarded Children for Instruction," *Journal of Psycho-Asthenics* 29 (June 1924): 176. For a fuller treatment of Wallin's contribution to early special education, see Philip M. Ferguson, "Creating the Continuum: J.E. Wallace Wallin and the Role of Clinical

Psychology in the Emergence of Public School Special Education in America," *International Journal of Inclusive Education* 18, no. 1 (2014): 86–100.

129. Ferguson, "Creating the Continuum."

130. Tremain, *Foucault ad Feminist Philosophy of Disability*, 116.

131. Arthur I. Gates, "A Study of Reading and Spelling with Special Reference to Disability," *Journal of Educational Research* 6, no. 1 (June 1922): 14.

132. Edgar A. Doll, "Education and Training of the Feebleminded," *Journal of Psycho-Asthenics* 37 (June 1931–June 1932): 106.

133. Samuel T. Orton, "An Impediment to Learning to Read—A Neurological Explanation of the Reading Disability," *School & Society* 28, no. 715 (September 8, 1928): 286.

134. Wallace, *The Education of Handicapped Children,* 80.

135. Scot Danforth, "Turning the Educability Narrative: Samuel A. Kirk at the Intersection of LD and MR," *Intellectual and Developmental Disabilities* 48 (2010): 180–94.

136. In November 2016, Benjamin Kelsey Kearl published on the blog *Education's Histories,* "Of Laggards and Morons: Definitional Fluidity, Borderlinity, and the Theory of Progressive Era Special Education." Kearl and his responders, Robert Osgood, Jason Ellis, and Donald Warren, offer readers an abundance of positions and counter-positions on early special education history and definitional intellectual borders. Categorical definitions, particularly as part of classification systems, are arbitrary and situational to the times created. That is why they remain fluid. What is not always apparent is the distance between the definitions within a classification taxonomy. If definitions are apparent in a classification system, then the borders around them, either as spaces of separation or overlap, are less noticeable or are ambiguous. Kearl wrote: "The concept of borderlinity as well as the term borderlands refers to the space of overlap between normality and abnormality. Borderland cases surfaced when individuals might be classified as either normal or abnormal depending on the evaluative measure employed. Discerning this space was the exclusive purview of experts who worked to varying degrees and sometimes in contradictory directions to define the borderlinity of feeble-mindedness. The case studies thus represent not only evidence of borderlands, they also indeterminately defined the subjectivities that gave these categorical spaces meaning and purpose. The borderlands of feeble-mindedness, however well conceptualized, could not exist unless populated." The power of Kearl's arguments is found in his rejoinder to Robert Osgood and Jason Ellis, the two premier historians of early special education history. Osgood takes Kearl to task for not probing deeper into the tension between special and general education in how both focused on creating more "efficient" students. Osgood argued that since 1902, "despite occupying separate spheres of educational influence, special and general education have defined one another, not behind a rigid demarcation but within the context of overlapping spheres of which special education has been viewed as "cutting into the world of regular education." Ellis equally

admonishes Kearl for ignoring the breadth of special education's complex history, failing to "historically multitask," to use a phrase by Donald Warren. That historical multitasking would diminish a "narrower than necessary focus," argued Ellis. Ellis goes on to posit that "historicizing special education's many features and functions reveals that it was simultaneously social uplift, social control, science, eugenic pseudo-science, a classification system, a set of theories about the nature and cause of learning problems, a collection of curricula and pedagogies, a way of legitimately and successfully treating very real learning difficulties." Osgood and Ellis are indeed correct. In his clarifying rejoinder to Osgood and Ellis, Kearl raised the question of racial difference—the only place where a racial analysis is applied.

2. The Road *from* Mental Retardation

1. The literature on the resegregation of people of color in American society and the implication of the *Brown v. Board of Education* decision has grown in recent years. See John Charles Boger and Gary Orfield, eds., *School Resegregation: Must the South Turn Back?* (Chapel Hill: University of North Carolina Press, 2005); Thomas V. O'Brien, "What Happened to the Promise of *Brown?* An Organizational Explanation and an Outline for Change," *Teachers College Record* 109, no. 8 (August 2007); Beth A. Ferri and David J. Connor, "In the Shadow of *Brown*: Special Education and Overrepresentation of Students of Color," *Remedial and Special Education,* 26, no. 2 (March/April 2005).

2. Derrick A. Bell Jr., "Brown v. Board of Education and the Interest-Convergence Dilemma," *Harvard Law Review,* 93, no. 3 (January 1980): 518–33.

3. Allison C. Carey, *On the Margins of Citizenship: Intellectual Disability and Civil Rights in Twentieth Century America* (Philadelphia: Temple University Press, 2009).

4. Bernadette Baker, "The Hunt for Disability: The New Eugenics and the Normalization of School Children," *Teachers College Record* 104, no. 4 (June 2002): 663–703; Bernadette Baker, *In Perpetual Motion: Theories of Power, Educational History, & the Child* (New York: Peter Lang, 2001).

5. Steven A. Gelb, "The Problem of Typological Thinking in Mental Retardation," *Mental Retardation* 35, no. 6 (December 1997): 448.

6. Alfred A. Strauss, "Typology in Mental Deficiency," *Journal of Psycho-Asthenics* 44 (June 1939): 86.

7. Strauss, "Typology in Mental Deficiency," 85.

8. Alfred A. Strauss and Heinz Werner, "The Mental Organization of the Brain-Injured Mentally Defective Child," *American Journal of Psychiatry* 97, no. 5 (March 1941): 1199–1200.

9. George Ordahl, "Heredity in Feeblemindedness," *Training School Bulletin* 16 (1919–1920): 12

10. Scot Danforth, *The Incomplete Child: An Intellectual History of Learning Disabilities* (New York: Peter Lang, 2009), 63, 70.

11. Italics in the original; Alfred A. Strauss, "The Education of the Brain-Injured Child," *American Journal of Mental Deficiency* 56 (1952): 716

12. Strauss, "The Education of the Brain-Injured Child," 712.

13. Alfred A. Strauss, "Typology in Mental Deficiency," *Journal of Psycho-Asthenics* 44 (June 1939): 86.

14. Alfred A. Strauss, "Arithmetic Fundamentals for the Brain-Crippled Child," *American Journal of Mental Deficiency* 49, no. 2 (October 1944): 149.

15. Alfred A. Strauss and Heinz Werner, "The Mental Organization of the Brain Injured Mentally Defective Child," *American Journal of Psychiatry* 97, no. 5 (March 1941): 1194.

16. Alfred A. Strauss and Laura E. Lehtinen, *Psychopathology and Education of the Brain-Injured* (New York: Grune & Stratton, 1947), 4.

17. Strauss and Lehtinen, *Psychopathology and Education of the Brain-Injured,* 13.

18. Strauss and Lehtinen, *Psychopathology and Education of the Brain-Injured,* 14.

19. Strauss and Lehtinen, *Psychopathology and Education of the Brain-Injured,* 14.

20. Stuart Hall, "Race, The Floating Signifier," Lecture, Media Education Foundation, Northhampton, MA, 1997, www.mediaed.org (accessed on July 11, 2020), 8–9. See also Stuart Hall, "Race—The Sliding Signifier," in *The Fateful Triangle: Race, Ethnicity, Nation,* ed. Kobena Mercer (Cambridge, Mass.: Harvard University Press, 2017), 31–79.

21. Hall, "Race, The Floating Signifier," Lecture, 10.

22. Hall, "Race, The Floating Signifier," Lecture, 2–3.

23. Hall, "Race, The Floating Signifier," Lecture, 3.

24. Sam D. Clements, *Minimal Brain Dysfunction in Children: Terminology and Identification* (National Institutes of Health, U.S. Department of Health, Education, and Welfare, 1966); Kenneth A. Kavale and Steven R. Forness, *The Science of Learning Disabilities* (San Diego: College Hill, 1985), 44.

25. Strauss and Lehtinen, *Psychopathology and Education of the Brain-Injured,* 129.

26. Joseph Wortis, "A Note on the Concept of the 'Brain-Injured Child,'" *American Journal of Mental Deficiency* 61 (1957): 204.

27. James Hinshelwood, *Congenital Word-Blindness* (London: H.K. Lewis & Co., 1917, repr. Forgotten Books, 2012). For a good historical overview of antecedent theories and an early history of learning disability see, J. Lee Wiederholt, "Historical Perspectives on the Education of the Learning Disabled," in *The Second Review of Special Education,* eds. Lester Mann and David A. Sabatino (Philadelphia: JSE, 1974), 103–52.

28. "Aphasia," http://www.mayoclinic.org (accessed July 2020); For an early history of Aphasia see Henry Head, "Aphasia: An Historical Review," *Brain: A*

Journal of Neurology 43 (July 1920): 390–411; Henry Head, "Aphasia and Kindred Disorders of Speech," *Brain: A Journal of Neurology* 43 (July 1920): 87–165.

29. Samuel Torrey Orton, *Reading, Writing, and Speech Problems in Children and Selected Papers,* (Baltimore, MD: The International Dyslexia Association, 1999), 20.

30. Orton, *Reading, Writing, and Speech Problems,* 159.

31. Samuel T. Orton, "An Impediment to Learning to Read," *School and Society* 28, no. 715 (1928): 286–87.

32. William F. Lyons, "Treatment of Speech Defects in a State School," *Journal of Psycho-Asthenics* 44, no. 2 (June 1938–June 1939): 163.

33. Lyons, "Treatment of Speech Defects in a State School," 163.

34. Lyons, "Treatment of Speech Defects in a State School," 163–64.

35. Thorleif Gruner Hegge, Richard Sears, and Samuel A. Kirk, "Reading Cases in an Institution for Mentally Retarded Problem Children: A Preliminary Report," *Journal of Psycho-Asthenics* 37 (June 1931–June 1932): 152–53, 156–57.

36. Rick Herber, *A Manual on Terminology and Classification in Mental Retardation,* Project on Technical Planning in Mental Retardation, American Association on Mental Deficiency, A Monograph Supplement to the *American Journal of Mental Deficiency*, September 1959.

37. Quoted in Herschel W. Nisonger, "Changing Concepts in Mental Retardation," *American Journal of Mental Deficiency* 67 (1962): 6.

38. Herber, *A Manual on Terminology and Classification in Mental Retardation,* 3.

39. Shelley Z. Reuter, *Testing Fate: Tay-Sachs Disease and the Right to be Responsible* (Minneapolis: University of Minnesota Press, 2016).

40. Herber, *A Manual on Terminology and Classification in Mental Retardation,* 7.

41. Herman Yannet, "Classification and Etiological Factors in Mental Retardation," *Journal of Pediatrics* 50, no. 2 (February 1957): 226.

42. Yannet, "Classification and Etiological Factors," 226.

43. R. C. Scheerenberger, *A History of Mental Retardation* (Baltimore: Paul H. Brookes, 1983), 221–22. In addition to Scheerenberger, one of the most thorough studies of mental retardation is Halbert B. Robinson and Nancy Robinson, *The Mentally Retarded Child: A Psychological Approach* (New York: McGraw-Hill, 1965). See part 2 on etiology and syndromes. See also, J. E. Wallace Wallin, *Children with Mental and Physical Handicaps* (New York: Prentice-Hall, 1949); Bernard Farber, *Mental Retardation: Its Social Context and Social Consequences* (Boston: Houghton Mifflin, 1968); Michael Craft, ed., *Tredgold's Mental Retardation* (London: Bailliere Tindall, 1979).

44. Rick Herber, *A Manual on Terminology and Classification in Mental Retardation,* 3.

45. Herber, *A Manual on Terminology and Classification in Mental Retardation,* 3.

46. Herber, *A Manual on Terminology and Classification in Mental Retardation*, 3.

47. In Rick Herber's 1959 definition of mental retardation, the concept of adaptive behavior had three parts: maturation, learning, and social adjustment. A through line in the concept of adaptive behavior is behavior and learning that is expected in different stages of the life cycle. For maturation, sitting, crawling, standing, walking, talking, and interacting with age peers in infancy and early childhood; for learning, the acquisition of expected knowledge at each age level; for social adjustment, mainly in adults, to be able to maintain themselves independently and to conform and keep up personal and social responsibilities set by society. A person's inability to do these things represented an impairment in adaptive behavior, thus rendering the person mentally retarded. See Herber, *A Manual on Terminology and Classification in Mental Retardation*, 3–4. Edgar A. Doll is credited with bringing these ideas to the fore of mental retardation discourse. See Doll, "The Relation of Social Competence to Social Adjustment," (1948) in *The History of Mental Retardation, Collected Papers*, Vol. 2, eds. Marvin Rosen, Gerald R. Clark, and Marvin S. Kivitz (Baltimore: University Park Press, 1976), 267–75. Herber's *Manual* was the first in a series of manuals published by the American Association on Mental Retardation. Most fascinating is to see how definitions, IQ cutoffs, diagnosis, and adaptive behavior have evolved from 1959 to the early 2000s. See Herbert J. Grossman, ed., *Manual on Terminology and Classification in Mental Retardation* (Washington, D.C.: American Association on Mental Deficiency, 1977); *Mental Retardation: Definition, Classification, and Systems of Supports* (Washington, D.C.: American Association on Mental Retardation, 1992); *Mental Retardation: Definition, Classification, and Systems of Supports* (Washington, D.C.: American Association on Mental Retardation, 2002); Harvey N. Switzky and Stephen Greenspan, eds., *What is Mental Retardation? Ideas for an Evolving Disability in the 21st Century* (Washington, D.C.: American Association on Mental Retardation, 2006).

48. Herber, *A Manual on Terminology and Classification in Mental Retardation*, 3.

49. Yannet, "Classification and Etiological Factors in Mental Retardation," 227.

50. Herber, *A Manual on Terminology and Classification in Mental Retardation*, 66–67.

51. Herber, *A Manual on Terminology and Classification in Mental Retardation*, 7.

52. Shelley Tremain, "On the Government of Disability," *Social Theory and Practice* 27, no. 4 (October 2001): 620.

53. Herber, *A Manual on Terminology and Classification in Mental Retardation*, 7.

54. Herschel W. Nisonger, "Changing Conceptions in Mental Retardation," *American Journal of Mental Deficiency* 67 (1962): 6.

55. Nisonger, "Changing Conceptions in Mental Retardation," 6.

56. I am not suggesting that epidemiologists and psychologists cooked the books. I am saying that disability measurement is predicated on how a disability is defined in each context. McDermott and Turk wrote: "The inclusion or exclusion of any group in the definition can make a tremendous difference in prevalence reports." Suzanne McDermott and Margaret A. Turk, "The Myth and Reality of Disability Prevalence: Measuring Disability for Research and Service," *Disability and Health Journal* 4 (2011): 3.

57. Nisonger, "Changing Conceptions in Mental Retardation," 7.

58. Nisonger, "Changing Conceptions in Mental Retardation," 6.

59. The actual number of mentally retarded students has never been established with certainty. For one, there has not been an agreement on the total number of "handicapped" students in general. Nisonger's number of mentally retarded students (five million) in 1962 does not square with Romaine Mackie's examination of a nationwide survey of statistical data collected by the U.S. Office of Education in 1963. Mackie said that the total number of handicapped children—physical, sensory, intellectual, or emotional—is five million, and even some of that was a projection. "About 10 percent, or approximately 5,000,000 of the school age children are so seriously handicapped by physical, mental, or emotional problems that they appear to require some form of special education." The estimated number of mentally retarded children in 1966 based on the collected data was 540,100, which, according to Mackie, represented 46.8 percent enrolled. Mackie added that the estimated number of children believed to be mentally retarded was 1,155,000 with a 2.3 percent prevalence rate. Sometimes, the estimate of five million mentally retarded by researchers included not only school children, but also adults. Despite its dubiousness, the five million mentally retarded number was used repeatedly. See Romaine Mackie, *Special Education in the United States: Statistics 1948–1966* (New York: Teachers College Press, 1969) and Romaine P. Mackie, "Spotlight Advances in Special Education," *Exceptional Children* (October 1965): 77–81. This kind of numerical confusion is what Ian Hacking called the fetishistic collection of statistical data. It is not an accident that this "statistical enthusiasm" occurred at the same time as the legislative enthusiasm picked up in the 1960s for the intellectual and learning disabled. I argue that the statistical enthusiasm plus the legislative enthusiasm equaled the money enthusiasm—the millions of dollars in federal appropriation made available with the increasing numbers of special education students. Donald MacMillan wrote, "When there are funds to be allocated to set up mental retardation services and programs, it is important for us to know how many retarded people there are. The problem is, no one knows for sure." See Ian Hacking, "Biopower and the Avalanche of Printed Numbers," *Humanities in Society* 5 (1982): 280 and Donald L. MacMillian, *Mental Retardation in School and Society* (Boston: Little, Brown, 1977), 58.

60. Janice Brockley, "Rearing the Child Who Never Grew: Ideologies of Parenting and Intellectual Disability in American History," in *Mental Retardation in*

America: A Historical Reader, ed., Steven Noll and James W. Trent Jr. (New York: New York University Press), 130–64; Katherine Castles, "Nice, Average Americans: Postwar Parents' Groups and the Defense of the Normal Family," in *Mental Retardation in America: A Historical Reader,* eds. Steven Noll and James W. Trent Jr. (New York: New York University Press, 2004), 351–70.

61. Richard H. Hungerford, "An Editorial," *American Journal of Mental Deficiency* (October 1949): 145.

62. Richard H. Hungerford, "On Locust," *American Journal of Mental Deficiency* (April 1950): 415.

63. Hungerford, "An Editorial," 145.

64. Joseph P. Shapiro, *No Pity: People with Disabilities Forging a New Civil Right Movement* (New York: Times Books, 1993), 19.

65. Arthur L. Rautman, "Society's Responsibility to the Mentally Retarded," *American Journal of Mental Deficiency* 54 (October 1949): 157

66. Derrick A. Bell Jr., "Brown v. Board of Education and the Interest-Convergence Dilemma," *Harvard Law Review* 93, no. 3 (January 1980): 523.

67. John W. Tenny, "The Minority Status of the Handicapped," *Exceptional Children* (April 1953): 260–64.

68. Tenny, "The Minority Status of the Handicapped," 260–64.

69. Lee J. Marino, "Organizing the Parents of Mentally Retarded Children for Participation in the Mental-Health Program," *Mental Hygiene* 35 (January 1951): 17.

70. Shapiro, *No Pity: People with Disabilities Forging a New Civil Rights Movement.*

71. Quoted in Charles W. Murdock, "Civil Rights of the Mentally Retarded: Some Critical Issues," *Notre Dame Lawyer* (October 1972): 169.

72. James W. Trent Jr., *Inventing the Feeble Mind: A History of Mental Retardation in the United States* (Berkeley: University of California Press, 1994); Barry B. Cohen, *Contingencies in the Labeling and the Placement of Borderline Educable Retarded Children* (Master's thesis, University of Minnesota, 1972), 12–15; See also Steven Noll, *Feeble-Minded in Our Midst: Institutions for the Mentally Retarded in the South, 1900–1940* (Chapel Hill: University of North Carolina Press, 1995); David Wright and Anne Digby, eds., *From Idiocy to Mental Deficiency: Historical Perspectives on People with Learning Disabilities* (New York: Routledge, 1996); Patrick McDonagh, *Idiocy: A Cultural History* (Liverpool: Liverpool University Press, 2008); Michael L Wehmeyer, *The Story of Intellectual Disability: An Evolution of Meaning, Understanding, & Public Perception* (Baltimore: Paul H. Brookes, 2013).

73. Cohen, *Contingencies in the Labeling and Placement of Borderline Educable Retarded Children,* 17–18. Cohen uses the million for the total number of mentally retarded. Also used by the President's Committee on Mental Retardation.

74. Kathleen W. Jones, "Education for Children with Mental Retardation: Parent Activism, Public Policy, and Family Ideology in the 1950s," in *Mental Retardation*

in America: A Historical Reader, eds. Steven Noll and James W. Trent Jr. (New York: New York University Press, 2004), 341.

75. Leo F. Cain, "Parent Groups: Their Role in a Better Life for the Handicapped," *Exceptional Children* 42 (1975–1976): 432–37; Rosemary F. Dybwad, *Perspectives on a Parent Movement: The Revolt of Parents of Children with Intellectual Limitations* (Cambridge, MA: Brookline, 1990); Melanie Panitch, *Disability, Mothers, and Organization: Accidental Activists* (New York: Routledge, 2008).

76. Marino, "Organizing the Parents of Mentally Retarded Children for Participation in the Mental Health Program," 14–15. For a comprehensive perspective on engaged parents see, Priya Lalvani, ed. *Constructing the (M)other: Narratives of Disability, Motherhood, and the Politics of Normal* (New York: Peter Lang, 2019).

77. Kathleen W. Jones, "Education for Children with Mental Retardation: Parent Activism, Public Policy, and Family Ideology in the 1950s," in *Mental Retardation in America: A Historical Reader,* eds. Steven Noll and James W. Trent Jr. (New York: New York University Press, 2004), 341.

78. Jones, "Education for Children with Mental Retardation: Parent Activism, Public Policy, and Family Ideology in the 1950s," 240; Leila Zenderland, "The Parable of the Kallikak Family: Explaining the Meaning of Heredity in 1912," in *Mental Retardation in America: A Historical Reader,* eds. Steven Noll and James W. Trent Jr. (New York: New York University Press, 2004), 165–85.

79. Alan H. Sampson, "Developing and Maintaining Good Relations with Parents of Mentally Deficient Children," *American Journal of Mental Deficiency* 52 (October 1947): 187–94.

80. Allison C. Carey, *On the Margins of Citizenship: Intellectual Disability and Civil Rights in Twentieth-Century America* (Philadelphia: Temple University Press, 2009), 120.

81. Carey, *On the Margins of Citizenship,* 120.

82. Jones, "Education for Children with Mental Retardation: Parent Activism, Public Policy, and Family Ideology in the 1950s," 328.

83. "A Senate Interim Committee . . . estimated there were 32,000 mentally retarded pupils in the public schools of the State. In 1947 and in 1949, the California Legislature enacted provisions designed to assist educable mentally retarded children in their educational, social, and vocational development." See Eli M. Bower, "California's Program for the Mentally Retarded," *American Journal of Mental Deficiency* 55, no. 5 (April 1951): 502; *Larry P. v. Riles,* 495 F. Supp. 926 (N.D. Cal. 1979); James Allan Simmons, "A Historical Perspective of Special Education in California," (PhD diss., University of Southern California, 1973).

84. Margret A. Winzer, *From Integration to Inclusion: A History of Special Education in the 20th Century* (Washington, D.C.: Gallaudet University Press, 2009), 101. For a good survey on state and city special education laws passed before 1957, the number of children in classroom, and the types of schools, see I. Ignacy Goldberg, "Current Status of Education and Training in the United States for Trainable Mentally Retarded Children," *Exceptional Children* 24, no. 4 (December

1957): 146–54. Also see, Morvin A. Wirtz and Richard Guenther, "The Incidence of Trainable Mentally Handicapped Children," *Exceptional Children* 23, no. 4 (January 1957): 171–75.

85. Carey, *On the Margins of Citizenship,* 118.

86. State of Minnesota, *Directives Relating to Special Education for Educable Mentally Retarded Children,* State of Minnesota, Department of Education, St. Paul, October 1963, p. 1, Minnesota Historical Society, Special Education Division/Section, Published Records and Reports, Location #120.D3.2F.

87. State of Illinois, *The Illinois Plan for Special Education of Exceptional Children: The Educable Mentally Handicapped,* compiled by Ray Graham, director of exceptional children, issued by Vernon Nickell, superintendent of public instruction, 1950, p. 5, Chicago History Museum, Archives and Manuscripts.

88. Chicago Public Schools, *Curriculum Guide for the Program for Educable Mentally Handicapped Children* (Chicago: Chicago Public Schools, 1967).

89. For two good overviews of special education from the nineteenth century through the twentieth century, see Robert L. Osgood, *The History of Special Education: A Struggle for Equality in American Public Schools* (Westport, Conn.: Praeger, 2008) and Margret A. Winzer, *From Integration to Inclusion: A History of Special Education in the 20th Century* (Washington, D.C.: Gallaudet University Press, 2009). For a summary of state legislative history in special education classes up to the mid-1950s, see Marguerite I. Gilmore, "Selected Legislative Provisions for Special Education in Local School Districts in Illinois with Those of Other States," *Exceptional Children* 22, no. 6 (March 1956): 237–48. See also, Romaine P. Mackie and Patricia P. Robbins, "Exceptional Children in Local Public Schools," *School Life* 43, no. 3 (November 1960): 14–16, and William R. Carriker, "Research Related to the Education of Mentally Retarded Children," *School Life* 42, no. 5 (January 1960): 26–28.

90. Cohen, *Contingencies in the Labeling and Placement of Borderline Educable Retarded Children,* 18.

91. Herold C. Hunt, *Special Education in the Chicago Public Schools: The Socially Maladjusted* (Chicago: Chicago Public Schools, 1951), 2.

92. *Report of the Commission on the Problems of the Mentally Retarded, Handicapped and Gifted Children,* Minnesota Legislature 1961, 20; *Directives Relating to Special Education for Educable Mentally Retarded Children,* State of Minnesota, Department of Education, St. Paul, October 1963.

93. Illinois Plan, *The Illinois Plan for Special Education of Exceptional Children,* 5–6.

94. *Pennsylvania Association for Retarded Children (PARC) v. Commonwealth of Pennsylvania,* E334 F.Supp. 1257 (E.D. Pa. 1971); *Mills v. Board of Education of District of Columbia,* 348 F. Supp. 866 (D.D.C 1972); Section 504, Rehabilitation Act of 1973 P.L. 93–112; Education for All Handicapped Children Act, 1975, P.L. 94–142.

95. Charles W. Murdock, "Civil Rights of the Mentally Retarded: Some Critical Issues," *Notre Dame Lawyer* (October 1972): 133.

96. Walter Lippman, "Tests of Hereditary Intelligence," *New Republic*, November 22, 1922. See also Scot Danforth, "Contributions of John Dewey to an Educational Philosophy of Intellectual Disability," *Educational Theory*, 58, no. 1 (2008): 45–62.

97. Horace Mann Bond, "Intelligence Tests and Propaganda," *Crisis* 28 (1924): 61; Wayne J. Urban, "The Black Scholar and Intelligence Testing: The Case of Horace Mann Bond," *Journal of the History of Behavioral Sciences* 25 (October 1989): 323–34.

98. Charles S. Johnson, "Mental Measurements of Negro Groups," *Opportunity* (1923): 21.

99. E. Franklin Frazier, "The Mind of the American Negro," *Opportunity* 6 (September 1928): 263.

100. Horace Mann Bond, "Again, On African-American 'Intelligence' (1958)" in *A Documentary History of the Negro People in the United States, 1951–1959*, ed. Herbert Aptheker (New York: Citadel, 1993), 430–31; William B. Thomas, "Black Intellectuals' Critique of Early Mental Testing: A Little-Known Saga of the 1920s," *American Journal of Education* 90, no. 3 (May 1982). Audrey M. Shuey, *The Testing of Negro Intelligence* (Lynchburg, VA: J. P. Bell and Co., 1958). For a thorough annotated bibliography on the history of black intelligence testing, see, Audrey M. Shuey, *The Testing of Negro Intelligence* (New York: Social Science, 1966) and R. Travis Osborne and Frank C. J. McGurk, eds., *The Testing of Negro Intelligence*, vol. 2 (Athens, GA: Foundation for Human Understanding, 1982).

101. J. McV. Hunt, *Intelligence and Experience* (New York: The Ronald Press, 1961) is one of the early studies to argue that intelligence was not hereditary or fixed but environmental. Influenced by the work of Piaget and the development of intelligence of children in their everyday environment, Hunt wrote, "For over half a century, the leading theory of man's nature has been dominated by the assumptions of fixed intelligence and predetermined development." Examining the evidence of "adaptive interaction between organism and environment," has led "to a serious questioning of the immutability of the IQ." (from the preface). See also, Benjamin S. Bloom, *Stability and Change in Human Characteristics* (New York: John Wiley, 1964). In 1939, Harold Skeels and Harold Dye published their findings from the University of Iowa Child Welfare Research Station study where the IQs of feebleminded children increased when they were placed in wards with adults who positively interacted with them. They concluded the stimulation provided by the adult ward attendants and residents contributed to the increase in children's intelligence. The "Iowa Studies," as they came to be known, merged the pre–World War II burgeoning interest in environmental perspectives with the postwar embrace of it by the late 1950s and 1960s. See Harold M. Skeels and Harold B. Dye, "A Study of the Effects of Differential Stimulation on Mentally Retarded Children," *Journal of Psycho-Asthenics* 44 (1939): 114–36.

102. John L. Rury and Shirley A. Hill, *The African American Struggle for Secondary Schooling, 1940–1980* (New York: Teachers College Press, 2012).

103. Alicia T. Doran, "Retardation Among Negro Pupils in the Junior High School," *Journal of Negro Education,* 5, no. 2 (April 1936): 228.

104. Doran, "Retardation Among Negro Pupils in the Junior High School," 228.

105. Doran, "Retardation Among Negro Pupils in the Junior High School," 229.

106. Doran, "Retardation Among Negro Pupils in the Junior High School," 229.

107. Doran, "Retardation Among Negro Pupils in the Junior High School," 231.

108. Otto Klineberg, *Negro Intelligence and Selective Migration* (New York: Columbia University Press, 1935). Kenneth Clark says Klineberg's research helped future researchers reexamine the theory of black academic retardation. Kenneth Clark, *Dark Ghetto: Dilemmas of Social Power* (New York: Harper & Row, 1965), 130.

109. Quoted in Everett S. Lee, "Negro Intelligence and Selective Migration: A Philadelphia Test of the Klineberg Hypothesis," *American Sociological Review* 16, no. 2 (April 1951): 228. See also Otto Klineberg, *Negro Intelligence and Selective Migration* (New York: Columbia University Press, 1935); and Thomas Pettigrew, "Negro American Intelligence," in *School Children in the Urban Slum*, ed. Joan I. Roberts (New York: The Free Press, 1967)

110. For a broader discussion of so-called black pathology, inferiority, and damaged personality, see Kenneth B. Clark, *Dark Ghetto: Dilemmas of Social Power* (New York: Harper & Row, 1965) and Daryl Michael Scott, *Contempt and Pity: Social Policy and the Image of the Damaged Black Psyche, 1880–1996* (Chapel Hill: University of North Carolina Press, 1997).

111. *Brown v. Board of Education of Topeka,* 347 U.S. 483 (1954), 3, 4, 6, and 7.

112. James D. Anderson, *The Education of Blacks in the South, 1860–1935* (Chapel Hill: University of North Carolina, 1988); Louis R. Harlan, *Separate and Unequal: Public School Campaigns and Racism in the Southern Seaboard States, 1910–1915* (Chapel Hill: University of North Carolina Press, 1958); Ronald E. Butchart, *Schooling the Freed People: Teaching, Learning, and the Struggle for Black Freedom, 1861–1876* (Chapel Hill: University of North Carolina, 2010); Camille Walsh, *Racial Taxation: Schools, Segregation, and Taxpayer Citizenship, 1869–1973* (Chapel Hill: University of North Carolina Press, 2018).

113. "Non-existent" language is in *Brown v. Board of Education,* 7. See also, Alethea H. Washington, "Negro Secondary Education in Rural Areas," *Journal of Negro Education* 9, no. 3 (July 1940).

114. *Brown v. Board of Education* (1954); Carl V. Harris, "Stability and Change in Discrimination Against Black Public Schools: Birmingham, Alabama, 1871–1931," *Journal of Southern History* 51, no. 3 (August 1985): 375–416; Henry Sullivan Williams, "The Development of the Negro Public School System in Missouri," *Journal of Negro History* 5, no. 2 (April 1920): 137–65.

115. Edgar A. Toppin, "Walter White and the Atlanta NAACP's Fight for Equal Schools, 1916–1917," *History of Education Quarterly* 7, no. 1 (Spring 1967). The fight for equal schools in Atlanta took place in the context of the deliberate creation

of special and vocational education for black students. See Barry F. Franklin, "Educating Atlanta's Backward Children, 1898–1924," in *From 'Backwardness' to 'At-Risk': Childhood Learning Difficulties and the Contradictions of School Reform* (Albany: State University of New York Press, 1994).

116. Ellis O. Knox, "A Historical Sketch of Secondary Education for Negroes," *Journal of Negro Education* 8, no. 3 (July 1940): 440; H. Councill Trenholm, "The Accreditation of the Negro High School," *Journal of Negro Education* 1, no. 1 (April 1932): 34–43.

117. Howard H. Long, "The Negro Secondary School Population," *Journal of Negro Education* 9, no. 3 (July 1940): 454–64. Hereditarians like Lewis Terman started to concede a little to the environmentalists by the 1940s but remained steadfast in their position on black intelligence. Terman quoted in Long: "The issue is not simply whether IQ's can be influenced by differences in environment and training. That to some degree they are so influenced, no one has ever denied. Whether in a typical American community the influence is relatively small (as I believe) or quite large (as some believe) is less important than whether it has a permanent effect upon capacity for achievement."

118. Martha Biondi, *To Stand and Fight: The Struggle for Civil Rights in Postwar New York City* (Cambridge, Mass.: Harvard University Press, 2003).

119. Quoted in Adina Back, "Exposing the 'Whole Segregation Myth': The Harlem Nine and New York City's School Desegregation Battles," in *Freedom North: Black Freedom Struggles Outside the South, 1940–1980,* eds., Jeanne F. Theoharis and Komozi Woodard (New York: Palgrave Macmillan, 2003), 65.

120. For a history of the civil rights movement in education in the North and West, see Clarence Taylor, *Knocking at Our Own Door: Milton A. Galamison and the Struggle to Integrate New York City Schools* (Lanham, MD: Lexington, 2001); David G. Garcia, *Strategies of Segregation: Race, Residence, and the Struggle for Educational Equality* (Berkeley: University of California Press, 2018); Kristopher Bryan Burrell, "Black Women as Activists Intellectuals: Ella Baker and Mae Mallory Combat Northern Jim Crow in New York City's Public Schools during the 1950s," in *The Strange Careers of the Jim Crow North,* eds. Brian Purcell and Jeanne Theoharis with Komozi Woodard (New York: New York University Press, 2019). For a history on the impact of integration on black teachers see, Barbara J. Shircliffe, *Desegregating Teachers: Contesting the Meaning of Equality of Educational Opportunity in the South post-Brown* (New York: Peter Lang, 2012).

121. Benjamin Pasamanick and Hilda Knobloch, "The Contribution of Some Organic Factors to School Retardation in Negro Children," *Journal of Negro Education* 27, no. 1 (Winter 1958): 4.

122. "On Race and Intelligence: A Joint Statement," *American Journal of Orthopsychiatry* 27, no. 2 (April 1957): 420.

123. Alfred H. Katz, *Parents of the Handicapped: Self-Organized Parents' and Relatives' Groups for Treatment of Ill and Handicapped Children* (Springfield, IL: Charles C. Thomas, 1961), 3.

124. Deborah S. Metzel, "Historical Social Geography," in *Mental Retardation in America: A Historical Reader* (New York: New York University Press, 2004), 433.

125. William Cruickshank recalls the enthusiasm of parents looking for answers to what ailed their children. "Parents of tens of thousands of children in the United States knew what they had, even if professional educators and psychologists and pediatricians did not. With the early appearance of articles dealing with brain-injured children, with dyslexic children, and with perceptually handicapped children, parents began to respond with the offer of their child as a subject for study. It soon became apparent to them that hundreds of their neighbors had similar problems which heretofore had not been discussed publicly." William M. Cruickshank, "Some Issues Facing the Field of Learning Disability," *Journal of Special Education* 5, no. 7 (August–September 1972): 381.

126. Milton S. Williams Jr., "Fund for Perceptually Handicapped Children, Louisville, Kentucky," in *Proceedings of the Conference on Exploration into the Problems of the Perceptually Handicapped Child,* April 6, 1963, 45–46; Jeanne Romans, "Maryland Association for Brain-Injured Children, Inc.," in *Proceedings of the Conference on Exploration into the Problems of the Perceptually Handicapped Child,* April 6, 1963, 51–52; William C. Conway, "Michigan Children's Neurological Development Program," in *Proceedings of the Conference on Exploration into the Problems of the Perceptually Handicapped Child,* April 6, 1963, 55–56.

127. William M. Cruickshank, "Some Issues Facing the Field of Learning Disability," *Journal of Learning Disabilities* 5, no. 7 (August–September 1972); Richard S. Lewis, *The Other Child: The Brain-Injured Child, A Book for Parents and Laymen* (New York: Grune & Stratton, 1951).

128. Katz, *Parents of the Handicapped,* 6.

129. Alton E. Lindstrom, "Minnesota Association for the Brain Injured," *Proceedings of the Conference on Exploration into the Problems of the Perceptually Handicapped Child,* April 6, 1963, 40–41; Charles W. Mentkowski, "Milwaukee Society for Brain-Injured Children, Inc.," *Proceedings of the Conference on Exploration into the Problems of the Perceptually Handicapped Child,* April 6, 1963, 42; Lamont Johnston, "Hamilton County Committee for Crippled Children and Adults," Chattanooga, Tennessee in *Proceedings of the Conference on Exploration into the Problems of the Perceptually Handicapped Child,* April 6, 1963, 47–48.

130. James M. Kauffman and Daniel P. Hallahan, eds., *Teaching Children with Learning Disabilities: Personal Perspectives* (Columbus, OH: Charles Merrill, 1976) 245–49; for the importance of William M. Cruickshank's work in mental retardation and learning disabilities, see same edited anthology, 95–105.

131. *Proceedings of the Conference on Exploration into the Problems of the Perceptually Handicapped Child, Volume 1,* Chicago, Illinois, April 6, 1963; Glenn T. Eskew, *But for Birmingham: The Local and National Movements in the Civil Rights Struggle* (Chapel Hill: University of North Carolina Press, 1997), 225.

132. "Theme," *Proceedings of the Conference on Exploration into the Problems of the Perceptually Handicapped Child, Volume 1,* Chicago, Illinois, April 6, 1963, i.

133. Dr. Oscar M. Chute, Superintendent of District 65, Elementary Schools, Evanston, Illinois, "Foreword," *Proceedings of the Conference on Exploration into the Problems of the Perceptually Handicapped in Child,* i.

134. Wretha Petersen, supervisor of special education, Montgomery County, Maryland, "Educating the Perceptually Handicapped Child," in *Proceedings of the Conference on Exploration into the Problems of the Perceptually Handicapped Child,* 9.

135. Samuel A. Kirk, "Characteristics of Slow Learners and Needed Adjustments in Reading," in *The Foundations of Special Education: Selected Papers and Speeches of Samuel A. Kirk,* eds. Gail A. Harris and Winifred D. Kirk (Reston, VA: Council for Exceptional Children, 1993), 145.

136. Kirk, "Characteristics of Slow Learners and Needed Adjustments in Reading," 146.

137. Kirk, "Characteristics of Slow Learners and Needed Adjustments in Reading," 146.

138. Samuel A. Kirk, "Reading Problems of Slow Learners," in *The Underachiever in Reading,* ed. H. Alan Robinson (Chicago: University of Chicago Press, 1962), 63. See also Julia M. Penn, "Reading Disability: A Neurological Deficit?," *Exceptional Children* (December 1966): 243–48. Penn said, "A child who cannot read but who can learn should be treated as dyslexic." This "dyslexic" child would be in Kirk's first group of slow learners.

139. Rudolf Flesch, *Why Johnny Can't Read and What You Can Do about It* (New York: Harper, 1955). Flesch promoted the use of phonics. See Kirk's critique of Flesch. Samuel A. Kirk and Winifred D. Kirk, "How Johnny Learns to Read," *Exceptional Children* 22, no. 4 (January 1956): 158–60.

140. Dr. Sylvia Rimm, *Why Bright Kids Get Poor Grades and What You Can Do about It* (Scottsdale, AZ: Great Potential, 2008).

141. Robert L. Thorndike, *The Concepts of Over- and Underachievement* (New York: Teachers College, Columbia University, Bureau of Publications, 1963), 2. See also Lennard J. Davis, *Enforcing Normalcy: Disability, Deafness, and the Body* (London: Verso, 1995).

142. In the 1950s and 1960s, the achievement literature was explicit about why children failed, going as far as labeling it the "achievement syndrome." The achievement syndrome was race and class based, locating the barriers to academic success in the lack of motivation and achievement values. Bernard Rosen represented this sentiment when he wrote: "It is hypothesized that social classes possess to a disparate extent two components of this achievement orientation. The first is a psychological factor involving a personality characteristic called *achievement motivation* . . . which provides an internal impetus to excel. The second is a cultural factor consisting of certain *value orientations* that define and implement achievement motivated behavior. Both of these factors are related to achievement; their incidence, we suggest, is greater among persons of the middle class than those of the lower class." Bernard C. Rosen, "The Achievement

Syndrome: A Psychocultural Dimension of Social Stratification," *American Sociological Review* 21, no. 2 (April 1956): 204.

143. Allison Davis, *Social-Class Influences Upon Learning* (Cambridge, MA: Harvard University Press, 1961); Joan C. Baratz and Roger W. Shuy, eds., *Teaching Black Children to Read* (Washington, D.C.: Center for Applied Linguistics, 1969); Carl Bereiter and Siegfried Engelmann, *Teaching Disadvantaged Children in the Preschool* (Englewood Cliffs, NJ: Prentice-Hall, 1966); Paul A. Witty, ed., *The Educationally Retarded and Disadvantaged* (Chicago: University of Chicago Press, 1967); E. Earl Baughman and W. Grant Dahlstrom, *Negro and White Children: A Psychological Study in the Rural South* (New York: Academic Press, 1968); William Ryan, *Blaming the Victim* (New York: Pantheon, 1971); Maurice R. Berube, *Education and Poverty: Effective Schooling in the United States and Cuba* (Westport, CT: Greenwood, 1984). Growing up in a poor black family and being raised in a poor black neighborhood made black children experientially and consequentially "retarded," manifesting in a lack of motivation and so many other habits of mind, so said the research literature. It was projected in the literature that a big difference between black and brown EMR students and white EMR students were cognitive-motivational factors. This kind of thinking was invoked in Head Start and other racialized special education programs. Two principal researchers in the 1960s were Edward Zigler and Donald MacMillan. MacMillan wrote, "Methods and materials presently in use in classes for EMR children may be appropriate for middle class children who, despite environmental support, are inefficient learners. Considering the overabundance of lower class and/or minority children placed in special classes for the EMR, attention must be focused upon another major reason for poor performance, i.e., motivation. Genotypically speaking, many such children are not retarded; their poor performance on IQ tests or in the regular classroom may be based on an inappropriate motivational set." Donald L. MacMillan, "The Problem of Motivation in the Education of the Mentally Retarded," *Exceptional Children* 37, no. 8 (April 1971): 579–80. See also Edward Zigler and E. C. Butterfield, "Motivational Aspects of Changes in IQ Test Performance of Culturally Deprived Nursery School Children," *Child Development* 39, no. 1 (March 1968): 1–14.

144. Samuel A. Kirk, "Behavioral Diagnosis and Remediation of Learning Disabilities," in *Proceedings of the Conference on Exploration into the Problems of the Perceptually Handicapped Child, April 6, 1963*, 1.

145. Jane Hart and Beverly Jones, *Where's Hannah? A Handbook for Parents and Teachers of Children with Learning Disorders* (New York: Hart, 1968), 69.

146. Hart and Jones, *Where's Hannah?*, 13.

147. Hart and Jones, *Where's Hannah?*, 18–19.

148. Hart and Jones, *Where's Hannah?*, quoted in foreword by Ray H. Barsch. See also Ray H. Barsch, "Perspectives on Learning Disabilities: The Vectors of a New Convergence," *Journal of Learning Disabilities* 1, no. 1 (January 1968): 4-20.

149. Samuel A. Kirk and Barbara Bateman, "Diagnosis and Remediation of Learning Disabilities," *Exceptional Children* (October 1962): 73

150. Samuel A. Kirk, "Mental Retardation vs. Learning Disabilities," Speech at the University of Minnesota, Spring Lecture Series, May 15, 1967, Samuel Kirk Papers, Box 3, University of Illinois—Urbana-Champaign.

151. Samuel A. Kirk and Barbara Bateman, "Diagnosis and Remediation of Learning Disabilities," *Exceptional Children* (October 1962): 73.

152. Samuel A. Kirk, "Behavioral Diagnosis and Remediation of Learning Disabilities," in *Proceedings of the Conference on Exploration into the Problems of the Perceptually Handicapped Child,* April 6, 1963, 1–2.

153. Kirk, "Behavioral Diagnosis and Remediation of Learning Disabilities," 2.

154. Kirk, "Behavioral Diagnosis and Remediation of Learning Disabilities," 3.

155. Walter Goodman, "Summation of the Meeting to Form a National Organization," in *Proceedings of the Conference on Exploration into the Problems of the Perceptually Handicapped Child,* April 6, 1963, 92.

156. "The History of the Learning Disabilities Association of Washington," https://www.ldawa.org/about (accessed June 4, 2010). For a later history of parent organizing in Seattle, see Susan Schwartzenberg, *Becoming Citizens: Family Life and the Politics of Disability* (Seattle: University of Washington Press, 2005).

157. James J. Gallagher, "The Public Policy Legacy of Samuel A. Kirk," *Learning Disabilities Research and Practice,* 13, no. 1 (Winter 1998): 11–14.

158. William C. Geer, Leo E. Connor, and Leonard S. Blackman, "Recent Federal Legislation—Provisions and Implications for Special Education," *Exceptional Children* 30, no. 9 (May 1964): 411–21. For an overview of education federal policies in the immediate postwar period, see George A. Kizer, "Federal Aid to Education: 1945–1963," *History of Education Quarterly* 10, no. 1 (Spring 1970): 84–102.

159. "Administration of Education Programs for Handicapped Children," *Congressional Record,* Samuel Kirk Papers.

160. Statement by Dr. Samuel A. Kirk to the Subcommittee on Health of the Committee on Labor and Public Welfare of the United States Senate on S-1400, *Report of the Committee on Labor and Public Welfare, United States Senate, Eighty-Ninth Congress, Second Session,* 2, Washington, D.C.: U.S. Government Printing Office, 1966. See also, Samuel A. Kirk, "Elementary and Secondary Education Act of 1966," in *The Foundations of Special Education: Selected Papers and Speeches of Samuel A. Kirk,* eds. Gail A. Harris and Winifred D. Kirk (Reston, VA: Council for Exceptional Children, 1993), 259.

161. "Administration of Education Programs for Handicapped Children," *Congressional Record,* Samuel Kirk Papers.

162. Bruce Watson, *Freedom Summer: The Savage Season of 1964 That Made Mississippi Burn and Made America a Democracy* (New York: Viking, 2010).

163. Samuel Kirk, House Committee on Education and Labor, Ad Hoc Subcommittee on the Handicapped, *Education and Training of the Handicapped: Elementary and Secondary Education Act of 1965,* 89th Congress, 1st Session, June 15,

1966, 383; see also Samuel A. Kirk, "Elementary and Secondary Education Act of 1966," in *The Foundations of Special Education: Selected Papers and Speeches of Samuel A. Kirk*, eds. Gail A. Harris and Winifred D. Kirk (Reston, VA: Council for Exceptional Children, 1993), 249.

3. Disabling Black Poverty, Supporting White Underachievement

1. Lyndon B. Johnson, "Remarks on Project Head Start," May 18, 1965, in *Project Hard Start: A Legacy of the War on Poverty,* eds. Edward Zigler and Jeanette Valentine (New York: Free Press, 1979), 68.

2. "The State of the Union," January 8, 1964, in *A Time for Action: A Selection from the Speeches and Writings of Lyndon B. Johnson, 1953–64* (New York: Atheneum, 1964), 168.

3. "The State of the Union," 170.

4. "The State of the Union," 170.

5. Alice O'Connor, *Poverty Knowledge: Social Science, Social Policy, and the Poor in Twentieth Century U.S. History* (Princeton, N.J.: Princeton University Press, 2001).

6. Lyndon B. Johnson, letter printed in *Exceptional Children* (March 1968): 477.

7. Legislative advocacy "is when an individual communicates the importance of a policy issue or law to people who are in policymaking positions." See Meghan M. Burke, Linda Sandman, Beatrize Perez, and Meghann O'Leary, "The Phenomenon of Legislative Advocacy Among Parents of Children with Disabilities," *Journal of Research in Special Educational Needs* 18, no. 1 (2018): 50–58. Much of that communication includes mobilizing people, contacting legislators, pushing lawmakers to introduce bills and enact them into law or revising current law. In the case of the educational disability rights movement, legislative advocacy manifested in modifying the Elementary and Secondary Education Act. Though parents were the most vocal advocates in the 1950s, special education organizations, school administrators, and psychologists did the heavy lifting in front of the U.S. Congress in the 1960s.

8. Sargent Shriver and Senate Committee on Labor and Public Welfare, *Amendments to the Economic Opportunity Act of 1964, Hearings before the Subcommittee on Employment, Manpower, and Poverty,* 89th Congress, 2nd Session, June 21–24, 1966, 44.

9. Shriver and Senate Committee on Labor and Public Welfare, *Amendments to the Economic Opportunity Act of 1964.*

10. Mel Ravitz, "The Role of the School in the Urban Setting," in *Education in Depressed Areas,* ed. A. Harry Passow (New York: Teachers College Press, 1963).

11. This understanding of neighborhood decay created by poverty was also what federal officials believed responsible for neighborhood crime. Elizabeth Hinton wrote, "Federal officials identified these pathologies—the various cultural

and familial patterns in low-income families that experts and policy-makers saw as deviant—in racial terms." Elizabeth Hinton, *From the War on Poverty to the War on Crime: The Making of Mass Incarceration* (Cambridge, Mass.: Harvard University Press, 2016), 38.

12. Majorie B. Smiley, "Objectives of Educational Programs for the Educationally Retarded and the Disadvantaged," in *The Educationally Retarded and Disadvantaged*, ed. Paul Witty (Chicago: University of Chicago Press, 1967), 125.

13. By the mid-1960s, research on environmental factors that created socially disadvantaged and culturally deprived conditions ranged topically from the state of the home and family status; language, cognition, and intelligence; perceptual styles and patterns of intellectual function; and motivation and aspiration. See a great review of the research literature by Edmund W. Gordon, "Characteristics of Socially Disadvantaged Children," *Review of Educational Research* 35, no. 5 (December 1965): 377–88.

14. Arthur R. Jensen, "How Much Can We Boost IQ and Scholastic Achievement?," *Harvard Educational Review*, 39, no. 1 (April 1969): 1–124.

15. John M. Beck and Richard W. Saxe, *Teaching the Culturally Disadvantaged Pupil* (Springfield, IL: Charles C. Thomas, 1965).

16. Norman Matlin and Carlos Albizu-Miranda, "Some Historical and Logical Bases for the Concept of Cultural Deprivation," in *Socio-Cultural Aspects of Mental Retardation: Proceedings of the Peabody-NIMH Conference,* ed. H. Carl Haywood (New York: Appleton-Century-Crofts, 1970), 497.

17. Mical Raz argued, "Yet until the late 1960s, little attention was given to the fact that the category, 'mild mental retardation' was applied primarily to African American children. Rather, most articles avoided any discussion of race. Some researchers noted that African American children were chosen as subjects for intervention for reasons of convenience and availability, while others focused on socioeconomic factors such as 'poverty' or life in an 'inner-city' environment— terms that became euphemisms for race." Mical Raz, *What's Wrong with the Poor? Psychiatry, Race, and the War on Poverty* (Chapel Hill: University of North Carolina Press, 2013), 133.

18. Raz, *What's Wrong with the Poor?*, 121.

19. *Larry P. v. Riles,* United States District Court for the Northern District of California (1972).

20. Robert J. Havighurst and Thomas E. Moorefield, "The Disadvantaged in Industrial Cities," in *The Educationally Retarded and Disadvantaged* (Chicago: University of Chicago Press, 1967), 9.

21. Havighurst and Moorefield, "The Disadvantaged in Industrial Cities," 9–10.

22. Havighurst and Moorefield, "The Disadvantaged in Industrial Cities," 11.

23. Havighurst and Moorefield, "The Disadvantaged in Industrial Cities," 11–12.

24. Havighurst and Moorefield, "The Disadvantaged in Industrial Cities," 12.

25. Robert J. Havighurst and Lindley J. Stiles, "National Policy for Alienated Youth," in *Education of the Disadvantaged: A Book of Readings,* eds. A. Harry Passow, Miriam Goldberg, and Abraham J. Tannenbaum (New York: Holt, Rinehart and Winston, 1967): 441–43.

26. Frank Riessman, *The Culturally Deprived Child* (New York: Harper & Row, 1962); Martin Deutsch, "The Disadvantaged Child and the Learning Process," in *Education in Depressed Areas,* ed. A. Harry Passow (New York: Teachers College Press, 1963); Kenneth B. Clark, "Educational Stimulation of Racially Disadvantaged Children," in *Education in Depressed Areas,* ed. A. Harry Passow (New York: Teachers College Press, 1963); Robert J. Havighurst, "Who Are the Socially Disadvantaged," *Journal of Negro Education* 33, no. 3 (Summer 1964): 210–17; Charles A. Valentine, *Culture and Poverty: Critique and Counter-Proposals* (Chicago: University of Chicago Press, 1968); The author that first coined the phrase "culture of poverty" was anthropologist Oscar Lewis. See Oscar Lewis, *Five Families: Mexican Case Studies in the Culture of Poverty* (New York: Basic Books, 1975) and Oscar Lewis, *La Vida: A Puerto Rican Family in the Culture of Poverty* (New York: Random House, 1966).

27. For an early critique of the cultural deprivation thesis besides Kenneth Clark, see Bernard Mackler and Morsley G. Giddings, "Cultural Deprivation: A Study in Mythology," *Teachers College Record* 66, no. 7 (April 1965): 608–13.

28. Kenneth B. Clark, *Dark Ghetto: Dilemmas of Social Power* (New York: Harper and Row, 1965), 130.

29. Clark, *Dark Ghetto,* 130–33; Richard R. Valencia, ed. *The Evolution of Deficit Thinking: Educational Thought and Practice* (London: Routledge Falmer, 1997); Richard R. Valencia, *Dismantling Contemporary Deficit Thinking* (New York: Routledge, 2010).

30. Educational Policies Commission, *Education and the Disadvantaged* (1962). For a history on how the National Education Association's Educational Policies Commission produced this report on the educational disadvantaged, see, Wayne J. Urban, "What's in a Name: Education and the Disadvantaged American (1962)," *Paedagogica Historica* 45, nos. 1–2 (February–April 2009): 251–64. The NEA often found itself on the wrong side of the issue when it came to black students. See the NEA's capitulation to segregation, R. McLaran Sawyer, "The National Educational Association and Negro Education, 1865–1884," *Journal of Negro Education* 39, no. 4 (Autumn 1970): 341–45. For the difficulty desegregation posed for the NEA, see, Wayne J. Urban, *Gender, Race, and the National Education Association: Professionalism and Its Limitations* (New York: Routledge, 2013), chap. 6. Edward Shorter, *The Kennedy Family and the Story of Mental Retardation* (Philadelphia: Temple University Press, 2000).

31. Stephen K. Bailey and Edith K. Mosher, *ESEA: The Office of Education Administers a Law* (Syracuse, N.Y.: Syracuse University Press, 1968), 8–9.

32. Edward Davens, "Head Start, A Retrospective View: The Founders," in *Project Head Start: A Legacy of the War on Poverty,* eds. Edward Zigler and Jeanette Valentine (New York: Free Press, 1979), 88–89.

33. Frederick Bertolaet, "The Education of Disadvantaged Youth," Senate Committee on Labor and Public Welfare, *Elementary and Secondary Education Act of 1965, Hearings before the Subcommittee on Education,* 89th Congress, 1st Session, January 26 to February 11, 1965, 1193–1200.

34. Sargent Shriver, "The Origins of Head Start," in *Project Head Start: A Legacy of the War on Poverty,* eds. Edward Zigler and Jeanette Valentine (New York: Free Press, 1979). 50.

35. Shriver, "The Origins of Head Start," 52. Also see, Bettye M. Caldwell, "The Fourth Dimension in Early Childhood Education," in *Early Education: Current Theory, Research, and Action,* eds. Robert D. Hess and Roberta Meyer Bear (Chicago: Aldine, 1968); Bettye M. Cardwell and Julius B. Richmond, "The Children's Center in Syracuse, New York," in *Early Child Care: The New Perspectives,* ed. Laura L. Dittman (New York: Atherton, 1968); Susan W. Gray, Barbara K. Ramsey, and Rupert A. Klaus, "The Early Training Project, 1962–1980," in *As the Twig is Bent: Lasting Effects of Preschool Programs,* The Consortium for Longitudinal Studies (Hillsdale, NJ: Lawrence Erlbaum Associates, 1983). See, Mical Raz, *What's Wrong with the Poor? Psychiatry, Race, and the War on Poverty* (Chapel Hill: University of North Carolina Press, 2013), 22–26. One of the first early childhood programs was the Harlem Youth Opportunities Unlimited (HARYOU) under the Kennedy administration with Kenneth Clark as the acting chairman of its board of directors. A multifaceted undertaking in areas such as employment and social services, understanding the educational problems of central Harlem black students was a focus of HARYOU's preschool endeavor. "Parents, teachers, principals, pupils, and laymen alike agree that the vast majority of Harlem's students leave its junior high schools two or more years retarded. There is ... a fundamental disagreement over where to place the blame for the situation, and hence where to direct corrective energies." For all the reasons central Harlem black students dropped out of middle and high school, such as employment, marriage, pregnancy, or health, being "overage" represented why 79.7 percent of black boys and 61.6 percent of black girls left school, respectively. "The pattern of test and I.Q. scores is what leads us to describe education in Central Harlem as marked by massive educational deterioration. The longer the pupils are in school, the greater the proportion who fail to meet established and comparative norms of academic competence." To counter this trend, it was wise for other childhood programs, HARYOU argued, to focus on those aged three to five. See Harlem Youth Opportunities Unlimited, *Youth in the Ghetto: A Study of the Consequences of Powerlessness and a Blueprint for Change* (New York, 1964), 184, 194–95. For the politics of community action and the tension between Kenneth Clark and Representative Adam Clayton Powell. See also Noel A. Cazenave, *Impossible Democracy: The Unlikely Success of the War on Poverty Community*

Action Programs (Albany: State University of New York Press, 2007). Damon Freeman, "Kenneth B. Clark and the Problem of Power," *Patterns of Prejudice* 42, nos. 4–5 (2008): 413–37.

36. To see how the environmental thesis led to deficit-thinking discourse, see, Richard R. Valencia, ed., *The Evolution of Deficit Thinking: Educational Thought and Practice* (London: Routledge Farmer, 1997).

37. Sargent Shriver, "The Origins of Head Start," 52. On the connection between Head Start and IQ see, Craig T. Ramey and Sharon Landesman Ramey, "Early Educational Interventions and Intelligence: Implications for Head Start," in *The Head Start Debates: Are We Failing the Children Most At Risk? 53 of America's Leading Experts Weigh In* (Baltimore: Paul H. Brookes, 2004).

38. Shriver, "The Origins of Head Start," 52–53. Shriver's comments are reminiscent of early twentieth-century commentary about enlarged tonsils being a cause of mental retardation and one's ability to learn.

39. Edward Zigler, a psychologist at Yale University, was also a member on Head Start's national planning committee. Head Start theorists like Zigler believed in the concept of "familial mental retardation." Familial retardation was not a new concept but one that stretched back to the early twentieth century, especially manifesting in the work of Alfred Strauss and others who made the distinction between exogeneous (organic) and endogamous (familial) brain injury. Defining and associating the endogamous with the hereditary mental retardation of family members, including the individual in question, Zigler and other environmentalists rejected genetic explanations of familial retardation and instead substituted environmental ones. The majority of black children and their families' retardation was understood under Strauss's older "endogamous" conception. The same existed under the newer environmental conception of familial-cultural mental retardation. It is not an accident that EOA and Head Start emerged as the greatest policy response to black familial-cultural mental retardation. See Edward Zigler, "Familial Mental Retardation: A Continuing Dilemma," *Science* 155, no. 3760 (January 20, 1967): 292–98. Environmentalists also argued black retardation was a problem of motivation and achievement "syndromes." See Donald L. MacMillan, "The Problem of Motivation in the Education of the Mentally Retarded," *Exceptional Children* (April 1971): 579–86; Edward Zigler and E. C. Butterfield, "Motivational Aspects of Changes in IQ Test Performance of Culturally Deprived Nursery School Children," *Child Development* 39 (1968): 1–14; Bernard C. Rosen, "The Achievement Syndrome: A Psychocultural Dimension of Social Stratification," *American Sociological Review* 21, no. 2 (April 1956): 203–11. There were hereditarians still pushing the fiction of hereditary mental retardation in the 1960s with the same but withering eugenics thrust. See Gordon C. Reed and Elizabeth W. Reed, "Who Are the Parents of the Retarded Children?," *Focus on Exceptional Children* 1, no. 8 (January 1970): 5–7. See the Reeds' longer Minnesota Human Genetics League inspired study, *Mental Retardation: A Family Study* (Philadelphia: W. B. Saunders Co., 1965).

40. For an overview of ESEA and Title I see, Carl L. LoPresti, "The Elementary and Secondary Education Act of 1965: The Birth of Compensatory Education," *Urban Law Annual: Journal of Urban and Contemporary Law,* 145 (January 1971): 145–61.

41. Edward Zigler admitted to this conflation, even implicating himself: "Everyone involved in Head Start's planning was aware that this was to be a program for poor children, *not* children with mental retardation. Unfortunately, with high-profile names like Shriver, Cooke, Zigler, and several others associated with the mental retardation field, their participation in Head Start created a subtle link in people's minds between poverty and developmental disabilities. Of course, these planners were just a small part of the reason that the fields of mental retardation and preschool intervention for children living in poverty became so theoretically intertwined. Given the thinking in the two fields at the time, this development was probably inevitable. Both fields were wedded to an environmental emphasis and discounted the importance of heredity in human development. Yet neither Cooke nor Zigler believed that intelligence could be raised dramatically. Shriver vacillated, although at times his speech writers got carried away with the idea." Edward Zigler and Sally J. Styfco, *The Hidden History of Head Start* (New York: Oxford University Press, 2010), 21–22.

42. Senate Committee on Labor and Public Welfare, *Elementary and Secondary Education Act of 1965, Hearings before the Subcommittee on Education,* 89th Congress, 1st Session, January 26 to February 11, 1965, 500–501.

43. Senate Committee on Labor and Public Welfare, *Elementary and Secondary Education Act of 1965,* 513, 511.

44. For a comprehensive history on the role black women played in the development of Head Start as well as politicization of Head Start centers, see Crystal R. Sanders, *A Chance for Change: Head Start and Mississippi's Black Freedom Struggle* (Chapel Hill: University of North Carolina Press, 2016).

45. Economic Opportunity Act, Public Law 88–452, Title II, Section 205 (a) (c), August 20, 1964.

46. Elementary and Secondary Education Act, Public Law 89–10, Title I, Section 205 (a) (1), April 11, 1965.

47. Quoted in Stephen K. Bailey and Edith K. Mosher, *ESEA: The Office of Education Administers a Law* (Syracuse, N.Y.: Syracuse University Press, 1968), 49.

48. Quoted in Maris A. Vinovskis, *The Birth of Head Start: Preschool Education Policies in the Kennedy and Johnson Administrations* (Chicago: University of Chicago Press, 2005), 84.

49. Vinovskis, *The Birth of Head Start,* 122.

50. Edward Zigler and Susan Muenchow, *Head Start: The Inside Story of America's Most Successful Educational Experiment* (New York: Basic Books, 1992), 238–42.

51. Elizabeth Hinton has challenged the long-standing belief in the "progressive" aspect of the War on Poverty, arguing that fighting poverty and fighting

crime were not only concomitant and overlapping but had a black face at its center. See Elizabeth Hinton, *From the War on Poverty to the War on Crime* (Cambridge, Mass.: Harvard University Press, 2016). A coordinating plan to implement special education services in Minnesota under ESEA's Title VI supports Hinton's thesis. Here is an ESEA document from the State of Minnesota referring specifically to the socially maladjusted and juvenile delinquent students and the jurisdiction they fell under. "Rehabilitative services for handicapped children and youth facilitated through the State Department of Education need to be coordinated with services provided under other administrative auspices. Schools for the seriously social maladjusted are administered by the Department of Corrections. Meeting the needs of the handicapped is defined as a public obligation. This responsibility is accepted and re-affirmed in Minnesota by statutory definition of handicapped children as a 'public problem,' along with dependents, delinquents." See "Plan for Development of a Comprehensive Special Education Services Plan," (1967), Minnesota Historical Society, Education Dept., Gov't Records, Desegregation/Integration Files, 1965–1996, Location: 126.J.9.6F.

52. Edwin W. Martin Jr., "Breakthrough for the Handicapped: Legislative History," in *New Directions in Special Education,* ed. Reginal L. Jones (Boston: Allyn and Bacon, 1970), 415. Reprinted from *Exceptional Children* 34 (1968): 493–503.

53. Edward W. Martin Jr., "Breakthrough for the Handicapped: Legislative History," *New Directions in Special Education,* ed. Reginald L. Jones (Boston: Allyn and Bacon, 1970), 414–15.

54. Edwin Martin called amendments to ESEA minority amendments, by which he meant the target audience for the amendments were the white handicapped. Distinguishing Title I from the other titles, Martin said, "It was apparent, however, that the basic thrust of ESEA was toward the economically disadvantaged ... and that more direct sources of support for the handicapped would be necessary." Though Martin called ESEA "brilliant" and "precedent shattering," his sentiments about ESEA were a curious mix of policy envy and interest convergence. "Special education, the minority group," by which he implied white in contrast to the majority black and brown, "had once more been caught in the philosophy of the greatest good for the greatest number." In other words, white handicapped students were marginalized in the policy because of the attention Title I gave to black and brown students. For Martin, the interest of the white handicapped plateaued in ESEA. "While the creation of the Elementary and Secondary Education Act indirectly contributed to a plateau in the growth of federal support for education of the handicapped in the administrative dimension, its program did provide new support." Though the support appeared insignificant and buried under the weight of Title I, ESEA's passage admitted by Martin, "added new strength to the momentum of federal aid for education and to the concept of categorical aid for minority groups." Expressing his sentiments in 1968, Martin appeared hopeful due to the momentum he witnessed on behalf of white

handicapped children. "People vitally interested in the education of handicapped children, certain members of the conference committee and their staffs, professional groups and their members, and persons operating programs within the government which serve these children, worked, watched, waited, hoped, and eventually exulted over what they know were major breakthrough for handicapped children. The breakthroughs of 1966 and 1967 were the high points of the legislative accomplishments of almost a decade, and of efforts toward these accomplishments of many people over a much longer period of time." See Martin, "Breakthrough for the Handicapped: Legislative History," 415, 417, 422–23.

55. Frank B. Withrow, "Enlarged Responsibilities for Educational Services to Handicapped Children," *Exceptional Children* 34, no. 7 (March 1968): 551.

56. Only P. L. 83–531 (Cooperative Research) in 1957 and P. L. 85–926 (Professional Personnel) in 1958 focused on the mentally retarded for research and the training of school and institutional leaders. The 1963 amendment, P. L. 88–164, added more money and new disability categories to the policy. Frank B. Withrow, "Enlarged Responsibilities for Educational Services to Handicapped Children," *Exceptional Children* 34, no. 7 (March 1968): 420. See also William R. Carriker, "Research Related to the Education of Mentally Retarded Children," *School Life* 42, no. 5 (January 1960): 26–28, and Romaine P. Mackie and Patricia P. Robbins, "Exceptional Children in Local Public Schools," *School Life* 43, no. 3 (November 1960): 14–16.

57. Romaine P. Mackie, "Converging Circles—Education of the Handicapped and Some General Federal Programs," *Exceptional Children* 31, no. 5 (January 1965): 251.

58. Mackie, "Converging Circles." See also, Romaine P. Mackie, "Opportunities for Education of Handicapped under Title I, Public Law 89–10," *Exceptional Children* 32, no. 9 (May 1966): 593–98.

59. For an explanation of the differences between categorial and noncategorical policies, see, Anne M. Hocutt and Joni Alberg, "Case Studies of the Application of Categorical and Noncategorical Special Education," *Exceptionality*, 5, no. 4 (June 2010): 199–221.

60. Mackie, "Converging Circles—Education of the Handicapped and Some General Federal Programs," 251.

61. Morvin A. Wirtz and James C. Chalfant, "Elementary and Secondary Education Act: Implications for Handicapped Children," *Exceptional Children*, 31, no. 5 (November 1965): 139.

62. Wirtz and Chalfant, "Elementary and Secondary Education Act: Implications for Handicapped Children," 140.

63. Wirtz and Chalfant, "Elementary and Secondary Education Act: Implications for Handicapped Children," 140.

64. Edward Martin, "Breakthrough for the Handicapped: Legislative History," *Exceptional Children* (March 1968): 498.

65. Martin, "Breakthrough for the Handicapped," 499.

66. Public Law 89–313 specifically identified handicapped children covered under the law as "mentally retarded, hard of hearing, deaf, speech impaired, visually handicapped, seriously emotionally disturbed, crippled, or other health impaired children who by reason thereof require special education."

67. Samuel Kirk, House Committee on Education and Labor, Ad Hoc Subcommittee on the Handicapped, *Education and Training of the Handicapped: Elementary and Secondary Education Act of 1965,* 89th Congress, 1st Session, June 15, 1966, 383.

68. Samuel Kirk, "The Education of Handicapped Children Under Title III—ESEA, PL 89–10," *Hearings Before the United States Commission on Civil Rights,* Rochester, New York, September 16–17, 1966, 1, 23.

69. "1966—Special Education's Greatest Legislative Year," *Exceptional Children* (December 1966): 269.

70. "1966—Special Education's Greatest Legislative Year"; A 1968 ESEA document said the "responsibility for administration of Title VI has been assigned to the Special Education Section which administers the existing state educational programs for handicapped children. Since the objective of Title VI is identical with that of the state special education program, it is regarded an integral part of that program and is not to be distinguished from it except as necessary to comply with the fiscal and technical requirements of the Act." Most telling in the document is who was defined as handicapped. "The term 'handicapped children' as used in this title includes the mentally retarded, hard-of-hearing, deaf, speech impaired, visually handicapped, seriously emotionally disturbed, crippled, or other health impaired children who because of their handicaps require special education and related service." As a precursor to future educational disability policies, Title VI excluded culturally deprived/environmentally induced mentally retarded children as well as the social maladjusted, the two major special education identities associated with black students in the 1960s. "Guidelines for Title VI ESEA to Enable Schools to Initiate, Expand, Improve Programs for Handicapped Children," Minnesota Department of Education, Division of Special and Compensatory Education, January 1968, 1, 3. Minnesota Historical Society, Education Dept., Gov't Records, Desegregation/Integration Files, 1965–1996, Location: 126.J.9.6F.

71. Thomas B. Irvin, "Assistance to the States for Education of Handicapped Children under ESEA Title VI-A," *Exceptional Children* (March 1968): 565.

72. E. W. Martin quoted in *Identification of Learning Disabilities: Research to Practice,* eds., Renee Bradley, Louis Danielson, and Daniel P. Hallahan (Mahwah, N.J.: Lawrence Erlbaum Associates, 2002): 26. See also, chapter 2, "History of the Field," in *Learning Disabilities: From Identification to Intervention,* eds. Jack M. Fletcher, G. Reid Lyon, Lynn S. Fuchs, and Marcia A. Barnes (New York: Guilford, 2007).

73. Samuel Kirk, House Committee on Education and Labor, Ad Hoc Subcommittee on the Handicapped, *Education and Training of the Handicapped:*

Elementary and Secondary Education Act of 1965, 89th Congress, 1st Session, June 15, 1966, 385.

74. Romaine Mackie commented on this two-tiered system: "Challenging opportunities for the education of the handicapped were created by the passage of the Elementary and Secondary Education Act of 1965 and its amendments. The program of Compensatory Education authorized by Title I of the Act is aimed directly at improving the opportunities for educationally and culturally disadvantaged children. As such, it reaches out to encompass the handicapped child—who very often may also be the victim of his environment. It even offers the possibility of preventing and reversing handicapping conditions in children who suffer from environmental and cultural deprivation." One gets the sense that the legislative focus on the culturally and educationally deprived, the resources that flowed to them from Title I, and the way the law overshadowed white disabled bodies engendered some envy on the part of education bureaucrats. Much of this envy was a function of race, with over a billion dollars flowing to an undeserving disabled population whose disability seemed to be "compensatory" more than "biological." A particular line of reasoning emerged: black and brown students with environmentally induced disabilities that needed compensatory fixing via enrichment programs should not be even considered disabled. "It is evident that in the United States major changes are occurring rapidly within the general education system. The Compensatory Education program is offering a much more diversified school program which may significantly aid some functionally handicapped children. In fact, many may never need to be labeled handicapped." If these "functionally" disabled students need not be understood as handicapped, then they "may never need special education." Two things are revealing about Mackie's statement. One is the segregation of the black educationally disabled from white disabled children even though poor white children were educationally deprived. And second, Mackie's use of the phrase "challenging opportunities" further suggested that special education bureaucrats like Mackie and Kirk worked hard to make lawmakers and the public understand that compensatory and enrichment programs were designed for a disabled "Other." This was one of the reasons lawmakers kept asking for clarity. See Romaine P. Mackie, "The Handicapped Benefit under Compensatory Education Programs," *Exceptional Children* 34, no. 8 (April 1968): 603, 606.

75. Samuel Kirk, House Committee on Education and Labor, Ad Hoc Subcommittee on the Handicapped, *Education and Training of the Handicapped: Elementary and Secondary Education Act of 1965,* 89th Congress, 1st Session, June 15, 1966, 385.

76. ESEA Title I "Helped to Define the Role of Teaching Assistants in the Schools." See Susan B. Gerber, Jeremy D. Finn, Charles M. Achilles, and Jayne Boyd-Zaharias, "Teacher Aides in Students' Academic Achievement," *Educational Evaluation and Policy Analysis* 23, no. 2 (Summer 2001): 124; "The hiring of minority women was seen as a way to bridge language and cultural communication

gaps between home and school and to make children feel more comfortable in desegregated settings." See Karla C. Lewis, "Seen but Not Heard: ESEA and Instructional Aides in Elementary Education," *Review of Research in Education* 29 (2005): 133.

77. Samuel Kirk, House Committee on Education and Labor, and Ad Hoc Subcommittee on the Handicapped, *Education and Training of the Handicapped: Elementary and Secondary Education Act of 1965*, 385.

78. In September 1968, Congress did pass a stand-alone policy, P.L. 90–538 called the "Handicapped Children's Early Education Assistance Act." Authorizing and establishing the operation of preschool and early education programs, special education lobbyists saw it as distinct from preschool priorities of Headstart with a focus on "(1) mentally retarded, (2) hard of hearing, (3) speech impaired, (4) visually impaired, (5) seriously emotionally disturbed, (6) crippled and other health impaired who, by reason thereof, require special education and related services." George Sheperd, "The Early Education of Handicapped Children," *Focus on Exceptional Children* 3, no. 1 (March 1971): 2.

79. House Committee on Education and Labor, *Preschool and Early Education Programs for Handicapped Children: Hearings Before the Select Subcommittee on Education on H.R. 17829—A Bill to Authorize Preschool and Early Education Programs for Handicapped Children*, 90th Congress, 2nd Session, July 16–17, 1968, 67.

80. House Committee on Education and Labor, *Preschool and Early Education Programs for Handicapped Children*, 67.

81. House Committee on Education and Labor, *Preschool and Early Education Programs for Handicapped Children*, 70–71.

82. House Committee on Education and Labor, *Preschool and Early Education Programs for Handicapped Children*, 74.

83. Committee on Mental Retardation, "Programs for the Handicapped," Handicapped Children's Early Education Program, Public Law 91–230, Part C, Title V, October 25, 1971.

84. House Committee on Education and Labor, General Subcommittee on Education, *Hearings: Children with Learning Disabilities Act of 1969*, 91st Congress, 1st Session, July 8–10, 1969, 3.

85. House Committee on Education and Labor, General Subcommittee on Education, *Hearings*, 1–2.

86. Lennard J. Davis, *Enforcing Normalcy: Disability, Deafness, and the Body* (London: Verso, 1995).

87. House Committee on Education and Labor, General Subcommittee on Education, *Hearings: Children with Learning Disabilities Act of 1969*, 91st Congress, 1st Session, July 8–10, 1969, 168.

88. House Committee on Education and Labor, General Subcommittee on Education, *Hearings*, 54.

89. House Committee on Education and Labor, General Subcommittee on Education, *Hearings*, 43–44.

90. House Committee on Education and Labor, General Subcommittee on Education, *Hearings,* 54.

91. House Committee on Education and Labor, General Subcommittee on Education, *Hearings,* 23.

92. House Committee on Education and Labor, General Subcommittee on Education, *Hearings,* 59.

93. House Committee on Education and Labor, General Subcommittee on Education, *Hearings,* 89.

94. House Committee on Education and Labor, General Subcommittee on Education, *Hearings,* 89.

95. Samuel A. Kirk, *Educating Exceptional Children* (Boston: Houghton Mifflin, 1962), 263.

96. Barbara Bateman, "An Educational View of a Diagnostic Approach to Learning Disorders," in *Learning Disorders:* Vol. 1, ed. Jerome Hellmuth (Seattle, WA: Special Child Publications, 1965), 219; Barbara Bateman, "Learning Disabilities: An Overview," *Journal of School Psychology,* 3, no. 3 (Spring 1965): 1–12.

97. House Committee on Education and Labor, General Subcommittee on Education, *Hearings: Children with Learning Disabilities Act of 1969,* 91st Congress, 1st Session, July 8–10, 1969, 5–6.

98. House Committee on Education and Labor, General Subcommittee on Education, *Hearings,* 2.

99. House Committee on Education and Labor, General Subcommittee on Education, *Hearings,* 9.

100. House Committee on Education and Labor, General Subcommittee on Education, *Hearings,* 12.

101. House Committee on Education and Labor, General Subcommittee on Education, *Hearings,* 52.

102. House Committee on Education and Labor, General Subcommittee on Education, *Hearings,* 19.

103. House Committee on Education and Labor, General Subcommittee on Education, *Hearings,* 167.

104. House Committee on Education and Labor, General Subcommittee on Education, *Hearings,* 27.

105. "When President Nixon signed Public Law 91–230, the Elementary and Secondary Education Act Amendments of 1969, a few months ago, he consolidated all legislation for the handicapped into one Act. Title VI of the new law recalls separate authorities for the various Office of Education programs for the handicapped and consolidated them into a single 'Education for the Handicapped Act.'" See summaries of parts A to G of PL-91–230 in the section called "Washington Report," in *Focus on Exceptional Children* 2, no. 7 (December 1970): 14.

106. Edwin Martin, Martin LaVor, Trudy Bryan, and Rhona Scheflin, "PL 91–230, The Elementary and Secondary Education Act Amendments of 1969: Title VI,

The Education of the Handicapped Act," *Exceptional Children* 37, no. 1 (September 1970): 56.

107. HARYOU, "Educational Excellence in Harlem," *Integrated Education* 3, no. 3 (1964): 15.

108. HARYOU, "Educational Excellence in Harlem," 15.

109. One of the more interesting interpretations of grassroots movements and professional advocacy that led to policy and special education disproportionality is contained in Zach McCall and Thomas M. Skrtic, "Intersectional Needs Politics: A Policy Frame for the Wicked Problem of Disproportionality," *Multiple Voices for Ethnically Diverse Exceptional Learners* 11, no. 2 (2009): 3–23. McCall and Skrtic identify "wicked problems" as a set of professionalization, politicization, legalization, and bureaucratization discourses. The authors described the culmination of special education and civil rights policies in the 1960s and 1970s as a form of "expert depoliticization of oppositional needs."

110. Michael J. Herrick, "Disabled or Disadvantaged: What's the Difference?," *Journal of Special Education,* 7, no. 4 (1973): 381.

111. Herrick, "Disabled or Disadvantaged," 381.

112. Herrick, "Disabled or Disadvantaged," 42.

113. Jeannie Oakes, *Keeping Track: How Schools Structure Inequality* (New Haven, CT: Yale University Press, 1985).

4. Challenging Special Education from Above and Below

1. Howard S. Adelman, "The Not So Specific Learning Disability," *Exceptional Children* 37, no. 7 (March 1971): 528.

2. Anthropologist Ray McDermott indeed argued as such. "We might just as well say there is no such thing as LD, only a social practice of displaying, noticing, documenting, remediating, and explaining it. . . . Although the folk theory has it that the traits (an inability to pay attention, an occasional lapse in word access, trouble with phonics, etc.) belong to the child and are the source of both the disordered behavior and the subsequent label, it is possible to argue that it is the labels that precede any child's entry into the world and that these labels, well-established resting places in adult conversations, stand poised to take their share from each new generation." McDermott and a team of researchers videotaped a classroom of eight- and nine-year-old children in different settings from 1976 to 1978, examining the various learning characteristics of the children. McDermott remembered "after following Adam for 18 months, we gave up on specifying his traits as the explanation of his behavior and began talking instead about what happened around him daily that seemed to organize his moments as an LD person." Believing that LD is a cultural fabrication, McDermott asks us to consider how LD and other disabilities have a way of finding "us" rather than those who already have learning disabilities being found by "them" the experts. "LD exists as a category in our culture, and it will acquire a certain proportion of our children as long as it is given life in the organization of tasks, skills, and evaluations in our

schools." Ray P. McDermott, "The Acquisition of a Child by a Learning Disability," in *In Understanding Practice*, eds. Seth Chaiklin and Jean Lave (New York: Cambridge University Press, 1993), 269–305. Other scholars argued that if LD is not made up, then it is a distinction without a difference or certainly not worth the attention it was being given in the late 1960s and early 1970s. "A review of the literature on learning disabilities strongly suggests that there is no need for another psychological or medical definition of that population whose achievement does not coincide with its assumed potential. Already there has been much time expended in attempts to delineate this learning disabilities population as has been spent in its actual diagnosis and treatment." See Thomas C. Lovitt, "Assessment of Children with Learning Disabilities," *Exceptional Children* 34, no. 4 (December 1967): 233.

3. William Cruickshank remembers keeping track of all the parents he met during his professional activities asking him if their child had a "learning disability." "In toto slightly more than 300 different inquiries have been received. In more than half of these a combination of neuropsychological factors brought the question within the arena of the topic on which I had spoken. However, parents attending a lecture on learning disabilities also have seen fit in a public forum to question me about their child who stuttered, who teased the family cat, who could not deal with geometry in the 10th grade but who otherwise was getting along well in school, who had night terrors, who was diagnosed by the family psychiatrist as depressed—all of these things under the label learning disabilities. I have had parents question me on the failure of the child of 9 years of age to be able to swim, another who could type but not legibly, another who masturbated, and still another who didn't like to go with girls. Parents in their concept of learning disability who talked with me about nail biting, poor eating habits, failure of the child to keep his room neat, unwillingness to take a bath and brush his teeth. Teachers have questioned me about disrespectful children, children who will not listen to the adult, children who cry, children who hate, children who are sexually precocious, children who are aggressive—all in the belief that these are learning disability children. One parent asked me if the fact that his college-student son wore long hair and he 'suspected' lived with a girl outside his dormitory was the result of a learning disability?" William M. Cruickshank, "Some Issues Facing the Field of Learning Disability," *Journal of Learning Disabilities* 5, no. 7 (August/September 1972): 382.

4. Lloyd M. Dunn, "Special Education for the Mildly Retarded—Is Much of It Justifiable?," *Exceptional Children* (September 1968): 6; *Hobson v. Hansen*, 269 F. Supp. 401, US District Court District of Columbia (1967). For a comprehensive analysis of Dunn's ideas and of special education for EMR students as it stood in 1970, see Donald L. MacMillan, "Special Education for the Mildly Retarded: Servant or Savant," *Focus on Exceptional Children* 2, no. 9 (February 1971): 1–11. Also see, Ernest Siegel, "Learning Disabilities: Substance or Shadow," *Exceptional Children* 34, no. 6 (February 1968): 433–38.

5. President's Committee on Mental Retardation, *The Six-Hour Retarded Child,* 1970, iii.

6. A. Harry Passow, *Toward Creating a Model Urban School System: A Study of Washington, D.C. Public Schools* (New York: Teachers College, Columbia University, 1967), 470.

7. *Hobson v. Hansen,* 269 F. Supp. 401, US District Court District of Columbia (1967), 443; Carl F. Hansen, *The Four-Track Curriculum in Today's High Schools* (Englewood Cliffs, N.J.: Prentice-Hall, 1964).

8. Hansen, *The Four-Track Curriculum in Today's High Schools,* 442.

9. David J. Franks, "Ethnic and Social Status Characteristics of Children in EMR and LD Classes," *Exceptional Children* (March 1971): 537–38.

10. Christine E. Sleeter, "Learning Disabilities: The Social Construction of a Special Education Category," in *Critical Voices on Special Education: Problems and Progress Concerning the Mildly Handicapped,* ed. Scott B. Sigmon (Albany: State University of New York Press, 1990), 28–29.

11. Grotberg is one of the first to observe that culturally deprived and educationally disadvantaged students do have learning disabilities. Experienced in working with Head Start children, she wrote, "Research studies with anything more than a broad description of the characteristics of disadvantaged children as the basis for research on learning disabilities are disappointingly few. The cumulative effects of social and cultural background provide further information about learning disabilities of disadvantaged children." Edith H. Grotberg, "Learning Disabilities and Remediation in Disadvantaged Children," *Review of Educational Research* 35, no. 5 (December 1965): 420, 422.

12. While some began arguing that the culturally deprived are also learning disabled, some cast doubt on the neurological basis of learning disability. Herbert Grossman, head of the pediatric-neurology service at the University of Illinois, College of Medicine wrote: "The physician often talks of 'soft' neurological signs. Such signs are often minimal and, in themselves, do not reflect any profound disturbance of motor function. They cannot be specifically correlated with learning or behavior problems. Actually, there is no syndrome, no aggregate of neurological signs, that can correlate with any specific learning and/or behavior disorder." See Herbert J. Grossman, "The Child, the Teacher, and the Physician," in *The Teacher of Brain-Injured Children: A Discussion of the Bases for Competency,* ed. William M. Cruickshank (Syracuse, N.Y.: Syracuse University Press, 1966), 63.

13. Edith Grotberg, "Neurological Aspects of Learning Disabilities: A Case for the Disadvantaged," *Journal of Learning Disabilities* 3, no. 6 (June 1970): 25.

14. Grotberg, "Neurological Aspects of Learning Disabilities."

15. Grotberg, "Neurological Aspects of Learning Disabilities."

16. Grotberg, "Neurological Aspects of Learning Disabilities," 25, 29.

17. Murray M. Kappelman, Eugene Kaplan, and Robert L. Ganter, "A Study of Learning Disorders among Disadvantaged Children," *Journal of Learning Disabilities,* 2, no. 5 (May 1969): 27.

18. Kappelman, Kaplan, and Ganter, "A Study of Learning Disorders among Disadvantaged Children," 32.

19. John L. Johnson, "Special Education and the Inner City: A Challenge for the Future or Another Means for Cooling the Mark Out?," *Journal of Special Education* 3, no. 3 (October 1969): 245.

20. M. Stephen Lilly, "Special Education: A Teapot in a Tempest," *Exceptional Children* (September 1970): 43.

21. Lilly, "A Teapot in a Tempest," 43–44.

22. Evelyn Deno, "Special Education as Developmental Capital," *Exceptional Children* (November 1970): 231.

23. Maynard C. Reynolds, "Categories and Variables in Special Education," in *Exceptional Children in Regular Classrooms,* eds. Maynard C. Reynolds and Malcolm D. Davis (Minneapolis: Distributed by Dept. of Audio-Visual Extension, University of Minnesota, 1971), 57. Also see two young professors at the University of Minnesota whose work greatly contributed to the field of special education in the 1970s, Robert H. Bruininks and John E. Rynders, "Alternatives to Special Class Placement for Educable Mentally Retarded Children," *Focus on Exceptional Children,* 3, no. 4 (September 1971): 1-12.

24. Deno, "Special Education as Developmental Capital," 236.

25. Reginald L. Jones, ed., *Mainstreaming and the Minority Child* (Minneapolis: Leadership Training Institute/Special Education, 1976), 2.

26. Jones, *Mainstreaming and the Minority Child.*

27. Wilton Anderson, "Who Gets a 'Special Education'?," in *Exceptional Children in Regular Classrooms,* ed. Maynard C. Reynolds and Malcolm D. Davis (Minneapolis: Distributed by Dept. of Audio-Visual Extension, University of Minnesota, 1971), 6.

28. Reginald L. Jones and Frank B. Wilderson Jr. wrote, "From the perspective of minority group members, self-contained special classes were to be indicted on several accounts, including but not limited to beliefs (a) that minority group children were overrepresented in special classes, particularly for the mentally retarded; (b) that assessment practices are biased; (c) that special education labels are stigmatizing; and (d) that teachers hold negative attitudes towards the potential of minority group children." See Jones and Wilderson, *Mainstreaming and the Minority Child,* 3.

29. *Pennsylvania Association for Retarded Children (PARC) v. Commonwealth of Pennsylvania,* 343 F. Supp. 279; 1972 U.S. Dist. Lexis 13874, 3.

30. Statute quoted in *PARC v. Commonwealth of Pennsylvania,* 3.

31. Consent agreement quoted in *PARC v. Commonwealth of Pennsylvania,* 6.

32. *Mills v. Board of Education of the District of Columbia,* 348 F. Supp. 866 (D.D.C. 1972), p. 10.

33. President Ford said, "I have today approved s. 6, the 'Education for All Handicapped Children Act of 1975.' I have signed this bill very reluctantly since it promises more than the Federal Government can deliver ...," Draft Signing

Statement, November 28, 1975, Box 33, folder "11/29/75 S6 Education for All Handicapped Children Act of 1975 (1)," White House Records Office: Legislation Case Files, Gerald R. Ford Presidential Library.

34. Erwin C. Hargrove, Scarlett G. Graham, Leslie E. Ward, Virginia Abernathy, Joseph Cunningham, and William K. Vaughn, "Regulation and Schools: The Implementation of Equal Education for Handicapped Children," *Peabody Journal of Education,* 60, no. 4 (Summer 1983): 1

35. Hargrove, et al., "Regulation and Schools," 5.

36. Kathryn M. Coates, "The Education for All Handicapped Children Act since 1975," *Marquette Law Review,* 69 (Fall 1985): 56.

37. Hargrove et al., "Regulation and Schools," 11.

38. Hargrove et al., "Regulation and Schools," 11.

39. Summary of the Principal Provisions of S. 6, "The Education for All Handicapped Children Act of 1975," Box 33, Folder, "11/29/75 S6 Education for All Handicapped Children Act of 1975."

40. Summary of the Principal Provisions of S. 6.

41. Tish Howard, Sandy Grogan, and Dennis R. Dunklee, *Poverty is not a Learning Disability: Equalizing Opportunities for Low SES Students* (Thousand Oaks, CA: Corwin, 2009).

42. Kenneth A. Kavale, "Learning Disability and Cultural-Economic Disadvantage: The Case for a Relationship," *Learning Disability Quarterly,* 11, no. 3 (Summer 1988): 196.

43. How the federal government defined disability and the how the states defined and covered students considered disabled sometimes matched. Too often, the federal government and the states were not in alignment. One scholar said it was naïve to expect them to be on the same page. "There exists today a multitude of classification systems predicated on varying and diverse definitions of handicapping conditions. To assume consensus of definition is naïve at best. Federal definitions are vague and ambiguous and are themselves filled with undefined terms. Individual states do not necessarily have to adopt definitions provided in federal statutes, and many of them choose not to do so. As a result, there is a wide range of definitions found among the 50 states." See David P. Frasse, "Legal Influence and Educational Policy in Special Education," *Exceptional Children* 54, no. 4 (January 1988): 304.

44. Rogers Elliott, *Litigating Intelligence: IQ Tests, Special Education and Social Science in the Courtroom* (Dover, MA: Auburn House, 1987), 13.

45. "In October 1970, the Bay Area Association of Black Psychologists proposed a moratorium on tests of intelligence and scholastic ability in the assessment of Black children. The Association of Psychologists of *La Raza* has petitioned the American Psychological Association and various governmental agencies to remedy inequalities in job placement and educational opportunities resulting from the misinterpretation of IQ tests given to persons of Chicano heritage. They have charged that standardized tests were used in the misplacement of Chicano

children in classes for the mentally retarded." See Jane R. Mercer, "A Policy Statement on Assessment Procedures and the Rights of Children," *Harvard Educational Review* 44, no. 1 (February 1974): 138.

46. Quoted in Robert I. Williams, "Black Pride, Academic Relevance and Individual Achievement," *Counseling Psychologist,* 2, no. 1 (Spring 1970): 20.

47. Williams, "Black Pride, Academic Relevance and Individual Achievement."

48. Williams, "Black Pride, Academic Relevance and Individual Achievement."

49. *Larry P. v. Riles,* 495 F. Supp. 926, 1979 U.S. Dist. Court, Northern District of California, 15, Lexis 9121.

50. *Larry P. v. Riles.*

51. *Larry P. v. Riles,* 11.

52. *Larry P. v. Riles,* 16.

53. Ashley Montagu, *Race and IQ* (New York: Oxford University Press, 1999), 6, 32–33; Paul Davis Chapman, *Schools as Sorters: Lewis M. Terman, Applied Psychology, and the Intelligence Testing Movement, 1890–1930* (New York: New York University Press 1988); R. C. Scheerenberger, *A History of Mental Retardation* (Baltimore: Paul H. Brookes, 1983).

54. Arthur R. Jensen, "How Much Can We Boost IQ and Scholastic Achievement," *Harvard Educational Review* 39 (1969): 29, 42; Ronald J. Samuda, *Psychological Testing of American Minorities: Issues and Consequences* (New York: Dodd, Mead & Company, 1975), 36–42.

55. Elliot, *Litigating Intelligence,* 6.

56. Elliot, *Litigating Intelligence,* 23–24.

57. Quoted in *Larry P. v. Riles,* 27; Herbert J. Grossman, *Manual on Terminology and Classification in Mental Retardation* (Washington, D.C.: American Association on Mental Deficiency, 1977).

58. Quoted in Mercer, "A Policy Statement on Assessment Procedures and the Rights of Children," 139.

59. *Larry P. v. Riles,* 29.

60. *Larry P. v. Riles,* 30.

61. *Larry P. v. Riles.*

62. *Larry P. v. Riles,* 31.

63. *Larry P. v. Riles.*

64. *Parents in Action on Special Education (PASE) v. Hannon,* 506 F. Supp. 831, 1980 U.S. Dist. Court, Northern District of Illinois, Eastern District, Lexis 12433.

65. *Parents in Action on Special Education (PASE) v. Hannon,* 2.

66. *Parents in Action on Special Education (PASE) v. Hannon,* 3.

67. *Parents in Action on Special Education (PASE) v. Hannon,* 4.

68. *Parents in Action on Special Education (PASE) v. Hannon.*

69. *Parents in Action on Special Education (PASE) v. Hannon,* 44.

70. Donald R. Moore, *Voice and Change in Chicago,* Designs for Change, March 1989, paper prepared for the Conference on Choice and Control in American

Education, University of Wisconsin Madison, May 17–19, 1989, Harold Washington Library Center, Chicago Public Library.

71. Designs for Change, "Caught in the Web: Misplaced Children in Chicago's Classes for the Mentally Retarded," December 1982, Harold Washington Library Center, Chicago Public Library, xiii.

72. Designs for Change, "Caught in the Web," ix.

73. Quoted in Dionne Danns, *Desegregating Chicago's Public Schools: Policy Implementation, Politics, and Protest, 1965–1985* (New York: Palgrave Macmillan, 2014), 122.

74. Michael Zielenziger, "Chicago on Collision Course with U.S. on Desegregation," *Washington Post,* October 13, 1979, washingtonpost.com/archive/politics/1979/10/13 (accessed on September 3, 2020).

75. Danns, *Desegregating Chicago's Public Schools,* 123.

76. Designs for Change, "Caught in the Web," 25.

77. *Corey H. v. Board of Education of the City of Chicago,* 995 F. Supp. 900 (N.D. Ill. 1998).

78. Adam R. Nelson, *The Elusive Ideal: Equal Educational Opportunity and the Federal Role in Boston's Public Schools, 1950–1985* (Chicago: University of Chicago Press, 2005).

79. Milton Budoff, "Engendering Change in Special Education Practices," *Harvard Educational Review* 45, no. 4 (December 1975): 510.

80. Nelson, *The Elusive Ideal,* 152. For the failure of case law and federal policy to change conditions for students of color in special education, see Donald L. Macmillan, Irving G. Hendrick, and Alice Watkins, "Impact of *Diana, Larry P.,* and P.L. 94–142 on Minority Students," *Exceptional Children* 54, no. 5 (February 1988): 426–32.

81. *PASE v. Hannon,* 1.

82. "The total litigation in California may be summarized as follows: a) total EMR enrollments decreased by 50% or more, b) the proportion of ethnic minority students in EMR was reduced, and c) the IQ cut-off was lowered, and the average IQ in EMR classes was reduced." See Donald L. MacMillan and Sharon Borthwick, "The New Educable Mentally Retarded Population: Can They Be Mainstreamed?" *Mental Retardation* 18, no. 4 (August 1, 1980): 155.

83. Mark Shinn and Doug Marston, "Differentiating Mildly Handicapped, Low-Achieving, and Regular Education Students: A Curriculum-Based Approach," *Remedial and Special Education* 6, no. 2 (March/April 1985): 31; Lonny R. Wilson, "Large-Scale Learning Disability Identification: The Reprieve of a Concept," *Exceptional Children* 52, no. 1 (September 1985): 44–51; Kenneth A. Kavale, Douglas Fuchs, and Thomas E. Scruggs, "Setting the Record Straight on Learning Disability and Low Achievement: Implications for Policy-Making," *Learning Disabilities Research & Practice* 9, no. 2 (1994): 70–77.

84. Diane Divoky, "Learning-Disability 'Epidemic,'" *New York Times,* January 15, 1975. Reprinted in *Journal of Learning Disabilities* 8, no. 5 (May 1975).

85. James A. Tucker, "Ethnic Proportions in Classes for the Learning Disabled: Issues in Nonbiased Assessment," *Journal of Special Education* 14, no. 1 (April 1980): 93–105.

86. Tucker, "Ethnic Proportions in Classes for the Learning Disabled"; Jean Kealy and John McLeod, "Learning Disability and Socioeconomic Status," *Journal of Learning Disabilities* 9, no. 9 (November 1976): 64–67; Faye L. Brosnan, "Overrepresentation of Low-Socioeconomic Minority Students in Special Education Programs in California," *Learning Disability Quarterly* 6, no. 4 (Autumn 1983): 517–25; Pamela Wright and Rafaela Santa Cruz, "Ethnic Composition of Special Education Programs in California," *Learning Disability Quarterly* 6, no. 4 (Autumn 1983): 387–94. A later study of California revealed the exponential growth of learning disability for black and Latinx students between 1976 to 1998, especially in districts with 50 percent or less black and brown students: "By 1998, black students were much more likely than white students to be identified as learning disabled, and Hispanic students were more likely than white students to be classified in that way in a wide range of school districts. Adding an interaction between race and minority proportion allows us to see more precisely that, in 1986 and 1998, local minority overrepresentation was especially pronounced in low-minority districts." See Colin Ong-Dean, "High Roads and Low Roads: Learning Disabilities in California, 1976–1998," *Sociological Perspectives* 49, no. 1 (Spring 2006): 101.

87. John T. Neisworth and John G. Greer, "Functional Similarities of Learning Disability and Mild Retardation," *Exceptional Children* 42, no. 1 (September 1975).

88. Kenneth A. Kavale, "Learning Disability and Cultural-Economic Disadvantage: The Case for a Relationship," *Learning Disability Quarterly* 11, no. 3 (Summer 1988): 195–210.

89. For a cross comparison of all disability categories by state, the rise of LD and the decline of EMR, see Daniel P. Hallahan, Clayton E. Keller, and Donald W. Ball, "A Comparison of Prevalence Rate Variability from State to State for Each of the Categories of Special Education," *Remedial and Special Education* 7, no. 2 (March/April 1986): 8–14. The differences in state LD and EMR numbers vary greatly. In some states, such as Rhode Island, Delaware, Louisiana, Connecticut, Massachusetts, Maryland, New Hampshire, New Jersey, Minnesota, Illinois, Iowa, Oregon, and Texas, the prevalence percentages for LD were astoundingly high, seemingly highest in New England and Midwestern states with no rhyme or reason. My theory is that many school districts in New England and Midwestern states outside of large metropolitan cities held student of color populations below 50 percent.

90. In addition to a lack of a clear federal disability definition for EMR and LD and divergent state prevalence numbers, what a student could be in one state may not be what he or she was in another. "The variations in terminology and classifications are quite large, so much so that the same student may be classified

as exceptional in one state, but regarded as below average in another, or a student's classification may change from LD to EMR simply by crossing state lines." See Daniel J. Reschly, "Beyond IQ Test Bias: The National Academy Panel's Analysis of Minority Overrepresentation," *Educational Researcher* 13, no. 3 (March 1984): 17.

91. James Ysseldyke and Bob Algozzine, *Critical Issues in Special and Remedial Education* (Boston: Houghton Mifflin, 1982), 11.

92. Nelson, *The Elusive Ideal,* 133.

93. Quoted in Divoky, "Learning-Disability 'Epidemic.'"

94. Neisworth and Greer, "Functional Similarities of Learning Disability and Mild Retardation," 18.

95. Neisworth and Greer, "Functional Similarities of Learning Disability and Mild Retardation"; Herbert J. Grossman, "The Child, the Teacher, and the Physician," in *The Teacher of Brain-Injured Children,* ed. William M. Cruickshank (Syracuse, N.Y.: Syracuse University Press, 1966).

96. Lester Mann et al., "LD or Not LD, That Was the Question: A Retrospective Analysis of Child Service Demonstration Centers' Compliance With the Federal Definition of Learning Disabilities," *Journal of Learning Disabilities* 16, no. 1 (January 1983): 15.

97. Mann et al., "LD or Not LD, That Was the Question," 15.

98. Mann et al., "LD or Not LD, That Was the Question," 17.

99. Mann et al., "LD or Not LD, That Was the Question," 16.

100. James Tucker, Linda J. Stevens, and James Ysseldyke, "Learning Disabilities: The Experts Speak Out," *Journal of Learning Disabilities* 16, no. 1 (January 1983): 6–13.

101. Bob Algozzine and James Ysseldyke, "Learning Disabilities as a Subset of School Failure: The Over-Sophistication of a Concept," *Exceptional Children* 50, no. 3 (November 1983): 243.

102. Mann et al., "LD or Not LD, That Was the Question," 9.

103. Jean Kealy and John McLeod, "Learning Disability and Socioeconomic Status," *Journal of Learning Disabilities* 9, no. 9 (November 1976): 65.

104. Kealy and McLeod, "Learning Disability and Socioeconomic Status," 66.

105. Samuel A. Kirk, *Educating Exceptional Children* (Boston: Houghton Mifflin, 1962); Association for Children with Learning Disabilities (ACLD).

106. Specific Learning Disabilities Act, 1969; National Advisory Committee on Handicapped Children.

107. William Frankenberger and Jerry Harper, "States' Criteria and Procedures for Identifying Learning Disabled Children: A Comparison of 1981/82 and 1985/86 Guidelines," *Journal of Learning Disabilities* 20, no. 2 (February 1987): 118–21; William Frankenberger and Kathryn Fronzaglio, "A Review of States' Criteria and Procedures for Identifying Children with Learning Disabilities," *Journal of Learning Disabilities* 24, no. 8 (October 1991): 495–500; James McLeskey and Nancy L. Waldron, "Identifying Students with Learning Disabilities: The Effect

of Implementing Statewide Guidelines," *Journal of Learning Disabilities* 24, no. 8 (October 1991): 501–506.

108. Samuel A. Kirk and Winifred D. Kirk, "On Defining Learning Disabilities," *Journal of Learning Disabilities* 16, no. 1 (January 1983): 20.

109. Bob Algozzine, Charles Forgnone, Cecil Mercer, and John Trifiletti, "Toward Defining Discrepancies for Specific Learning Disabilities: An Analysis and Alternatives," *Learning Disability Quarterly* 2, no. 4 (Autumn 1979): 25–32; James E. Ysseldyke and Mark Shinn, "Identifying Children with Learning Disabilities: When Is a Discrepancy Severe?," *Journal of School Psychology* 20, no. 4 (1982): 299–305; A Position Statement by the Board of Trustees of the Council of Learning Disabilities, "Use of Discrepancy Formulas in the Identification of Learning Disabled Individuals," *Learning Disability Quarterly* 9, no. 3 (Summer 1986): 245.

110. Kirk and Kirk, "On Defining Learning Disabilities," 20.

111. Federal Register, Department of Health, Education and Welfare, Office of Education: Part III, December, 1977.

112. Louis C. Danielson and Jane Bauer, "A Formula-Based Classification of Learning Disabled Children: An Examination of the Issues," *Journal of Learning Disabilities* 11, no. 3 (March 1978): 50. This essay is an analysis of the comments and testimony made about the federal regulations.

113. Algozzine and Ysseldyke, "Learning Disabilities as a Subset of School Failure," 243; Bob Algozzine, "Low Achiever Differentiation: Where's the Beef?," *Exceptional Children* 52, no. 1 (September 1985): 75.

114. Samuel A. Kirk and John Elkins, "Characteristics of Children Enrolled in the Child Service Demonstration Centers," *Journal of Learning Disabilities* 8, no. 10 (December 1975): 31.

115. Kirk and Elkins, "Characteristics of Children Enrolled in the Child Service Demonstration Centers," 31.

116. Kirk and Elkins, "Characteristics of Children Enrolled in the Child Service Demonstration Centers," 36.

117. Kirk and Elkins, "Characteristics of Children Enrolled in the Child Service Demonstration Centers," 36.

118. Kirk and Elkins, "Characteristics of Children Enrolled in the Child Service Demonstration Centers," 37.

119. Kirk and Elkins, "Characteristics of Children Enrolled in the Child Service Demonstration Centers," 37.

120. A Position Statement by the Board of Trustees of the Council of Learning Disabilities, "Inclusion of Non-Handicapped Low-Achievers and Underachievers in Learning Disability Programs," *Learning Disability Quarterly* 9, no. 3 (Summer 1986): 246.

121. Bob Algozzine and James E. Ysseldyke, "Questioning Discrepancies: Retaking the First Step 20 Years Later," *Learning Disability Quarterly* 10, no. 4 (Autumn 1987): 309.

122. Algozzine and Ysseldyke, "Questioning Discrepancies: Retaking the First Step 20 Years Later," 309.

123. Algozzine and Ysseldyke, "Questioning Discrepancies: Retaking the First Step 20 Years Later," 310.

124. Algozzine and Ysseldyke, "Learning Disabilities as a Subset of School Failure," 246.

125. T. T. Lovitt quoted in Algozzine and Ysseldyke, "Questioning Discrepancies," 311.

126. Ray McDermott, Jason D. Riley and Ingrid Seyer-Ochi, "Race and Class in a Culture of Risk," *Review of Research in Education* 33 (2009): 106.

127. Thomas G. Finlan, *Learning Disability: The Imaginary Disease* (Westport, CT: Bergin & Garvey, 1994), 1–10. Much of the work on the myth of learning disabilities is built from the many works of Thomas S. Szasz. See Thomas S. Szasz, *The Manufacture of Madness: A Comparative Study of the Inquisition and the Mental Health Movement* (New York: Harper & Row, 1970).

128. Finlan, *Learning Disability: The Imaginary Disease,* 9.

129. Lloyd M. Dunn, "Children with Mild General Learning Disabilities," in *Exceptional Children in the Schools: Special Education in Transition,* ed. Lloyd M. Dunn (New York: Holt, Rinehart and Winston, 1973), 131; see also Mary S. Poplin, "The Severely Learning Disabled: Neglected or Forgotten?," *Learning Disability Quarterly* 4, no. 4 (Autumn 1981): 330.

130. Dunn, "Children with Mild General Learning Disabilities," 133.

5. Emotional Behavior Disorder and Other Conduct Problems

1. Samuel K. Roberts Jr., *Infectious Fear: Politics, Disease, and the Health Effects of Segregation* (Chapel Hill: University of North Carolina Press, 2009); Michael Yudell, *Race Unmasked: Biology and Race in the 20th Century* (New York: Columbia University Press, 2014).

2. Jonathan M. Metzl, *The Protest Psychosis: How Schizophrenia Became a Black Disease* (Boston: Beacon, 2009); E. Y. Williams, "The Incidence of Mental Disease in the Negro," *Journal of Negro Education* 6, no. 3 (July 1937): 377–92.

3. EBD, written by some researchers as E/BD means emotional *or* behavior disorder. The term is a combination of two related but independent categories, ED (emotional disturbance), which has been around since the early twentieth century, and BD (behavior disorder), which began appearing more frequently in the mid-twentieth century. ED and BD, or the merged term EBD, are designations used by states and not by the federal government. Some states used EH (emotionally handicapped) to describe emotionally disturbed students. The federal equivalent is SED, seriously emotionally disturbed. SED was first used in the early 1960s, well before the passage of the Education of All Handicapped Children's Act in 1975 (EHA-P.L. 94–142). The federal label, SED, first appeared in the 1963, then in 1970 in the regulations implementing P.L. 91–230 (ESEA-Title VI) but received its greatest policy recognition under P.L. 94–142 (EHA-1975). I generally

use the term EBD in the chapter but will use the terms ED, BD, EH, and SED when historically appropriate, or referred to by a school, an author, or utilized by a source.

4. Russell Skiba and Kenneth Grizzle, "The Social Maladjustment Exclusion: Issues of Definition and Assessment," *School Psychology Review* 20, no. 4 (1991): 580–94.

5. Edward B. Reuter, "Why the Presence of the Negro Constitutes a Problem in the American Social Order," *Journal of Negro Education* 8, no. 3 (July 1939): 294.

6. Richard R. Valencia, ed., *The Evolution of Deficit Thinking: Educational Thought and Practice* (London: Routledge Falmer, 1997).

7. Valencia, *The Evolution of Deficit Thinking*; William Ryan, *Blaming the Victim* (New York: Vintage, 1972).

8. Valencia, *The Evolution of Deficit Thinking.*

9. Gunnar Myrdal, *An American Dilemma: The Negro Problem and Modern Democracy* (New York: Harper & Brothers, 1944).

10. Helen V. McLean, "Psychodynamic Factors in Racial Relations," *Annals of the American Academy of Political and Social Science* 244 (March 1946): 159.

11. Helen V. McLean, "The Emotional Health of Negroes," *Journal of Negro Education* 18, no. 3 (Summer 1949): 287–88.

12. Harry Manuel Shulman, "Intelligence and Delinquency," *Journal of Criminal Law and Criminology* 41, no. 6 (March/April 1951): 768; Karl Birnbaum wrote, "Major problems in the handling of juvenile offenders in court are presented by cases that are not psychotic but plainly pathologic; they are diagnostically labeled mental defectives, defective delinquents, constitutional psychopaths, or sexual psychopaths." See Karl Birnbaum, "A Court Psychiatrist's View of Juvenile Delinquents," *Annals of the American Academy of Political and Social Science* 261 (January 1949): 55.

13. Birnbaum, "A Court Psychiatrist's View," 770–71.

14. Birnbaum, "A Court Psychiatrist's View," 769.

15. Clifford R. Shaw and Henry D. McKay, *Juvenile Delinquency and Urban Areas* (Chicago: University of Chicago Press, 1969).

16. Shaw and McKay, *Juvenile Delinquency and Urban Areas*, 173.

17. Harry Manuel Shulman, "Intelligence and Delinquency," *Journal of Criminal Law and Criminology* 41, no. 6 (March/April 1951): 775.

18. Shulman, "Intelligence and Delinquency," 776.

19. Shulman, "Intelligence and Delinquency," 776.

20. R. L. Jenkins and Sylvia Glickman, "Common Syndromes in Child Psychiatry: Deviant Behavior Traits," *American Journal of Orthopsychiatry* 16, no. 2 (April 1946): 250–51. See also Bernice Milburn Moore, *Juvenile Delinquency: Research, Theory and Comment* (Washington, D.C.: Association for Supervision and Curriculum Development, NEA, 1958), 17–18.

21. Thorsten Sellin, "Unraveling Juvenile Delinquency: A Symposium of Review," *Journal of Criminal Law and Criminology (1931–1951)* 41, no. 6 (March/April 1951): 741.

22. Sellin, "Unraveling Juvenile Delinquency."

23. Sellin, "Unraveling Juvenile Delinquency."

24. Shulman, "Intelligence and Delinquency," 775, 777.

25. Edwin Powers, "The School's Responsibility for the Early Detection of Delinquency-Prone Children," *Harvard Educational Review* 19, no. 2 (Spring 1949): 80–86; Selma J. Glick, "Spotting Potential Delinquents," *Exceptional Children* 20, no. 8 (May 1954): 342–59; Gordon P. Waldo and Nason E. Hall, "Delinquency Potential and Attitudes toward the Criminal Justice System," *Social Forces* 49, no. 2 (December 1970): 291–98.

26. Roderick Pugh, "A Comparative Study of the Adjustment of Negro Students in Mixed and Separate High Schools," *Journal of Negro Education* 12, no. 4 (Autumn 1943): 608.

27. Hans von Hentig, "The Criminality of the Negro," *Journal of Criminal Law and Criminology* 30, no. 5 (January/February 1940): 662.

28. Manuel Lopez-Rey, "Juvenile Delinquency, Maladjustment, and Maturity," *Journal of Criminal Law, Criminology, and Police Science* 51, no. 1 (May/June 1960): 38.

29. Lopez-Rey, "Juvenile Delinquency, Maladjustment and Maturity," 39.

30. Erdman Palmore, "Factors Associated with School Dropouts and Juvenile Delinquency among Lower-Class Children," *Social Security Bulletin* 26, no. 10 (October 1963): 9.

31. Palmore, "Factors Associated with School Dropouts," 7. Palmore went on to racialize and gender juvenile delinquency as black and male and who are mentally retarded and school dropouts: "The first four factors—race, sex, intelligence, and school status—are primarily individual characteristics and are most strongly related to delinquency. Being nonwhite almost doubles the probability of delinquency, and being male quadruples the probability. The probability of delinquency for those with below-average intelligence, and dropping out of school more than doubles the probability of delinquency."

32. Edward H. Stullken, "Schools and the Delinquency Problem," *Journal of Criminal Law, Criminology, and Police Science* 43, no. 5 (January/February 1953): 573.

33. Stullken, "Schools and the Delinquency Problem," 572.

34. Jack W. Birch, "Special Classes and Schools for Maladjusted Children," *Exceptional Children* 22, no. 8 (May 1956): 332.

35. Herbert C. Quay, William C. Morse, and Richard L. Cutler, "Personality Patterns of Pupils in Special Classes for the Emotionally Disturbed," in *Educating Emotionally Disturbed Children,* ed. Henry Dupont (New York: Holt, Rinehart and Winston, 1969), 33.

36. Edward H. Stullken, "Education of the Socially Handicapped," *Phi Delta Kappan* 23, no. 2 (October 1940): 68.

37. Montefiore Special School, also known later as Moses Montefiore Academy, was a "social adjustment" school, opening in September 1929 on 461 North Sangamon Street, on the Northwest side of Chicago, serving "underprivileged and unadjusted boys," or "truants and incorrigibles." The school subsequently moved to 655 West Fourteenth Street, then 1310 South Ashland Avenue, both westside locations. The students were transferred from Chicago Public Schools and from some Cook County Schools. In the early years, the racial demographics of Montefiore were predominantly Polish, Italian, and black, all of whom were overrepresented at Montefiore versus their numbers in the city population. As the demographics of the city changed, so too did the racial composition of Montefiore, which became more African American and Latinx after 1960. "While the socially maladjusted boys at Montefiore . . . exhibited those characteristics associated with the 'poor' and 'culturally disadvantaged,' they also had serious educational problems," said Mary Ann Pollett. "Many boys had language and reading disabilities and 76% [*sic*] of the boys were 'academically retarded,' i.e., their educational age was one to three+ years less their chronological age." The median IQ was 80. See Mary Ann Pollett, "A Study of Social Adjustment Education in Chicago, 1929–1981," (PhD diss., Loyola University Chicago, 1982); see also Edward H. Stullken, "Special Education in Chicago," *Exceptional Children* 2, no. 3 (December 1935): 73–75; Edward H. Stullken, "How the Montefiore School Prevents Crime," *Journal of Criminal Law and Criminology* 26, no. 2 (July 1935): 228–34. The Montefiore School was the subject of a VICE-TV documentary entitled *Last Chance High* in 2014 highlighting the dwindling number of students and the problems the school faced in the twenty-first century. Montefiore closed in 2016.

38. Stullken, "Schools and the Delinquency Problem," 565.

39. Edward H. Stullken, "Philosophy of a Special School," *Phi Delta Kappan* 22, no. 7 (March 1940): 346.

40. Stullken, "Philosophy of a Special School," 347.

41. Ruth Newman, director of education and educational research at the National Institute of Mental Health described ED and other special education students, on the role of the classroom teacher and predictable outcomes that underscored the fine line between behavior and suspension: "The school may be aware of other types of emotional disturbance, but it is the hyper-active, aggressive, behavior problem for whom drastic measures are taken. The course of action usually taken is suspension . . . or he may be put in a special class. Few school systems have special classes for the 'emotionally disturbed.' More often he is put in classes for the brain-injured, the physically handicapped, or the retarded, where it is hoped that he will cease to be torment for anyone but the special teacher to whom he is assigned, and that, incidentally, he may be able to learn." See Ruth G. Newman, "The *Acting-Out* Boy," *Exceptional Children* 22, no. 5 (February 1956): 188–89.

42. U.S. Congress, House, *Exceptional Children Educational Assistance Act,* HR 9591, 85th Congress, 1st Session, August 30, 1957, 1.

43. U.S. Congress, House, *Exceptional Children Educational Assistance Act,* HR 9591, 85th Congress, 1st Session, August 30, 1957, 1–2.

44. U.S. Congress, House, *Exceptional Children Educational Assistance Act,* HR 9591, 85th Congress, 1st Session, August 30, 1957, 4.

45. Barney Rabinow, "A Proposal for a Training Program for Teachers of the Emotionally Disturbed and the Socially Maladjusted," *Exceptional Children* 26, no. 6 (February 1960): 288.

46. Rabinow, "A Proposal for a Training Program."

47. Rabinow, "A Proposal for a Training Program."

48. Herbert C. Quay, "Some Basic Considerations in the Education of Emotionally Disturbed Children," in *Educating Emotionally Disturbed Children,* ed. Henry Dupont (New York: Holt, Rinehart and Winston, 1969), 136–37. This essay was originally published in *Exceptional Children* 30 (1963): 27–31.

49. Quay, "Some Basic Considerations in the Education of Emotionally Disturbed Children."

50. Rabinow, "A Proposal for a Training Program," 288.

51. Rabinow, "A Proposal for a Training Program," 288.

52. Thomas E. Stone, *Organizing and Operating Special Classes for Emotionally Disturbed Elementary School Children* (West Nyack, NY: Parker, 1971), 50.

53. Eli M. Bower, "The Emotionally Handicapped Child and the School," *Exceptional Children* 26, no. 1 (September 1959): 8.

54. Rabinow, "A Proposal for a Training Program," 289.

55. Leo Kanner, "Emotionally Disturbed Children: A Historical Review," *Child Development* 33, no. 1 (March 1962): 101. For the role that Hans Asperger played in developing autism as well as an intersectional history see Anne McGuire, *War on Autism: On the Cultural Logic of Normative Violence* (Ann Arbor: University of Michigan Press, 2016); see also Melanie Yergeau, *Authoring Autism: On Rhetoric and Neurological Queerness* (Durham, N.C.: Duke University Press, 2018).

56. Bower, "The Emotionally Handicapped Child and the School," 8.

57. Bower, "The Emotionally Handicapped Child and the School," 9.

58. Shelley L. Tremain, *Foucault and Feminist Philosophy of Disability* (Ann Arbor: University of Michigan Press, 2017).

59. Bower, "The Emotionally Handicapped Child and the School," 8.

60. Mental retardation also had an "adaptive behavior" component to it, and it is not clear how Bower squared the differences between a maladaptive mentally retarded child and an emotionally disturbed child, or if there existed a hierarchy between the two since he used the words "if all other possibilities have been ruled out."

61. Bower, "The Emotionally Handicapped Child and the School," 9.

62. Bower, "The Emotionally Handicapped Child and the School," 9.

63. Bower, "The Emotionally Handicapped Child and the School," 9.

64. U.S. Congress, House, Subcommittee on Special Education of the Committee on Education and Labor. *Special Education and Rehabilitation, Part 1,* New York, N.Y. 86th Congress, 1st Session, October 28 and 29, 1959, 35.

65. U.S. Congress, House, Subcommittee on Special Education of the Committee on Education and Labor, *Special Education and Rehabilitation, Part 1,* Hearings held in New York, N.Y. 86th Congress, 1st Session, October 28 and 29, 1959, 35.

66. U.S. Congress, House, Subcommittee on Special Education of the Committee on Education and Labor, 37.

67. U.S. Congress, House, Subcommittee on Special Education of the Committee on Education and Labor, 96.

68. U.S. Congress, House, Subcommittee on Special Education of the Committee on Education and Labor, 93, 96.

69. U.S. Congress, House, Subcommittee on Special Education of the Committee on Education and Labor. *Special Education and Rehabilitation, Part 3,* Cullman, Alabama. 86th Congress, 2nd Session, January 27 and 28, 1960, 628, 630.

70. U.S. Congress, House, Subcommittee on Special Education of the Committee on Education and Labor, 815–17.

71. U.S. Congress, House, Subcommittee on Special Education of the Committee on Education and Labor. *Special Education and Rehabilitation, Part 7,* Portland, Oregon. 86th Congress, 2nd Session, July 21 and 22, 1960, 1967.

72. U.S. Congress, House, Subcommittee on Special Education of the Committee on Education and Labor, 1968.

73. U.S. Congress, House, Subcommittee on Special Education of the Committee on Education and Labor, 1836.

74. U.S. Congress, House, Subcommittee on Special Education of the Committee on Education and Labor. *Special Education and Rehabilitation, Part 1,* New York, N.Y. 86th Congress, 1st Session, October 28 and 29, 1959, 161–62.

75. U.S. Congress, House, Subcommittee on Special Education of the Committee on Education and Labor, 161–62.

76. U.S. Congress, House, Subcommittee on Special Education of the Committee on Education and Labor, 214–15.

77. U.S. Congress, House, Subcommittee on Special Education of the Committee on Education and Labor, 216–17.

78. U.S. Congress, House, Subcommittee on Special Education of the Committee on Education and Labor, 216–17.

79. U.S. Congress, House. Subcommittee of the Committee on Interstate and Foreign Commerce. *Mental Health (Supplemental).* 88th Congress, 1st Session, July 10 and 11, 1963, 199.

80. Russell Skiba and Kenneth Grizzle, "The Social Maladjustment Exclusion: Issues of Definition and Assessment," *School Psychology Review* 20, no. 4 (1991): 580–94.

81. Daniel H. Cline, "A Legal Analysis of Policy Initiatives to Exclude Handicapped/Disruptive Students from Special Education," *Behavior Disorders* 15, no. 3 (May 1990): 166.

82. Cline, "A Legal Analysis," 166; Russell Skiba, Kenneth Grizzle, and Kathleen M. Minke, "Opening the Floodgates? The Social Maladjustment Exclusion and State SED Prevalence Rates," *Journal of School Psychology* 32, no. 3 (1994): 267–82; Eli M. Bower, "Defining Emotional Disturbance: Public Policy and Research," *Psychology in the Schools* 19, no. 1 (January 1982): 55–60; John W. Magg and Kenneth W. Howell, "Special Education and the Exclusion of Youth with Social Maladjustments: A Cultural-Organizational Perspective," *Remedial and Special Education* 13, no. 1 (January/February 1992): 47–54. Skiba et al. wrote "it has been argued . . . that both the exclusionary clause and the term *serious* were added to the federal SED definition to provide a fiscal control on the potentially high cost of service to students with emotional disturbance by restricting services to certain populations, such as adjudicated juvenile delinquents." While the research in this regard counters the argument that the exclusion was an accident in history and supports the argument that fiscal restraint could be at the heart of it, the literature fails to ask if African Americans are being racially singled out by the exclusion. Many African American students were labeled socially maladjusted and were adjudicated juvenile delinquents. To not include these designations was to exclude black students and increase funding opportunities that would go to other disabled students.

83. Rep. Leonor K. Sullivan (Mo). "Meeting the Educational Challenge of the 'Exceptional' Child—Testimony by Congresswoman on H.R. 15—Exceptional Children Educational Assistance Bill," *Congressional Record,* 87th Congress, 1st Session (August 21, 1961), 16578.

84. Elizabeth M. Eddy, *Walk the White Line: A Profile of Urban Education* (Garden City, NY: Anchor, 1967), 64.

85. Eddy, *Walk the White Line,* 83–84.

86. G. Alexander Moore Jr., *Realities of the Urban Classroom: Observations in Elementary Schools* (Garden City, N.Y.: Anchor, 1967), 6–7.

87. Eddy, *Walk the White Line,* 85.

88. Eddy, *Walk the White Line,* 109.

89. Moore, *Realities of the Urban Classroom,* 69.

90. Eddy, *Walk the White Line,* 110.

91. Jonathan Kozol, *Death at an Early Age: The Destruction of the Hearts and Minds of Negro Children in the Boston Public Schools* (Boston: Houghton Mifflin Co., 1967), 22–23.

92. Estelle Fuchs, *Teachers Talk: Views from Inside City Schools* (Garden City, NY: Anchor, 1969), 201.

93. Kozol, *Death at an Early Age,* 183.

94. James A. Banks, *Teaching the Black Experience: Methods and Materials* (Belmont, CA: Fearon, 1970); James A. Banks, "Teaching Ethnic Minority Studies

with a Focus on Culture," *Educational Leadership* 29, no. 2 (November 1971): 113–17; Geneva Gay, "Ethnic Minority Studies: How Widespread? How Successful?," *Educational Leadership* 29, no. 2 (November 1971): 108–112.

95. Norman E. Whitten Jr. and John F. Szwed, eds., *Afro-American Anthropology: Contemporary Perspectives* (New York: Free Press, 1970); Janice E. Hale-Benson, *Black Children: Their Roots, Culture, and Learning Styles* (Baltimore: Johns Hopkins University Press, 1982).

96. James A. Banks, "Cultural Pluralism and the Schools," *Educational Leadership* 32, no. 3 (December 1974): 163–66; Geneva Gay, "On Behalf of Children: A Curriculum Design for Multicultural Education in the Elementary School," *Journal of Negro Education* 48, no. 3 (Summer 1979): 324–40; Barbara A. Sizemore, "The Four M Curriculum: A Way to Shape the Future," *Journal of Negro Education* 48, no. 3 (Summer 1979): 341–56; Gwendolyn C. Baker, "Policy Issues in Multicultural Education in the United States," *Journal of Negro Education* 48, no. 3 (Summer 1979): 253–66. For a comprehensive history on the intersection of civil rights, black power, and education, see Charles M. Payne and Carol Sills Strickland, eds., *Teach Freedom: Education for Liberation in the African-American Tradition* (New York: Teachers College Press, 2008) and Russell Rickford, *We Are An African People: Independent Education, Black Power, and the Radical Imagination* (New York: Oxford University Press, 2016).

97. Eli M. Bower, "A Brief History of How We Have Helped Emotionally Disturbed Children and Other Fairy Tales," in *Celebrating the Past, Preparing for the Future: 40 Years of Serving Students with Emotional and Behavioral Disorders,* eds. Sheldon Braaten, Frank W. Woos, Gordon Wrobel (Minneapolis: Minnesota Council for Children with Behavioral Disorders, and Minnesota Educators of Emotionally/Behaviorally Disordered, 1989), 13.

98. *Lora v. Board of Education,* 456 F. Supp. 1211, 1978 U.S. Dist. Lexis 17417, 21–22.

99. Frank H. Wood, "Looking Back-Looking Ahead: Programs for Students with Emotional and Behavioral Problems at the Millennium," *Preventing School Failure: Alternative Education for Children and Youth* 45, no. 2 (2001): 59.

100. B. F. Skinner, "Are Theories of Learning Necessary?," *Psychological Review* 57, no. 4 (July 1950): 193–216; Geneva Gay and Willie L. Baber, eds., *Expressively Black: The Cultural Basis of Ethnic Identity* (New York: Praeger, 1987); John U. Ogbu, ed., *Minority Status, Oppositional Culture, & Schooling* (New York: Routledge, 2008).

101. James M. Kauffman and Timothy J. Landrum, *Children and Youth with Emotional and Behavioral Disorders: A History of Their Education* (Austin, TX: Pro-Ed, 2006), 78.

102. James M. Kauffman and Clayton D. Lewis, eds., *Teaching Children with Behavior Disorders: Personal Perspectives* (Columbus, OH: Charles E. Merrill, 1974), 15.

103. Kauffman and Landrum, *Children and Youth with Emotional and Behavioral Disorders,* 84.

104. Kauffman and Lewis, *Teaching Children with Behavior Disorders,* 188–89.

105. Kauffman and Lewis, *Teaching Children with Behavior Disorders,* 188–89.

106. Bower, "Defining Emotional Disturbance: Public Policy and Research," 57.

107. Bower, "The Emotionally Handicapped Child and the School," 182.

108. Bower, "Defining Emotional Disturbance: Public Policy and Research," 57.

109. Kauffman and Lewis, *Teaching Children with Behavior Disorders: Personal Perspectives,* 229–30.

110. Kauffman and Lewis, *Teaching Children with Behavior Disorders: Personal Perspectives,* 230.

111. Judy W. Kugelmass, *Behavior Bias and Handicaps: Labeling the Emotionally Disturbed Child* (New Brunswick, N.J.: Transaction, 1987), 69.

112. Shi-Chang Wu, William Pink, Robert Crain, and Oliver Moles, "Student Suspension: A Critical Reappraisal," *The Urban Review* 14, no. 4 (1982): 245–303.

113. Quoted in Joseph L. Tropea, "Bureaucratic Order and Special Children: Urban Schools, 1950s–1960s," *History of Education Quarterly* 27, no. 3 (Autumn 1987): 341.

114. Joseph L. Tropea, "Bureaucratic Order and Special Children: Urban Schools, 1950s–1960s," 341.

115. *Goss v. Lopez,* 419 U.S. 565, 1975 U.S. Lexis 23.

116. *Mills v. Board of Education of the District of Columbia,* 348 F. Supp. 866, 1972, U.S. Dist. Lexis 12499, 4–6.

117. *Mills v. Board of Education of the District of Columbia,* 9.

118. *Brown v. Board of Education,* 347 U.S. 483 (1954).

119. *Bolling v. Sharpe,* 347 U.S. 497 (1954).

120. *Hobson v. Hansen,* 269 F. Supp. 401 (DDC 1967).

121. U.S. Congress, Senate, Subcommittee on the Handicapped of the Committee on Labor and Public Welfare. *Education for All Handicapped Children Act.* Hearings to Provide Financial Assistance to the States for Improved Educational Services for Handicapped Children and Related Bills, 94th Congress, 1st Session, April 8, 9, and 15, 1975, 2.

122. Statement by Honorable T. H. Bell, U.S. Commissioner of Education, Department of Health, Education, and Welfare, Subcommittee on the Handicapped, United States Senate, April 9, 1975, 168.

123. *Lora v. Board of Education,* 456, F. Supp. 1211, 1978 U.S. Dist. Lexis 17417.

124. U.S. Congress, Senate, Committee on Labor and Public Welfare. *Education for All Handicapped Children Act.* Report Together with Additional Views, 94th Congress, 1st Session, June 2, 1975, 9.

125. U.S. Congress, Senate, Committee on Labor and Public Welfare, 10.

126. U.S. Congress, Senate, Committee on Labor and Public Welfare, *Mental Retardation Facilities and Community Mental Health Centers Construction Act of 1963*, 88th Congress, 1st Session, Calendar No. 161, Report No. 180.

127. Bower, "Defining Emotional Disturbance: Public Policy and Research," 58.

128. Bower, "The Emotionally Handicapped Child and the School."

129. Bower, "Defining Emotional Disturbance: Public Policy and Research," 55.

130. Bower, "Defining Emotional Disturbance: Public Policy and Research," 58.

131. Bower, "The Emotionally Handicapped Child and the School," 9. The distinction between choice/necessity ED were signifiers for maladjustment-delinquency/idiosyncratic-internal conflict ED. To behave in egregiously disruptive ways (social maladjustment) or to come under the supervision of the criminal justice system (juvenile delinquency) was a choice that seemed endemic to black youth. To behave in ways that suggested one's behavior was odd, eccentric, strange or unconventional (emotional disturbance) was to have something going on within the personality beyond the student's control that explained bad white youth behavior. I am suggesting that these arguments were not objective observations; they were based on racialized perceptions of black and white children, who they were, and how their families lived their lives during the early and mid-twentieth century. Eli Bower created this distinction in 1959, which was then codified in legislation in 1963 and then again in 1975 that created the social maladjustment exclusion. Special education is still burdened with Bower's ideas and the quandary it created.

132. U.S. Congress, Senate, Committee on Labor and Public Welfare, *Education for All Handicapped Children Act*, 94th Congress, 1st session, Calendar No. 162, Report No. 94–168, 8.

133. U.S. Congress, House, Subcommittee on Select Education of the Committee on Education and Labor, *Extension of Education of the Handicapped Act*, Hearings on the Education and Training of the Handicapped and H.R. 7217, 94th Congress, 1st session, April 9 and 10, 1975 and June 9, 1975, 23–24. Representative Lehman continued to lecture Harris about the time he served on the Dade County School Board. "I know that these kids go to these classes, if they go to a regular school system, and I don't know if you have ever heard the term 'occie,' but they are called 'occies,' by the regular schools and elementary schools. The special education kids are 'occies,' which means that this is a term that comes from occupational therapy. These kids get some pretty rough treatment, and they don't need that, you know," p. 24.

134. U.S. Congress, House, Subcommittee on Select Education of the Committee on Education and Labor, 35.

135. U.S. Congress, House, Subcommittee on Select Education of the Committee on Education and Labor, 35.

136. U.S. Congress, House, Subcommittee on Select Education of the Committee on Education and Labor, 36.

137. Bower, "Defining Emotional Disturbance: Public Policy and Research," 59.

138. Bower, "Defining Emotional Disturbance: Public Policy and Research," 59.

139. Bower, "Defining Emotional Disturbance: Public Policy and Research," 59.

140. Bower, "Defining Emotional Disturbance: Public Policy and Research," 60.

141. Debra Viadero, "New Definition of 'Emotionally Disturbed' Sought," *Education Week,* April 29, 1992, www.edweek.org/ew/articles/1992/04/29; Dave F. Brown, "The Significance of Congruent Communication in Effective Classroom Management," *Clearing House* 79, no. 1 (September/October 2005): 12–15.

142. Benjamin L. Brooks and David A. Sabatino, eds., *Personal Perspectives on Emotional Disturbance/Behavioral Disorders* (Austin, TX: Pro-Ed, 1996).

143. Viadero, "New Definition of 'Emotionally Disturbed' Sought."

144. Gloria Ladson-Billings, *The Dream-Keepers: Successful Teachers of African-American Children* (San Francisco: Jossey-Bass, 2009); Barbara J. Shade, "Afro-American Cognitive Style: A Variable in School Success," *Review of Educational Research* 52, no. 2 (Summer 1982): 219–44; Shirley Brice Heath, *Ways with Words: Language, Life, and Work in Communities and Classrooms* (Cambridge: Cambridge University Press, 1983); Thomas Kochman, *Black and White: Styles in Conflict* (Chicago: University of Chicago Press, 1981).

145. Federal Register, February 10, 1993, 58(28), 7938, quoted in Thomas McIntyre and Steven R. Forness, "Is There a New Definition Yet or Are Our Kids Still Seriously Emotionally Disturbed?," *Beyond Behavior* 7, no. 3 (Fall 1996): 5.

146. Bower, "The Emotionally Handicapped Child and the School," 8.

147. Bower, "The Emotionally Handicapped Child and the School," 9.

148. McIntyre and Forness, "Is There a New Definition Yet," 6.

149. McIntyre and Forness, "Is There a New Definition Yet?"

150. Thomas McIntyre, "Guidelines for Providing Appropriate Services to Culturally Diverse Students with Emotionally and/or Behavioral Disorders," *Behavioral Disorders* 21, no. 2 (February 1996): 137–44.

151. McIntyre and Forness, "Is There a New Definition Yet?," 7; Debra Viadero, "New Definition of 'Emotionally Disturbed' Sought," *Education Week,* April 29, 1992; Gloria Ladson-Billings, "Fighting for Our Lives: Preparing Teachers to Teach African American Students," *Journal of Teacher Education* 51, no. 3 (May/June 2000): 206–214. For a comprehensive assessment of black behavior and black culture, see Carla R. Monroe, "Why Are 'Bad Boys' Always Black? Causes of Disproportionality in School Discipline and Recommendations for Change," *The Clearing House* 79, no. 1 (September/October 2005): 45–50; Carla R. Monroe, "Misbehavior or Misinterpretation? Closing the Discipline Gap through Cultural Synchronization," *Kappa Delta Pi Record,* (Summer 2006): 161–65; Carla R. Monroe

and Jennifer E. Obidah, "The Influence of Cultural Synchronization on a Teacher's Perceptions of Disruption: A Case Study of an African American Middle School Classroom," *Journal of Teacher Education* 55, no. 3 (May/June 2004): 256–68.

152. David R. Adamson, "Expulsion, Suspension, and the Handicapped Student," *NASSP Bulletin* 68, no. 471 (April 1984): 86–96.

153. *Goss v. Lopez,* 419 U.S. 565, 95 S. Ct. 729, 42 L. Ed. 2d 725, 1975 U.S. Lexis 23, 5.

154. Ohio statute quoted in Jane E. Slenkovich, *The Law of Suspension, Expulsion, and Discipline of the Special Education Student* (Saratoga, CA: Kinghorn, 1985), 17.

155. Moral panic did set in during the integration of white schools in the late 1960s and 1970s. Many school leaders could not distinguish between so-called bad black behavior and political unrest as revealed by a public statement from James E. Allen, U.S. Commissioner of Education on September 10, 1969: "I have become increasingly concerned about student unrest at the secondary school level. Educational leaders have an obligation to confront the issues which underlie unrest and to plan actions which reduce avoidable tensions in our school district. All of us need to be thinking through what we can do about the problem."

156. Judith Preissle Goetz and E. Anne Rowley Breneman, "Desegregation and Black Students' Experience in Two Rural Southern Elementary Schools," *Elementary School Journal* 88, no. 5 (May 1988): 493.

157. *Stuart v. Nappi,* 443 F. Supp. 1235, 1978; *Doe v. Koger,* 480 F. Supp. 225, 1979.

158. *Lora v. Board of Education,* 456 F. Supp. 1211, 1978, U.S. Dist. Lexis 17417, 40.

159. *Lora v. Board of Education,* 14.

160. *Lora v. Board of Education,* 40.

161. Frank B. Wilderson Jr., "Behavior Disorders in Children from Deprived Backgrounds," in *Special Education and Programs for Disadvantaged Children and Youth,* ed. Abraham J. Tannenbaum (Washington, D.C.: The Council for Exceptional Children, 1968), 20.

162. The list of behavior labels is from Frank H. Wood and K. Charlie Lakin, "Defining Emotionally Disturbed/Behaviorally Disordered Populations for Research Purposes," in *Disturbing, Disordered or Disturbed? Perspectives on the Definition of Problem Behavior in Educational Settings,* eds. Frank H. Wood and K. Charlie Lakin (Reston, VA: Council for Exceptional Children, 1982), 32.

163. Leonard P. Ullmann and Len Krasner quoted in Frank H. Wood, "Defining Disturbing, Disordered, and Disturbed Behavior," in *Disturbing, Disordered or Disturbed?* ed. Frank H. Wood and K. Charlie Lakin (Reston, VA: The Council for Exceptional Children, 1982), 13–14.

6. The Implications of Unteachability

1. The National Commission on Excellence in Education, *A Nation at Risk: The Imperative for Educational Reform,* A Report to the Nation and the Secretary

of Education, United States Department of Education, April 1983. The report advanced the notion of a high percentage of "functional illiteracy" among "minority" students as a kind of drag on American achievement and standing in the world. See also, Sally Lubeck and Patricia Garnett, "The Social Construction of the 'At-Risk' Child," *British Journal of Sociology in Education* 11, no. 3 (1990): 327–40; Frank Margonis, "The Cooptation of 'At-Risk': Paradoxes of Policy Criticism," *Teacher College Record,* 94, no. 2 (Winter 1992): 343–64.

2. Charles Tilly, *Durable Inequality* (Berkeley: University of California Press, 1998), 8–9. Charles Tilly suggested that oppositional binaries exist in categorical conflict, responsible for producing durable inequality. "Durable inequality among categories arises because people who control access to value-producing resources solve pressing organizational problems by means of categorical distinctions. Inadvertently or otherwise, those people set up systems of social closure, exclusion, and control. Through all these variations, we discover, and rediscover paired, recognized, organized, unequal categories such as black/white, male/female, married/unmarried, and citizen/noncitizen. Where they apply, however, paired and unequal categories do crucial organizational work, producing marked, durable differences in access to valued resources. Durable inequality, depends heavily on the institutionalization of categorial pairs."

3. Ellen Brantlinger, *Dividing Classes: How the Middle Class Negotiates and Rationalizes School Advantage* (New York: Routledge Falmer, 2003), 12.

4. Not the cleanest of analogies. Immanuel Kant's "a thing in itself" referred to what he called "noumenon": "We know not this thing as it is in itself, but only its appearances" through the senses, or what Kant called phenomenon. Immanuel Kant, *Prolegomena to Any Future Metaphysics* (1783).

5. Allan V. Horowitz argued similarly with psychiatric disorders. "At the beginning of the twenty-first century, the ascendancy of diagnostic psychiatry is almost unquestioned. The many heterogenous entities that it studies, whether schizophrenia, major depression, panic disorder, substance abuse and dependence, or attention deficit disorder, are accepted as 'real' disorders." Allan V. Horowitz, *Creating Mental Illness* (Chicago: University of Chicago Press, 2002), 38.

6. George Lipsitz, "The Racialization of Space and the Spatialization of Race: Theorizing the Hidden Architecture of Landscape," *Landscape Journal* 26, no. 1 (2007): 13.

7. James G. Carrier, "Sociology and Special Education: Differentiation and Allocation in Mass Education," *American Journal of Education* 94, no. 3 (May 1986): 291.

8. Beth Harry and Janette K. Klingner, *Why Are So Many Minority Students in Special Education? Race and Disability in Schools* (New York: Teachers College Press, 2006).

9. Beth Harry and Janette K. Klingner, *Why Are So Many Minority Students in Special Education? Race and Disability in Schools* (New York: Teachers College Press, 2006), 11.

10. Thomas M. Skrtic, "The Special Education Paradox: Equity as a Way to Excellence," *Harvard Educational Review* 61, no. 2 (July 1991): 148–207.

11. Skrtic quoted in Harry and Klingner, *Why Are So Many Minority Students in Special Education?*, 11.

12. Harry and Klingner, *Why Are So Many Minority Students in Special Education?*, 11.

13. Brown, Lohman, Mayer, and Decker document how ideas of risk traveled from Europe to the United States in the nineteenth century. See Keffrelyn D. Brown, *After the "At-Risk" Label: Reorienting Educational Policy and Practice* (New York: Teachers College Press, 2016); Jeroen J. H. Dekker, "Children At Risk in History: A Story of Expansion," *Paedagogica Historica* 45, nos. 1–2 (February–April 2009); Ingrid Lohmann and Christine Mayer, "Lessons from the History of Education for a Century of the Child At Risk," *Paedagogica Historica* 45, nos. 1–2 (February–April 2009): 1–16; William Hayes, *Are We Still a Nation At-Risk Two Decades Later?* (Lanham, MD: Rowman & Littlefield, 2004).

14. Carla O'Connor, Lori Diane Hill, and Shanta R. Robinson, "Who's At Risk in School and What's Race Got to Do With It?," *Review of Research in Education* 33 (2009): 1–34.

15. Ray McDermott, Jason D. Raley, and Ingrid Seyer-Ochi, "Race and Class in a Culture of Risk," *Review of Research in Education* 33 (2009): 101.

16. David J. Connor, Beth A. Ferri, and Subini A. Annamma, eds., *DisCrit: Disability Studies and Critical Race Theory in Education* (New York: Teachers College Press, 2016), 14. For a more detailed treatment of DisCrit theory, see Subini Ancy Annamma, David Connor, and Beth Ferri, "Dis/ability Critical Race Studies (DisCrit): Theorizing at the Intersections of Race and Dis/ability," *Race, Ethnicity, and Education* 16, no. 1 (2013): 1–31.

17. Annamma, Connor, and Ferri, "Dis/ability Critical Race Studies (DisCrit): Theorizing at the Intersections of Race and Dis/ability," 17.

18. Sami Schalk, *Bodyminds Reimagined: (Dis)ability, Race, and Gender in Black Women's Speculative Fiction* (Durham, N.C.: Duke University Press, 2018), 6. See also Sami Schalk, "Critical Disability Studies as Methodology," *Lateral* 6, no. 1 (Spring 2017).

19. Connor, Ferri, and Annamma, *DisCrit: Disability Studies and Critical Race Theory in Education,* 14.

20. Connor, Ferri, and Annamma, *DisCrit: Disability Studies and Critical Race Theory in Education,* 19–25.

21. Derrick A. Bell Jr., "Brown v. Board of Education and the Interest Convergence Dilemma," *Harvard Law Review* 93, no. 3 (January 1980): 518–33.

22. "The Normal and the Subnormal Child," *Journal of Educational Psychology* 3, no. 9 (November 1912): 535.

23. Leonard Porter Ayers, *Laggards in Our School: A Study of Retardation and Elimination in City School Systems* (New York: Russell Sage Foundation, 1909).

24. Edgar A. Doll, "Mental Hygiene Aspects of Special Education," *Journal of Psycho-Asthenics* 35–37 (June 1929– 1930): 73.

25. Beth Ferri and David Connor wrote, "The disability labels associated with the highest levels of disproportionate assignment of students of color are also the most subjective. . . . Conversely, less subjective categories, such as blindness or deafness, are ascribed proportionately to all student groups." Beth A. Ferri and David Connor, "In the Shadow of Brown: Special Education and Overrepresentation of Students of Color," *Remedial and Special Education* 26, no. 2 (March/April 2005): 94. Alfredo Artiles et al. agreed when they said, "High incidence disabilities are also described as 'judgmental' categories, which means the diagnosis of these conditions (EMR, LD, EBD) relies heavily on professional clinical decisions." See Artiles et al., "Justifying and Explaining Disproportionality, 1968–2008: A Critique of Underlying Views of Culture," *Exceptional Children* 76, no. 3 (2010): 281.

26. Goddard was clear on what was at risk: schools for sure but democracy as well. "The discoveries that each individual has his mental level which, once established, he cannot exceed and that the level [of intelligence] of the average person is probably between thirteen and fourteen years, explain a great many things not previously understood, but also raise some questions that are at first sight, somewhat disturbing. One of these is: What about democracy, can we hope to have a successful democracy where the average mentality is thirteen?" See H. H. Goddard, "Mental Levels and Democracy," *Shaping the American Educational State: 1900 to the Present,* ed. Clarence J. Karier (New York: Free Press, 1975), 165.

27. Goddard, "Mental Levels and Democracy," 77.

28. R. Lapouse and M. Weitzner, "Epidemiology," in *Mental Retardation—An Annual Review I,* ed. J. Wortis (New York: Grune & Stratton, 1970); S. Wishik, *Georgia Study of Handicapped Children. Report on a Study of Prevalence, Disability Needs, Resources, and Contributory Factors,* Publications for Program Administration and Community Organization. Georgia Department of Public Health, Atlanta, 1964; Jane Mercer, *Labeling the Mentally Retarded: Clinical and Social System Perspectives on Mental Retardation* (Berkeley: University of California Press, 1973).

29. Marleen C. Pugach, "The Limitations of Federal Special Education Policy: The Role of Classroom Teachers in Determining Who is Handicapped," *Journal of Special Education* 19, no. 1 (1985): 124.

30. Thomas M. Skrtic, *Behind Special Education: A Critical Analysis of Professional Culture and School Organization* (Denver: Love, 1991), chap. 3.

31. P. L. 108–446, Dec. 3, 2004 118 Stat., 2651.

32. Thomas Hehir, "IDEA and Disproportionality: Federal Enforcement, Effective Advocacy, and Strategies for Change," in *Racial Inequality in Special Education,* eds. Daniel J. Losen and Gary Orfield (Cambridge, MA: Harvard University Press, 2002), 219.

33. Hehir, "IDEA and Disproportionality."

34. Amanda L. Sullivan, "Wading Through Quicksand: Making Sense of Minority Disproportionality in Identification of Emotional Disturbance" 43, no. 1 (January 2017): 244–52.

35. Kirby A. Heller, Wayne H. Holtzman, and Samuel Messick, eds., *Placing Children in Special Education: A Strategy for Equity* (Washington, D.C.: National Academy Press, 1982), x.

36. Heller, Holtzman, and Messick, *Placing Children in Special Education*, x.

37. M. Suzanne Donovan and Christopher T. Cross, eds., *Minority Students in Special and Gifted Education* (Washington, D.C.: National Academy Press, 2002), 18.

38. Martha J. Coutinho and Donald P. Oswald, "Disproportionate Representation in Special Education: A Synthesis and Recommendations," *Journal of Child and Family Studies* 9, no. 2 (2000): 135–56; Federico R. Waitoller, Alfredo J. Artiles, and Douglas A. Chaney, "The Miner's Canary: A Review of Overrepresentation Research and Explanations," *Journal of Special Education* 44, no. 1 (May 2010): 29–49; Alfredo J. Artiles, Elizabeth B. Kozleski, Stanley C. Trent, David Osher, and Alba Ortiz, "Justifying and Explaining Disproportionality, 1968–2008: A Critique of Underlying Views of Culture," *Exceptional Children* 76, no. 3 (Spring 2010): 279–99. See also Alfredo J. Artiles, "Re-Framing Disproportionality Research: Outline of a Cultural-Historical Paradigm," *Multiple Voices for Ethnically Diverse Exceptional Learners* 11, no. 2 (2009): 24–37; Alfredo J. Artiles and Aydun Bal, "The Next Generation of Disproportionality Research: Toward a Comparative Model in the Study of Equity in Ability Differences," *Journal of Special Education* 42, no. 1 (May 2008): 4–14.

39. Gerald N. Grob, "Origins of *DSM-I*: A Study in Appearance and Reality," *American Journal of Psychiatry* 148, no. 4 (April 1991); Alvin E. House, *DSM-IV: Diagnosis in the Schools* (New York: Guilford, 1999); Renee M. Tobin and Alvin E. House, *DSM-5: Diagnosis in the Schools* (New York: Guilford, 2016); Joel Paris and James Phillips, eds., *Making the DSM-5: Concepts and Controversies* (New York: Springer, 2013); Martin Gold and David W. Mann, "Alternative Schools for Troublesome Secondary Students," *Urban Review* 14, no. 4 (1982).

40. Richard L. Jenkins, "Psychiatric Syndromes in Children and their Relation to Family Background," *American Journal of Orthopsychiatry* 36 (1966): 456. See also William Ryan, "Emotional Disorder as a Social Problem: Implications for Mental Health Programs," *American Journal of Orthopsychiatry* 41, no. 4 (July 1971).

41. Angela Davis, "Masked Racism: Reflections on the Prison Industrial Complex," *Colorlines,* September 10, 1998; Eric Schlosser, "The Prison-Industrial Complex," *Atlantic,* December 1998. Perhaps what I am calling a "behavior industrial complex" is just a subset of the "medical industrial complex," or the "mental health industrial complex," the former coined in the late 1960s and the latter in the twenty-first century. See Arnold S. Relman, "The New Medical-Industrial

Complex," *New England Journal of Medicine* 303, no. 17 (October 1980): 963–70, and Eric M. Greene, "The Mental Health Industrial Complex: A Study in Three Cases," *Journal of Humanistic Psychology* 59, no. 2 (February 2019): 1–19.

42. Writing about the prison industrial complex, Angela Davis mentions how capital and the flow of money is generated from imprisoned black bodies in the "corporatization of punishment." Similarly, the behavior industrial complex has produced an expert class and a profit stream, merging education, psychiatry, and corporate pharmacology, creating stimulant pharmacotherapy to treat deviant behavior and mental health disorders, like attention deficit hyperactivity disorder, conduct disorder, or antisocial personality disorder. See Rick Mayes, Catherine Bagwell, and Jennifer Erkulwater, *Medicating Children: ADHD and Pediatric Mental Health* (Cambridge, MA: Harvard University Press, 2009). See also Dr. Terence D. Fitzgerald, *White Prescriptions? The Dangerous Social Potential for Ritalin and Other Psychotropic Drugs to Harm Black Males* (Boulder, CO: Paradigm, 2009). Eric Greene argues that psychiatrists exploit "zones of social abandonment" to craft "mental illness as an individual problem, not one of structural racism and classism." He goes on to write, "over the past four decades, the mental health industrial complex has continued to oppress disenfranchised populations while generating billions in revenue by means of its biomedical model or explanations of mental suffering," p. 2.

43. Monique W. Morris, *Pushout: The Criminalization of Black Girls in Schools* (New York: New Press, 2016).

44. Herb Kutchins and Stuart A. Kirk, *Making Us Crazy—DSM: The Psychiatric Bible and the Creation of Mental Disorders* (New York: Free Press, 1997).

45. Alan V. Horowitz, *Creating Mental Illness* (Chicago: University of Chicago Press, 2002), 72.

46. Renee M. Tobin and Alvin House, *DSM-5 Diagnosis in the Schools* (New York: Guilford, 2016). Tobin and House write on page 147 about how changes in the DSM-5 closed the distance between emotional disturbance, oppositional defiant disorder, and conduct disorder in schools. "The DSM-5 formulation of Oppositional Defiant Disorder has added an emphasis on the underlying emotional disturbance, which could facilitate the inclusion of children showing both Conduct Disorder and Oppositional Defiant Disorder under the 'emotional disturbance' provisions of IDEA. What is most important for the reader to recognize is that the categories in IDEA and DSM-5 are not identical. The basic purpose, structure, and methods of the two systems are different, and the 'mapping' of one upon the other is imperfect and open to differences of interpretation. Establishing an objective case for a mental disorder diagnosis will usually support and facilitate qualification of a student as eligible for services under IDEA, provided that the disorder is connected to significant academic and/or interpersonal issues." See chapter 11 for a fuller explanation.

47. Terry Fitzgerald Welch, "The Impact of Positive Behavioral Interventions and Supports on Academic Achievement among African American Male Students

Diagnosed as Emotionally Disturbed" (PhD diss., California State University, Fresno, 2015).

48. Alan V. Horowitz, *Creating Mental Illness* (Chicago: University of Chicago Press, 2002), 35.

49. Horowitz, *Creating Mental Illness*, 35.

50. Herbert C. Quay, "Some Basic Considerations in the Education of Emotionally Disturbed Children," *Exceptional Children* (September 1963): 29, 30.

51. Richard L. Jenkins, "Psychiatric Syndromes in Children and Their Relation to Family Background," *American Journal of Orthopsychiatry* 36, no. 3 (April 1966); Richard L. Jenkins, "The Varieties of Children's Behavioral Problems and Family Dynamics," *American Journal of Psychiatry* 124, no. 10 (April 1968); Richard L. Jenkins, "Classification of Behavior Problems of Children," *American Journal of Psychiatry* 125, no. 8 (February 1969).

52. Herbert C. Quay, William C. Morse, and Richard L. Cutler, "Personality Patterns of Pupils in Special Classes for the Emotionally Disturbed," *Exceptional Children* 32, no. 5 (January 1966): 301.

53. Amanda L. Sullivan and Shanna S. Sadeh, "Differentiating Social Maladjustment from Emotional Disturbance: An Analysis of Case Law," *School Psychology Review* 43, no. 4 (2014): 454.

54. Paul A. McDermott, "Racial and Social Class Prevalence of Psychopathology among School-Age Youth in the United States," *Youth & Society* 28, no. 4 (June 1997): 404.

55. Olympia et al., "Social Maladjustment and Students with Behavioral and Emotional Disorders: Revisiting Basic Assumptions and Assessment Issues," *Psychology in the Schools* 41, no. 8 (2004): 837.

56. Ralph Mason Dreger, "The Classification of Children and Their Emotional Problems," *Clinical Psychology Review* 1 (1981): 416.

57. Dreger, "The Classification of Children and Their Emotional Problems," 417.

58. Nock et al., "Prevalence, Subtypes, and Correlates of DSM-IV: Conduct Disorder in the National Comorbidity Survey Replication," *Psychological Medicine* 36 (2006): 703.

59. Carl B. Gacono and Tammy L. Hughes, "Differentiating Emotional Disturbance from Social Maladjustment: Assessing Psychopathy in Aggressive Youth," *Psychology in the Schools* 41, no. 8 (2004): 851. See Table 1 on p. 850 for trait comparisons on CD, ASPD, Cleckley's characteristics, and Hare's psychopathy traits. For a comparison of ODD and CD, see Loeber et al., "Oppositional Defiant and Conduct Disorder: A Review of the Past 10 Years, Part I," *Journal of American Academy of Child Adolescence Psychiatry* 39, no. 12 (December 2000): 1468–88. Psychiatrist Hervey M. Cleckley defined the field of psychopathy and the diagnostic basis of ASPD. Psychiatrist Robert D. Hare built on Cleckley's work, creating his own psychopathy checklist in the 1970s.

60. Raines et al., "Universal Screening for Behavioral and Emotional Risk: A Promising Method for Reducing Disproportionate Placement in Special Education," *Journal of Negro Education* 81, no. 3 (2012): 285.

61. Donald R. Lynam, "Early Identification of the Fledgling Psychopath: Locating the Psychopathic Child in the Current Nomenclature," *Journal of Abnormal Psychology* 107, no. 4 (November 1998).

62. Renee M. Tobin and Alvin House, *DSM-5 in the Schools* (New York: Guilford, 2016), chap. 11; Joel Paris and James Phillips, eds., *Making the DSM 5: Concepts and Controversies* (New York: Springer, 2013). In the Paris and Phillips anthology, Joseph Pierre of the David Geffen School of Medicine at UCLA observed, "At their core, many of the recent critiques of DSM-5 involve claims of overdiagnosis—that psychiatry has been ever-widening its borders with diagnostic labels for mental states and responses to life situations that have been and should be considered within normal variation (such overdiagnosis has been synonymously called 'diagnostic expansion,' 'diagnostic creep,' 'prevalence inflation,' 'over-pathologizing,' 'medicalization,' 'disease mongering,' or a problem of 'false positives,' and 'false epidemics,'" 106.

63. Richard Lynn, "Racial and Ethnic Differences in Psychopathic Personality," *Personality and Individual Differences* 32 (2002): 279, 309; see two great rebuttals, Skeem et al., "Psychopathic Personality and Racial/Ethnic Differences Reconsidered: A Reply to Lynn," *Personality and Individual Differences* 35 (2003): 1439–62; Jennifer Skeem et al., "Are There Ethnic Differences in Levels of Psychopathy? A Meta-Analysis," *Law and Human Behavior* 28, no. 5 (October 2004): 505–27.

64. Two other studies attempting to demonstrate the genetic basis of black antisocial behavior are Ronald L. Simmons et al., "Social Adversity, Genetic Variation, Street Code, and Aggression: A Genetically Informed Model of Violent Behavior," *Youth Violence and Juvenile Justice* 10, no. 1 (January 2012): 3–24. Keven M. Beaver et al., "The Interaction Between Neighborhood Disadvantage and Genetic Factors in the Prediction of Antisocial Outcomes," *Youth Violence and Juvenile Justice* 10, no. 1 (January 2012): 25–40.

65. Joseph Murray and David P. Farrington, "Risk Factors for Conduct Disorder and Delinquency: Key Findings from Longitudinal Studies," *Canadian Journal of Psychiatry* 55, no. 10 (October 2010): 633–42.

66. Abiodun Raufu, "School-to-Prison Pipeline: Impact of School Discipline on African American Students," *Journal of Education & Social Policy* 7, no. 1 (March 2017): 47.

67. Nirmala Erevelles, "Crippin' Jim Crow: Disability, Dis-Location, and the School-to-Prison Pipeline," *Disability Incarcerated: Imprisonment and Disability in the United States and Canada*, eds. Liat Ben-Moshe, Chris Chapman, and Allison Carey (New York: Palgrave Macmillan, 2014).

68. Subini Ancy Annamma, *The Pedagogy of Pathologization* (New York: Routledge, 2018), 62.

69. Daniel J. Losen and Kevin G. Welner, "Legal Challenges to Inappropriate and Inadequate Special Education for Minority Children," in *Racial Inequality in Special Education*, eds. Daniel J. Losen and Gary Orfield (Cambridge, MA: Harvard University Press, 2002), 171.

70. This "warehousing" happened in a variety of alterative pull-out locations, resource rooms, special classes, separate schools, residential facilities, and prisons more than it has been a site of support and services.

71. Losen and Welner, "Legal Challenges to Inappropriate and Inadequate Special Education for Minority Children," 171.

72. "An Interview with Marian Wright Edelman," *Harvard Educational Review* 44, no. 1 (February 1974): 55, 57.

73. Frances Vavrus and KimMarie Cole, "'I Didn't Do Nothin': The Discursive Construction of School Suspension," *The Urban Review* 34, no. 2 (June 2002): 89.

74. Jawanza Kunjufu, *Black Students, Middle Class Teachers* (Chicago: African American Images, 2002), 19–20.

75. Frances Vavrus and KimMarie Cole, "'I Didn't Do Nothin': The Discursive Construction of School Suspension," *Urban Review* 34, no. 2 (June 2002): 89.

76. Mark G. Yudof, "Suspension and Expulsion of Black Students from Public Schools: Academic Capital Punishment and the Constitution," *Law and Contemporary Problems* 39, no. 2 (Spring 1975): 380. Yudof later served as the president of the University of Minnesota, the University of California, and chancellor at the University of Texas.

77. Pedro A. Noguera, *The Trouble with Black Boys and Other Reflections on Race, Equity, and the Future of Public Education* (San Francisco: Jossey-Bass, 2008), 111.

78. Children's Defense Fund, *School Suspensions: Are They Helping Children?* (Cambridge, MA: Children Defense Fund of the Washington Research Project, Inc., 1975), 9.

79. Children's Defense Fund, *School Suspensions*, 10.

80. Children's Defense Fund, *School Suspensions*, 12.

81. *Black Girls Matter: Pushed Out, Overpoliced and Underprotected* (African American Policy Forum, Center for Intersectionality and Social Policy Studies, 2015), 4.

82. Subini Ancy Annamma, *The Pedagogy of Pathologization*, 44.

83. Charles W. Mills, *The Racial Contract* (Ithaca, N.Y.: Cornell University Press, 1997), 41.

84. Ann Ferguson, *Bad Boys: Public Schools in the Making of Black Masculinity* (Ann Arbor: University of Michigan Press, 2000); Pedro Noguera, *The Trouble with Black Boys* (San Francisco: Jossey-Bass, 2008).

85. Tera Eva Agyepong, *The Criminalization of Black Children: Race, Gender, and Delinquency in Chicago's Juvenile Justice System, 1899–1945* (Chapel Hill: University of North Carolina Press, 2018); Geoff K. Ward, *The Black Child-Savers* (Chicago: University of Chicago Press, 2012).

86. Morris, *Pushout: The Criminalization of Black Girls in Schools*, 18.

87. Gloria Ladson-Billings, *The Dreamkeepers: Successful Teachers of African American Children* (San Francisco: Jossey-Bass, 2009), 24. Ladson-Billings wrote that custodian "teachers do not believe that much can be done to help their students and do not look to others to help them maintain classes. The second group, 'Referral Agents' . . . do not believe that much can be done to help their students improve, but they shift the responsibility to other school personnel by sending children to the school psychologists or the special education teacher." See also Kunjufu, *Black Students, Middle-Class Teachers*, 44–45.

88. Mills, *The Racial Contract*, 47.

89. Mills, *The Racial Contract*, 48.

90. Morris, *Pushout: The Criminalization of Black Girls in Schools*, 71.

91. "School Discipline Laws & Regulations by State & Category," www.safe supportinglearning.ed.gov/discipline-compendium/choose-type/Louisiana/ Grounds for possible suspension or expulsion, accessed on November 22, 2020; "SB-607 Pupil Discipline: Suspensions and Expulsions: Willful Defiance (2017–2018)," www.leginfo.legislature.ca.gov/faces/billTextClient, accessed on November 22, 2020.

92. "School Discipline Laws & Regulations by State & Category," www.safe supportinglearning.ed.gov/discipline-compendium/choose-type/Louisiana/ Grounds for possible suspension or expulsion, accessed on November 22, 2020. These laws have singlehandedly led to the disproportional increase of black students suspended or expelled from schools across the country. Here are selected states and the language they use. Alaska: "Willful disobedience; open and persistent defiance of authority"; Colorado: "Continued willful disobedience or open and persistent defiance of proper authority"; Connecticut: "Disruptive behavior"; Florida: "Willful disobedience; open defiance of authority"; Idaho: "Disruption of good order"; Illinois: "Gross disobedience and misconduct"; Maine: "Forming secret societies and; deliberate and disorderly conduct"; Massachusetts: "hitting or pushing a teacher, school official or employee"; Michigan: "Gross misdemeanor or persistent disobedience"; Minnesota: "Disruptive behavior"; New Hampshire: "Gross misconduct"; New Jersey: "Continued and willful disobedience; open defiance of authority"; New York: "Insubordinate or disorderly conduct"; North Carolina: "Willful violation policies of conduct"; North Dakota: "Insubordination; habitual indolence; disorderly conduct"; Ohio: "Disruptive behavior"; Utah: "Frequent or flagrant willful disobedience; defiance of proper authority, or disruptive behavior, including the use of foul, profane, vulgar, or abusive language"; Vermont: "Ongoing threat; disruptive behavior." See, The Civil Rights Project, Harvard University, *Opportunities Suspended: The Devastating Consequences of Zero Tolerance and School Discipline*, Report from A National Summit on Zero Tolerance, Washington, D.C., June 15–16, 2000, Appendix III.

93. Barry C. Feld, *The Evolution of the Juvenile Court: Race, Politics, and the Criminalizing of Justice* (New York: New York University Press, 2017), 180.

94. Annamma, *The Pedagogy of Pathologization*, 53.

95. Morris, *Push-Out: The Criminalization of Black Girls*, 56, 59. Megan Thee Stallion flipped black female tropes on their head in "Savage" (2020). The song became a rap anthem of willful defiance for young black girls: "I'm a savage, / Classy, bougie, ratchet, / Sassy, moody, nasty, / Actin' stupid, what's happening?"

96. Ann Arnett Ferguson, *Bad Boys: Public Schools in the Making of Black Masculinity* (Ann Arbor: University of Michigan Press, 2000), 175.

97. Children Defense Fund, *School Suspensions: Are They Helping Children?* (1975), 66. "I have observed . . . a white teacher challenged the possession by a black student of a 'pick'—a style of Afro comb used by many black students for grooming purposes. The teacher's attempt to confiscate the comb resulted in resistance by the student and a confrontation."

98. Morris, *Pushout: The Criminalization of Black Girls*, 92–93.

99. The Civil Rights Project, Harvard University, *Opportunities Suspended: The Devastating Consequences of Zero Tolerance and School Discipline*, Report from A National Summit on Zero Tolerance, June 15–16, 2000, Washington, D.C., II-6. "Students of color are far more likely than white students to be referred for subjective infractions such as 'defiance of authority.' Because teachers and other school officials are the first to identify disciplinary infractions, if these officials are more prone to report violations committed by students of color than by white students, there will be no record of white students' misconduct, thus making it very difficult to prove that similar situated white students were not referred." II-4.

100. Annamma, *The Pedagogy of Pathologization*, 40–41.

101. Miles B. Santamour, "The Mentally Retarded Offender," in *Special Education in the Criminal Justice System*, eds. C. Michael Nelson, Robert B. Rutherford Jr., and Bruce I. Wolford (Columbus, OH: Merrill, 1987), 109.

102. James E. Gilliam and Brenda K. Scott, "The Behaviorally Disordered Offender," in *Special Education in the Criminal Justice System*, eds. C. Michael Nelson, Robert B. Rutherford Jr., and Bruce I. Wolford (Columbus, OH: Merrill, 1987), 141.

103. Ingo Keilitz and Noel Dunivant, "The Learning Disabled Offender," in *Special Education in the Criminal Justice System*, eds. C. Michael Nelson, Robert B. Rutherford Jr., and Bruce I. Wolford (Columbus, OH: Merrill, 1987), 122.

104. Keilitz and Dunivant, "The Learning Disabled Offender," 121.

105. Peter E. Leone, Barbara A. Zaremba, Michelle S. Chapin, and Curt Iseli, "Understanding the Overrepresentation of Youths with Disabilities in Juvenile Detention," *District of Columbia Law Review* 3, no. 2 (Fall 1995): 394.

106. C. Nelson, Robert B. Rutherford Jr., and Bruce I. Wolford, eds., *Special Education in the Criminal Justice System* (Columbus, OH: Merrill, 1987), 18.

107. Office of Special Education and Rehabilitative Services Blog, U.S. Department of Education, "Supporting Youth with Disabilities in Juvenile Corrections," (https://sites.ed.gov/osers), accessed on January 29, 2022.

108. Randy K. Otto, J. J. Greenstein, M. K. Johnson, and R. M. Friedman, "Prevalence of Mental Disorders Among Juvenile Youth in the Juvenile Justice System," *Focal Point* 11, no. 1 (Spring 1997): 1–9.

109. Office of Juvenile Justice and Delinquency Prevention, "Educational Advocacy for Youth with Disabilities," (https://ojjdp.ojp.gov/sites, accessed on January 29, 2022).

110. Joseph B. Tulman, "Disability and Delinquency: How Failures to Identify, Accommodate, and Serve Youth with Educational-Related Disabilities Leads to Their Disproportionate Representation in the Delinquency System," *Whittier Journal of Child and Family Advocacy* 3, no. 1 (2003): 3–76; Dean Hill Rivkin, "Decriminalizing Students with Disabilities," *New York Law School Review* 54, no. 4 (2009-2010): 909–54.

111. Annamma, *The Pedagogy of Pathologization*, 45–46.

112. Arthur S. Hill, "A Critical Glance at Special Education," *Exceptional Children* 22, no. 8 (May 1956): 315.

113. Alfredo J. Artiles, "Special Education's Changing Identity: Paradoxes and Dilemmas in Views of Culture and Space," *Harvard Educational Review* 73, no. 2 (Summer 2003); 164–202; For paradoxes associated with EBD see also Theresa Glennon, "Disabling Ambiguities: Confronting Barriers to the Education of Students with Emotional Disabilities," *Tennessee Law Review*, 60, no. 2 (Winter 1993): 295-364.

114. Burton Blatt, *In and Out of Mental Retardation: Essays on Educability, Disability, and Human Policy* (Baltimore: University Park Press, 1981), 17.

Index

Prepared by Denise E. Carlson
Page numbers in italics refer to figures.

students with disabilities, 16, 18, 57, 228, 230, 267
exogenous factors, 62–65, 67–68, 74
expulsions, 228–29, 241–42, 243, 254, 265, 268, 275, 364n92. *See also* discipline; punishment; suspensions

Falkner, Roland P., 18–19
Farrington, David P., 265
feeblemindedness: ableist epistemologies of, 15, 16; borderlinity of, 306–7n136; categories of, 51, 72–73, 79, 83; classifications of, 42–43, 48; commitment of, 296–97n40; female, 23–24; history of, 20–24, 66; psychologists' assessment of, 45; racialization of, 8–9; segregation of, 14, 165; training of, 59–64, 71–72, 100, 301–2n99; treatment for, 304–5n118; use of term, 8, 166. *See also* "dullard/dull-normal" children/students; intelligence (IQ) testing and scores: feebleminded range; mental retardation; morons; slow learners
Ferguson, Ann, 271, 274
Fernald, Walter E., 24, 43
Ferri, Beth A., 247, 251, 358n25
Fields, Barbara J. and Karen E., 37, 39
Finlan, Thomas, 186–87
Flesch, Rudolf, 103, 319n139
Forness, Steven, 288–89n13
Foucault, Michel, 17
Franks, David, 153
Frazier, E. Franklin, 90, 119
Freedom Summer, 109. *See also* civil rights movement

Gacono, Carl, 263
Gallagher, James J., 142, 143
Ganter, Robert, 154
Gargoylism, 73
Gates, Arthur, 53

Geer, William C., 135–36
gender, 4, 24, 34, 251; behavior and, 194, 270–74, 346n31, 365n95
general education, 165, 170, 235, 239; distinguished from special education, 155, 157–58, 271, 306–7n136, 331n74; limiting black and brown access to, 2–4, 14–15, 30, 38, 45, 48, 188, 244, 252–53, 255, 264–68, 278. *See also* special education; special education, black and brown students overrepresented in
genetic factors, 8, 21, 23, 166; of black behavior, 10–11, 18, 264–65; of mental retardation, 53, 73, 75–76, 96–97, 166, 326n39. *See also* hereditary factors
genius, 25, 43
giftedness, 36, 38
Gilliam, James E, 275–76
Glazer, Nathan, 119–20
Glickman, Sylvia, 194
Goddard, Henry: intelligence testing promoted by, 34, 72, 91, 164, 358n26; *The Kallikak Family,* 85; mental retardation categories developed by, 41, 58, 61; moron description given by, 63–64
Goetz, Judith Preissle, 243
Goldstein, Kurt, 65, 66
Goodman, Walter, 108
Gordon, Edmond, 154
Gordon, Robert A., 166
Gorman, Ethel, 210–11
Goss v. Lopez, 241–42, 243
grade-level retardation, 8, 19–20, 40, 266. *See also* age: grade-level; educable mentally retarded (EMR)
Gray, Susan, 121
Great Cities Program for School Improvement, 120
Great Migration, 91–92, 93
Greene, Eric, 360n42